The
Collegeville
Hymnal

The Collegeville Hymnal

Reverend Edward J. McKenna

Editor

THE LITURGICAL PRESS

Collegeville   *Minnesota*

Nihil obstat: Rev. Robert C. Harren J.C.L., *Censor deputaus.*
Imprimatur: ✝ Jerome Hanus, O.S.B., Bishop of St. Cloud. May 25, 1990.

The English translations of the liturgical texts in this hymnal have been approved by the National Conference of Catholic Bishops, confirmed by the Apostolic See and published by authority of the Committee on the Liturgy of the National Conference of Catholic Bishops.

New English translations of the Order of Mass from the 1974 Sacramentary. Copyright 1974, 1985, International Committee on English in the Liturgy, Inc. The English translation of the Psalm responses, gospel acclamations, and gospel verses from *Lectionary for Mass* © 1969, International Committee on English in the Liturgy, Inc. (ICEL); text of "You Have Put on Christ" from *Rite of Baptism for Children* © 1969, ICEL; the English translation of "May the Angels" and "Saints of God" from the *Rite of Funerals* © 1970, ICEL; the English translation of the texts of the Order of Mass from the Roman Missal © 1973, ICEL; excerpts from the English translation of *The Liturgy of the Hours* © 1974, ICEL; excerpts from the English translation of *Eucharistic Prayers for Masses with Children* © 1975, ICEL; music for "Saints of God" and "May the Angels" and "You Have Put on Christ" from *Music for the Rite of Funerals and Rite of Baptism for Children* © 1977, ICEL; text of nos. 112 (verses 4, 6), 241, 255, and 333, music of 255 and 333, and Accompaniment for 6, 20, 25, 60, 74, 79, 89, 164, and 398 from *Resource Collection of Hymns and Service Music for the Liturgy* © 1981, ICEL; music for Psalm 118 (no. 126) and Psalm 103 (no. 153) from *ICEL Lectionary Music* © 1982, ICEL. All rights reserved.

English translation of Kyrie, Gloria in Excelsis, Nicene Creed, Apostles' Creed, Sanctus and Benedictus, and Agnus Dei prepared by the International Consultation on English Texts.

Selected Psalms and scripture selections are taken from the New American Bible Copyright © 1970 by The Confraternity of Christian Doctrine, Washington, D.C. 20005.

The publisher gratefully acknowledges the copyright owners who have given permission to include their material in this collection. Every effort has been made to determine copyright ownership of texts and music used in this edition and to get permission for their use. The publisher regrets any oversight that may have occurred and will gladly make proper acknolwledgments in future printings.

Copyright Acknowledgments will be found in the index.
Printed in the United States of America.

ISBN 0-8146-1569-4

| 1 | 2 | 3 | 4 | 5 | 6 | 7 | 8 | 9 | 10 |

CONTENTS

HYMNS FOR THE LITURGY OF THE HOURS

HYMNS FOR GENERAL USAGE

INDEXES

FOREWORD

In my first pastoral letter to the Church of Chicago, "Our Communion, Our Peace, Our Promise," (1983) I wrote that "what we do in liturgy is too vast and too deep to be left to our speaking voices. We need music so that we can fully express what we are about." These thoughts were developed from the document of the U.S. Bishops' Committee on the Liturgy, "Music in Catholic Worship" (1972). The bishops had pointed out that the dimension of music in liturgy

> is integral to the human personality and to growth in faith. It cannot be ignored if the signs of worship are to speak to the whole person. Ideally every communal celebration of faith, including funerals and the sacraments of baptism, confirmation, penance, anointing, and matrimony should include music and singing. (#24)

In 1959, long before that document was published by the bishops, The Liturgical Press of St. John's Abbey, Collegeville, Minnesota, issued the first edition of its successful vernacular hymnal, *Our Parish Prays and Sings*. Thirty years later, a seventh completely revised and updated edition is now published. Hymns from every English-speaking tradition—some old and some newly composed—are here linked together with pieces from the repertory of Gregorian chant, that inexhaustible treasury of Catholic melody. Congregational hymn-singing for rites of the Church in every liturgical season is to be encouraged along with cantorial and choral singing of psalms and service music for the Eucharist.

This labor of the general editor, Father Edward McKenna, a priest of the Archdiocese of Chicago, as well as of many musical consultants and his Benedictine directors, Fathers Daniel Durken and Michael Naughton, has resulted in *The Collegeville Hymnal*. I am pleased to recommend it. I am confident that it will assist in promoting quality, communal celebrations of the Sunday Eucharist in many parishes. May we all continue to pray and sing!

Joseph Card. Bernardin

✝ Joseph Cardinal Bernardin
Archbishop of Chicago
March 17, 1989

INTRODUCTION

In their fifteen-hundred-year history, Benedictines have passed on to parishes all over the globe their tradition of praising God in song. In 1959 the Liturgical Press published a prime example of that with the first edition of *Our Parish Prays and Sings*. Through several editions, including the *Book of Sacred Song,* the American parish has come to know the best of classical Christian hymnody, in both the vernacular and the Latin chant. Much of the tradition of thirty years in promoting congregational song has been included in *The Collegeville Hymnal,* with emphasis as well on music and texts of notable merit gleaned from the work of contemporary composers and writers. Indeed, particular attention has been paid to texts from which archaic or non-inclusive language has been eliminated, except where poetic importance precludes change.

Our primary aim has been to provide the Sunday assembly with a liturgically alive and comprehensive hymnbook that invites and encourages congregational song in typical parish settings, without neglecting the choral and cantorial music recommended by the Constitution on Sacred Liturgy and the statements of the American hierarchy. Herein the parish music director can find nearly 500 seasonal, sanctoral and sacramental hymn selections, many intended for choral and assembly part-singing, with organ or other keyboard and instrumental accompaniment. *The Collegeville Hymnal* includes responsorial psalmody for all seasons, canticles and Gospel acclamations, sequences, and of course, Mass ordinary parts with eucharistic acclamations (eleven in English and three in Latin). Songs for common prayer and national festivity, for funeral and wedding, and a body of accessible anthems from the Roman Catholic thesaurus are all to be found within these pages!

In this newly engraved edition all hymntune titles and first lines are given along with pertinent information on composers, arrangers, authors and translators. Thorough indices on musicological, liturgical and scriptural topics are found in the back of the book. As Mass prayers or readings are not included, *The Collegeville Hymnal* works well along with the seasonal Mass Guide, though the Order of Mass and a schema of daily common prayer are handily printed. It is hoped that the liturgical and topical indices, together with the presentation of each Mass as a unified composition, will bring both musical beauty and liturgical coherence to each Sunday celebration.

A national board of experts assisted us in the selection and collection of these musical and lyrical gems, and to these persons we are most grateful: Father Joseph C. Cirou, Sister Delores Dufner, OSB, William Ferris, Msgr. Robert F. Hayburn, Kim Kasling, Bro. David Klingeman, OSB, Father Robert Koopman, OSB, Ramona LaGundo, Sister Christine Manderfeld, OSB, Father Stanley P. Rudcki, Sister Laurian Schumacher, OSB, Father Stephen Somerville, Sister Marguerite Streifel, OSB, Robert Strusinski, Michael Sullivan, Joseph P. Swain, and Joan Witek. We hope that what we propose for the feast of the People of God has musical competence and lyrical taste that results in prayerful integrity. May the broad ecumenical basis on which this work stands assure its place in parish pew and choir stall into the next century!

Reverend Edward J. McKenna, Editor
Vatican City State
November 1, 1989
The Solemnity of All Saints

THE ORDER OF MASS

INTRODUCTORY RITES

Acts of prayer and penitence prepare us to meet Christ as he comes in Word and Sacrament. We gather as a worshiping community to celebrate our unity with him and with one another in faith.

Options are indicated by A, B, C, D in the margin. Appropriate settings of the Mass Parts and hymns may be found in the Music section of the hymnal.

ENTRANCE SONG

Joined together as Christ's people, we open the celebration by raising our voices in praise of God who is present among us. This song should deepen our unity as it introduces the Mass we celebrate today.

GREETING   *After the entrance song, all make the sign of the cross.*

The priest welcomes us in the name of the Lord. We show our union with God, our neighbor, and the priest by a united response to his greeting.

A
Priest: The grace of our Lord Jesus Christ and love of God and the fellowship of the Holy Spirit be with you all.
People: And also with you.

B
Priest: The grace and peace of God our Father and the Lord Jesus Christ be with you.
People: Blessed be God the Father of our Lord Jesus Christ
or:
And also with you.

C
Priest: The Lord be with you.   *(Bishop:* Peace be with you.)
People: And also with you.

RITE OF BLESSING AND SPRINKLING HOLY WATER

The rite of blessing and sprinkling holy water may be celebrated all Masses celebrated on Sunday or Saturday evening. This rite takes the place of the penitential rite. The Kyrie is also omitted. During the sprinkling of the people an antiphon, or another appropriate song may be sung.

PENITENTIAL RITE

The priest invites the people to recall their sins and to repent of them in silence. Then one of the following forms is used.

Priest and People:

A
I confess to almighty God,
and to you, my brothers and sisters,
that I have sinned through my own fault
They strike their breast:
in my thoughts and in my words,
in what I have done,
and in what I have failed to do;
and I ask blessed Mary, ever virgin,
all the angels and saints,
and you, my brothers and sisters,
to pray for me to the Lord our God.

B
Priest: Lord, we have sinned against you:
Lord, have mercy.
People: Lord, have mercy.

Priest: Lord, show us your mercy and love.
People: And grant us your salvation.

Priest or other minister: Invocation.
　　　Lord, have mercy.
　People: Lord, have mercy.

Priest or other minister: Invocation.
　　　Christ, have mercy.
　People: Christ, have mercy.

Priest or other minister: Invocation.
　　　Lord, have mercy.
　People: Lord, have mercy.

The penitential rite always concludes:

Priest: May almighty God have mercy on us, forgive us our sins, and bring us to everlasting life. *People:* Amen.

KYRIE

Unless included in the penitential rite, the Kyrie or Lord, have mercy is sung or said by all.

℣.	Lord, have mercy.	or	℣.	Kyrie eleison.
℟.	Lord, have mercy.		℟.	Kyrie eleison.
℣.	Christ, have mercy.		℣.	Christe eleison.
℟.	Christ, have mercy.		℟.	Christe eleison.
℣.	Lord, have mercy.		℣.	Kyrie eleison.
℟.	Lord, have mercy.		℟.	Kyrie eleison.

GLORIA

As the Church assembled in the Spirit, we praise and pray to the Father and the Lamb.

Glory to God in the highest,
　and peace to his people on earth.
Lord, God, heavenly King,
almighty God and Father,
　we worship you, we give you thanks,
　we praise you for your glory.
Lord Jesus Christ, only Son of the Father,
Lord God, Lamb of God,
you take away the sin of the world:
　have mercy on us;
you are seated at the right hand of the Father:
　receive our prayer.
For you alone are the Holy One,
you alone are the Lord,
you alone are the Most High,
　Jesus Christ,
　with the Holy Spirit,
　in the glory of God the Father. Amen.

OPENING PRAYER

The priest invites us to pray silently for a moment and then, in our name, expresses the theme of the day's celebration and petitions God the Father through the mediation of Christ in the Holy Spirit.
Priest: Let us pray. *Priest and people pray silently for a while. Then the priest says the opening prayer which concludes:* for ever and ever. *People:* Amen.

LITURGY OF THE WORD

The proclamation of God's Word is always centered on Christ, present through his Word. Old Testament writings prepare for him; New Testament books speak of him directly. All of Scripture calls us to the faithful following of God's commandments. After the reading we reflect upon God's words and respond to them.

FIRST READING

At the end of the reading.

Reader: This is the Word of the Lord.   *People:* Thanks be to God.

The Responsorial Psalm is sung or recited after a period of silence.

SECOND READING

Reader: This is the Word of the Lord.   *People:* Thanks be to God.

GOSPEL

Jesus will speak to us in the Gospel. We rise now out of respect and prepare for his message with the Gospel acclamation.

Deacon (or priest): The Lord be with you.

People: And also with you.

Deacon (or priest): A reading from the holy gospel according to *N*.

People: Glory to you, Lord.

At the end:

Deacon (or priest): This is the Gospel of the Lord.

People: Praise to you, Lord Jesus Christ.

HOMILY

God's word is spoken again in the homily. The preacher explains and applies today's biblical readings to the needs of this particular congregation. He calls us to respond to Christ through the life we lead.

PROFESSION OF FAITH

As a people we express our acceptance of God's message in the Scriptures and homily. We summarize our faith by proclaiming a creed handed down from the early Church.

All say the profession of faith on Sundays and solemnities:

> We believe in one God,
>> the Father, the Almighty,
>> maker of heaven and earth,
>> of all that is seen and unseen.
>
> We believe in one Lord, Jesus Christ,
>> the only Son of God, eternally begotten of the Father,
>> God from God, Light from Light,
>> true God from true God,
>> begotten, not made, one in Being with the Father.
>> Through him all things were made.
>> For us men and for our salvation
>> he came down from heaven:

All bow at the following words, up to; and became man.

>> by the power of the Holy Spirit
>>> he was born of the Virgin Mary, and became man.
>
>> For our sake he was crucified under Pontius Pilate;
>>> he suffered, died, and was buried.
>> On the third day he rose again
>>> in fulfillment of the Scriptures;
>> He ascended into heaven,
>>> and is seated at the right hand of the Father.

He will come again in glory to judge the living and the dead,
and his kingdom will have no end.
We believe in the Holy Spirit, the Lord, the giver of life,
who proceeds from the Father and the Son.
With the Father and the Son he is worshiped and glorified.
He has spoken through the Prophets.
We believe in one holy catholic and apostolic Church.
We acknowledge one baptism for the forgiveness of sins.
We look for the resurrection of the dead,
and the life of the world to come. Amen.

At Masses with children, the Apostle's Creed may be used:

We believe in God, the Father almighty,
creator of heaven and earth.
We believe in Jesus Christ, his only Son, our Lord.
He was conceived by the power of the Holy Spirit
and born of the Virgin Mary.
He suffered under Pontius Pilate,
was crucified, died, and was buried.
He descended to the dead.
On the third day he arose again.
He ascended into heaven,
and is seated at the right hand of the Father.
He will come again to judge the living and the dead.
We believe in the Holy Spirit,
the holy catholic Church,
the communion of saints,
the forgiveness of sins,
the resurrection of the body,
and the life everlasting. Amen.

GENERAL INTERCESSION

As a priestly people we unite with one another to pray for today's needs in the Church and the world.

After the priest gives the introduction, the deacon or other minister sings or says the invocations.

The people respond: Lord, here our prayer; *or another response, according to local custom. After the concluding prayer, the people answer:* Amen.

LITURGY OF THE EUCHARIST

Made ready by reflection on God's Word, we enter now into the Eucharistic sacrifice itself, the Supper of the Lord. We celebrate the memorial which the Lord instituted at his Last Supper. We are God's new people, the redeemed brothers and sisters of Christ, gathered by him around his table. We are here to bless God and to receive the gift of Jesus' Body and Blood so that our faith and life may be transformed.

PREPARATION OF THE ALTAR AND THE GIFTS

While the gifts of the people are brought forward and placed on the altar and prepared, a hymn may be sung. If there is no singing, the priest may pray the prayers aloud. The people respond:

Blessed be God for ever.

The priest then invites the people to pray that the sacrifice will be acceptable.

People: May the Lord accept the sacrifice at your hands
for the praise and glory of his name,
for our good, and the good of all his Church.

PRAYER OVER THE GIFTS

The priest, speaking in our name, asks the Father to bless and accept these gifts.

At the end: *People:* **Amen.**

THE EUCHARISTIC PRAYER

We begin the Eucharistic Prayer of praise and thanksgiving, the center of the entire celebration, the central prayer of worship. At the priest's invitation we lift our hearts to God and unite with him in the words he address-es to the Father through Jesus Christ. Together we join Christ in his sacrifice, celebrating his memorial in the holy meal and acknowledging with him the wonderful works of God in our lives.

INTRODUCTORY DIALOGUE

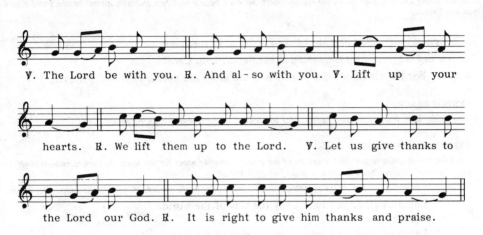

℣. The Lord be with you. ℟. And al-so with you. ℣. Lift up your

hearts. ℟. We lift them up to the Lord. ℣. Let us give thanks to

the Lord our God. ℟. It is right to give him thanks and praise.

PREFACE

SANCTUS

Priest and people: Holy, holy, holy Lord, God of power and might
heaven and earth are full of your glory.
  Hosanna in the highest.
Blessed is he who comes in the name of the Lord.
  Hosanna in the highest.

The people kneel after the Sanctus is sung or said. The priest then continues with one of the Eucharistic Prayers.

After the Institution, the priest says: Let us proclaim the mystery of faith. *Memorial acclamation of the people:*

A Christ has died,
Christ is risen
Christ will come again.

B Dying you destroyed our death,
rising you restored our life.
Lord Jesus, come in glory.

C When we eat this bread and drink this cup,
we proclaim your death, Lord Jesus,
until you come in glory.

D. Lord, by your cross and resurrection
you have set us free.
You are the Savior of the world.

The priest concludes the Eucharist Prayer singing or saying: **Through him, with him, in him, in the unity of the Holy Spirit, all glory and honor is yours, almighty Father, for ever and ever.** *The people respond:* **Amen.**

COMMUNION RITE

To prepare for the paschal meal, to welcome the Lord, we pray for forgiveness and exchange a sign of peace. Before eating Christ's Body and drinking his Blood, we must be one with him and with all our brothers and sisters in the Church.

The priest invites all to pray the Lord's Prayer. *At its conclusion:*

Deliver us Lord . . . for the coming of our Savior, Jesus Christ.

People: **For the kingdom, the power, and the glory are yours, now and for ever.**

SIGN OF PEACE

The priest says the prayer for peace, and invites all to exchange a sign of peace.

BREAKING OF THE BREAD

Christians are gathered for the "breaking of the bread," another name for the Mass. In Communion, though many we are made one body in the one bread, which is Christ.

The priest breaks the host over the paten and places a small piece in the chalice. Meanwhile the people sing or say:

Lamb of God, you take away the sins of the world:
have mercy on us.
Lamb of God, you take away the sins of the world:
have mercy on us.
Lamb of God, you take away the sins of the world:
grant us peace.

COMMUNION

We pray in silence and then voice words of humility and hope as our final preparation before meeting Christ in the Eucharist.

Priest: **This is the Lamb of God
who takes away the sins of the world.
Happy are those who are called to his supper.**

Priest and people (once only):
**Lord, I am not worthy to receive you,
but only say the word and I shall be healed.**

Priest: **The body of Christ.** *Communicant:* **Amen.**
Priest: **The blood of Christ.** *Communicant:* **Amen.**

During communion a suitable song may be sung. After communion, the priest and people may spend some time in silent prayer. (Sit or Kneel.) If desired, a hymn, psalm, or other song of praise may be sung.

PRAYER AFTER COMMUNION

The priest prays in our name that we may live the life of faith since we have been strengthened by Christ himself.
Priest: **Let us pray.**

Priest and people pray silently for a while unless a period of silence has been observed. Then the priest says the prayer after communion. At the end: **Amen.**

CONCLUDING RITE

We have heard God's Word and eaten the Body of Christ. Now it is time for us to leave, to do good works, to praise and bless the Lord in our daily lives.

GREETING

Priest: The Lord be with you.

People: And also with you.

> *When the Bishop blesses the people:* Blessed be the name of the Lord.
> *People:* Now and for ever.
>
> *Bishop:* Our help is in the name of the Lord.
> *People:* Who made heaven and earth.

BLESSING

The blessing may be a simple or solemn form. All respond to the blessing or to each part of the blessing: Amen.

DISMISSAL

Priest or Deacon:

> Go in the peace of Christ.
> *or*
> The Mass is ended, go in peace.
> *or*
> Go in peace to love and serve the Lord.

People: Thanks be to God.

MASS IN HONOR OF AMERICAN NUNS

Rite of Blessing and Sprinkling of Holy Water   1
(Outside the Easter Season)

ANTIPHON

Cantor/Choir; All repeat

Cleanse us, Lord, from all our sins; wash us, and we shall be whit-er than snow.

1.–2. *To Verses*

Final Ending

snow.

VERSE 1

Cantor

Have mer-cy on me, O God, in your good-ness; in the great-ness of your com-pas-sion wipe out my of-fense.

Repeat Antiphon

Thor-ough-ly wash me from my guilt and of my sin cleanse me.

VERSE 2

Cantor

For I ac-knowl-edge my of-fense, And my sin is be-fore me al-ways: "A-gainst you

Repeat Antiphon

on-ly have I sinned, and done what is e-vil in your sight."

Music: Robert E. Kreutz, b. 1922, ©

2 Rite of Blessing and Sprinkling of Holy Water
(Easter Season)

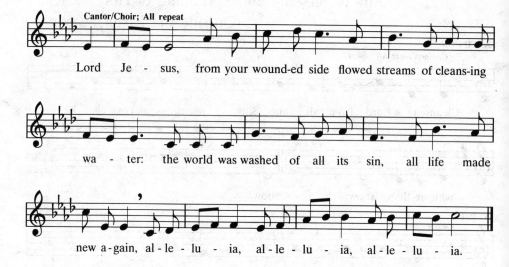

Lord Je - sus, from your wound-ed side flowed streams of cleans-ing wa - ter: the world was washed of all its sin, all life made new a-gain, al - le - lu - ia, al - le - lu - ia, al - le - lu - ia.

3 Kyrie

Lord, have mer - cy. Lord, have mer - cy. Christ, have mer - cy. Christ, have mer - cy. Lord, have mer - cy. Lord, have mer - cy.

Gloria 4

REFRAIN All
Glo-ry to God in the high-est, and peace to his peo-ple on earth.

Glo-ry to God in the high-est, and peace to his peo-ple on earth.

Cantor/Choir
Lord God, heav-en - ly King, al - might-y God and Fa - ther,

we wor-ship you, we give you thanks, we praise you for your glo - ry.

REFRAIN All
Glo-ry to God in the high-est, and peace to his peo-ple on earth.

Glo-ry to God in the high-est, and peace to his peo-ple on earth.

Cantor/Choir
Lord Je - sus Christ, on - ly Son of the Fa - ther, Lord God,

Lamb of God, you take a - way the sin of the world: have

mer - cy on us; you are seat - ed at the

right hand of the Fa - ther: re - ceive our prayer.

REFRAIN
All

Glo - ry to God in the high-est, and peace to his peo-ple on earth.

Glo - ry to God in the high-est, and peace to his peo-ple on earth.

Cantor/Choir

For you a - lone are the Ho - ly One, you a - lone are the

Lord, you a - lone are the Most High, Je - sus Christ, with the

Ho - ly Spir - it, in the glo - ry of God the Fa - ther.

REFRAIN
All

Glo - ry to God in the high-est, and peace to his peo-ple on earth.

Glo - ry to God in the high-est, and peace to his peo-ple on earth.

A - men, a - men.

Gospel Acclamation 5

Al - le - lu - ia, al - le - lu - ia, al - le - lu - ia.

VERSE

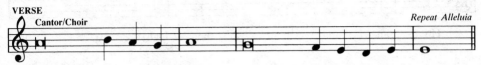

Gospel Acclamations for Lent 6

[A]

Praise to you, Lord Je - sus Christ, King of end - less glo - ry!

[B]

Praise and hon - or to you, Lord Je - sus Christ!

[C]

Glo - ry and praise to you, Lord Je - sus Christ!

[D]

Glo - ry to you, Word of God, Lord Je - sus Christ!

Sanctus 7

Ho - ly, ho - ly, ho - ly Lord, God of pow-er and might,

heav-en and earth are full of your glo - ry. Ho - san - na in the high-est.

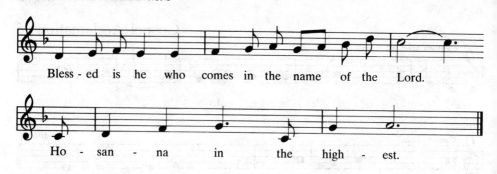

Bless - ed is he who comes in the name of the Lord.

Ho - san - na in the high - est.

8 Memorial Acclamations and Great Amen

[A]

Christ has died, Christ is ris - en, Christ will come a - gain.
A - men, a - men, a - men.

[B]

Dy - ing you de - stroyed our death, ris - ing you re - stored our life.
A - men, a - men,

Lord Je - sus, come in glo - ry.
a - men.

[C]

When we eat this bread and drink this cup, we pro - claim your death, Lord

Je - sus, un - til you come in glo - ry.

[D]

Lord, by your cross and re - sur - rec - tion you have set us free.

You are the Sav - ior of the world.

The Lord's Prayer 9

10 Agnus Dei

Lamb of God, you take a - way the sins of the world:

have mer-cy on us. Lamb of God, you take a - way the sins

of the world: have mer - cy on us. Lamb of God,

you take a - way the sins of the world:

grant us peace, grant us peace.

MASS FOR CANTOR AND CONGREGATION

Rite of Blessing and Sprinkling of Holy Water 11
(Outside of Easter Season)

ANTIPHON
Cantor/Choir; All repeat

Cleanse us, Lord from all our sins, cleanse us from all our sins;

Fine

wash us, and we shall be whit - er than snow.

VERSE
Cantor

Have mer - cy on me, O God, in your good - ness; in the

great-ness of your com - pas - sion wipe out my of - fense.

Glo - ry be to the Fa - ther, and to the Son, and to the

Ho - ly Spir - it; as it was in the be - gin-ning, is now, and

Repeat Antiphon

ev - er shall be, world with - out end. A - men.

Music: Michael Sullivan, b. 1937, ©

12 Kyrie

Lord, have mer - cy. Lord, have mer - cy.

Christ, have mer - cy. Christ, have mer - cy.

Lord, have mer - cy. Lord, have mer - cy.

13 Gloria

Glo - ry to God in the high - est, and peace to his peo-ple on

earth. Lord God, heav-en - ly King, al - might - y God and

Fa - ther, we wor-ship you, we give you thanks, we praise you for your

glo - ry. Lord Je - sus Christ, on - ly Son of the Fa - ther,

Lord God, Lamb of God, you take a-way the sin of the world: have

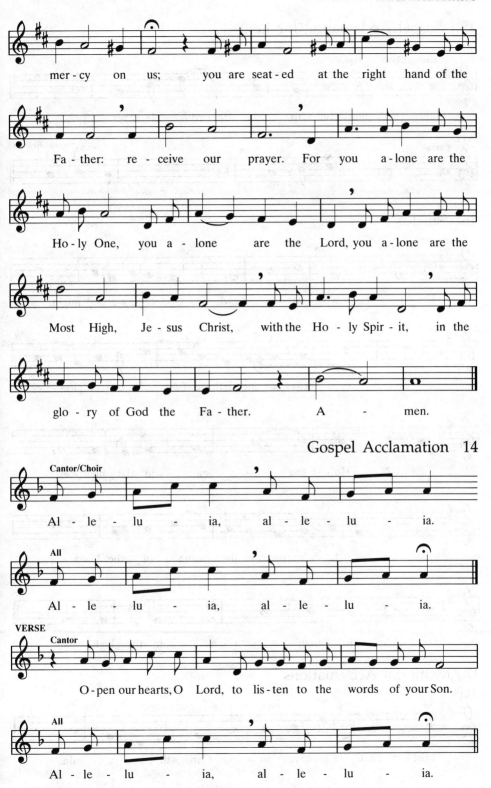

mer - cy on us; you are seat - ed at the right hand of the

Fa - ther: re - ceive our prayer. For you a - lone are the

Ho - ly One, you a - lone are the Lord, you a - lone are the

Most High, Je - sus Christ, with the Ho - ly Spir - it, in the

glo - ry of God the Fa - ther. A - men.

Gospel Acclamation 14

Cantor/Choir

Al - le - lu - ia, al - le - lu - ia.

All

Al - le - lu - ia, al - le - lu - ia.

VERSE

Cantor

O - pen our hearts, O Lord, to lis - ten to the words of your Son.

All

Al - le - lu - ia, al - le - lu - ia.

15 Gospel Acclamation for Lent

REFRAIN

Cantor/Choir; All repeat

Praise and hon - or to you, Lord Je - sus Christ!

VERSE

Cantor

Repeat Refrain

16 Sanctus

All

Ho - ly, ho - ly, ho - ly Lord, God of pow-er and might,

heav - en and earth are full of your glo - ry.

Ho - san - na in the high - est.

Bless - ed is he who comes in the name of the Lord.

Ho - san - na in the high - est.

17 Memorial Acclamations

[A]

All

Christ has died, Christ is ris - en, Christ will come a - gain.

[C]

All

When we eat this bread and drink this cup, we pro-claim your death,

Lord Je - sus, un - til you come in glo - ry.

[D]

All

Lord, by your cross and re - sur - rec - tion

you have set us free. You are the Sav - ior of the world.

Great Amen 18

All

A - men, a - men, a - men.

Agnus Dei 19

All

Lamb of God, you take a - way the sins of the

world: have mer - cy on us.

Lamb of God, you take a-way the sins of the world: grant us peace.

PEOPLE'S MASS

20 Kyrie

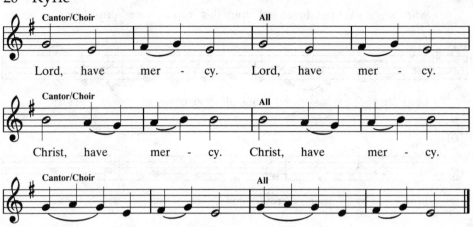

Lord, have mer - cy. Lord, have mer - cy.

Christ, have mer - cy. Christ, have mer - cy.

Lord, have mer - cy. Lord, have mer - cy.

21 Gloria

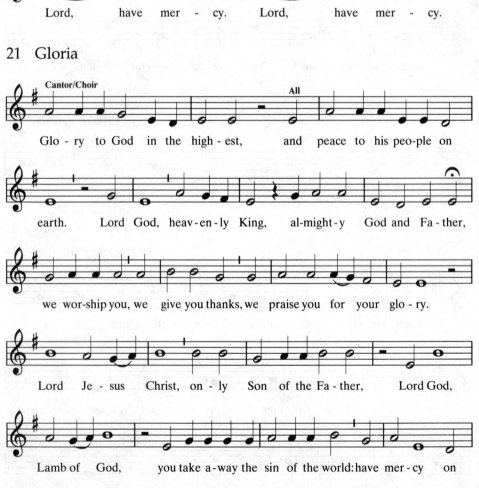

Glo - ry to God in the high - est, and peace to his peo-ple on

earth. Lord God, heav-en-ly King, al-might-y God and Fa - ther,

we wor-ship you, we give you thanks, we praise you for your glo - ry.

Lord Je - sus Christ, on - ly Son of the Fa - ther, Lord God,

Lamb of God, you take a-way the sin of the world: have mer - cy on

Music: Jan Martin Vermulst, b. 1925 © *1970, World Library Publications, Inc.*

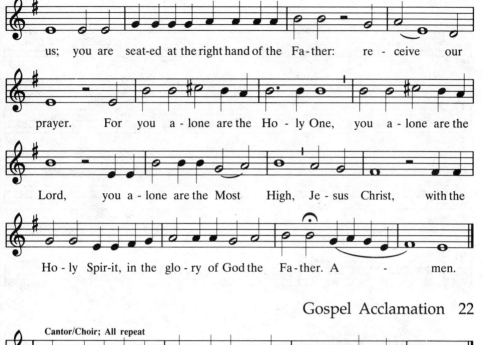

us; you are seat-ed at the right hand of the Fa-ther: re - ceive our

prayer. For you a - lone are the Ho - ly One, you a - lone are the

Lord, you a - lone are the Most High, Je - sus Christ, with the

Ho - ly Spir-it, in the glo - ry of God the Fa-ther. A - men.

Gospel Acclamation 22

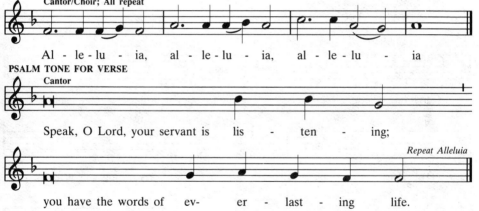

Cantor/Choir; All repeat

Al - le - lu - ia, al - le - lu - ia, al - le - lu - ia

PSALM TONE FOR VERSE

Cantor

Speak, O Lord, your servant is lis - ten - ing;

Repeat Alleluia

you have the words of ev- er - last - ing life.

Gospel Acclamations for Lent 23

1. Praise to you, Lord Je - sus Christ, King of end - less glo - ry!
2. Praise and hon - or to you, Lord Je - sus Christ!
3. Glo - ry and praise to you, Lord Je - sus Christ!
4. Glo - ry to you, Word of God, Lord Je - sus Christ!

24 Sanctus

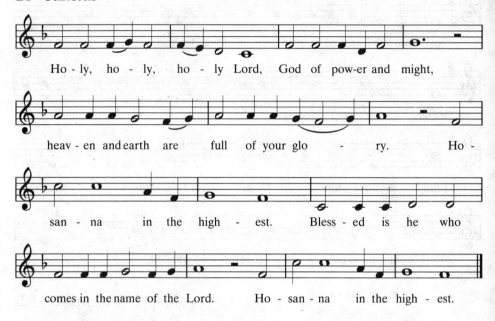

Ho - ly, ho - ly, ho - ly Lord, God of pow-er and might,

heav - en and earth are full of your glo - ry. Ho -

san - na in the high - est. Bless - ed is he who

comes in the name of the Lord. Ho - san - na in the high - est.

25 Memorial Acclamations

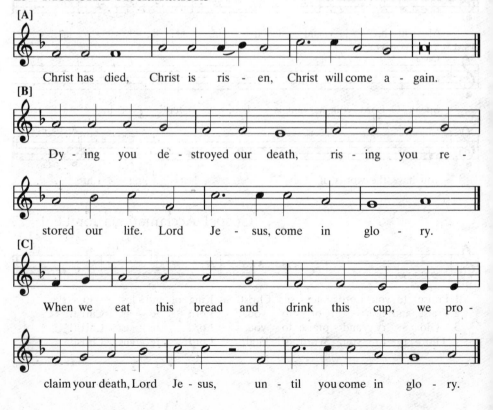

[A]

Christ has died, Christ is ris - en, Christ will come a - gain.

[B]

Dy - ing you de - stroyed our death, ris - ing you re -

stored our life. Lord Je - sus, come in glo - ry.

[C]

When we eat this bread and drink this cup, we pro -

claim your death, Lord Je - sus, un - til you come in glo - ry.

[D]

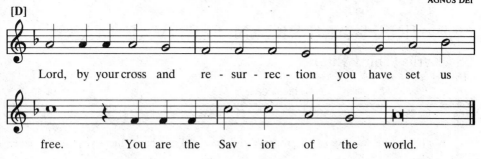

Lord, by your cross and re - sur - rec - tion you have set us free. You are the Sav - ior of the world.

Great Amen 26

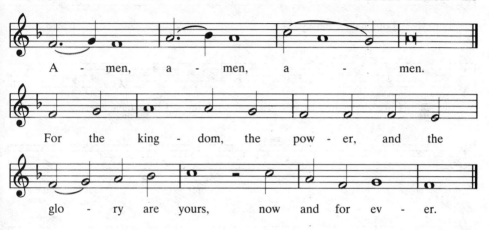

A - men, a - men, a - men.

For the king - dom, the pow - er, and the glo - ry are yours, now and for ev - er.

Agnus Dei 27

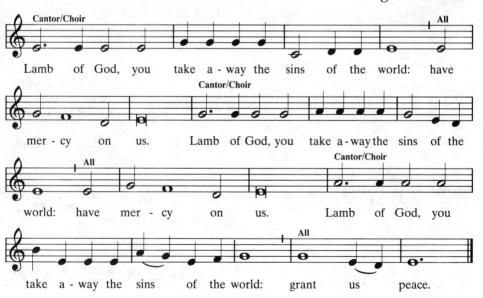

Cantor/Choir ... *All*

Lamb of God, you take a - way the sins of the world: have mer - cy on us.

Cantor/Choir

Lamb of God, you take a - way the sins of the world: have mer - cy on us.

All ... *Cantor/Choir*

Lamb of God, you take a - way the sins of the world: grant us peace.

All

IRISH–AMERICAN FESTIVAL MASS

28 Kyrie (Third Rite)

This may also be used with First Rite

First invocation is read, or sung. Lord, have mer-cy. Lord, have mer-cy. Lord, have

mer-cy. Lord, have mer-cy. *Second invocation is read, or sung.* Christ, have

mer-cy. Christ, have mer-cy. Christ, have mer-cy. Christ, have mer-cy.

Third invocation is read, or sung. Lord, have mer - cy. Lord have

mer - cy. Lord, have mer - cy. Lord, have mer - cy.

29 Gloria

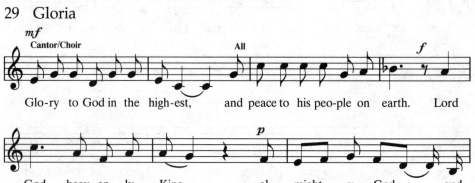

Glo-ry to God in the high-est, and peace to his peo-ple on earth. Lord

God, heav-en-ly King, al - might - y God and

Fa-ther, we wor-ship you, we give you thanks, we praise you for your

Music: Edward J. McKenna, b. 1939, ©

glo - ry. O Lord Je - sus Christ, on - ly Son of the Fa - ther,

Lord God, Lamb of God, you take a - way the sin of the world:

Slower

Cantor/Choir

have mer - cy on us; you are seat - ed at the right hand of the

mp **All** *a tempo*

Fa-ther: re - ceive our prayer. For you a-lone are the Ho - ly One,

you a - lone are the Lord, you a - lone are the Most High,

mf

Je - sus Christ, with the Ho - ly Spir - it, in the

glo - ry of God the Fa - ther. A - men. In the glo-ry of God the Fa - ther.

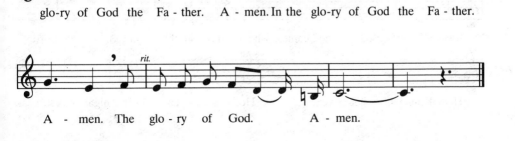

rit.

A - men. The glo - ry of God. A - men.

30 Gospel Acclamation

Cantor/Choir; All repeat

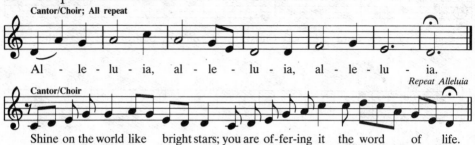

Al - le - lu - ia, al - le - lu - ia, al - le - lu - ia.

Repeat Alleluia

Cantor/Choir

Shine on the world like bright stars; you are of-fer-ing it the word of life.

31 Gospel Acclamation for Lent

Cantor/Choir; All repeat

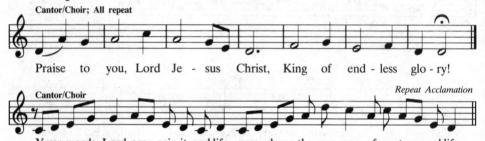

Praise to you, Lord Je - sus Christ, King of end - less glo - ry!

Repeat Acclamation

Cantor/Choir

Your words, Lord, are spir-it and life, you have the mes-sage of e - ter - nal life.

32 Sanctus

All *mf*

Ho - ly, ho - ly, ho - ly Lord, God of pow-er and

might, hea - ven and earth are full of your

f

glo - ry. Ho - san - na in the high - est.

Cantor/Choir

Bless-ed is he who comes, who comes in the name of the Lord,

All

High King of hea - ven. Ho - san - na in the high - est.

Memorial Acclamations   33

Celebrant

Let us pro - claim the mys - ter - y of faith:

[A] All

Christ has died, Christ is ris - en, Christ will come a - gain.

[B] All *mf*

Dy - ing you de - stroyed our death, ris - ing you re -

f

stored our life. Lord Je - sus, come in glo - ry.

[D] All *mf*

Lord, by your cross and re - sur - rec - tion, you have set us

f   *dim.*

free. You are the Sav - ior of the world.

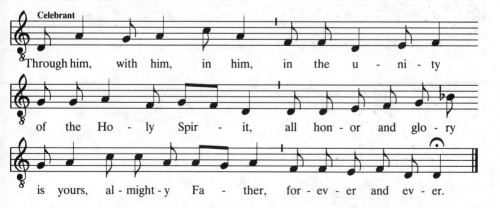

Celebrant

Through him, with him, in him, in the u - ni - ty

of the Ho - ly Spir - it, all hon - or and glo - ry

is yours, al - might - y Fa - ther, for - ev - er and ev - er.

34 Great Amen

A - men, a - men, a - men.

May be repeated ad lib.

35 The Lord's Prayer

Our Fa - ther, who art in hea - ven, hal-lowed be thy name; thy

king-dom come; thy will be done on earth as it is in heav'n. Give

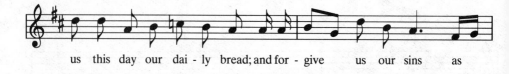

us this day our dai - ly bread; and for - give us our sins as

we for-give those who sin a-gainst us. Save us from the time of trial.

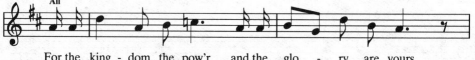

For the king - dom, the pow'r, and the glo - ry are yours,

now and for - ev - er. A - men.

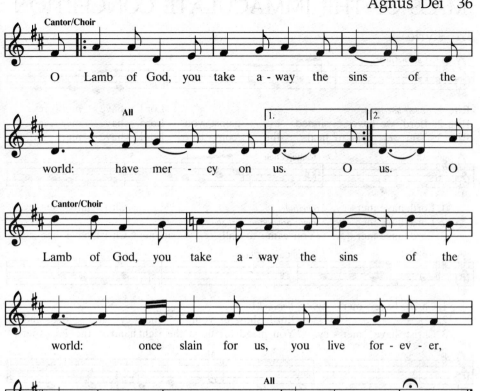

Cantor/Choir

O Lamb of God, you take a - way the sins of the

All

world: have mer - cy on us. 1. O us. 2. O

Cantor/Choir

Lamb of God, you take a - way the sins of the

world: once slain for us, you live for - ev - er,

All

grant us peace. Grant us peace.

MASS OF THE IMMACULATE CONCEPTION

37 Kyrie

Cantor/Choir

Rite 1: *(organ interlude)*   Lord,   have   mer - cy.
Rite 2: Lord, we have   sinned   a - gainst you.   Lord,   have   mer - cy.
Rite 3: You were sent to heal   the   con - trite: Lord,   have   mer - cy.

All   Cantor/Choir

1. Lord, have mer - cy.   *(interlude)*   Christ, have mer - cy.
2. Lord, have mer - cy.   *(omit; proceed to next stave.)*
3. Lord, have mer - cy.   You came to call   sin - ners: Christ, have mer - cy.

All   Cantor/Choir

1. Christ, have mer - cy.   *(interlude)*
2.   Lord, show us your   mer - cy   and   love, and
3. Christ, have mer - cy.   You plead for us at the right hand of the Fa - ther:

All

1. Lord,   have   mer - cy.   Lord,   have   mer - cy.
2. grant   us   your sal - va - tion.   Grant   us   your sal - va - tion.
3. Lord,   have   mer - cy.   Lord,   have   mer - cy.

Celebrant

May almighty God have mercy on us,   for - give   us   our   sins,

and bring us   to   ev - er - last-ing life.   A - men.

All

38 Gloria

REFRAIN
All   *

Glo - ry to God in the high - est,   and peace to his peo - ple on earth.

*The last time, proceed to "Amen.

Music: Fintan P. O'Carroll, © 1977

39 Gospel Acclamations

Al - le - lu - ia, al - le - lu - ia, al - le - lu - ia!

PSALM TONE FOR VERSE

Repeat Alleluia

Cantor

Alleluia

Cantor/Choir

Al - le - lu - ia, al - le - lu - ia, al - le -

lu - ia, al - le - lu - ia. Al - le - lu - ia,

al - le - lu - ia, al - le - lu - ia, al - le - lu - ia!

VERSE   Cantor

The Word was made flesh and lived a-mong us, and we saw his glo-ry.

All

Al - le - lu - ia, al - le - lu - ia,

al - le - lu - ia, al - le - lu - ia!

Sanctus 40

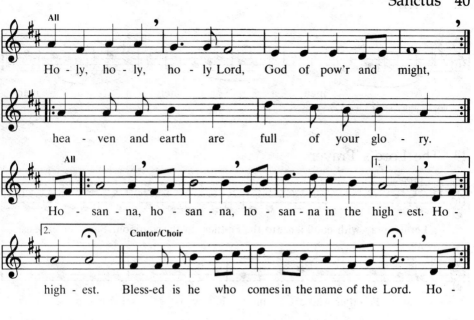

Ho - ly, ho - ly, ho - ly Lord, God of pow'r and might,

hea - ven and earth are full of your glo - ry.

Ho - san - na, ho - san - na, ho - san - na in the high - est. Ho -

high - est. Bless-ed is he who comes in the name of the Lord. Ho -

Memorial Acclamation 41

Let us pro - claim the mys - ter - y of faith:

Christ has died, Christ is ris - en, Christ will come a - gain.

Through him, with him, in him, in the u - ni - ty

of the Ho - ly Spir - it, all glo - ry and hon - or is yours,

al - might - y Fa - ther, for - ev - er and ev - er.

42 Amen

A - men, a - men, a - men.

This may be performed as a round in 3 parts.

43 The Lord's Prayer

Let us pray with confidence to the Fa-ther in the words our Sav - ior gave us:

Our Fa - ther, who art in hea - ven, hal-lowed be thy

name; thy king - dom come; thy will be done on

earth as it is in hea - ven. Give us this day our dai - ly

bread, and for - give us our tres-pas-ses; as we for-give those who

tres - pass a - gainst us; and lead us not in - to temp-

ta - tion, but de - li - ver us from e - vil.

For the king-dom, the pow'r, and the glo - ry are yours, now and for ev - er.

Agnus Dei 44

Lamb of God, you take a - way the sins of the world: have mer - cy on us, have mer - cy on us. Lamb of God, you take a - way the sins of the world: have mer - cy on us, have mer - cy on us.

Lamb of God, you take a - way the sins of the world:

grant us peace, grant us peace.

MASS OF SAINT OLIVER PLUNKETT

45 Kyrie (Third Rite)*

mf Cantor/Choir

Sing/Read First Invocation. Lord, have mer - cy. Lord, have mer - cy.

Sing/Read Second Invocation. Christ, have mer - cy.

Christ, have mer - cy. *Sing/Read Third Invocation.*

Lord, have mer - cy. Lord, have mer - cy.

*May also be used with First Rite.

46 Gloria

Con Spirito *f* All

Glo-ry to God in the high - est, and peace to his peo-ple on earth.

Lord God, hea-ven-ly King, al-might-y God and Fa - ther, we

wor - ship you, we give you thanks, we praise you for your glo - ry.

Lord Je - sus Christ, on - ly Son of the Fa - ther,

Music: Edward J. McKenna, b. 1939; Sanctus and Agnus Dei, Gaelic tune, adapt., ©
Dedicated to the memory of Tomás Cardinal Ó Fiaich.

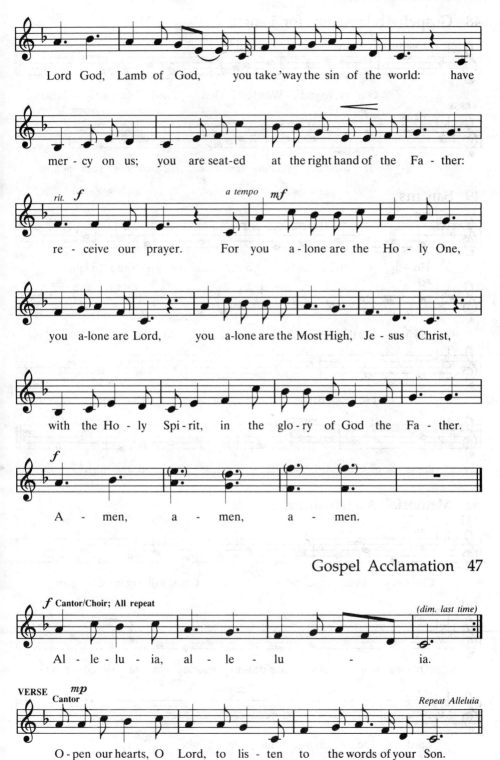

Lord God, Lamb of God, you take 'way the sin of the world: have
mer - cy on us; you are seat-ed at the right hand of the Fa - ther:
rit. **f**   *a tempo* ***mf***
re - ceive our prayer. For you a - lone are the Ho - ly One,
you a-lone are Lord, you a-lone are the Most High, Je - sus Christ,
with the Ho - ly Spi - rit, in the glo - ry of God the Fa - ther.
f
A - men, a - men, a - men.

Gospel Acclamation 47

f Cantor/Choir; All repeat   *(dim. last time)*
Al - le - lu - ia, al - le - lu - ia.

VERSE ***mp***
Cantor   *Repeat Alleluia*
O - pen our hearts, O Lord, to lis - ten to the words of your Son.

48 Gospel Acclamation for Lent

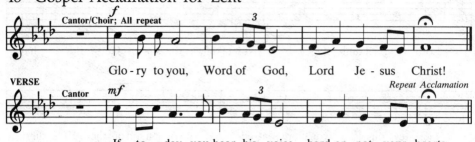

Glo-ry to you, Word of God, Lord Je-sus Christ!

If to-day you hear his voice, hard-en not your hearts.

49 Sanctus

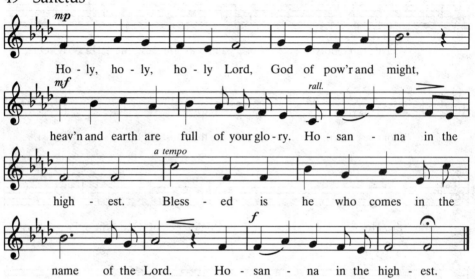

Ho-ly, ho-ly, ho-ly Lord, God of pow'r and might,

heav'n and earth are full of your glo-ry. Ho-san-na in the

high-est. Bless-ed is he who comes in the

name of the Lord. Ho-san-na in the high-est.

50 Memorial Acclamations

[A]

Christ has died, Christ is ris-en, Christ will come a-gain.

[B]

Dy-ing you de-stroyed our death, ris-ing you re-stored our life.

Lord Je-sus, come in glo-ry.

[C]

mf
All
When we eat this bread and drink this cup, we pro-

f
claim your death, Lord Je - sus, un - til you come in glo - ry.

The Great Amen 51

Slowly
f Cantor/Choir; All repeat   *ff*
A - men, a - men, a - men.

Agnus Dei 52

Andante *mp*
Cantor/Choir   3
O Lamb of God, you take a - way the sins of the world:

meno mosso
All Second Time *f*   3   *a tempo*
                                   mf Cantor/Choir
have mer - cy on us. O Lamb of God, you

f *mf*   3
take a - way the sins of the world: have mer - cy on

a tempo
All *meno mosso*   3   Cantor/Choir
us. Have mer - cy on us. O Lamb of God, you

f
take a - way the sins of the world; once slain for us you

ff All
live for - ev - er, grant us peace, grant us peace.

MASS OF HOPE

53 Kyrie

Cantor/Choir Lord, have mer - cy. **All** Lord, have mer - cy.

Cantor/Choir Christ, have mer - cy. **All** Christ, have mer - cy.

Cantor/Choir Lord, have mer - cy. **All** Lord, have mer - cy.

54 Gloria

Celebrant/Cantor Glo - ry to God in the high - est, **All** and peace to his peo - ple on earth. Lord God, heav - en - ly King, al - might - y God and Fa - ther, we wor - ship you, we give you thanks, we praise you for your glo - ry. Lord Je - sus Christ, on - ly Son of the

Music: Eugene Englert, b. 1931, ©

Fa - ther, Lord God, Lamb of God, you take a -
way the sin of the world: have mer - cy on us;
you are seat - ed at the right hand of the Fa - ther:
re - ceive our prayer. For you a -
lone are the Ho - ly One, you a - lone are the Lord,
you a - lone are the Most High, Je - sus Christ, with the
Ho - ly Spir - it, in the glo - ry of God the Fa - ther.
A - men, a - men.

55 Gospel Acclamation

Al - le - lu - ia, al - le - lu - ia, al - le - lu - ia.

PSALM TONE FOR VERSE

56 Gospel Acclamation For Lent

Glo - ry and praise to you, Lord Je - sus Christ!

57 Sanctus

Ho - ly, ho - ly, ho - ly Lord, God of pow'r and might,

heav - en and earth are full of your glo - ry. Ho -

san - na in the high - est, ho - san - na in the high - est.

Bless - ed is he who comes in the name of the Lord. Ho -

san - na in the high - est, ho - san - na in the high - est.

Memorial Acclamations 58

[A] Christ has died, Christ is ris-en, Christ will come a-gain.

[B] Dy-ing you de-stroyed our death, ris-ing you re-stored our life. Lord Je-sus, come in glo-ry.

[C] When we eat this bread and drink this cup, we pro-claim your death, Lord Je-sus, un-til you come in glo-ry.

[D] Lord, by your cross and re-sur-rec-tion you have set us free. You are the Sav-ior of the world.

Great Amen 59

A-men, a-men, a-men.

60 Agnus Dei

Lamb of God, you take a - way the sins of the world: have mer-cy on us. Lamb of God, you take a - way the sins of the world: have mer-cy on us. Lamb of God, you take a - way the sins of the world: grant us peace.

MASS IN HONOR OF SAINT PHILIP NERI

Kyrie 61

Cantor/Choir · All

Lord, have mer - cy Lord, have mer - cy.

Cantor/Choir · All

Christ, have mer - cy. Christ, have mer - cy.

Cantor/Choir · All

Lord, have mer - cy. Lord, have mer - cy.

Gloria 62

Lively

Cantor · Choir

Glo-ry to God in the high-est, and peace to his peo-ple on earth.

All · Cantor

Lord God, heav-en - ly King, al - might - y God and Fa - ther, we

Choir

wor - ship you, we give you thanks, we praise you for your glo - ry.

All · *Slower*

Lord Je - sus Christ, on - ly Son of the Fa - ther, Lord God,

Cantor/Choir

you take the world's sin:

Lamb of God, you take a - way the sin of the world:

Music: Edward J. McKenna, b. 1939, ©

Slow

All

have mer - cy on us; have mer - cy on us. Fa- ther re- ceive our

Cantor/Choir

You are seat-ed at the right hand of the Fa-ther: re - ceive our prayer.

prayer. For you a - lone are the Ho-ly One, you a - lone are Lord,

All with Cantor

you a - lone are the Most High, Je - sus Christ,

Tempo I

with the Ho - ly Spir - it, in the glo - ry of God the

Slowing

Fa - ther. A - men, a - men, a - men.

63 Sanctus

All

Cantor

Ho - ly, ho - ly, ho-ly Lord, God of pow-er and might, hea-ven and

All

earth are full of your glo - ry. Ho - san - na in the high - est.

Cantor/Choir

Bless - ed is he who comes in the name

All

of the Lord. Ho - san - na in the high - est.

Memorial Acclamation 64

When we eat this bread and drink this cup, we pro - claim your death,
Lord Je - sus, un - til you come in glo - ry.

Amen 65

Celebrant sings Doxology   All

May be repeated.

A - men, a - men, a - men.

Agnus Dei 66

Cantor/Choir

O Lamb of God, you take a - way the sins of the world:

All   Cantor

have mer - cy on us, have mer - cy on us. O

Lamb of God, you take a - way the sins of the world:

All   Cantor   All

grant us peace, once slain for us, you live for-ev-er, grant us peace, your

Slow

bod - y bro - ken, bread for us, grant us peace.

MISSA LAUDIS

67 Kyrie

Cantor/Choir

Lord, O Lord, have mer - cy, have mer - cy on us.

All

Lord, O Lord, have mer - cy, have mer - cy on us.

Cantor/Choir

Christ, O Christ, have mer - cy, have mer - cy on us.

All

Christ, O Christ, have mer - cy, have mer - cy on us.

Cantor/Choir

Lord, O Lord, have mer - cy, have mer - cy on us.

All

Lord, O Lord, have mer - cy, have mer - cy on us.

68 Gloria

ANTIPHON

All

Glo-ry to God in the high - est, and peace to his peo-ple on earth.

VERSE 1

Cantor

Lord God, heav-en - ly King, al-might - y God and Fa - ther:

Music: Becket Senchur, OSB, b. 1946, ©

69 Sanctus

Ho - ly, ho - ly, ho - ly Lord, God of pow-er and

might, heav-en and earth are full of your glo - ry.

Ho - san - na, ho - san - na in the high - est.

Bless-ed is he who comes in the name

of the Lord. Ho - san - na, ho -

san - na in the high - est.

70 Memorial Acclamation

Your death, O Lord, is a birth to e - ter - nal life:

you have set us free, al - le - lu - ia!

Great Amen 71

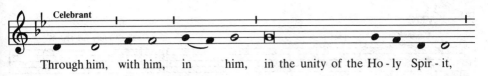

Through him, with him, in   him,   in the unity of the Ho - ly Spir - it,

all glory and honor is   yours, almight-y Fa-ther, for ev - er and ev - er.

A -   men,   a -   men.

Agnus Dei 72

Lamb of God, you   take   a - way   the sins   of the world: have

mer - cy on us.   Lamb of   God,   you   take   a - way   the

sins   of the world: have mer - cy on us.   Lamb of   God,   you

take   a - way   the sins   of the world: grant   us   peace.

MASS OF THE GOOD SHEPHERD

73 Kyrie

Lord, have mer - cy. Christ, have mer - cy. Lord, have mer - cy.

74 Gloria

Glo-ry to God in the high - est, and peace to his peo-ple on earth.

Lord God, heav-en - ly King, al - might-y God and Fa - ther, we

wor - ship you, we give you thanks, we praise you for your glo - ry.

Lord Je - sus Christ, on - ly Son of the Fa - ther,

Lord God, Lamb of God, you take a - way the sin of the

world: have mer - cy on us; you are

Music: Stephen Somerville, ©

seat - ed at the right hand of the Fa - ther: re - ceive our

prayer. For you a - lone are the Ho - ly One,

you a - lone are the Lord, you a - lone are the Most

High, Je - sus Christ, with the Ho - ly Spir - it, in the

glo-ry of God the Fa - ther. A - men, a - men, a - men.

Sanctus 75

Ho - ly, ho - ly, ho - ly Lord, God of pow'r and might,

heav - en and earth are full of your glo - ry. Ho -

san - na in the high - est. Bless - ed is he who

comes in the name of the Lord. Ho - san - na in the high - est.

76 Agnus Dei

Lamb of God, you take a-way the sins of the world: have

mer - cy on us. Lamb of God, you take a-way the

sins of the world: have mer - cy on us.

Lamb of God you take a-way the sins of the world: grant us peace.

CHANT MASS

Lord, have mer-cy. Lord, have mer-cy. Christ, have mer-cy. Christ, have mer-cy.

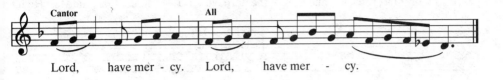

Lord, have mer - cy. Lord, have mer - cy.

Glo - ry to God in the high - est, and peace to his peo-ple on earth.

Lord God, heav-en - ly King, al - might-y God and Fa - ther,

we wor-ship you, we give you thanks, we praise you for your glo - ry.

Lord Je - sus Christ, on - ly Son of the Fa-ther, Lord God, Lamb of God,

you take a-way the sin of the world: have mer-cy on us; you are seat-ed at the

Music: Jubilate Deo Chant Mass; adapt. and acc. Edward J. McKenna, ©

right hand of the Fa-ther: re - ceive our prayer. For you a - lone are the

Ho-ly One, you a - lone are the Lord, you a - lone are the Most High,

Je - sus Christ, with the Ho - ly Spir - it,

in the glo - ry of God the Fa-ther. A - men.

79 Sanctus

Ho - ly, ho - ly, ho - ly Lord, God of pow'r and might,

hea - ven and earth are full of your glo - ry.

Ho - san - na in the high - est. Bless - ed is he who

comes in the name of the Lord. Ho - san - na in the high - est.

Memorial Acclamation 80

Let us pro-claim the mys-te - ry of faith:

Christ has died, Christ is ris - en, Christ will come a - gain.

Agnus Dei 81

Lamb of God, you take a - way the sins of the world: have mer - cy on us.

Lamb of God, you take a - way the sins of the world: have mer - cy on us.

Lamb of God, you take a - way the sins of the world: grant us peace.

MATHIAS MASS

82 Kyrie

Lord, have mer - cy. Lord, have mer - cy. Lord, have mer - cy.

Christ, have mer - cy. Christ, have mer - cy. Christ, have mer - cy.

Lord, have mer - cy. Lord, have mer - cy. Lord, have mer - cy.

83 Sanctus

Ho - ly, ho - ly, ho - ly Lord,

God of power and might, heav'n and earth are full of your glo - ry.

Ho-san-na in the high-est. Bless-ed is he who

comes in the name of the Lord. Ho-san-na in the high - est.

Music: William Mathias, © Oxford University Press

Memorial Acclamation 84

Christ has died, Christ is ri - sen, Christ will come a - gain.

Agnus Dei 85

Sopranos and Altos

Je - sus, Lamb of God: have mer - cy on us.

Tenors and Basses

Je - sus, bear-er of our sins: have mer - cy on us.

All

Je - sus, re-deem-er of the world: give us your peace.

86 AMBROSIAN GLORIA

Glo-ry to God in the high-est, and peace to his peo-ple on earth.

Lord God, heav-en-ly King, al-might-y God and

Fa - ther, we wor-ship you, we give you thanks,

we praise you for your glo - ry. Lord Je-sus Christ,

on-ly Son of the Fa-ther, Lord God, Lamb of God,

you take a-way the sin of the world: have mer-cy on us;

you are seat-ed at the right hand of the Fa - ther:

re-ceive our pray'r. For you a-lone are the Ho-ly One, you a-lone

are the Lord, you a-lone are the Most High, Je - sus Christ,

with the Ho-ly Spir-it, in the glo - ry of God the Fa-ther. A - men.

Music: Graduale Romanum, 1979; Chant Mass IV; adapt. and acc. Rev. Bartholomew Sayles, O.S.B., Sr. Cecile Gertken, O.S.B., ©

GLORIA 87

REFRAIN

Glo-ry to God in the high - est, and peace to his peo-ple on earth.

VERSE 1   *Repeat Refrain*

Lord   God, heav-en-ly King, al - might-y   God and Fa - ther.

VERSE 2   *Repeat Refrain*

We wor-ship you, we give you thanks, we praise you for your glo - ry.

VERSE 3

Lord Je - sus Christ,   on - ly Son of the Fa -   ther,

Lord   God,   Lamb of God, you take a - way the

Repeat Refrain

sin of the world: have mer - cy on us.

VERSE 4

You are seat - ed   at the right   hand of the Fa - ther,

Repeat Refrain **VERSE 5**

re - ceive   our prayer.   For you a - lone are the

Ho - ly One,   you a - lone are the   Lord,

Music: Columba Kelly, O.S.B., ©

GLORIA

you a - lone are the Most High, Je - sus Christ.

REFRAIN

Glo-ry to God in the high - est, and peace to his peo-ple on earth.

VERSE 6

With the Ho - ly Spir - it, in the glo - ry of

Repeat Refrain

God the Fa - ther. A - men!

We be-lieve in one God, the Fa-ther, the Al-

might-y, ma-ker of heav-en and earth, of all that is

seen and un-seen. We be-lieve in one Lord, Je-sus Christ,

the on-ly Son of God, e-ter-nal-ly be-got-ten of the

Fa-ther, God from God, Light from Light, true God from

true God, be-got-ten, not made, one in Be-ing

with the Fa-ther. Through him all things were made.

For us men and for our sal-va-tion he came down from

Music: *Authentic melody, 10 c.*

heav - en: by the pow - er of the Ho - ly Spir - it

he was born of the Vir - gin Ma - ry, and be - came man.

For our sake he was cru - ci - fied un - der Pon - tius Pi - late;

he suf - fered, died, and was bu - ried. On the third day he

rose a - gain in ful - fill - ment of the Scrip - tures; he as -

cend - ed in - to heav - en and is seat - ed at the right hand

of the Fa - ther. He will come a - gain in glo - ry to

judge the liv - ing and the dead, and his king-dom will have no end.

We be - lieve in the Ho - ly Spir - it, the Lord, the

89 CREDO II

We be - lieve in one God, the Fa - ther, the Al - might - y,

mak-er of heav-en and earth, of all that is seen and un - seen.

We be-lieve in one Lord, Je - sus Christ, the on - ly Son of God,

e - ter-nal-ly be-got-ten of the Fa - ther, God from God, Light from Light,

true God from true God, be-got-ten, not made, one in be-ing with the Fa-ther,

through him all things were made. For us men and for our sal-va-tion

he came down from heav - en: by the pow'r of the Ho - ly Spir-it

he was born of the Vir - gin Ma - ry, and be - came man.

For our sake he was cru - ci - fied un - der Pon-tius Pi - late;

Music: Plainchant; adapt. and arr. Rev. Bartholomew Sayles, O.S.B.; Sr. Cecile Gertken, O.S.B., ©

DANISH AMEN MASS

90 Sanctus

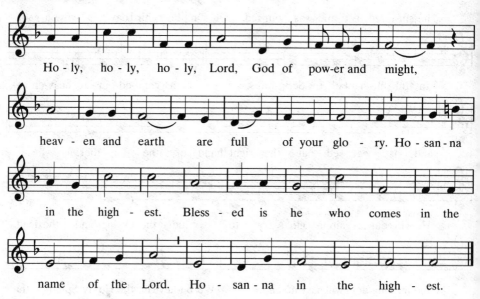

Ho - ly, ho - ly, ho - ly, Lord, God of pow-er and might,

heav - en and earth are full of your glo - ry. Ho - san - na

in the high - est. Bless - ed is he who comes in the

name of the Lord. Ho - san - na in the high - est.

91 Memorial Acclamations

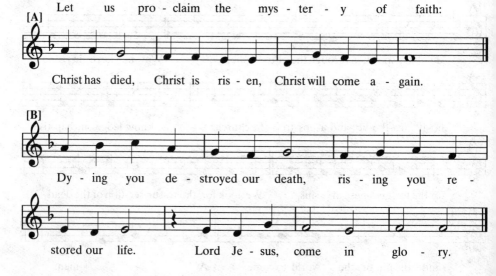

INVITATION
Celebrant

Let us pro - claim the mys - ter - y of faith:

[A]

Christ has died, Christ is ris - en, Christ will come a - gain.

[B]

Dy - ing you de - stroyed our death, ris - ing you re -

stored our life. Lord Je - sus, come in glo - ry.

Music: Charles G. Frischmann, b. 1938 and David Kraehenbuehl, b. 1923, © 1970, 1973, J. S. Paluch Co. Inc.

[C]

When we eat this bread and drink this cup, we pro-claim your death, Lord

Je - sus, un - til you come in glo - ry.

[D]

Lord, by your cross and re - sur - rec - tion, you have set us

free. You are the Sav - ior of the world.

Great Amen 92

A - men, a - men, a - men.

The Lord's Prayer 93

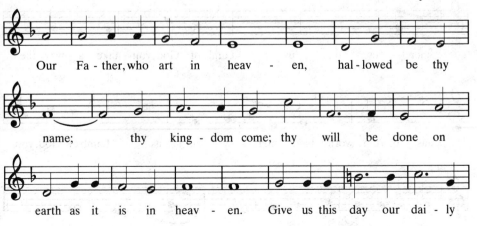

Our Fa - ther, who art in heav - en, hal - lowed be thy

name; thy king - dom come; thy will be done on

earth as it is in heav - en. Give us this day our dai - ly

bread; and for - give us our tres-pass-es as we for-give those who

tres - pass a - gainst us; and lead us not in - to temp-

ta - tion, but de - liv - er us from e - vil. For the king - dom, the

pow - er, and the glo - ry are yours, now and for ev - er.

94 Agnus Dei

Lamb of God, you take a - way the sins of the world: have

mer - cy on us. Lamb of God, you take a - way the

sins of the world: have mer - cy on us. Lamb of God, you

take a - way the sins of the world: grant us peace.

TRINITY MASS

Ho - ly, ho - ly, ho - ly Lord, God of pow-er and might,

heav - en and earth are full, full of your glo - ry. Ho -

san - na, ho - san - na, ho - san - na in the high - est.

Bless - ed is he who comes in the name of the Lord. Ho -

san - na, ho - san - na, ho - san - na in the high - est.

Memorial Acclamations 96

[A]

Christ has died, Christ is ris - en, Christ will come a - gain.

[C]

When we eat this bread and drink this cup, we pro - claim your

death, Lord Je - sus, un - til you come in glo - ry.

Music: Becket Senchur, O.S.B., b. 1946, ©

[D]

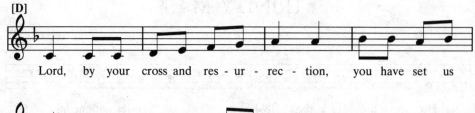

Lord, by your cross and res - ur - rec - tion, you have set us free. You are the Sav - ior of the world.

97 Agnus Dei

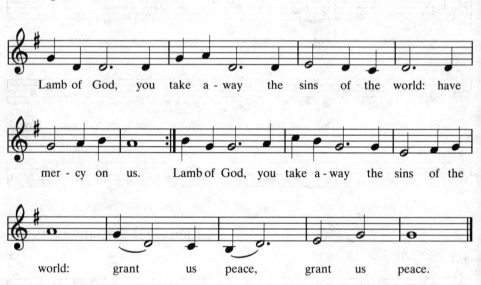

Lamb of God, you take a - way the sins of the world: have mer - cy on us. Lamb of God, you take a - way the sins of the world: grant us peace, grant us peace.

Celebrant

Let us pro - claim the mys - ter - y of faith.

[A]

Christ has died, Christ is ris - en, Christ will come a - gain.

[B]

Dy - ing you de - stroyed our death, ris - ing you

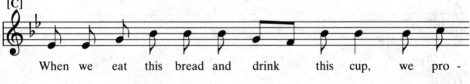

re - stored our life. Lord Je - sus, come in glo - ry.

[C]

When we eat this bread and drink this cup, we pro -

claim your death, Lord Je - sus, un - til you come in glo - ry.

Music: Plainchant Mode VI; acc. Rev. Bartholomew Sayles, O.S.B., b. 1918; Sr. Cecile Gertken, O.S.B., b. 1902, ©

99 THE LORD'S PRAYER

Celebrant

Let us pray with confidence to the Fa - ther
Je - sus taught us to call God our Fa - ther
Let us pray for the coming of the king - dom

in the words our Sav - ior gave us:
and so we have the cour - age to say:
as Je - sus taught us.

All

Our Fa - ther who art in heav-en hal-lowed be thy name;

thy king-dom come; thy will be done on earth as it is in

heav - en. Give us this day our dai - ly bread, and for -

give us our tres - pass - es as we for - give those who tres - pass

a - gainst us; and lead us not in - to temp-ta - tion,

Celebrant

but de - liv - er us from e - vil. De - liv - er us, Lord,

from ev' - ry e - vil, and grant us peace in our day.

Music: Plainchant; acc. Rev. Bartholomew Sayles, O.S.B., b. 1918; Sr. Cecile Gertken, O.S.B., b. 1902, ©

In your mer-cy keep us free from sin and pro-tect us from all anx - i - e - ty

as we wait in joy-ful hope for the com-ing of our Sav-ior, Je - sus Christ.

For the king-dom, the pow'r, and the glo-ry are yours, now and for-ev - er.

Sign of Peace

Celebrant: The peace of the Lord be with you al - ways. All: And al - so with you.

Celebrant: Let us of - fer each oth - er a sign of peace.

100 THE LORD'S PRAYER

Celebrant

Let us pray with confidence to the Fa - ther
Je - sus taught us to call God our Fa - ther
Let us pray for the coming of the king - dom

in the words our Sav - ior gave us:
and so we have the cour - age to say:
as Je - sus taught us.

All

Our Fa - ther who art in heav - en hal - lowed be thy

name; thy king - dom come; thy will be done on

earth as it is in heav - en. Give us this day our

dai - ly bread, and for - give us our tres - pass - es as

we for - give those who tres - pass a - gainst us; and

lead us not in - to temp - ta - tion, but de - liv - er

Music: Chant; Our Father adapt. Robert J. Snow, 1964; acc. Rev. Bartholomew Sayles, O.S.B., b. 1918;
  Sr. Cecile Gertken, O.S.B., b. 1902, ©

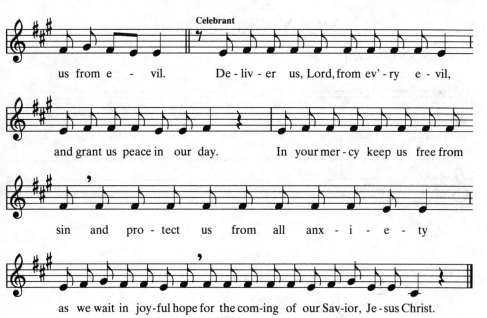

Celebrant

us from e - vil. De - liv - er us, Lord, from ev' - ry e - vil,

and grant us peace in our day. In your mer - cy keep us free from

sin and pro - tect us from all anx - i - e - ty

as we wait in joy - ful hope for the com - ing of our Sav - ior, Je - sus Christ.

Doxology

All

For the king - dom, the pow'r, and the glo - ry are yours, now and for - ev - er.

Alternate Doxology

For the king - dom, the pow'r, and the glo - ry are yours, now and for ev - er.

Sign of Peace

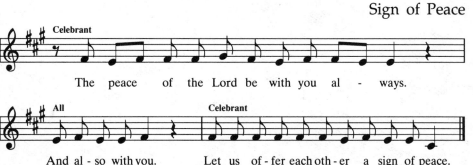

Celebrant

The peace of the Lord be with you al - ways.

All   **Celebrant**

And al - so with you. Let us of - fer each oth - er a sign of peace.

HOLY CROSS MASS

101 AGNUS DEI

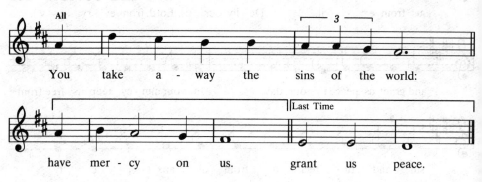

You take a - way the sins of the world:

have mer - cy on us. grant us peace.

OPTIONAL INVOCATIONS

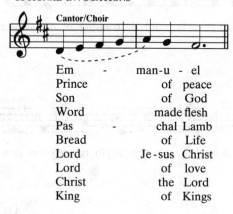

Cantor/Choir

Em	-	man-u - el
Prince		of peace
Son		of God
Word		made flesh
Pas	-	chal Lamb
Bread		of Life
Lord		Je - sus Christ
Lord		of love
Christ		the Lord
King		of Kings

For the final invocation, once again sing
"Lamb of God" to which all conclude "grant us peace."

Text: Invocations, ©
Music: David C. Isele, ©

CHILDREN'S EUCHARISTIC PRAYER I

Preface 102

INVITATION
Celebrant
So we all sing to-geth-er:

Lively
All
Ho - ly, ho - ly, ho - ly Lord, God of pow-er and might,

heav - en and earth are full of your glo - ry. Ho - san-na, ho -

san - na, ho - san - na in the high - (high - high-) est.

INVITATION
Celebrant
So we are glad to sing:

A small unison choir or solo
Bless - ed is he who comes in the name of the

All
Lord. Ho - san - na, ho - san - na, ho -

san - na in the high - (high - high-) est.

Music: Edward J. McKenna, b. 1939, ©

INVITATION

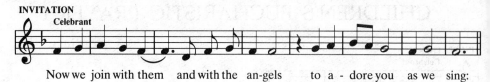

Now we join with them and with the an-gels to a - dore you as we sing:

All: Repeat "Holy, Holy" and "Blessed" without pause.

Memorial Acclamation

INVITATION

Let us pro - claim our faith.

Christ has died, Christ is ris - en, Christ will come a - gain.

Great Amen

A - men, Fa - ther, a - men, Je - sus,

Ho - ly Spi - rit, a - men, a - men, a - men.

CHILDREN'S EUCHARISTIC PRAYER II

Preface 103

INVITATION

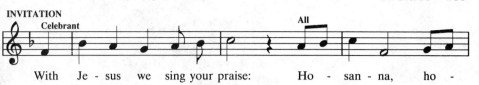

With Je - sus we sing your praise: Ho - san - na, ho -

san - na, ho - san - na, in the high - (high - high-) est.

*This acclamation is sung three times during the Preface, after
the celebrant sings: "With Jesus we sing your praise."
Celebrant sings, "as they praise you and sing: ...
"Holy, Holy" sung by all, complete – as in Eucharistic Prayer no. 1 (above);
Celebrants sings "...so that we can live as your children;"
All repeat only "Blessed is he."*

After the Consecrated host is shown, and again after the chalice is shown:

Je - sus has giv - en his life for us.

*The acclamation below is sung after each of the following texts:
Celebrant "...to be the sacrifice we offer you."
      "...to all who serve your people."
      "...to be with you for ever."
      "...will sing a song of joy."*

We praise you, we bless you, we

thank you, we praise you, bless you, thank you.

Then, "Great Amen" as in Children's Eucharistic Prayer 1

Music: Edward J. McKenna, b. 1939, ©

COMMON RESPONSORIAL PSALMS

Ps. 25: Your Ways, O Lord, Make Known To Me 104

Antiphon 1: Your Ways, O Lord, Are Love and Truth
Antiphon 2: To You, O Lord, I Lift My Soul

ANTIPHON Cantor/Choir; All repeat

Your ways, O Lord, are love and truth.
To you, O Lord, I lift my soul.

Psalm 25: 4-5, 6-7, 8-9

VERSE 1 Cantor/Choir

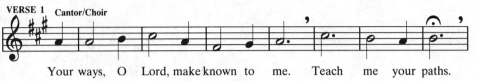

Your ways, O Lord, make known to me. Teach me your paths.

Guide me in your truth and teach me; for you are my sav - ior.

VERSE 2 Cantor/Choir

Re - mem - ber that your com - pas - sion, O Lord, and your kind - ness are from of

old. In your kind - ness re - mem - ber me, be - cause of your good - ness, O Lord.

VERSE 3 Cantor/Choir

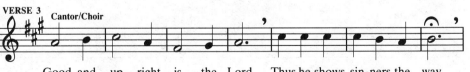

Good and up - right is the Lord. Thus he shows sin - ners the way.

He guides the hum - ble to jus - tice, he teach - es the hum - ble his way.

Music: William Ferris, b. 1937, ©   ADVENT AND LENT

105 Ps. 25: Make Me Know Your Ways

Antiphon: Remember Your Mercy, Lord

ANTIPHON

Re - mem - ber your mer - cy, Lord.

Psalm 25: 4-5, 6-7, 8-9

VERSES

1. Make me know your ways, Lord, and teach me your paths.
2. Remember, Lord, your mercy and love,
   for they have been ever from of old.
3. The Lord is good and upright;

Lead me in your truth and teach me;
Remember not the sins of my youth or my of - fenses
therefore he teaches sin - ners his way.

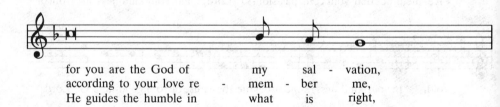

for you are the God of my sal - vation,
according to your love re - mem - ber me,
He guides the humble in what is right,

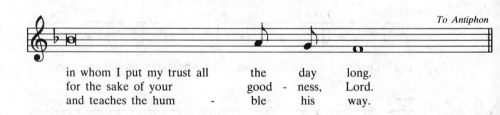

To Antiphon

in whom I put my trust all the day long.
for the sake of your good - ness, Lord.
and teaches the hum - ble his way.

Music: Fintan P. O'Carroll, d. 1981, ©   ADVENT AND LENT

Ps. 25: Make Me Know Your Ways 106

Antiphon: To You, O Lord, I Lift Up My Soul

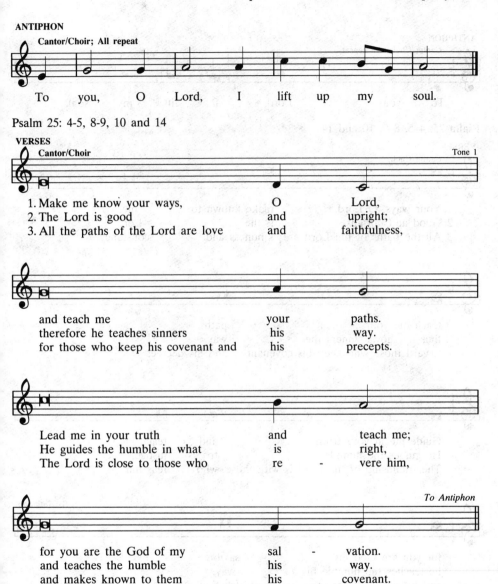

ANTIPHON

Cantor/Choir; All repeat

To you, O Lord, I lift up my soul.

Psalm 25: 4-5, 8-9, 10 and 14

VERSES

Cantor/Choir   Tone 1

1. Make me know your ways,   O   Lord,
2. The Lord is good   and   upright;
3. All the paths of the Lord are love   and   faithfulness,

and teach me   your   paths.
therefore he teaches sinners   his   way.
for those who keep his covenant and   his   precepts.

Lead me in your truth   and   teach me;
He guides the humble in what   is   right,
The Lord is close to those who re   -   vere him,

To Antiphon

for you are the God of my   sal   -   vation.
and teaches the humble   his   way.
and makes known to them   his   covenant.

Music: Fintan P. O'Carroll, d. 1981, ©   ADVENT

107 Ps. 25: Your Ways, O Lord, Make Known To Me

Antiphon: To You, O Lord, I Lift My Soul

ANTIPHON

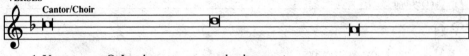

Cantor/Choir; All repeat

To   you,   O   Lord,   I   lift   my   soul.

Psalm 25: 4–5, 8–9, 10 and 14

VERSES

Cantor/Choir

1. Your ways, O Lord,   make known to   me;
2. Good and upright   is the   Lord;
3. All the paths of the Lord are kindness and   constancy

teach me your   paths.
thus he shows sinners the   way.
toward those who keep his covenant   and his decrees.

Guide me in your truth   and   teach me,
He guides the humble   to   justice,
The friendship of the Lord is with those who   fear him

To Antiphon

for you are God my   savior.
he teaches the humble his   way.
and his covenant for their in - struction.

Music: Gerard Farrell, O.S.B., b. 1919, ©   ADVENT

Ps. 85: I Will Hear What God Proclaims 108

Antiphon: Come, O Lord, and Set Us Free

ANTIPHON

Cantor/Choir; All repeat

Come, O Lord, and set us free.

Psalm 85: 9–10, 11–12, 13–14

VERSES

Cantor/Choir

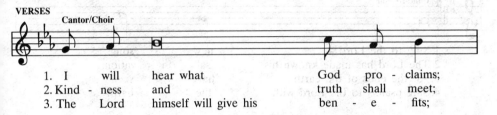

1. I will hear what God pro - claims;
2. Kind - ness and truth shall meet;
3. The Lord himself will give his ben - e - fits;

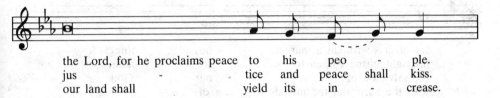

the Lord, for he proclaims peace to his peo - ple.
jus - tice and peace shall kiss.
our land shall yield its in - crease.

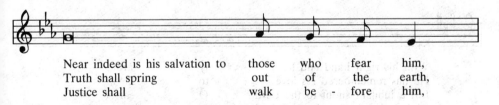

Near indeed is his salvation to those who fear him,
Truth shall spring out of the earth,
Justice shall walk be - fore him,

To Antiphon

glory dwelling in our land.
and justice shall look down from heav'n.
and salvation along the way of his steps.

Music: John Lee, b. 1908, ©   ADVENT

109 Ps. 98: Sing to the Lord a New Song

Antiphon: All the Ends of the Earth Have Seen the Salvation of Our God

ANTIPHON

All the ends of the earth have seen the sal - va - tion of our God.

Psalm 98: 1, 2–3, 3–4, 5–6

VERSES

Cantor/Choir   Tone 3

1. Sing to the Lord a   new   song,
2. The Lord has made known his   sal - vation,
3. All the ends of the earth   have   seen
4. Sing psalms to the Lord with   the   harp;

for he has wrought a marvel - ous thing.
his righteousness open to the nations.
the salvation of our God.
with the harp and the melody of songs.

With his right hand and ho - ly arm,
He has remembered his love to Jacob,
Lift a jubilant shout to the Lord, O earth;
With trumpets and the sound of the horn,

To Antiphon

he himself has brought sal - vation.
his faithfulness to the house of Israel.
rejoice and ring out his praises.
shout with joy before the King, the Lord.

Music: Fintan P. O'Carroll, d. 1981, ©   CHRISTMAS

Ps. 98: Sing to the Lord a New Song 110

Antiphon: All the Ends of the Earth Have Seen the Power of God

ANTIPHON

Cantor/Choir; All repeat

All the ends of the earth have seen the pow-er of God.

Psalm 98: 1, 2–3, 3–4, 5–6

VERSES

Cantor/Choir

1. Sing to the Lord a new song, for he has done

2. The Lord has made his sal - va - tion known, his jus - tice re -

3. All of the ends of earth have seen sal - va - tion

4. Sing to the Lord with harp and song, with trum - pet

won - drous deeds; his right hand has won the vic - t'ry for

vealed to all. Re - mem-bered his kind-ness and faith - ful -

by our God. Joy - ful - ly sing out all you

and with horn. Sing in your joy be - fore the

Music: David Haas, b. 1957; Marty Haugen, b. 1952, ©   CHRISTMAS

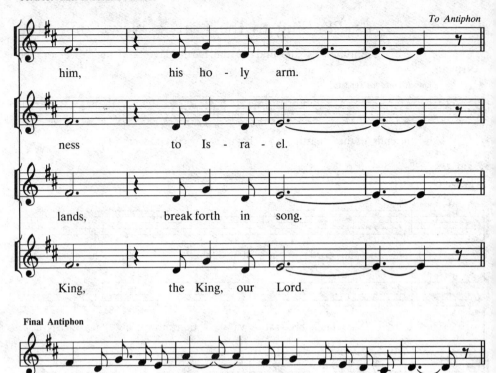

To Antiphon

him,　　　　his　ho - ly　arm.

ness　　　to　Is - ra - el.

lands,　　break forth　in　song.

King,　　the King,　our　Lord.

Final Antiphon

All　the ends of the　earth　have seen the pow-er of　God.

Ps. 72: Give Your Justice to the King 111

Antiphon: All Nations Shall Fall Prostrate before You, O Lord.

ANTIPHON

Cantor/Choir; All repeat

All na - tions shall fall pros-trate be - fore you, O Lord.

Psalm 72: 1–2, 7–8, 10–11, 12–13

VERSES

Cantor/Choir   Tone 4

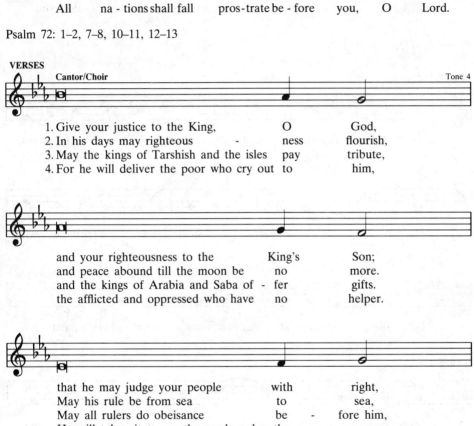

1. Give your justice to the King,   O   God,
2. In his days may righteous   -   ness   flourish,
3. May the kings of Tarshish and the isles pay   tribute,
4. For he will deliver the poor who cry out to   him,

and your righteousness to the   King's   Son;
and peace abound till the moon be   no   more.
and the kings of Arabia and Saba of - fer   gifts.
the afflicted and oppressed who have no   helper.

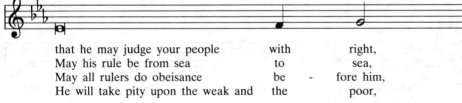

that he may judge your people   with   right,
May his rule be from sea   to   sea,
May all rulers do obeisance   be   -   fore him,
He will take pity upon the weak and the   poor,

To Antiphon

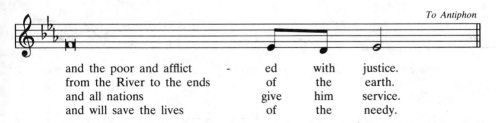

and the poor and afflict   -   ed   with   justice.
from the River to the ends   of   the   earth.
and all nations   give   him   service.
and will save the lives   of   the   needy.

Music: Fintan P. O'Carroll, d. 1981, ©   EPIPHANY

112 Ps. 72: O God, With Your Judgment

Antiphon: Lord, Every Nation on Earth

ANTIPHON

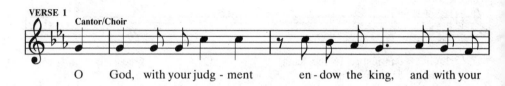

Lord, ev-'ry na-tion on earth, ev-'ry na-tion on earth will a-dore you.

Psalm 72: 1–2, 7–8, 10–11

VERSE 1

O God, with your judg-ment en-dow the king, and with your

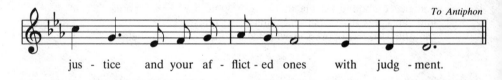

jus-tice the king's son; he shall gov-ern your peo-ple with

jus-tice and your af-flict-ed ones with judg-ment.

VERSE 2

Jus-tice shall flow-er in his days, and

peace, till the moon be no more. May he rule from

sea to sea, and from the Ri-ver to the ends of the earth.

Music: Donald J. Reagan, b. 1923, ©   EPIPHANY

VERSE 3
Cantor/Choir

The kings of Tar - shish and the Isles shall of - fer gifts; the
kings of A - ra - bi - a and Sa - ba shall bring tri - bute. All

To Antiphon

kings shall pay him hom - age, all na - tions shall serve him.

VERSE 4
Cantor/Choir

For he shall res - cue the poor when they cry out, and the af -
flict - ed with no one to help. He shall have pi - ty for the

To Antiphon

low - ly and the poor: the lives of the poor he shall save.

113 Ps. 51: Have Mercy on Me, O God

Antiphon: Have Mercy on Us, O Lord, for We Have Sinned

ANTIPHON

Cantor/Choir; All repeat

Have mer - cy on us, O Lord, for we have sinned.

Psalm 51: 3–4, 5–6, 12–13, 14, 17

VERSES

Cantor/Choir   Tone 2

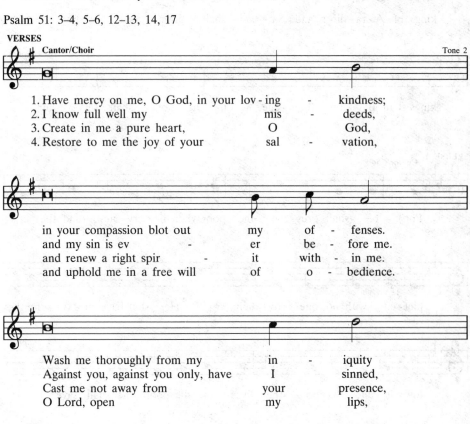

1. Have mercy on me, O God, in your lov - ing   -   kindness;
2. I know full well my   mis   -   deeds,
3. Create in me a pure heart,   O   God,
4. Restore to me the joy of your   sal   -   vation,

in your compassion blot out   my   of - fenses.
and my sin is ev   -   er   be - fore me.
and renew a right spir   -   it   with - in me.
and uphold me in a free will   of   o - bedience.

Wash me thoroughly from my   in   -   iquity
Against you, against you only, have   I   sinned,
Cast me not away from   your   presence,
O Lord, open   my   lips,

To Antiphon

and cleanse me   from   my   sin.
and done what is evil   in   your   sight.
and take not your holy Spir   -   it   from   me.
and my mouth shall pro   -   claim   your   praise.

Music: Fintan P. O'Carroll, d. 1981, ©   LENT/ASH WEDNESDAY

Ps. 51: Create in Me a Pure Heart, O God 114

Antiphon: A Pure Heart Create for Me, O God

ANTIPHON

Cantor/Choir; All repeat

A pure heart cre - ate for me, O God.

Psalm 51: 12–13, 14–15, 18–19

VERSES

Cantor/Choir   Tone 1

1. Create in me a pure heart,   O   God,
2. Restore to me the joy of your   sal - vation,
3. You have no delight   in   sacrifices;

and renew a right spirit   with - in me.
and uphold me in a free will of   o - bedience,
a burnt offering from me would   not   please you.

Cast me not away from   your   presence,
that I may teach transgressors   your   ways,
The sacrifice you accept is a hum - ble   spirit;

To Antiphon

and take not your holy Spirit   from   me
and turn sinners back   to   you
a broken and contrite heart, O God, you will not re - ject.

Music: Fintan P. O'Carroll, d. 1981, ©   LENT

115 Ps. 91: You Who Dwell in the Shelter

Antiphon: The Lord is Near to All Who Call on Him

ANTIPHON

Cantor/Choir; All repeat

The Lord is near to all who call on him.

Psalm 91: 1–2, 10–11, 12–13, 14, 16

VERSES

Cantor/Choir

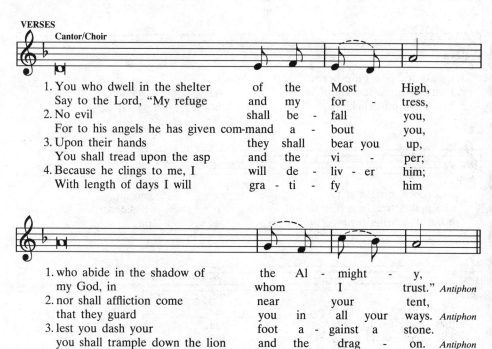

1. You who dwell in the shelter · of · the · Most · High,
   Say to the Lord, "My refuge · and · my · for - · tress,
2. No evil · shall · be - · fall · you,
   For to his angels he has given com-mand · a - · bout · you,
3. Upon their hands · they · shall · bear you · up,
   You shall tread upon the asp · and · the · vi - · per;
4. Because he clings to me, I · will · de - · liv - er · him;
   With length of days I will · gra - · ti - · fy · him

1. who abide in the shadow of · the · Al - · might - · y,
   my God, in · whom · I · trust." *Antiphon*
2. nor shall affliction come · near · your · tent,
   that they guard · you · in · all · your · ways. *Antiphon*
3. lest you dash your · foot · a - · gainst a · stone.
   you shall trample down the lion · and · the · drag - · on. *Antiphon*
4. I will set him on high because he ac-knowl-edges · my · name.
   and will show him · my · sal - · va - · tion. *Antiphon*

Music: William A. Jurgens, 1908 – 1982, ©

LENT

Ps. 91: Whoever Dwells under the Shelter 116
Of the Most High

Antiphon: Be with Me, O Lord, in My Distress

ANTIPHON

Be with me, O Lord, in my dis - tress.

Psalm 91: 1–2, 10–11, 12–13, 14–15

VERSES

Cantor/Choir — Tone 6

1. Whoever dwells under the shelter of the Most High,
2. No evil will happen to you,
3. In their hands they will hold you,
4. Because he holds fast to me in love, I will save him;

and abides in the shade of the Al - mighty,
nor calamity come near your dwelling.
lest you stub your foot on a stone.
because he knows my name, I will pro - tect him.

shall say to the Lord, "My refuge, my fortress,
He will give charge over you to his angels,
You will tread on poisonous ser - pents;
When he calls upon me, I will an - swer him.

To Antiphon

my God in whom is my trust."
to guard you in all your ways.
you will trample young li - ons and dragons.
In trouble I will be with him; I will rescue and hon - or him.

Music: Fintan P. O'Carroll, d. 1981, ©

LENT

117 Ps. 130: Out of the Depths Have I Called to You

Antiphon: If You, O Lord, Should Mark Our Guilt

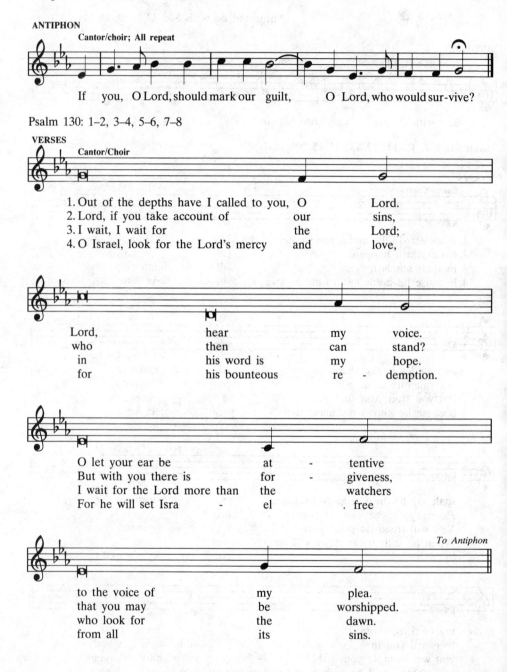

ANTIPHON

Cantor/choir; All repeat

If you, O Lord, should mark our guilt, O Lord, who would sur-vive?

Psalm 130: 1–2, 3–4, 5–6, 7–8

VERSES

Cantor/Choir

1. Out of the depths have I called to you, O   Lord.
2. Lord, if you take account of   our   sins,
3. I wait, I wait for   the   Lord;
4. O Israel, look for the Lord's mercy   and   love,

Lord,   hear   my   voice.
who   then   can   stand?
in   his word is   my   hope.
for   his bounteous   re - demption.

O let your ear be   at - tentive
But with you there is   for - giveness,
I wait for the Lord more than   the   watchers
For he will set Isra - el . free

To Antiphon

to the voice of   my   plea.
that you may   be   worshipped.
who look for   the   dawn.
from all   its   sins.

Music: Michael Naughton, O.S.B., b. 1939, ©

LENT

Ps. 130: Out of the Depths Have I Called to You   118

Antiphon: With the Lord There Is Mercy and Fullness of Redemption

ANTIPHON

Cantor/Choir; All repeat

With the Lord there is mer - cy and full-ness of re-demp-tion.

Psalm 130: 1–2, 3–4, 5–6, 7–8

VERSES

Cantor/Choir
Tone 12

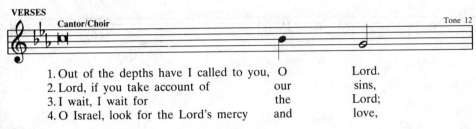

1. Out of the depths have I called to you, O		Lord.
2. Lord, if you take account of	our	sins,
3. I wait, I wait for	the	Lord;
4. O Israel, look for the Lord's mercy	and	love,

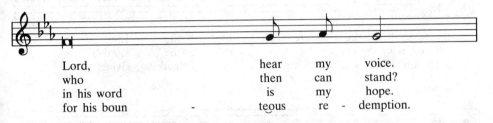

Lord,	hear	my	voice.
who	then	can	stand?
in his word	is	my	hope.
for his boun -	teous	re -	demption.

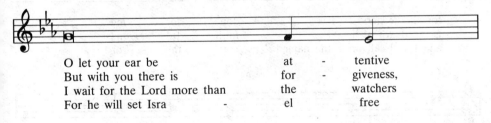

O let your ear be	at -	tentive
But with you there is	for -	giveness,
I wait for the Lord more than	the	watchers
For he will set Isra -	el	free

To Antiphon

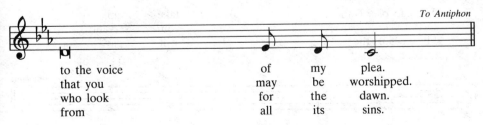

to the voice	of	my	plea.
that you	may	be	worshipped.
who look	for	the	dawn.
from	all	its	sins.

Music: Fintan P. O'Carroll, d. 1981, ©   LENT

119 Ps. 116: How Shall I Make a Return to the Lord

Antiphon: The Blessing Cup that We Bless Is a Communion with the Blood of Christ

ANTIPHON

The bless - ing cup that we bless is a com -

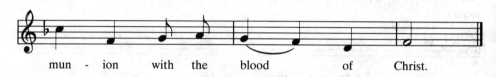

mun - ion with the blood of Christ.

Psalm 116: 12–13, 15–16, 17–18

VERSES

Cantor/Choir   Tone 8

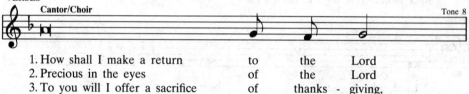

1. How shall I make a return   to   the   Lord
2. Precious in the eyes   of   the   Lord
3. To you will I offer a sacrifice   of   thanks - giving,

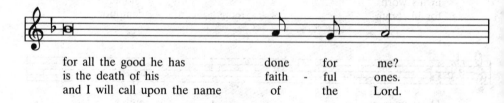

for all the good he has   done   for   me?
is the death of his   faith - ful   ones.
and I will call upon the name   of   the   Lord.

The cup of salvation I   will   take   up,
O Lord, I   am   your   servant;
My vows to the Lord   I   will   pay

To Antiphon

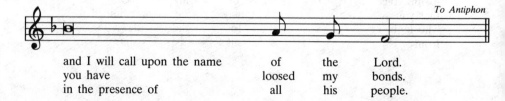

and I will call upon the name   of   the   Lord.
you have   loosed   my   bonds.
in the presence of   all   his   people.

Music: Fintan P. O'Carroll, d. 1981, ©   HOLY WEEK, HOLY THURSDAY

Ps. 22: All Who See Me Laugh At Me 120

Antiphon: My God, My God, O Why Have You Abandoned Me?

ANTIPHON

My God, my God, O why have you a - ban - doned me?

Psalm 22: 8-9, 17-18, 19-20, 23-24

VERSE 1

All who see me laugh at me, they mock me and they shake their heads:

"He re - lied on the Lord, let the Lord be his ref - uge."

VERSE 2

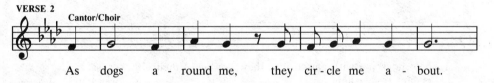

As dogs a - round me, they cir - cle me a - bout.

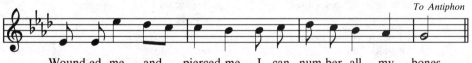

Wound-ed me and pierced me, I can num - ber all my bones.

VERSES 3 and 4

My cloth - ing they di - vid - ed, for my gar - ments cast-ing
I will praise you to my peo - ple, and pro - claim you in their

lots, O Lord do not de - sert me, but has - ten to my aid.
midst, O fear the Lord and praise him, give glo - ry to his name.

Music: Marty Haugen, b. 1952, ©

121 Ps. 22: All Who See Me Scoff at Me

Antiphon: My God, My God, Why Have You Abandoned Me?

ANTIPHON

My God, my God, why have you a - ban-doned me?

Psalm 22: 8–9, 17–18, 19–20, 23–24

VERSES

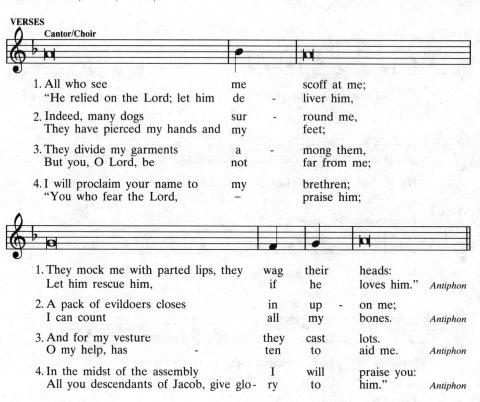

1. All who see me scoff at me;
   "He relied on the Lord; let him de - liver him,

2. Indeed, many dogs sur - round me,
   They have pierced my hands and my feet;

3. They divide my garments a - mong them,
   But you, O Lord, be not far from me;

4. I will proclaim your name to my brethren;
   "You who fear the Lord, – praise him;

1. They mock me with parted lips, they wag their heads:
   Let him rescue him, if he loves him." *Antiphon*

2. A pack of evildoers closes in up - on me;
   I can count all my bones. *Antiphon*

3. And for my vesture they cast lots.
   O my help, has - ten to aid me. *Antiphon*

4. In the midst of the assembly I will praise you:
   All you descendants of Jacob, give glo- ry to him." *Antiphon*

Music: Owen Alstott, b. 1947, ©   **HOLY WEEK**

Ps. 22: All Who See Me Deride Me 122

Antiphon: My God, My God, Why Have You Forsaken Me?

ANTIPHON

Cantor/Choir; All repeat

My God, my God, why have you for - sa - ken me?

Psalm 22: 8–9, 17–18, 19–20, 23–24

VERSES

Cantor/Choir   Tone 6

1. All who see me deride me and   make   sport of me,
2. Packs of dogs close in on me; a gang of villains   en -   circle me.
3. They divide my garments   a -   mong them,
4. I shall proclaim your name to   my   people;

curling their lips and tossing   their   heads:
They pierce my hands and   my   feet.
and cast lots for   my   clothes.
in the midst of the assembly I   shall   praise you.

"He trusted in the Lord; let   him   save him,
I can count all   my   bones,
Be not far off from   me,   Lord;
Praise the Lord, you   who   fear him!

To Antiphon

let him rescue him if he de -   lights   in   him!"
as they glare and gloat   o -   ver   me.
you are my strength, hasten   to   help   me.
Give him glory, you off -   spring   of   Jacob!

Music: Fintan P. O'Carroll, d. 1981, ©

HOLY WEEK

123 Ps. 31: In You, O Lord, I Take Refuge

Antiphon: Father, Into Your Hands I Commend My Spirit

ANTIPHON

Fa - ther,   in - to your hands I com - mend   my   spir - it.

Psalm 31: 2 and 6, 12–13, 15–16, 17 and 25

VERSES

Cantor/Choir   Tone 2

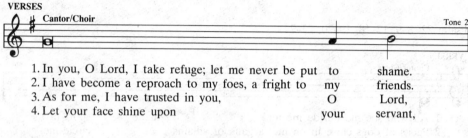

1. In you, O Lord, I take refuge; let me never be put to   shame.
2. I have become a reproach to my foes, a fright to   my   friends.
3. As for me, I have trusted in you,   O   Lord,
4. Let your face shine upon   your   servant,

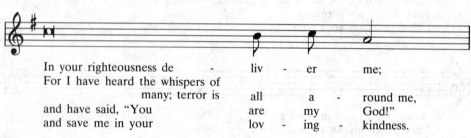

In your righteousness de   -   liv - er   me;
For I have heard the whispers of
                        many; terror is   all   a - round me,
and have said, "You   are   my   God!"
and save me in your   lov - ing - kindness.

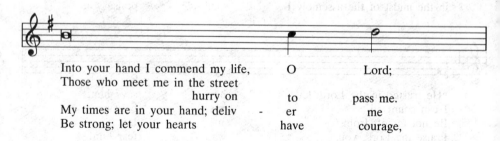

Into your hand I commend my life,   O   Lord;
Those who meet me in the street
                        hurry on   to   pass me.
My times are in your hand; deliv -   er   me
Be strong; let your hearts   have   courage,

To Antiphon

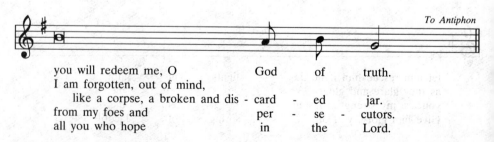

you will redeem me, O   God   of   truth.
I am forgotten, out of mind,
    like a corpse, a broken and dis - card - ed   jar.
from my foes and   per - se - cutors.
all you who hope   in   the   Lord.

Music: Fintan P. O'Carroll, d. 1981, ©   HOLY WEEK: GOOD FRIDAY

Ps. 118: Give Thanks to the Lord for He Is Good 124

Antiphon: This Day Was Made by the Lord: We Rejoice and Are Glad

ANTIPHON

Cantor/Choir; All repeat

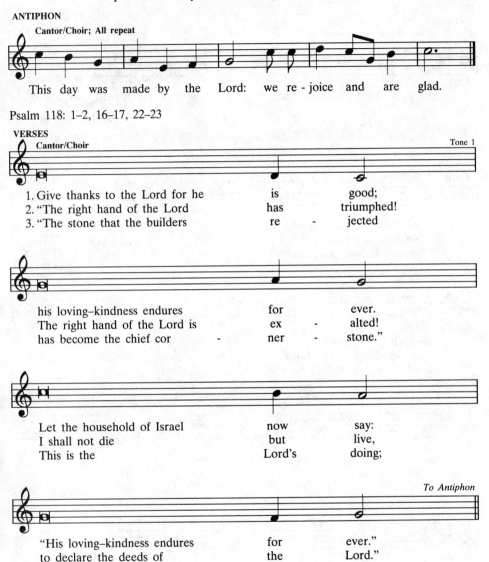

This day was made by the Lord: we re-joice and are glad.

Psalm 118: 1–2, 16–17, 22–23

VERSES

Cantor/Choir   Tone 1

1. Give thanks to the Lord for he — is — good;
2. "The right hand of the Lord — has — triumphed!
3. "The stone that the builders — re - jected

his loving–kindness endures — for — ever.
The right hand of the Lord is — ex - alted!
has become the chief cor - ner - stone."

Let the household of Israel — now — say:
I shall not die — but — live,
This is the — Lord's — doing;

To Antiphon

"His loving–kindness endures — for — ever."
to declare the deeds of — the — Lord."
it is marvelous in — our — sight.

Music: Fintan P. O'Carroll, d. 1981 ©   **EASTER DAY**

125 Ps. 118: Give Thanks to the Lord for He Is Good

Antiphon: Give Thanks to the Lord for He Is Good, for His Love Has No End

ANTIPHON

Cantor/Choir; All repeat

Give thanks to the Lord for he is good, for his love has no end.

Psalm 118: 1–2, 16–17, 22–23

VERSES

Cantor/Choir   Tone 5

1. Give thanks to the Lord for he   is   good;
2. "The right hand of the Lord   has   triumphed!
3. "The stone that the builders   re   -   jected

his loving–kindness en   -   dures   for   ever.
The right hand of the Lord   is   ex   -   alted!
has become the chief   cor - ner - stone."

Let the household of Israel   now   say:
I shall not die   but   live,
This is the   Lord's   doing;

To Antiphon

"His loving–kindness en   -   dures   for   ever."
to declare the deeds   of   the   Lord."
it is marvelous   in   our   sight.

Music: Fintan P. O'Carroll, d. 1981, ©   EASTER SEASON

Ps. 118: Give Thanks to the Lord 126

Antiphon: The Stone that the Builders Rejected Has Become the Cornerstone

ANTIPHON
Cantor/Choir; All repeat

The stone that the build-ers re - ject - ed has be-come the cor - ner - stone.

Psalm 118: 1, 8–9, 21–23, 26, 28

VERSE 1
Cantor/Choir

Give thanks to the Lord for he is good, for his mercy en-dures for - ev - er.

To Antiphon

It is better to take re-fuge in the Lord, than to trust in men of high es-tate

VERSE 2
Cantor/Choir

I will give thanks to you for you have an-swered me, and have been my

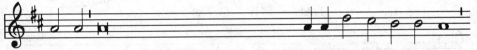

Sav - ior. The stone which the builders rejected has be-come the cor - ner-stone.

To Antiphon

By the Lord has this been done; it is won-der-ful in our eyes.

VERSE 3
Cantor/Choir

Blest is he who comes in the name of the Lord; we bless you from the

house of the Lord. You are my God, and I give thanks to you;

To Antiphon

give thanks to the Lord, for his good-ness en-dures for - ev - er.

Music: William Ferris, b. 1937, ©

EASTER SEASON

127   Ps. 118: Give Thanks to the Lord

Antiphon: This Is the Day the Lord Has Made

ANTIPHON

Cantor/Choir; All repeat

This is the day   the Lord has made;   let us re - joice and be   glad.

Psalm 118: 1–2, 16–17, 22–23

VERSE 1

Cantor/Choir

Give   thanks to the Lord for he   is   good;   his

lov - ing - kind - ness   en - dures   for   ev   -   er.

Let   the   house - hold   of   Is - ra - el   now   say:

To Antiphon

"His lov - ing - kind - ness   en - dures   for   ev - er."

VERSE 2

Cantor/Choir

"The   right hand of   the Lord   has   tri - umphed!   The

right   hand   of   the   Lord   is   ex - alt   -   ed!

The   right hand   of   the   Lord   is   vic - to - ri - ous!"

Music: Robert E. Kreutz, b. 1922 ©   **EASTER SEASON**

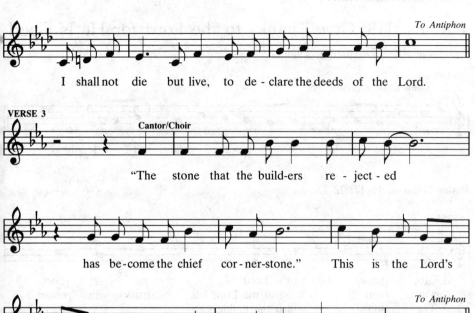

To Antiphon

I shall not die but live, to de - clare the deeds of the Lord.

VERSE 3

Cantor/Choir

"The stone that the build-ers re - ject - ed

has be-come the chief cor - ner-stone." This is the Lord's

To Antiphon

do - ing; it is mar - vel - ous in our sight.

128 Ps. 118: Give Thanks to the Lord for He Is Good

Antiphon: Alleluia, Alleluia, Alleluia

ANTIPHON

Al - le - lu - ia, al - le - lu - ia, al - le - lu - ia.

Psalm 118: 1–2, 16–17, 22–23

VERSES

1. Give thanks to the Lord for he is good,
2. The right hand of the Lord has struck with power:
3. The stone which the builders re - ject - ed

for his mercy en - dures for - ev - er.
the right hand of the Lord is ex - alt - ed.
has be - come the cor - ner - stone.

To Antiphon

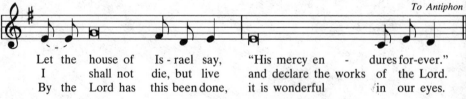

Let the house of Is - rael say, "His mercy en - dures for-ever."
I shall not die, but live and declare the works of the Lord.
By the Lord has this been done, it is wonderful in our eyes.

Music: John Lee, b. 1908, ©

EASTER SEASON

Ps. 66: Raise a Shout to God, All the Earth 129

Antiphon: Cry Out with Joy to the Lord All the Earth

ANTIPHON
Cantor/Choir; All repeat

Cry out with joy to the Lord all the earth.

Psalm 66: 1–3, 4–5, 6–7, 16, 20

VERSES
Cantor/Choir   Tone 1

1. Raise a shout to God, all   the   earth;
2. All the earth wor -   ships   you;
3. He turned the sea into   dry   land,
4. Come and hear, all you who   fear   God;

sing the glory of   his   name,
to you they sing praises,
    they sing praises to   your   name."
so they went through the water   on   foot.
I will tell you what he has done   for   me.

make his   praise   glorious.
Come, see the works   of   God,
There we rejoiced   in   him,
Blessed be God, who has not rejected   my   prayer

To Antiphon

Say to God: "How awesome are   your   deeds!
his awesome deeds   a -   mong us.
who rules by his might   for   ever.
nor turned away his love   from   me.

Music: Fintan P. O'Carroll, d. 1981, ©

EASTER SEASON

130 Ps. 47: Clap Your Hands, All You Peoples

Antiphon: God Goes Up with Shouts of Joy: The Lord Goes Up with Trumpet Blast

ANTIPHON

God goes up with shouts of joy: the Lord goes up with trum-pet blast.

Psalm 47: 2–3, 6–7, 8–9

VERSES

1. Clap your hands, clap your hands, all you peoples;
2. God has gone up with a shout,
3. For God is king over all the world;

shout to God, shout to God with songs of joy!
the Lord with a blast of the horn.
sing praises to him with psalms.

The Lord, the Most High is awesome;
Sing praises, sing prais - es to God;
God reigns o - ver the nations;

To Antiphon

he is a great King over all the world.
sing praises, sing praises to our King!
God is seated on his ho - ly throne.

Music: Fintan P. O'Carroll, d. 1981, ©   ASCENSION

Ps. 104: Bless the Lord, O My Soul 131

Antiphon: Send Forth Your Spirit, O Lord, and Renew the Face of the Earth

ANTIPHON

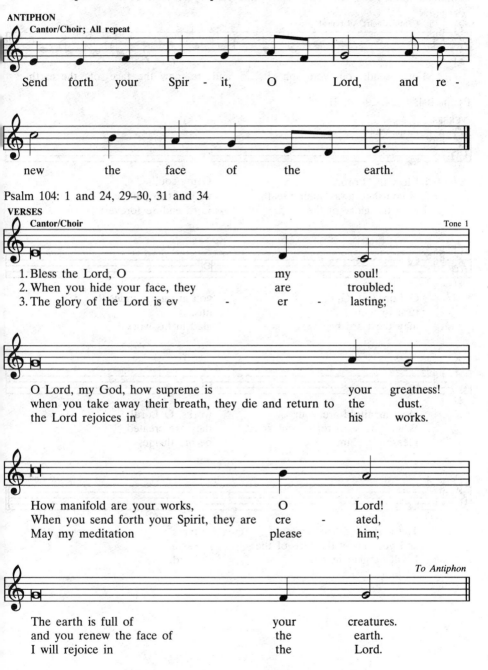

Cantor/Choir; All repeat

Send forth your Spir - it, O Lord, and re -

new the face of the earth.

Psalm 104: 1 and 24, 29–30, 31 and 34

VERSES

Cantor/Choir   Tone 1

1. Bless the Lord, O my soul!
2. When you hide your face, they are troubled;
3. The glory of the Lord is ev - er - lasting;

O Lord, my God, how supreme is your greatness!
when you take away their breath, they die and return to the dust.
the Lord rejoices in his works.

How manifold are your works, O Lord!
When you send forth your Spirit, they are cre - ated,
May my meditation please him;

To Antiphon

The earth is full of your creatures.
and you renew the face of the earth.
I will rejoice in the Lord.

Music: Fintan P. O'Carroll, d. 1981, ©   PENTECOST

132 Ps. 104: Bless the Lord, O My Soul

Antiphon: Lord, Send Out Your Spirit, and Renew the Face of the Earth

ANTIPHON

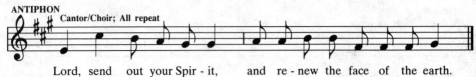

Lord, send out your Spir - it, and re - new the face of the earth.

Psalm 104: 1, 24, 29–30, 31, 34

VERSES

1. Bless the Lord,   O my soul!
2. If you take away their breath,   they perish and re   -
3. May the glory of the   Lord endure forever;

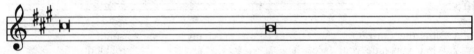

O Lord, my God,   you are great indeed!
turn to their   dust.
may the Lord be   glad in his works!

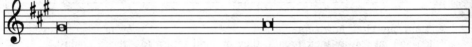

How manifold are your   works, O Lord!
When you send forth your spirit, they are created,
Pleasing to him   be my theme;

To Antiphon

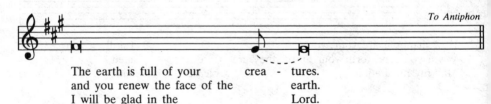

The earth is full of your   crea - tures.
and you renew the face of the earth.
I will be glad in the   Lord.

Music: Gerard Farrell, O.S.B., b. 1919, ©   PENTECOST

Ps. 19: The Law of the Lord Is Perfect 133

Antiphon: Lord, You Have the Words of Everlasting Life

ANTIPHON

Cantor/Choir; All repeat

Lord, you have the words of ev-er-last-ing life.

Psalm 19: 8, 9, 10, 11

VERSE 1

Cantor/Choir

The law of the Lord is per-fect, re-fresh-ing the soul; the de-

To Antiphon

cree of the Lord is trust-worth-y, giv-ing wis-dom to the sim-ple.

VERSE 2

Cantor/Choir

The pre-cepts of the Lord are right, re-joic-ing, the heart; the com-

To Antiphon

mand of the Lord is clear, en-light'-ning the eye.

VERSE 3

Cantor/Choir

The fear of the Lord is pure, en-dur-ing for-ev-er; the

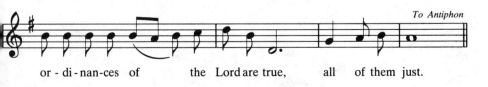

To Antiphon

or-di-nan-ces of the Lord are true, all of them just.

Music: Robert E. Kreutz b. 1922, ©   ORDINARY TIME

VERSE 4

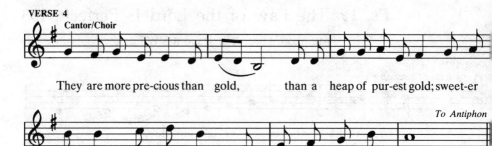

They are more pre-cious than gold, than a heap of pur-est gold; sweet-er
al - so than syr - up or hon - ey from the comb.

134 Ps. 19: The Law of the Lord Is Perfect

Antiphon: Lord, You Have the Words of Everlasting Life.

ANTIPHON

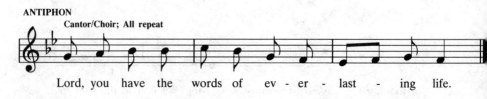

Lord, you have the words of ev - er - last - ing life.

Psalm 19: 8, 9, 10, 11

VERSES

1. The law of the Lord is perfect, re - fresh-ing the soul;
2. The precepts of the Lord are right, re - joic-ing the heart;
3. The fear of the Lord is pure, en - dur-ing for ever;
4. They are more pre - cious than gold, than a heap of pur - est gold;

To Antiphon

the de - cree of the Lord is trust-worth - y, giving wisdom to the simple.
the com-mand of the Lord is clear, enlighten - ing the eye.
the ordinances of the Lord are true, all of them just.
sweet-er also than syr - up, or honey from the comb.

Music: John Lee, b. 1908, ©

ORDINARY TIME

Ps. 23: The Lord Is My Shepherd 135

Antiphon: The Lord Is My Shepherd; There Is Nothing I Shall Want

ANTIPHON

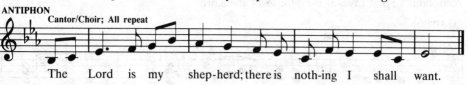

Cantor/Choir; All repeat

The Lord is my shep-herd; there is noth-ing I shall want.

Psalm 23: 1–3, 4, 5, 6

VERSES

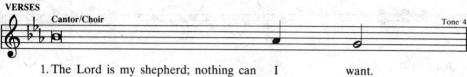

Cantor/Choir   Tone 4

1. The Lord is my shepherd; nothing can   I   want.
2. Though I walk through valleys   of   darkness,
3. You spread out a banquet   be -   fore me
4. Surely your goodness   and   mercy

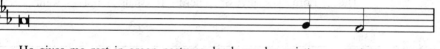

He gives me rest in green pastures, leads me by qui-et   waters.
I fear   no   evil.
in sight of   my   foes.
follow me all my   life   long;

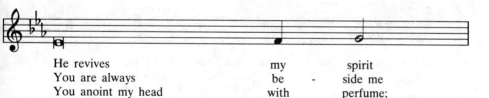

He revives   my   spirit
You are always   be -   side me
You anoint my head   with   perfume;
And I will dwell in the house of the   Lord,

To Antiphon

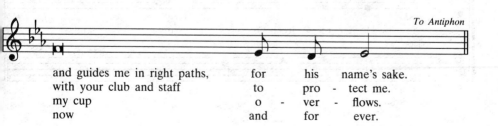

and guides me in right paths,   for   his   name's sake.
with your club and staff   to   pro - tect me.
my cup   o -   ver - flows.
now   and   for   ever.

Music: Fintan P. O'Carroll, d. 1981, ©   ORDINARY TIME

136 Ps. 23: The Lord Is My Shepherd

Antiphon: I Shall Live in the House of the Lord

Psalm 23:1–3, 3–4, 5, 6

Music: William Ferris, b. 1937, ©

ORDINARY TIME

Ev - en though I walk in the dark val - ley, I fear no e - vil;

for you are at my side, your rod and your staff give me cour-age.

VERSE 3

Soprano and Alto

You spread the ta-ble be-fore me, in the sight of my foes;

Tenor and Bass

you a - noint my head with oil; my cup o - ver flows.

VERSE 4

To Antiphon

S

On - ly good-ness and kind-ness fol-low me, All the days of my life;

A

T

On - ly good-ness and kind-ness fol-low me, All the days of my life;

B

137 Ps. 23: The Lord Is My Shepherd

Antiphon: The Lord Is My Shepherd, and Nothing Do I Want

ANTIPHON

The Lord is my shep - herd, and noth - ing do I want.

Psalm 23: 1-3, 3-4, 5, 6

VERSES

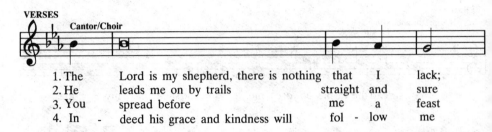

1. The Lord is my shepherd, there is nothing that I lack;
2. He leads me on by trails straight and sure
3. You spread before me a feast
4. In - deed his grace and kindness will fol - low me

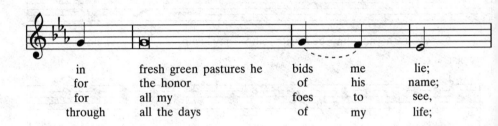

in fresh green pastures he bids me lie;
for the honor of his name;
for all my foes to see,
through all the days of my life;

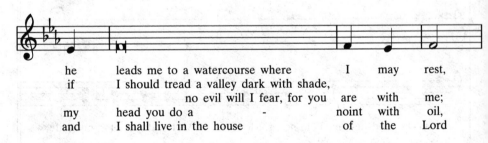

he leads me to a watercourse where I may rest,
if I should tread a valley dark with shade,
no evil will I fear, for you are with me;
my head you do a - noint with oil,
and I shall live in the house of the Lord

To Antiphon

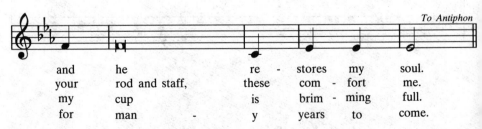

and he re - stores my soul.
your rod and staff, these com - fort me.
my cup is brim - ming full.
for man - y years to come.

Music: Stephen Somerville, b. 1931, ©

Ps. 27: The Lord Is My Light and My Salvation 138

Antiphon: The Lord Is My Light and My Help

ANTIPHON

Cantor/Choir; All repeat

The Lord is my light and my help.

Psalm 27: 1, 4, 13–14

VERSES

Cantor/Choir   Tone 4

1. The Lord is my light and my sal - vation:
2. One thing I ask of the Lord; one thing I seek:
3. I do believe that I shall see

whom shall I fear?
that I may dwell in the house of the
Lord all the days of my life,
the goodness of the Lord in the land of the living.

The Lord is the strength of my life:
To behold the beauty of the Lord,
Put your hope in the Lord.

To Antiphon

of whom shall I be a - fraid?
to consult in his temple.
Be strong and take courage. Put your hope in the Lord.

Music: Fintan P. O'Carroll, d. 1981, ©   ORDINARY TIME

139 Ps. 27: The Lord Is My Light

Antiphon 1: The Lord Is My Light and My Salvation
Antiphon 2: One Thing I Seek: to Dwell in the House of the Lord

ANTIPHON 1

Cantor/Choir; All repeat

The Lord is my light and my sal - va - tion; no one shall fright-en me.

ANTIPHON 2

Cantor/Choir; All repeat

One thing I seek: to dwell in the house of the Lord all the days of my life.

Psalm 27: 1, 2, 4, 5, 6, 7–8, 9–10, 11–12, 13–14

VERSES

Cantor/Choir

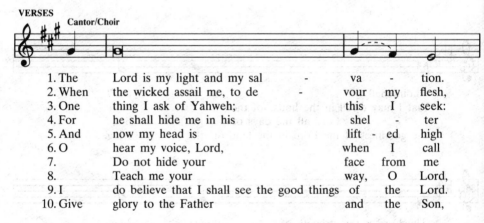

1. The	Lord is my light and my sal	-	va	- tion.
2. When	the wicked assail me, to de	-	vour my	flesh,
3. One	thing I ask of Yahweh;		this I	seek:
4. For	he shall hide me in his		shel	- ter
5. And	now my head is		lift - ed	high
6. O	hear my voice, Lord,		when I	call
7.	Do not hide your		face from	me
8.	Teach me your		way, O	Lord,
9. I	do believe that I shall see the good things	of	the	Lord.
10. Give	glory to the Father		and the	Son,

1. No	one shall frighten	me
2. It	is my foes and enemies who trip and	fall.
3. To	dwell in the house of the Lord all the days of my	life.
4.	On an evil	day,
5. A -	bove my enemies surrounding	me.
6. Have	pity on me, answer	me.
7. Nor	drive your servant angrily a -	way;
8. And	lead me on an even road because of my	foes;
9.	In the land of the	living
10. Give	glory to the Holy	Spirit;

Text: tr., Stephen Somerville, b. 1931, ©
Music: Stephen Somerville, b. 1931, ©

ORDINARY TIME

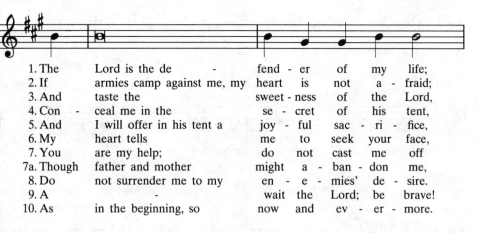

1. The	Lord is the de -	fend - er	of	my	life;
2. If	armies camp against me, my	heart is	not	a -	fraid;
3. And	taste the	sweet - ness	of	the	Lord,
4. Con -	ceal me in the	se - cret	of	his	tent,
5. And	I will offer in his tent a	joy - ful	sac - ri -		fice,
6. My	heart tells	me to	seek	your	face,
7. You	are my help;	do not	cast	me	off
7a. Though	father and mother	might a -	ban - don		me,
8. Do	not surrender me to my	en - e -	mies'	de -	sire.
9. A	-	wait the	Lord;	be	brave!
10. As	in the beginning, so	now and	ev -	er -	more.

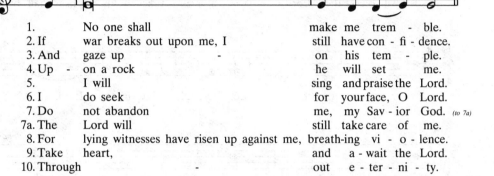

To Antiphon

1.	No one shall	make me trem - ble.	
2. If	war breaks out upon me, I	still have con - fi - dence.	
3. And	gaze up -	on his tem - ple.	
4. Up -	on a rock	he will set me.	
5.	I will	sing and praise the Lord.	
6. I	do seek	for your face, O Lord.	
7. Do	not abandon	me, my Sav - ior God.	*(to 7a)*
7a. The	Lord will	still take care of me.	
8. For	lying witnesses have risen up against me,	breath-ing vi - o - lence.	
9. Take	heart,	and a - wait the Lord.	
10. Through	-	out e - ter - ni - ty.	

140 Ps. 34: I Will Bless the Lord at All Times

Antiphon: I Will Bless the Lord at All Times

ANTIPHON

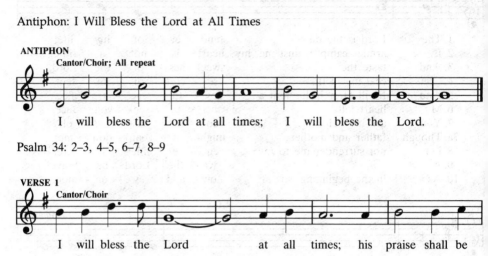

I will bless the Lord at all times; I will bless the Lord.

Psalm 34: 2–3, 4–5, 6–7, 8–9

VERSE 1

I will bless the Lord at all times; his praise shall be

ev - er in my mouth. Let my soul glo-ry in the Lord;

the low - ly will hear me and be glad.

VERSE 2

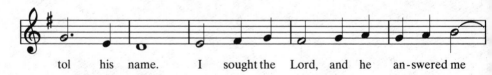

Glo - ri - fy the Lord with me, let us to - geth - er ex -

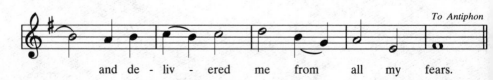

tol his name. I sought the Lord, and he an-swered me

and de - liv - ered me from all my fears.

Music: Donald J. Reagan, b. 1923, ©

ORDINARY TIME

VERSE 3

Cantor/Choir

Look to him that you may ra - di - ate with joy, and your

fac - es may not blush with shame. When the af - flict - ed one called

To Antiphon

out, the Lord heard, and from all dis - tress he saved him.

VERSE 4

Cantor/Choir

The an - gel of the Lord camps a - round those who fear him, and de -

liv - ers them. Taste and see the good-ness of the

To Antiphon

Lord; hap - py the one who takes re - fuge in him.

141 Ps. 34: I Will Bless the Lord at All Times

Antiphon: Taste and See That the Lord Is Good

ANTIPHON

Cantor/Choir; All repeat

Taste and see that the Lord is good.

Psalm 34: 2–3, 4–5, 6–7, 8–9

VERSES

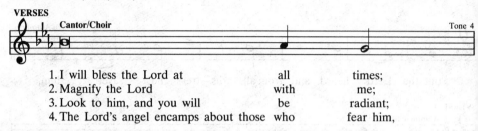

Cantor/Choir   Tone 4

1. I will bless the Lord at   all   times;
2. Magnify the Lord   with   me;
3. Look to him, and you will   be   radiant;
4. The Lord's angel encamps about those who   fear him,

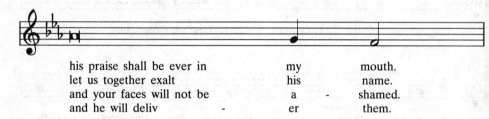

his praise shall be ever in   my   mouth.
let us together exalt   his   name.
and your faces will not be   a   -   shamed.
and he will deliv   -   er   them.

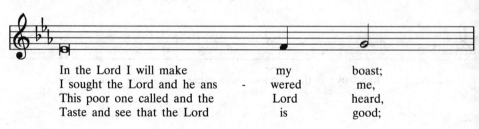

In the Lord I will make   my   boast;
I sought the Lord and he ans   -   wered   me,
This poor one called and the   Lord   heard,
Taste and see that the Lord   is   good;

To Antiphon

let the humble hear   and   re - joice.
and delivered me from   all   my   fears.
and I was saved from   all   my   troubles.
happy are they who   trust in   him.

Music: Fintan P. O'Carroll, d. 1981, ©   ORDINARY TIME

Ps. 34: I Will Bless The Lord at All Times 142

Antiphon: Taste and See the Goodness of the Lord

ANTIPHON

Taste and see the good-ness of the Lord,

taste and see the good-ness of the Lord.

Psalm 34: 2–3, 4–5, 6–7, 8–9

VERSE 1

I will bless the Lord at all times; his praise shall

be ev-er in my mouth. Let my soul glo-ry in the

To Antiphon

Lord; the low-ly will hear me and be glad.

VERSE 2

Glo-ri-fy the Lord with me, let us to-geth-er ex-tol his name. I sought the

To Antiphon

Lord, and he an-swered me and de-liv-ered me from all my fears.

Music: Robert E. Kreutz, b. 1922, ©　　　　　　　　　　　　ORDINARY TIME

VERSE 3 *mf*

Cantor/Choir

Look to him that you may be ra - di - ant with joy, and your fac-es may not blush with shame. When the af-flict-ed man called out, the Lord

To Antiphon

heard, and from all his dis - tress he saved him.

VERSE 4 *mp*

Cantor/Choir

The an - gel of the Lord en - camps a - round those who fear him, and de - liv - ers them. Taste and see how good the Lord

To Final Antiphon

is; hap - py the man who takes ref - uge in him.

FINAL ANTIPHON *mf*

Taste and see the good - ness of the Lord, taste and see the good - ness of the Lord.

Ps. 40: You Do Not Ask for Sacrifice 143

Antiphon: Here Am I, O Lord, to Do Your Will

ANTIPHON

Here am I, O Lord, to do your will.

Psalm 40: 7, 8, 9, 10, 11

VERSE 1

You do not ask for sac-ri-fice and off-'rings, but an o - pen ear. You

do not ask for ho - lo - caust and vic - tim. In - stead, here am I.

VERSE 2

In the scroll of the book it stands writ - ten that I should do your will. My

God, I de - light in your law in the depth of my heart.

VERSEn 3

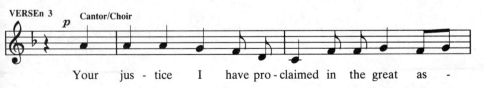

Your jus - tice I have pro - claimed in the great as -

sem - bly. My lips I have not sealed; you know it, O Lord.

Text: The Grail, ©
Music: Fintan P. O'Carroll, d. 1981, ©

ORDINARY TIME

VERSE 4   *p*   Cantor/Choir

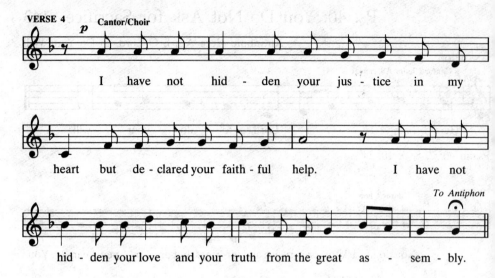

I have not hid - den your jus - tice in my

heart but de - clared your faith - ful help. I have not

To Antiphon

hid - den your love and your truth from the great as - sem - bly.

Ps. 63: O God, You Are My God 144

Antiphon: My Soul Is Thirsting for You, O Lord, My God

ANTIPHON

Cantor/Choir; All repeat

My soul is thirst - ing for you, O Lord, my God.

Psalm 63: 2, 3–4, 5–6, 8–9

VERSES

Cantor/Choir

1. O God, you are my God whom I seek;
2. Thus have I gazed toward you in the sanctuary
3. Thus will I bless you while I live;
4. That you are my help,

for you my flesh pines and my soul thirsts
to see your power and your glory,
lifting up my hands, I will call upon your name.
and in the shadow of your wings I shout for joy.

like the earth, parched, lifeless
for your kindness is a greater good than life;
As with the riches of a banquet shall my soul be satisfied,
My soul clings fast to you;

To Antiphon

and without water.
my lips shall glorify you.
and with exultant lips my mouth shall praise you.
your right hand up - holds me.

Music: Gerard Farrell, O.S.B., b. 1919, ©   ORDINARY TIME

145 Ps. 63: O God, You Are My God Whom I Seek

Antiphon: For You My Soul Is Thirsting, O Lord, My God

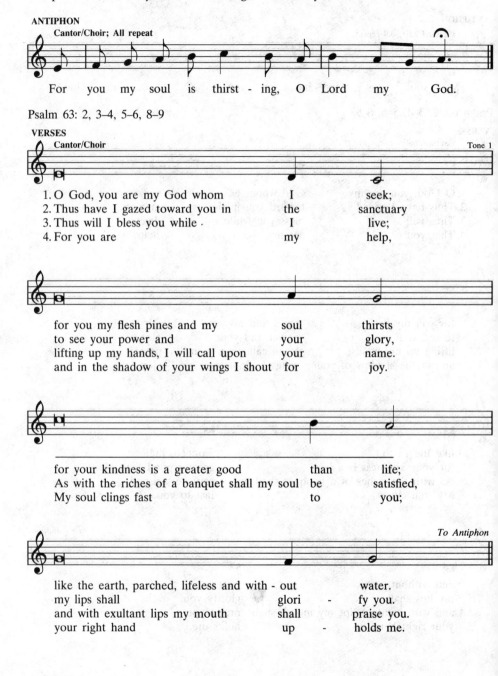

ANTIPHON

Cantor/Choir; All repeat

For you my soul is thirst-ing, O Lord my God.

Psalm 63: 2, 3–4, 5–6, 8–9

VERSES

Cantor/Choir   Tone 1

1. O God, you are my God whom   I   seek;
2. Thus have I gazed toward you in   the   sanctuary
3. Thus will I bless you while ·   I   live;
4. For you are   my   help,

for you my flesh pines and my   soul   thirsts
to see your power and   your   glory,
lifting up my hands, I will call upon   your   name.
and in the shadow of your wings I shout for   joy.

for your kindness is a greater good   than   life;
As with the riches of a banquet shall my soul be   satisfied,
My soul clings fast   to   you;

To Antiphon

like the earth, parched, lifeless and with - out   water.
my lips shall   glori   -   fy you.
and with exultant lips my mouth   shall   praise you.
your right hand   up   -   holds me.

Music: Fintan P. O'Carroll, d. 1981, ©   ORDINARY TIME

Ps. 84: How Lovely Is Your Dwelling Place 146

Antiphon: How Lovely Is Your Dwellng Place

ANTIPHON

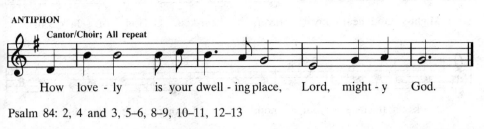

How love - ly is your dwell - ing place, Lord, might - y God.

Psalm 84: 2, 4 and 3, 5–6, 8–9, 10–11, 12–13

VERSE 1

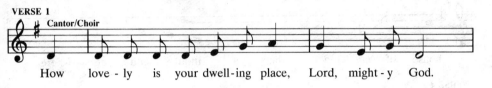

How love - ly is your dwell-ing place, Lord, might - y God.

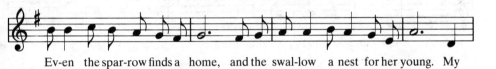

Ev-en the spar-row finds a home, and the swal-low a nest for her young. My

To Antiphon

soul yearns and pines, my heart and my flesh cry out for the liv - ing God.

VERSE 2

Hap-py they who dwell in your house! Ev - er they sing a song of

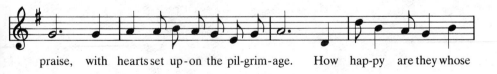

praise, with hearts set up-on the pil-grim-age. How hap-py are they whose

To Antiphon

strength you are! They shall see God in Zi - on.

Music: Donald J. Reagan, b. 1923, ©

ORDINARY TIME

VERSE 3

Cantor/Choir

Might-y God hear my prayer; hear-ken, O God of Ja - cob!

Look on the face of your a - noint - ed. I would rath-er one day in the

To Antiphon

house of my God than a thou - sand else - where.

VERSE 4

Cantor/Choir

A sun and a shield is the Lord; grace and glo - ry be -

stowed. No good thing does God with-hold from those who walk in sin -

To Antiphon

cer - i - ty, hap - py they who trust in you!

Ps. 89: I Will Sing Forever of Your Love 147

Antiphon: I Will Sing Forevermore of Your Kindness and of Your Love

ANTIPHON

I will sing for-ev-er-more of your

kind-ness and of your love, O Lord.

Psalm 89: 2–3, 14–15, 16–17, 18–19

VERSES

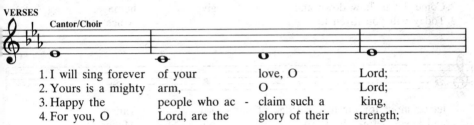

1. I will sing forever of your love, O Lord;
2. Yours is a mighty arm, O Lord;
3. Happy the people who ac - claim such a king,
4. For you, O Lord, are the glory of their strength;

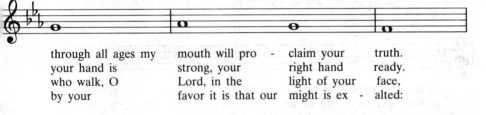

through all ages my mouth will pro - claim your truth.
your hand is strong, your right hand ready.
who walk, O Lord, in the light of your face,
by your favor it is that our might is ex - alted:

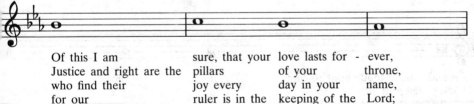

Of this I am sure, that your love lasts for - ever,
Justice and right are the pillars of your throne,
who find their joy every day in your name,
for our ruler is in the keeping of the Lord;

To Antiphon

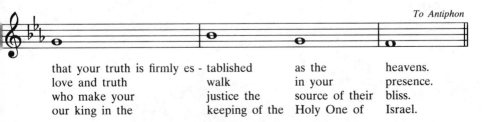

that your truth is firmly es - tablished as the heavens.
love and truth walk in your presence.
who make your justice the source of their bliss.
our king in the keeping of the Holy One of Israel.

Text: Ps. The Grail, ©; Vs. 2 & Ant. Roberta Knakal, O.S.B., b. 1930, ©
Music: Roberta Knakal, O.S.B., b. 1930, Ant. acc. Francis Winkels, b. 1958, ©

ORDINARY TIME

148 Ps. 95: Come, Let Us Sing to the Lord

Antiphon: O That Today You Would Listen to His Voice! Harden Not Your Hearts

ANTIPHON

O that to-day you would lis-ten to his voice! Har-den not your hearts.

Psalm 95: 1–2, 6–7, 7c–9

VERSES

Cantor/Choir   Tone 1

1. Come, let us sing to .... the .... Lord;
2. Come, let us bow down and .... give .... homage,
3. Today will you listen to .... his .... voice?

let us shout for joy to the Rock of our .... sal - vation.
and kneel before the Lord .... our .... Maker.
"Harden not your hearts, as at Meribah,
        as on the day at Massah in .... the .... desert,

Let us come before his presence with .... thanks - giving,
For he is our God; and we are .... his .... people,
when your forebears tried me and put me to .. the ...... test,

To Antiphon

and raise a loud shout to him .... in .... psalms.
the sheep of .... his .... pasture.
though they had seen the wonders I .... per - formed."

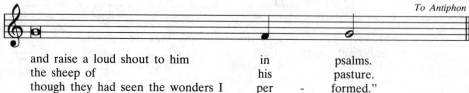

Music: Fintan P. O'Carroll, d. 1981, ©   ORDINARY TIME

Ps. 96: Proclaim His Help Day by Day 149

Antiphon: Sing a New Song to the Lord!

ANTIPHON

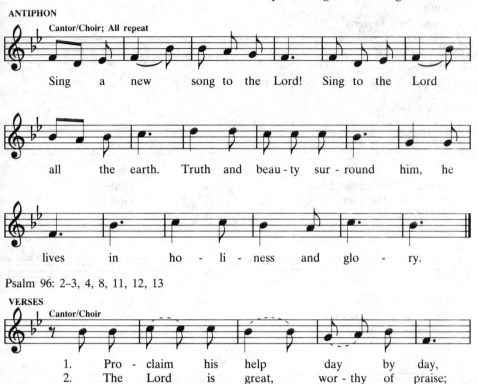

Sing a new song to the Lord! Sing to the Lord

all the earth. Truth and beau-ty sur-round him, he

lives in ho-li-ness and glo-ry.

Psalm 96: 2–3, 4, 8, 11, 12, 13

VERSES

Cantor/Choir

1. Pro - claim his help day by day,
2. The Lord is great, wor - thy of praise;
3. Let the heav-ens re - joice, earth be glad;
4. With jus - tice he will rule the world;

To Antiphon

tell a - mong the na - tions his glo - ry.
give the Lord the glo - ry of his name.
all the trees of the wood shout for joy.
he will judge the peo - ple with his truth.

ORDINARY TIME

150 Ps. 100: Shout for Joy to the Lord

Antiphon: We Are His People, The Sheep of His Flock

ANTIPHON

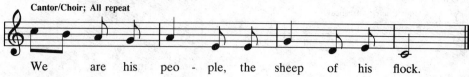

Cantor/Choir; All repeat

We are his peo - ple, the sheep of his flock.

Psalm 100: 1–2, 3, 5

VERSES

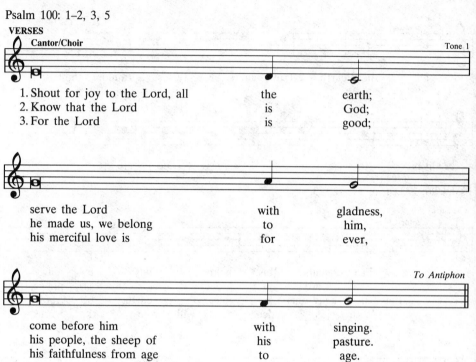

Cantor/Choir   Tone 1

1. Shout for joy to the Lord, all   the   earth;
2. Know that the Lord   is   God;
3. For the Lord   is   good;

serve the Lord   with   gladness,
he made us, we belong   to   him,
his merciful love is   for   ever,

To Antiphon

come before him   with   singing.
his people, the sheep of   his   pasture.
his faithfulness from age   to   age.

Music: Fintan P. O'Carroll, d. 1981, ©   ORDINARY TIME

Ps. 100: Sing Joyfully to the Lord, All You Lands 151

Antiphon: We Are His People, the Sheep of His Flock

ANTIPHON
Cantor/Choir; All repeat | Last Time

We are his peo - ple, the sheep of his flock. flock.

Psalm 100: 1–2, 3, 5

VERSE 1
Cantor/Choir

Sing joy - ful - ly to the Lord all you lands; serve the Lord, with

To Antiphon

glad - ness, come be - fore him with joy - ful song.

VERSE 2
Cantor/Choir

Know that the Lord is God; he made us, his we

To Antiphon

are: his peo - ple, the flock he tends.

VERSE 3
Cantor/Choir

The Lord is good; his

kind - ness en - dures for - ev - er, and his

To Antiphon

faith - ful - ness to all gen - er - a - tions.

Music: Robert LeBlanc, b. 1948, © 1979   ORDINARY TIME

152 Ps. 100: Let All the Earth Cry Out

Antiphon: Let All the Earth Cry Out to the Lord with Joy

ANTIPHON

Cantor/Choir; All repeat

Let all the earth cry out to the Lord with joy; Give thanks to him and bless his name.

Psalm 100: 3, 4, 4–5

VERSES

Cantor/Choir

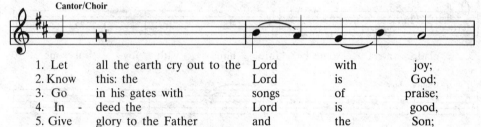

1. Let all the earth cry out to the Lord with joy;
2. Know this: the Lord is God;
3. Go in his gates with songs of praise;
4. In - deed the Lord is good,
5. Give glory to the Father and the Son;

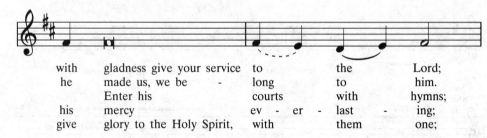

with gladness give your service to the Lord;
he made us, we be - long to him.
Enter his courts with hymns;
his mercy ev - er - last - ing;
give glory to the Holy Spirit, with them one;

To Antiphon

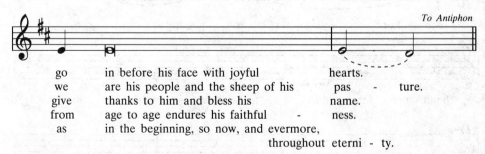

go in before his face with joyful hearts.
we are his people and the sheep of his pas - ture.
give thanks to him and bless his name.
from age to age endures his faithful - ness.
as in the beginning, so now, and evermore,
        throughout eterni - ty.

Music: Stephen Somerville, b. 1931

ORDINARY TIME

Ps. 103: My Soul, Give Thanks to the Lord 153

Antiphon: The Lord Is Kind and Merciful

ANTIPHON

Cantor/Choir; All repeat

The Lord is kind and mer - ci - ful.

Psalm 103: 1–2, 3–4, 12–13

VERSE 1

Cantor/Choir

My soul, give thanks to the Lord all my

be - ing, bless his ho - ly name. My soul, give thanks to the

To Antiphon

Lord and nev - er for - get all his bless - ings.

VERSE 2

Cantor/Choir

It is he who for - gives all your guilt, who

heals ev - 'ry one of your ills, who re - deems your life from the

To Antiphon

grave, who crowns you with love and com - pas - sion.

Music: Noel Goemanne, b. 1926, ©

ORDINARY TIME

VERSE 3

As far as the east is from the west so far does he re-move our sins. As a fa-ther has com-pas-sion on his sons, the Lord has pit - y on those who fear him.

To Antiphon

Ps. 103: Bless the Lord, O My Soul   154

Antiphon 1: The Lord Is Kind and Merciful
Antiphon 2: Hear Us, Lord, and Save Us

ANTIPHON

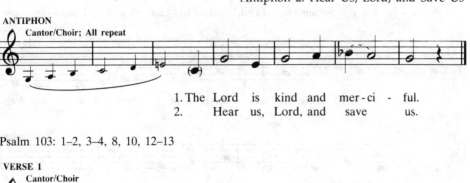

1. The Lord is kind and mer-ci-ful.
2.   Hear us, Lord, and save us.

Psalm 103: 1–2, 3–4, 8, 10, 12–13

VERSE 1

Bless the Lord, O my soul; and all my be-ing, bless his

ho - ly name. Bless the Lord, O my soul,

To Antiphon

and for - get not all his ben - e - fits.

VERSE 2

Cantor/Choir

He par - dons all your in - i - qui - ties, he

heals all your ills. He re - deems your life from de -

To Antiphon

struc - tion, he crowns you with kind-ness and com - pas - sion.

Music: Robert E. Kreutz, b. 1922, ©

ORDINARY TIME

VERSE 3

Mer-ci-ful and gra-cious is the Lord, slow to an-ger and a-bound-ing in kind-ness. Not ac-cord-ing to our sins does he deal with us, nor does

To Antiphon

he re-quite us ac-cord-ing to our crimes.

VERSE 4

As far as the east is from the west, so far has he put our trans-gres-sions from us. As a fa-ther has com-pas-sion on his chil-dren,

To Antiphon

so the Lord has com-pas-sion on those who fear him.

Ps. 145: I Will Extol You, O My God 155

Antiphon: I Will Praise Your Name For Ever

ANTIPHON

Cantor/Choir; All repeat

I will praise your name for ev - er, my King and my God.

Psalm 145: 1–2, 8–9, 10–11, 13–14

VERSE 1

Cantor/Choir

I will ex - tol you, O my God and King,

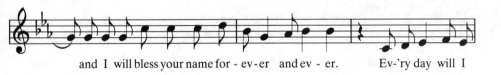

and I will bless your name for - ev-er and ev - er. Ev-'ry day will I

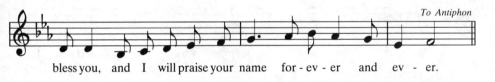

To Antiphon

bless you, and I will praise your name for - ev - er and ev - er.

VERSE 2

Cantor/Choir

The Lord is gra - cious and mer - ci - ful, slow to

an - ger and of great kind - ness. The Lord is

To Antiphon

good to all and com - pas-sion-ate to all his works.

Music: Robert E. Kreutz, b. 1922, © 1988   ORDINARY TIME

VERSE 3

Cantor/Choir

Let all your works give you thanks, O Lord, and let your faith-ful ones bless you. Let them dis-course of the glo-ry of your king-dom and speak of your might.

To Antiphon

VERSE 4

Cantor/Choir

The Lord is faith-ful in all his words and ho-ly in all his works. The Lord lifts up all who are fall-ing and rais-es up all who are bowed down.

To Antiphon

Ps. 145: I Will Give You Glory, O God 156

Antiphon: I Will Praise Your Name For Ever

ANTIPHON

I will praise your name for ev - er, my King and my God.

Psalm 145: 1–2, 8–9, 10–11, 13–14

VERSES

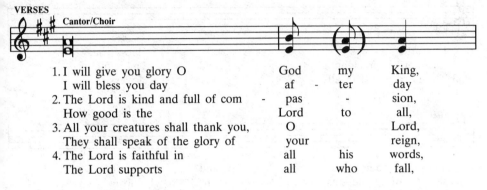

1. I will give you glory O God my King,
   I will bless you day af - ter day
2. The Lord is kind and full of com - pas - sion,
   How good is the Lord to all,
3. All your creatures shall thank you, O Lord,
   They shall speak of the glory of your reign,
4. The Lord is faithful in all his words,
   The Lord supports all who fall,

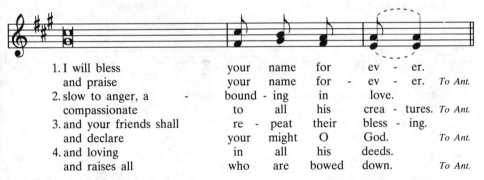

1. I will bless your name for ev - er.
   and praise your name for - ev - er. *To Ant.*
2. slow to anger, a - bound - ing in love.
   compassionate to all his crea - tures. *To Ant.*
3. and your friends shall re - peat their bless - ing.
   and declare your might O God. *To Ant.*
4. and loving in all his deeds.
   and raises all who are bowed down. *To Ant.*

Text: The Grail, © 1963
Music: Michael Sullivan, b. 1937, © 1986

ORDINARY TIME

157 Ps. 145: Day after Day Will I Bless You

Antiphon: The Lord Is Close to All Who Call Him

ANTIPHON

Cantor/Choir; All repeat

The Lord is close to all who call him.

Psalm 145: 2–3, 8–9, 17–18

VERSES

Cantor/Choir

Tone 1

1. Day after day will I bless you,
2. The Lord is gracious and merciful,
3. The Lord is just in all his ways,

and praise your name for ever and ever.
slow to anger and steadfast in love.
and gracious in all his deeds.

Great is the Lord and worthy of great praise;
The Lord is good to ev - 'ry one;
The Lord is near to all who call to him,

To Antiphon

there is no limit to his greatness.
his compassion reaches all whom he has made.
to all who call to him sin - cerely.

Music: Fintan P. O'Carroll, d. 1981, ©

ORDINARY TIME

Ps. 145: The Lord Is Gracious and Merciful 158

Antiphon: I Will Bless Your Name For Ever, O God My King

ANTIPHON

Cantor/Choir; All repeat

I will bless your name for ev - er, O God my King.

Psalm 145: 8–9, 10–11, 13–14

VERSES

Cantor/Choir   Tone 2

1. The Lord is gracious   and   merciful,
2. All your creation praises you,   O   Lord;
3. The Lord is faithful in all   his   words,

slow to anger and stead   -   fast   in   love.
all your faithful   peo - ple   bless you.
and gracious in   all   his   deeds.

The Lord is good to ev   -   'ry   -   one;
They proclaim the glory of   your   kingdom,
The Lord upholds all who   have   fallen,

To Antiphon

his compassion reaches all whom   he   has   made.
and tell of   all   your   pow'r.
and raises up those who   are   bowed   down.

Music: Fintan P. O'Carroll, d. 1981, ©   ORDINARY TIME

159 Ps. 122: I Rejoiced When They Said to Me

Antiphon: I Rejoiced When I Heard Them Say: "Let Us Go to God's House"

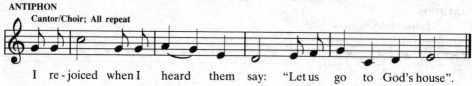

ANTIPHON
Cantor/Choir; All repeat

I re-joiced when I heard them say: "Let us go to God's house".

Psalm 122: 1–2, 3–4, 4–5, 8–9

VERSES
Cantor/Choir   Tone 1

1. I rejoiced when they said	to	me,
2. Jerusalem is built as	a	city
3. As he decreed	for	Israel,
4. For love of my family	and	friends

"Let us go to the house of	the	Lord."
bound firmly together	in	unity.
to praise the name of	the	Lord.
I say, "Peace	be	with you!"

Now at last we	are	standing
There the tribes	go	up,
There are the seats	of	justice,
For love of the house of the Lord	our	God,

To Antiphon

within your gates, O	Je -	rusalem.
the tribes of	the	Lord.
the thrones of the house	of	David.
I will seek to do	you	good.

Music: Fintan P. O'Carroll, d. 1981, ©

LAST WEEKS IN ORDINARY TIME

Ps. 122: I Rejoiced Because They Said to Me   160

Antiphon: Let Us Go Rejoicing, Rejoicing, Rejoicing

ANTIPHON

Cantor/Choir; All repeat

Let us go re - joic - ing, re - joic - ing, re - joic - ing;

let us go re - joic - ing to the house of the Lord.

Psalm 122: 1–2, 3–4, 4–5, 6–7, 8–9

VERSES

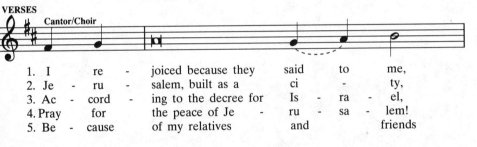

Cantor/Choir

1. I re - joiced because they said to me,
2. Je - ru - salem, built as a ci - ty,
3. Ac - cord - ing to the decree for Is - ra - el,
4. Pray for the peace of Je - ru - sa - lem!
5. Be - cause of my relatives and friends

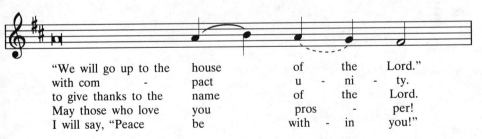

"We will go up to the house of the Lord."
with com - pact u - ni - ty.
to give thanks to the name of the Lord.
May those who love you pros - per!
I will say, "Peace be with - in you!"

Music: Donald J. Reagan, b. 1923, © 1988

And now we have		set		foot	
To it the		tribes	go	up,	
In it are set up		judg -	ment	seats,	
May peace be with -	in		your	walls,	
Because of the house of the	Lord,		our	God,	

To Antiphon

within your gates,	O	Je - ru - sa - lem.
the	tribes	of the Lord.
seats for the house	of	Da - vid.
prosperity in	your	build - ings
I will	pray	for your good.

The V. and R⧵., "Alleluia," can be sung to the chant as follows:

Al - le - lú - ia,   al - le - lú - ia,   al - le - lú - ia.

During Lent the V. and R⧵., "Praise to you, Lord Jesus Christ, King of endless glory," can be sung as follows:

Praise to   you, Lord Je - sus Christ, King of   end - less glo - ry.

How to Point to the Text of the VERSE of the Gospel Acclamations for Singing It to a Simplified Gregorian Chant Psalmody

1. Place an asterisk (*) at the end of the first line to indicate the end of the first half of the verse. Cf. Gospel Acclamation verse for the First Sunday of Lent (C Cycle).

    Man does not live on bread alone *

2. Indicate the LAST word or syllable accent on that line thus [´].

    Man does not live on bread alóne *

3. Underline the syllable immediately preceding that accent thus [_].

    Man does not live on bread a̲lóne *

4. Indicate the LAST word or syllable accent on the second line with [´].

    but on every word that comes from the mouth of Gód.

5. Underline the second syllable preceding that accent thus [_].

    but on every word that comes from the mou̲th of Gód.

The following is the Gospel Acclamation verse for the First Sunday of Lent with three different simplified psalm tones.

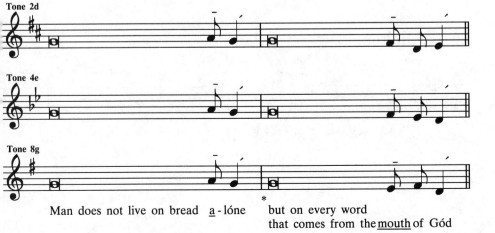

Tone 2d

Tone 4e

Tone 8g

Man does not live on bread   a̲ - lóne   but on every word
                                            that comes from the mou̲th of Gód

162 Alleluia

TONE 4

Al - le - lú - ia.

163 Alleluia

TONE 5

Al - le - lú - ia.

164 Alleluia, Alleluia, Alleluia

TONE 6

Al - le - lú - ia, al - le - lú - ia, al - le - lú - ia.

Music: Plainchant, Tones 4, 5, 6 from Graduale Romanum;
acc. Rev. Bartholomew Sayles, O.S.B., b. 1918; S. Cecile Gertken, O.S.B., b. 1902, ©

165 Alleluia, Alleluia, Alleluia

Al - le - lú - ia, al - le - lú - ia, al - le - lú - ia.

Music: William Ferris, b. 1937, ©

Praise and Honor to You, Lord Jesus Christ 166

Praise and hon - or to you, Lord Je - sus Christ.

Praise to You, Lord Jesus Christ, 167
King of Endless Glory!

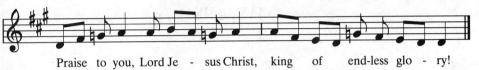

Praise to you, Lord Je - sus Christ, king of end-less glo - ry!

Music: Plainchant; acc. Rev. Bartholomew Sayles, O.S.B., b. 1918; S. Cecile Gertken, O.S.B., b. 1902, ©

Glory to You, Word of God, Lord Jesus Christ 168

Glo - ry to you, Word of God, Lord Je - sus Christ!

Music: William Ferris, b. 1937, ©

Praise to You, Lord Jesus Christ, 169
King of Endless Glory

Praise to you, Lord Je - sus Christ, King of end - less glo - ry!

Music: William Ferris, b. 1937, ©

Glory and Praise to You, Lord Jesus Christ! 170

Glo - ry and praise to you, Lord Je - sus Christ!

Music: William Ferris, b. 1937, ©

HYMNS

Comfort My People 171

1. Com - fort my peo - ple and qui - et her fear;
2. Say to the cit - ies of Ju - dah: "Be - hold!
3. Moun - tains and hills shall be - come like a plain.

Tell her the time of sal - va - tion draws near.
Gen - tle, yet might - y, the arm of the Lord
Van - ished are mourn - ing and hun - ger and pain;

Tell her I come to re - move all her shame;
Res - cues the cap - tives of dark - ness and sin,
Nev - er a - gain shall these war a - gainst you;

"She that is pit - ied" shall be her new name.
Bring - ing them jus - tice and joy with - out end."
"See, he comes quick - ly to make all things new!"

Text: St. Joseph Abbey, ©
Music: F. V. Strahan; harm. Jerry R. Brubaker, b. 1946, ©

10 10 10 10
CONSOLAMINI

172 As Joseph Lay Uneasy

1. As Jo-seph lay un-eas-y, Sore trou-bled and dis-tressed,
2. "Fear not O son of Da-vid, To take your gen-tle bride:
3. "His Name it shall be Je-sus, The Name you'll give to Him;
4. "I-sa-iah had fore-told it: 'A maid shall bear a Son,

There came an an-gel-mes-sage To soothe his sad un-rest,
This Child of hers is ho-ly, Con-ceived of God most high.
For thus it has been writ-ten, He'll save the world from sin.
Em-man-u-el, God-with-us' And thus it has been done.

There came an an-gel-mes-sage To soothe his sad un-rest.
This Child of hers is ho-ly, Con-ceived of God most high.
For thus it has been writ-ten, He'll save the world from sin.
'Em-man-u-el, God-with-us' And thus it has been done."

5. Then Joseph rose from slumber
   And took his holy bride;
   Her Babe, he named it Jesus
   At blessed Christmastide.

Text: The Dominican Nuns of Summit, New Jersey, ©
Music: Old English Carol; harm. ©

76 76 and Repeat
CHERRY TREE CAROL

173 O Come, Divine Messiah

VERSES

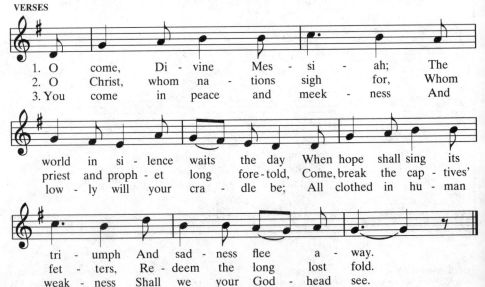

1. O come, Di-vine Mes-si-ah; The
2. O Christ, whom na-tions sigh for, Whom
3. You come in peace and meek-ness And

world in si-lence waits the day When hope shall sing its
priest and proph-et long fore-told, Come, break the cap-tives'
low-ly will your cra-dle be; All clothed in hu-man

tri-umph And sad-ness flee a-way.
fet-ters, Re-deem the long lost fold.
weak-ness Shall we your God-head see.

REFRAIN

Dear Sav-ior, haste! Come, come to earth. Dis-pel the night and show your face,

And bid us hail the dawn of grace. O come, Di-vine Mes-si-ah; The world in si-lence

waits the day When hope shall sing its tri-umph And sad-ness flee a - way.

Text: Abbé Pellegrin, 1663–1745; tr. Sister Mary of St. Phillip
Music: 16th. c. Noel, ca. 1544; arr. Arthur Hutchings, b. 1906, ©

Irregular with Refrain
VENEZ, DIVIN MESSIE

Creator of the Stars of Night 174

1. Cre - a - tor of the stars of night, Your peo - ple's
2. Our Fa - ther heard the help - less cry Of all cre -
3. When earth was near its ev - 'ning hour, You did, in
4. At your great name, ex - alt - ed now, All knees should

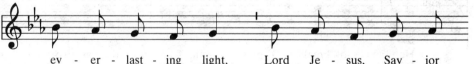

ev - er - last - ing light, Lord Je - sus, Sav - ior
a - tion doomed to die, And saved our lost and
love's re - deem - ing pow'r, Like bride - groom from his
bend, all heads should bow, All things in heav'n and

of us all, Now hear your ser - vants when they call.
guil - ty race By heal - ing gifts of heav'n - ly grace.
cham - ber, come Forth from a maid - en moth - er's womb.
earth a - dore, And praise you, King for - ev - er - more.

5. To you, O holy One, we pray,
   Our judge in that tremendous day,
   Ward off, while yet we dwell below,
   The weapons of our crafty foe.

6. To God the Father, God the Son,
   And God the Spirit, three in one,
   Praise, honor, might, and glory be
   From age to age eternally.

Text: Latin 9th Century; John Mason Neale, 1818–1866, alt.
Music: Plainchant Mode IV

88 88
CONDITOR ALME SIDERUM

175 Hail to the Lord's Anointed

1. Hail to the Lord's A - noint - ed, Great Da - vid's great - er Son!
2. He shall come down like show - ers Up - on the fruit - ful earth,
3. Kings shall bow down be - fore him And gold and in - cense bring;
4. O'er ev - 'ry foe vic - to - ri - ous, He on his throne shall rest,

Hail, in the time ap - point - ed, His reign on earth be - gun!
And joy and hope, like flow - ers, Spring in his path to birth.
All na - tions shall a - dore him, His praise all peo - ples sing;
From age to age more glo - rious, All bless - ing and all - blest,

He comes to break op - pres - sion, To set the cap - tive free,
Be - fore him on the moun - tains Shall peace, the her - ald, go
To him shall prayer un - ceas - ing And dai - ly vows as - cend,
The tide of time shall nev - er His cov - e - nant re - move;

To take a - way trans - gres - sion, And rule in eq - ui - ty.
And right - eous - ness, in foun - tains, From hill to val - ley flow.
His king - dom still in - creas - ing, A king - dom with - out end.
His name shall stand for - ev - er, That name to us is love.

Text: James Montgomery, 1771–1854; Psalm 72
Music: Gesangbuch der Herzogl, 1784, adapt. 1863; harm. William Henry Monk, 1823–1889

76 76 D
ELLACOMBE

Hark! A Herald Voice Is Calling 176

1. Hark! A her - ald voice is call - ing:
2. Star - tled at the sol - emn warn - ing
3. Lo, the Lamb so long ex - pect - ed
4. So when love comes forth in judg - ment,

"Christ is near," it seems to say, "Cast a - way the
Let the earth-bound soul a - rise; Christ, her sun, all
Comes with par - don down from heav'n; Let us meet him
Debts and doubts and wrongs to clear, Faith - ful may he

dreams of dark - ness, Wak - en, chil - dren of the day!"
sloth dis - pel - ling, Shines up - on the morn - ing skies.
with re - pen - tance, Pray that we may be for - giv'n.
find his ser - vants Watch-ing till the dawn ap - pear.

5. Honor, glory, praise, and blessing
   To the Father and the Son,
   With the everlasting Spirit,
   While eternal ages run.

Text: Anon.; tr. Edward Caswall, 1814–1878, and others
Music: William Henry Monk, 1823–1889

87 87
MERTON

177 Hark, the Glad Sound!

1. Hark, the glad sound! The Sav - ior comes, The
2. On him the Spir - it large - ly poured Ex -
3. He comes to set the pris - 'ners free In
4. He comes the bro - ken heart to bind, The

Sav - ior prom - ised long; Let ev - 'ry
erts its sa - cred fire; Wis - dom and
Sa - tan's bond - age held; The gates of
bleed - ing soul to cure; And with the

heart pre - pare a throne And ev - 'ry voice a song.
might and zeal and love His ho - ly heart in - spire.
brass be - fore him burst, The i - ron fet - ters yield.
treas - ures of his grace En - rich - es all the poor.

5. His silver trumpets publish loud
The jub'lee of the Lord,
Our debts are all remitted now,
Our heritage restored.

6. Our glad hosannas, Prince of peace,
Your welcome shall proclaim,
And heav'n's exalted arches ring
With your beloved name.

Text: Philip Doddridge, 1705–1751
Music: Thomas Ravenscroft's Psalmes, 1621

86 86
BRISTOL

He Will Come 178

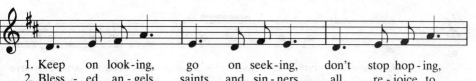

1. Keep on look-ing, go on seek-ing, don't stop hop-ing,
2. Bless - ed an-gels, saints and sin-ners, all re-joice to
3. Hearts will won-der, eyes must o-pen, ears shall catch His

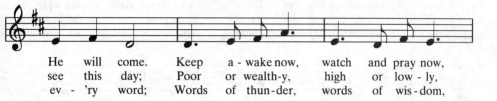

He will come. Keep a-wake now, watch and pray now,
see this day; Poor or wealth-y, high or low-ly,
ev - 'ry word; Words of thun-der, words of wis-dom,

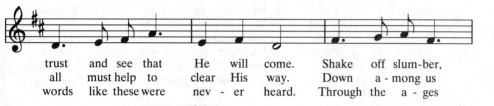

trust and see that He will come. Shake off slum-ber,
all must help to clear His way. Down a-mong us
words like these were nev - er heard. Through the a-ges

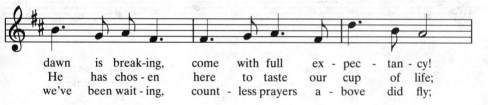

dawn is break-ing, come with full ex - pec - tan-cy!
He has chos-en here to taste our cup of life;
we've been wait-ing, count - less prayers a - bove did fly;

Years of grop-ing, years of hop-ing, all ful-filled when He will come.
Who would guess that He'd be com-ing here to share both joy and strife?
Now He's com-ing down a-mong us, here to live and here to die.

Text: Willard F. Jabusch, b. 1930, ©
Music: Welsh Folk Song; acc. S. R. Rudcki, b. 1928, ©

179 O Come, O Come, Emmanuel

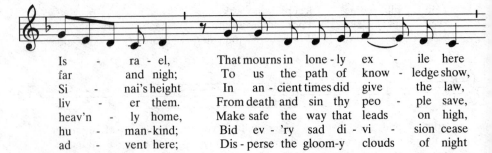

1. (Dec.21) O come, O come, Em - man - u - el, And ran-som cap-tive
2. (Dec.17) O come, thou wis - dom from on high, And or - der all things
3. (Dec.18) O come, thou ho - ly Lord of might, Who to thy tribes on
4. (Dec.19) O come, thou rod of Jes - se's stem, From ev - 'ry foe de -
5. (Dec.20) O come, thou key of Da - vid, come, And o - pen wide our
6. (Dec.22/Dec.23) O come, de - sire of na - tions, bind In one the hearts of
7. (Dec.24) O come, thou day-spring, come and cheer Our spir - its by thine

Is - ra - el, That mourns in lone - ly ex - ile here
far and nigh; To us the path of know - ledge show,
Si - nai's height In an - cient times did give the law,
liv - er them. From death and sin thy peo - ple save,
heav'n - ly home, Make safe the way that leads on high,
hu - man-kind; Bid ev - 'ry sad di - vi - sion cease
ad - vent here; Dis - perse the gloom-y clouds of night

Un - til the Son of God ap - pear.
And teach us in her ways to go.
In cloud and ma - jes - ty and awe.
And give them vict - 'ry o'er the grave.
And close the path to mis - er - y.
And be thy - self our Prince of peace.
And death's dark shad - ow put to flight.

Re-joice! Re-joice! Em - man-u - el shall come to thee, O Is - ra - el.

Text: O Antiphons, 12th c.; tr. John Mason Neale, 1818-1866
Music: Thos. Helmore, 1811-1890, 15th c. Plainchant, adapt.; acc. Edward J. McKenna, b. 1939, ©

88 88 with Refrain
VENI, VENI, EMMANUEL

O Heavens, Send Your Rain 180
Upon Us/Rorate Caeli

REFRAIN

O heav - ens send your rain up - on us,
Ro - rá - te cae - li dé - su - per,

send down the Just One to Is - ra - el.
et nu - bes plu - ant ju - stum.

1. Do not be an - gry with us Lord, remember no longer all our
Ne i - ra - scá - ris Dó - mi - ne, ne ultra memíneris in -

past trans-gres - sions: See your city of Holies now has been deser-ted:
i - qui - tá - tis: ec - ce cívitas Sancti facta est desér - ta

Zi - on has been a - ban - doned Je - ru - sa - lem has been made
Si - on de - sér - ta fa - cta est: Je - rú - sa - lem de - so -

des - o - late: The house of your kind and merciful blessing and of your
lá - ta est: do - mus sanctificatiónis tuae et gló - ri - ae

To Refrain

glo - ry, the place where a - bun - dant praise rose from our fa - thers.
tu - ae, u - bi lau - da - vé - runt te pa - tres no - stri.

Text: Rorate Caeli; tr. Refrain and v. 1, Owen M. Lee, C.S.B.; vv. 2-4, Monks of St. John's Abbey, ©
Music: Plainchant, Tone I; acc. Rev. Bartholomew Sayles, O.S.B., ©

2. We all have sinned, and are be - come like those who are un-clean.
    Pec-cá - vi - mus, et fácti su - mus tán-quam im - mún - dus nos,

We have fall-en low, as a dy - ing leaf falls earth-ward; and our in - iqui - ties,
et ce - cí - di-mus quási fóli-um u - ni - vér - si: et in i-quitas nós-trae

as a wind, have swept us swift - ly far. You have hidden your face from us,
quási véntus ab - stu - lé - runt nos: ab - scon - disti fáciem tú - am

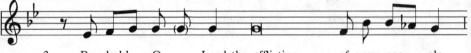

To Refrain

your chil-dren; you have broken us by the weight of our own sin-ning.
a no - bis, et al - lisisti nos in mánu in - i - qui-tá - tis nós-trae.

3. Be - hold, O Lord, the affliction of your peo - ple
    Vi - de Dó-(mi) - ne afflictiónem pó - pu - li tú - i,

Send quick - ly him who is to come, Send forth the Lamb who rules all
et mit - te quem mis sú - rus es: e - mit - te (A)-gnum do - mi - na -

earth-ly king-doms, from Petra in the des-ert, to the mount of the daugh-ter of
tó - rem tér - rae, de pétra desér - ti ad móntem fi - li-ae

To Refrain

Zi - on: that he may take a-way the yoke of our sub-jec - tion.
Si - on: ut áu - fe - rat ip-se júgum cap - ti - vi-tá - tis nos-trae.

4. Be now com-fort-ed, Be now com-fort-ed, O you my peo - ple:
Con-so - lá - mi - ni, con - so - lá - mi - ni, pó - pu - le mé - us:

for most speed-i - ly comes sal - va - tion, Why are you con - sumed with
ci - to vé - ni - et sá - lus tú - a: qua - re moe-ró - re con-

sor - row-ing, so that your grief has quite trans - formed you?
sú - me - ris, qui - a in - no - vá - vit te dó - lor?

I come to save, be no more fear - ful. For know you not that
Sal - vá - bo te nó - li ti - mé - re, é - go é - nim sum

To Refrain

I am your God and Mas - ter. Is - rael's Ho - ly One, your sole Re - deem-er.
Dó - mi-nus De - us tu - us, Sán-ctus Is - ra - el, re - dém-ptor tu - us.

181 O Savior, Rend the Heavens Wide

1. O Sav - ior, rend the heav-ens wide; Come down, come
2. O Morn - ing Star, O ra - diant Sun, When will our
3. Sin's dread - ful doom up - on us lies; Grim death looms
4. There shall we all our prais - es bring Ev - er to

down with might-y stride; Un - lock the gates, the doors break
hearts be - hold your dawn? O Sun, a - rise; with-out your
fierce be - fore our eyes. Oh, come, lead us with might - y
you, our Sav - ior King; There shall we laud you and a -

down; Un - bar the way to heav - en's crown.
light We grope in gloom and dark of night.
hand From ex - ile to our prom - ised land.
dore For - ev - er and for - ev - er - more.

Text: German spiritual song, Köln, 1623; tr. Martin L. Seltz, 1909–1967, alt., ©
Music: German Catholic Hymnbook, 1623, ©

88 88
O HEILAND, REISS

On Jordan's Bank 182

1. On Jor - dan's bank the Bap - tist's cry An -
2. Then cleansed be ev - 'ry heart from sin; Make
3. For you are our sal - va - tion, Lord, Our
4. To God the Son all glo - ry be! His

noun - ces that the Lord is nigh; A - wake and heark - en
straight the way of God with - in. Let ev - 'ry one a
ref - uge and our great re - ward; Once more up - on your
ad - vent set all na - tions free. Him with the Fa - ther

for he brings Glad tid - ings of the King of kings.
home pre - pare For Christ to come and en - ter there.
peo - ple shine, And fill the world with love di - vine.
we a - dore, And Ho - ly Spir - it ev - er - more.

Alt. tune: This Is My Will, no. 480
Text: Charles Coffin, 1676–1749; tr. John Chandler, 1806–1876
Music: Vehe, 1537, alt.   **88 88**

183 People, Look East

1. Peo - ple, look East. The time is near Of the crown - ing of the year. Make your house fair as you are a - ble, Trim the hearth, and set the ta - ble. Peo - ple, look East, and sing to - day: Love, the Guest, is on the way.

2. Stars, keep the watch. When night is dim. One more light the bowl shall brim. Shin - ing be - yond the frost - y weath - er, Bright as the sun and moon to - geth - er. Peo - ple, look East, and sing to - day: Love, the Star, is on the way.

3. An - gels, an - nounce with shouts of mirth Him who brings new life to earth. Set ev - 'ry peak and val - ley hum - ming With the word, "The Lord is com - ing." Peo - ple, look East, and sing to - day: Love, the Lord, is on the way.

Text: Eleanor Farjeon, 1881–1965, ©
Music: French Carol, arr. John Stainer, 1840–1901, ©

87 98 87
BESANCON CAROL

Savior of the Nations Come 184

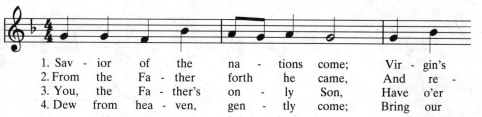

```
1. Sav - ior    of    the    na  - tions come;    Vir - gin's
2. From   the    Fa - ther  forth   he   came,    And   re -
3. You,    the    Fa - ther's on - ly   Son,    Have  o'er
4. Dew    from  hea - ven,  gen - tly come;    Bring  our
```

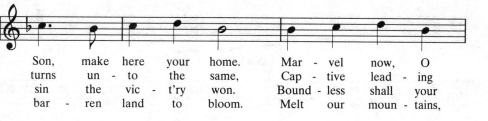

```
Son,    make  here  your   home.   Mar - vel   now,   O
turns   un - to   the    same,   Cap - tive  lead - ing
sin     the    vic - t'ry  won.    Bound - less shall  your
bar - ren   land   to    bloom.   Melt   our   moun - tains,
```

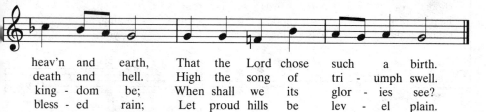

```
heav'n and    earth,  That  the   Lord chose  such   a    birth.
death  and    hell.   High  the   song  of    tri - umph swell.
king - dom   be;    When shall we   its   glor - ies  see?
bless - ed    rain;   Let  proud hills  be    lev - el   plain.
```

5. Long desired of ages past,
   Show yourself to us at last;
   And from sin's captivity,
   Call us back and set us free.

6. Brightly does your manger shine;
   Glorious is its light divine.
   Let not sin o'er cloud this light;
   Ever be our faith thus bright.

Text: St. Ambrose, 340–397; para. Martin Luther, 1483–1546; tr. William M. Reynolds, 1812–1876, vv 1–3&6;
Sr. Delores Dufner, O.S.B., b. 1939, vv 4 & 5, ©   77 77
Music: Erfurt Enchiridia, 1524; harm. Melchior Vulpius, 1560?-1616   NUN KOMM, DER HEIDEN HEILAND

Alternate words, for Epiphany and Baptism of the Lord

Infant Wrapped in God's Own Light 185

For Epiphany, sing stanzas 1, 2, and 4.
For the Baptism of the Lord, sing stanzas 2, 3, and 4.

1. Infant wrapped in God's own light,
   Savior sent to conquer night,
   King before whom kings bowed low,
   Let a star before us go!

2. Light of all the nations, shine!
   Show to us who wait a sign.
   God on earth, our host and guest,
   Be in flesh made manifest.

3. Servant Savior, chosen one,
   You are God's beloved Son.
   Let your Spirit on us rest;
   Be in us made manifest.

4. Radiance of the Father's face,
   Shine his love in every place.
   Splendor of God's glory bright,
   Lead us to eternal light!

Text: Sr. Delores Dufner, O.S.B., b. 1939, ©

186 Sleepers, Wake! A Voice Astounds Us

1. "Sleep-ers, wake!" a voice a-stounds us, The
2. Zi-on hears the watch-men sing-ing; Her
3. Lamb of God, the heav'ns a-dore you; Let

shout of ram-part guards sur-rounds us: "A-
heart with joy-ful hope is spring-ing, She
saints and an-gels sing be-fore you, As

wake, Je-ru-sa-lem, a-rise!" Mid-night's peace their
wakes and hur-ries through the night. Forth he comes, her
harps and cym-bals swell the sound. Twelve great pearls, the

cry has bro-ken, Their ur-gent sum-mons
Bride-groom glo-rious In strength of grace, in
ci-ty's por-tals: Through them we stream to

Text: Philipp Nicolai, 1556–1608; tr. Carl P. Daw, Jr., b. 1944
Music: melody, Hans Sachs, 1494–1576; adapt. Philipp Nicolai; acc. J. S. Bach, 1685–1750

Irregular
WACHET AUF

clear ly spo - ken: "The time has come, O maid - ens wise!
truth vic - to - rious: Her star is ris'n, her light grows bright.
join the im - mor - tals As we with joy your throne sur - round.

Rise up, and give us light; The Bride - groom is in sight.
Now come, most wor - thy Lord, God's Son, in - car - nate Word,
No eye has known the sight, No ear heard such de - light:

Al - le - lu - ia! Your lamps pre - pare and
Al - le - lu - ia! We fol - low all and
Al - le - lu - ia! There - fore we sing to

has - ten there, That you the wed - ding feast may share."
heed your call To come in - to the ban - quet hall.
greet our King; For ev - er let our prais - es ring.

187 The Advent of Our God

1. The ad-vent of our God With ea-ger prayers we greet. And
2. The ev-er-last-ing Son Came down to make us free; And
3. Daugh-ter of Si-on, rise To meet your low-ly King; Nor
4. As judge on clouds of light, He soon will come a-gain, His

sing-ing, haste up-on his road His com-ing reign to meet.
he a ser-vant's form put on To gain our lib-er-ty.
let your faith-less heart des-pise The peace he comes to bring.
scat-tered peo-ple to u-nite, With them in heav'n to reign.

5. Then evil flee away
   Before the rising dawn!
   Let this old Adam day by day
   God's image still put on.

6. Praise to th'incarnate Son
   Who comes to set us free,
   With Father, Spirit, ever one,
   To all eternity.

Lower Key: Blest Are the Pure in Heart, no. 450
Text: Charles Coffin, 1676–1749; tr. John Chandler, 1806–1876, alt.
Music: Johann B. Konig, 1691–1758; adapt. and harm. by William Henry Havergal, 1793–1870

66 86
FRANCONIA

The Advent Wreath 188

REFRAIN

Ev-'ry ta-per, ev-'ry can-dle flame,

Or an-y blaz-ing light Re-minds us of Christ, the Light of the world, Who

gives our blind-ed vi - sion sight. May ev-'ry Ad-vent flame

Final Ending

To Verses

Lead us to God: We ask in Je-sus' name. name.

VERSES

1. (First Sunday) The Church in ex-pec-ta-tion waits For
2. (Second Sunday) The sec-ond can-dle on our wreath, The
3. (Third Sunday) We light the An-gel Can-dle now, For
4. (Fourth Sunday) We light four can-dles on this day; The
5. (Christmas) The can-dle num-ber five is saved For

Je - sus to come up-on our earth. In four long weeks we
Beth-le-hem Can-dle, now is lit. The ho - ly pair must
"Glo - ry to God" will soon be heard. The song an-nounc-es
cir - cle of light is now com-plete. Soon in the sta-ble
Christ-mas, when glad - ly it is lit. We praise the one we

will fore-see The in-fant Je-sus' low-ly birth. We
leave their home; Their wills to God's do they sub-mit. Now
God's Good News, Ful-fill-ing An-gel Ga-briel's word. The
we shall see Di-vin-i-ty with our flesh meet. The
wait-ed for, Our Lord and King, the In-fi-nite. With

Text: Omer Westendorf, b. 1916, ©
Music: Robert E. Kreutz, b. 1922, ©

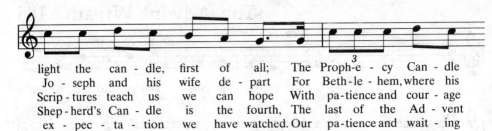

light	the	can - dle,	first	of	all;	The	Proph-e - cy	Can - dle
Jo - seph	and	his	wife	de - part	For	Beth-le - hem,	where	his
Scrip - tures	teach	us	we	can	hope	With	pa-tience and	cour - age
Shep - herd's	Can - dle	is	the	fourth,	The	last of the	Ad - vent
ex - pec - ta - tion	we	have watched.	Our	pa-tience and	wait - ing

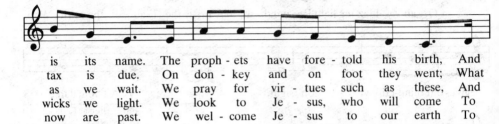

is	its	name.	The	proph - ets	have	fore - told	his	birth,	And
tax	is	due.	On	don - key	and	on	foot	they	went;	What
as	we	wait.	We	pray	for	vir - tues	such	as	these,	And
wicks	we	light.	We	look	to	Je - sus,	who	will	come	To
now	are	past.	We	wel - come	Je - sus	to	our	earth	To

To Refrain

Good	News	Je - sus	would	pro - claim.
lay	a - head	they	lit - tle	knew.
God	will	be	our	ad - vo - cate.
change	to	day	our	dark - est	night.
stay	and	live	with	us	at	last.

How Great Our Joy! 189

1. While by the sheep we watched at night, Glad tid - ings brought an
2. There shall be born, so he did say, In Beth - le - hem a
3. There shall the Child lie in a stall, This Child who shall re -
4. This gift of God we'll cher - ish well, That ev - er joy our

an - gel bright. *f*
Child to - day. *p* How great our joy! Great our joy!
deem us all.
hearts shall fill.

f *p* *f*
Joy, joy, joy! Joy, joy, joy! Praise we the Lord in

p
heav'n on high! Praise we the Lord in heav'n on high!

Text: German carol
Music: German melody; acc. Hugo Jungst

88 with Refrain

190 Good Christian Friends, Rejoice

1. Good Christian friends, re - joice With heart and soul and voice;
2. Good Christian friends, re - joice With heart and soul and voice;
3. Good Christian friends, re - joice With heart and soul and voice;

O give heed to what we say: Je - sus Christ is born to - day!
Now you hear of end - less bliss: Je - sus Christ was born for this!
Now you need not fear the grave: Je - sus Christ was born to save!

Ox and ass be - fore him bow, And he is in the man - ger now.
He has o - pened hea - ven's door, And we are blest for ev - er - more.
Calls you one and calls you all To gain his ev - er - last - ing hall.

Christ is born to - day! Christ is born to - day!
Christ was born for this! Christ was born for this!
Christ was born to save! Christ was born to save!

Text: *Medieval Latin and German Carol; tr. John M Neale, 1818–1866, alt.*
Music: *German Carol, 14th c.; harm. Robert L. Pearsall, 1795–1856*

66 77 78 55
IN DULCI JUBILO

Lo, How a Rose E'er Blooming   191

1. Lo, how a Rose e'er bloom-ing From ten - der stem hath sprung!
2. I - sa - iah 'twas fore-told it, The Rose I have in mind,
3. O Flower, whose fra-grance ten - der With sweet-ness fills the air,

Of Jes-se's lin-eage com - ing, As pro-phets long have sung.
With Ma - ry we be-hold it, The Vir - gin Moth - er kind.
Dis - pel in glo-rious splen-dor The dark-ness ev - 'ry-where;

It came, a flow-'ret bright, A - mid the cold of
To show God's love a - right, She bore to us a
True man, yet ver - y God, From sin and death now

win - ter, When half - spent was the night.
Sav - ior, When half - spent was the night.
save us, And share our ev - 'ry load.

Text: German, 15th c.; vv. 1–2, trans. Theodore Baker, 1851–1934; v. 3, Friedrich Layritz, 1808–1859;
  tr. Harriet Reynolds Krauth Spaeth, 1845–1925; ver. Hymnal, 1940, ©
Music: German melody, 16th c.; acc. Michael Praetorius, 1571–1621

76 76 676
ES IST EIN ROS

192 I Wonder As I Wander

1. I won-der as I wan-der out un-der the sky,
2. When Ma-ry birthed Je-sus, 'twas in a cows' stall,
3. If Je-sus had want-ed for an-y wee thing:
4. I won-der as I wan-der out un-der the sky,

How Je-sus, the Sav-ior, did come for to die. For
With wise-men and far-mers and shep-herds and all. But
A star in the sky, or a bird on the wing; Or
How Je-sus, the Sav-ior, did come for to die. For

poor, or-n'ry peo-ple like you and like I, I
high from God's heav-en a star's light did fall, And the
all of God's an-gels in heav-en to sing, He
poor, or-n'ry peo-ple like you and like I, I

won-der as I wan-der, Out un-der the sky.
prom-ise of a-ges It then did re-call.
sure-ly could have had it, 'Cause He was the King!
won-der as I wan-der, Out un-der the sky.

Text: Appalachian carol; collected by John Jacob Niles
Music: Appalachian folksong; adapt. John Jacob Niles; arrangement Fred Bock, ©

In the Bleak Mid-Winter 193

1. In the bleak mid - win - ter / Frost - y wind made moan,
2. Our God, heav'n can - not hold him, / Nor earth sus - tain;
3. An - gels and arch - an - gels / May have ga - thered there,
4. What can I give him, / Poor as I am?

Earth stood hard as i - ron, / Wa - ter like a stone;
Heav'n and earth shall flee a - way / When he comes to reign:
Cher - u - bim and ser - a - phim / Thronged the air;
If I were a shep - herd, / I would bring a lamb;

Snow had fal - len snow on snow, / Snow on snow,
In the bleak mid - win - ter A / sta - ble - place suf - ficed The
But his mo - ther on - ly, / In her mai - den bliss,
If I were a wise man, / I would do my part; Yet

In the bleak mid - win - ter, / Long a - go.
Lord God Al - migh - ty, / Je - sus Christ.
Wor - shipped the be - lov - ed / With a kiss.
what I can I give him, / Give my heart.

Text: Christina Rossetti, 1830–1894
Music: Gustav Holst, 1874–1934

Irregular
CRANHAM

194 Infant Holy, Infant Lowly

1. In - fant ho - ly, in - fant low - ly For his bed a cat - tle stall;
2. Flocks were sleep - ing, shep-herds keep-ing Vi-gil till the morn-ing new

Ox - en low - ing, lit - tle know-ing, Christ the babe, is Lord of all.
Saw the glo - ry, heard the sto - ry, Ti - dings of a gos-pel true.

Swift are wing - ing an - gels sing - ing, No - els ring - ing,
Thus re - joic - ing, free from sor - row, Prais-es voic - ing

tid - ings bring - ing: Christ the babe is Lord of all.
greet the mor - row: Christ the babe was born for you.

Text: Traditional Polish carol; tr. Edith M. G. Reed, 1885–1933, alt.
Music: Traditional Polish Carol; acc. John Ribble

87 87 88 77
W ZLOBIE LEZY

It Came upon the Midnight Clear 195

1. It came up-on the mid-night clear, That glo - rious song of old,
2. Still through the clo - ven skies they come, With peace-ful wings un - furled,
3. Yet with the woes of sin and strife, The world has suf - fered long;
4. For, lo, the days are has-t'ning on, By proph-ets seen of old,

From an - gels bend - ing near the earth To touch their harps of gold:
And still their heav-'n - ly mu - sic floats O'er all the wea - ry world:
Be - neath the heav-'n - ly hymn have rolled Two thou-sand years of wrong;
When with the ev - er - cir - cling years Shall come the time fore - told,

"Peace on the earth, good will to all From heav-en's all gra - cious King."
A - bove its sad and low - ly plains They bend on hov - 'ring wing,
And war - ring hu - man-kind hears not The ti - dings which they bring;
When peace shall o - ver all the earth Its an - cient splen-dors fling,

The world in sol - emn still - ness lay, To hear the an - gels sing.
And ev - er o'er its Ba - bel sounds The bless-ed an - gels sing.
O hush the noise and cease your strife And hear the an - gels sing.
And all the world give back the song Which now the an - gels sing.

Text: Edmund Hamilton Sears, 1810–1876, alt.
Music: Richard S. Willis, 1819–1900

86 86 86 86
CAROL

196 O Bethlehem of Holy Worth

1. O Beth - le - hem of ho - ly worth! O
2. No inn bade wel - come at its door To
3. No pomp of kings, nor prin - ces there, With
4. O Beth - le - hem, we pray the babe, Once

hal - lowed town of Je - sus' birth! In thee a vir - gin
Ma - ry on that ho - ly night; But in a sta - ble
Jo - seph and the moth - er fair; But an - gel voi - ces
born with - in thy cheer - less cave, May grant the prom - ised

moth - er's child Brought God from heav'n to earth.
Christ was born, With on - ly stars for light.
from on high, With glo - ry filled the air.
"Peace on earth" To us he came to save.

Text: Edward C. Currie, d. 1967, ©
Music: Traditional Irish melody; acc. by Cornelius O'Sullivan, ©

88 86
INNISKEEN

O Come, Little Children 197

1. O come, lit - tle chil - dren; O come one and all,
2. He lies there, be - fore you, a - sleep in the hay,
3. A - dore like the shep - herds! Your glad voi - ces raise

Who lies in the man - ger in Beth - le - hem's stall;
With Ma - ry and Jo - seph to guard him and pray.
With those of the an - gels who sing in his praise.

For there, lit - tle chil - dren on this hol - iest night,
The won - der - ing shep - herds look in at the door,
Your cho - rus will ech - o from earth to the sky,

Our God sends from heav - en his Son, your de - light.
And see - ing the in - fant they kneel and a - dore.
With "Glo - ry to God in his heav - en most high."

Text: Johann Christoph von Schmid, 1768–1854; tr. Edward C. Currie, d. 1967, ©
Music: Johann A.P. Schulz, 1747–1800; harm. J. Alfred Schehl, 1882–1959, alt., ©

11 11 11 11
IHR KINDERLEIN, KOMMET

198 O Little Town of Bethlehem

1. O lit-tle town of Beth-le-hem, How still we see thee lie! A-
2. For Christ is born of Ma - ry, And gath-ered all a - bove, While
3. How si - lent-ly, how si - lent-ly The won-drous gift is giv'n! So
4. O ho - ly Child of Beth-le-hem, De-scend to us, we pray; Cast

bove thy deep and dream-less sleep The si - lent stars go by; Yet
mor-tals sleep, the an - gels keep Their watch of won-d'ring love. O
God im - parts to hu - man hearts The bless-ings of his heav'n. No
out our sin and en - ter in; Be born in us to - day. We

in thy dark streets shin - eth The ev - er - last - ing Light; The
morn-ing stars, to - geth - er Pro - claim the ho - ly birth; And
ear may hear his com - ing, But in this world of sin, Where
hear the Christ-mas an - gels The great glad ti - dings tell; O

hopes and fears of all the years Are met in thee to - night.
prais - es sing to God the King, And peace to all on earth.
meek souls will re - ceive him, still The dear Christ en - ters in.
come to us, a - bide with us, Our Lord Em - man - u - el!

Alt. Tune: I Sing the Almighty Power of God, no. 565

Text: Phillip Brooks, 1835–1908
Music: Lewis H. Redner, 1831–1908

86 86 86 86
ST. LOUIS

While Shepherds Watched 199
Their Flocks by Night

1. While shepherds watched their flocks by night, All
2. "Fear not," said he, for mighty dread Had
3. "To you in David's town this day Is
4. "The heav'nly child you there shall find To

seated on the ground, The angel of the
seized their troubled mind; "Glad tidings of great
born of David's line A Savior, who is
human view displayed, All meanly wrapped in

Lord came down, And glory shone around.
joy I bring To you and humankind.
Christ the Lord; And this shall be the sign:
swaddling clothes And in a manger laid."

5. Thus spoke the seraph; and forthwith
   Appeared a shining throng
   Of angels praising God, who thus
   Addressed their joyful song:

6. "All glory be to God on high,
   And on the earth be peace;
   Good will henceforth from heav'n to all
   Begin and never cease."

Text: New Version of the Psalms, 1696; tr. Nahum Tate, 1652–1715, and Nicholas Brady, 1659–c. 1726;
Music: George Kirbye, c. 1560–1634, attr.

86 86
WINCHESTER OLD

200 A Virgin Most Pure

1. A Vir - gin most pure, as the pro - phets fore - told,
2. To Beth' - lem of Ju - da, from Ga - li - lee land,
3. But when they sought shel - ter at Beth - le - hem's inn,
4. A sta - ble they found in their trou - ble - some plight

Hath brought forth an in - fant mid win - ter's deep cold,
Came Jo - seph and Ma - ry, at Cae - sar's com - mand,
No place could they find, and no sym - pa - thy win:
To serve as a re - fuge from cold and the night:

To be our Re - deem - er from sin and dis - grace
Their names to en - roll in King Da - vid's own town,
The keep - er re - plied to their hum - ble re - quest:
And there be - fore dark - ness had yield - ed to morn,

Which A - dam's trans - gres - sion hath passed to our race.
Be - cause they were sprung from that House of re - nown.
"No room can I make for your lodg - ing and rest."
The in - fant Re - deem - er from Ma - ry was born.

REFRAIN

Now let us be joy - ful, put sad - ness a - way.

For Je - sus our Sav - ior is born on this day!

Text: Traditional; tr. Desmond A. Schmal, S.J., 1897–1958, slightly adapt., ©
Music: Traditional British/Celtic carol; harm. Ralph Vaughan Williams, 1872–1958, ©

11 11 11 11

5. With gladness the mother now gazed on her boy,
The Lord of Creation, the Source of her joy;
She swaddled his body with linen most fair,
And laid him to sleep in the manger with care. *Refrain*

6. An angel appeared while the night was all still,
To shepherds who watched o'er their flocks on the hill,
Announcing that joy to the world had come down;
"A Savior is born in yon Bethlehem town." *Refrain*

7. An army of angels draws suddenly nigh,
Their splendor adorning the silvery sky:
"To God in the highest be glory," they sing:
And "Peace to the world," are the tidings they bring. *Refrain*

Resonet in Laudibus   201

1. Ré - son - et   in   laú - di - bus   Cum   ju - cún - dis   pláu - si - bus,
2. Si - on   lau - da   Dó - mi - num   Sal - va - tó - rem   ó - mni - um;
3. Na - tus   est   Em - má - nu - el,   Quem prae - dí - xit   Gá - bri - el,
4. San - cta   ti - bi   Trí - ni - tas   Os   ó - mni - um   grá - ti - as

Si - on cum fi - dé - li - bus.
Vir - go pa - rit Fí - li - um.
Te - stis est E - zé - chi - el.   Ap - pá - ru - it quem gé - nu - it Ma - rí - a.
Ré - son - et al - tís - si - mas.

Gau - dé - te,   gau - dé - te,   Chri - stus na - tus hó - di - e!

Gau - dé - te,   gau - dé - te,   ex Ma - rí - a Vír - gi - ne.

Text: Anon., 14th c.
Music: Plainchant Mode V; acc. Jean-Hebert Desrocquettes, O.S.B., ©

202 A Christmas Anthem

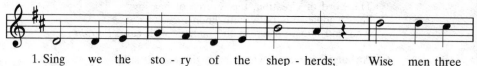

1. Sing we the sto - ry of the shep - herds; Wise men three
2. Stars shine a - round the man - ger ta - ble; Glo - ry of
3. Cold be the win - ter of our birth - place; High be the
4. Christ leads us to our com - mon Par - ent, Mak - ing us

tell us of a star; Gos - pel of peace is more than mere words.
hea - ven rings the world; Hearts join as one to there as - sem - ble.
vi - sion of this night; Wis - dom from God to flesh in pure grace,
one in what we do. Borne from the womb to life tran - scen - dant,

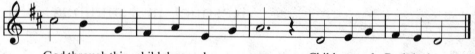

God through this child shows who we are: Child-ren of Beth-le-hem!
Christ is re - born a thou-sand-fold. Come, ye to Beth-le-hem!
Word leaps down from her bed of light. Born we in Beth-le-hem!
Love comes to live with us a - new. Make we for Beth-le-hem!

Text: Edward J. McKenna, b. 1939, ©
Music: Edward J. McKenna, b. 1939, ©

98 98 6
MARYHAVEN

203 A Child Is Born/The Magi Kings

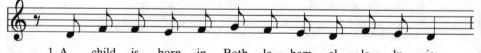

1. A child is born in Beth - le - hem, al - le - lu - ia;
2. Our broth - er in the flesh is he, al - le - lu - ia;
3. By grace this child is born a - gain, al - le - lu - ia;
4. The Ma - gi kings come from a - far, al - le - lu - ia;
5. Gold, in - cense, myrrh, they of - fer him, al - le - lu - ia;

Re - joice, re - joice Je - ru - sa - lem, al - le - lu - ia, al - le - lu - ia.
Our King for all e - ter - ni - ty, al - le - lu - ia, al - le - lu - ia.
In ev - 'ry heart he frees from sin, al - le - lu - ia, al - le - lu - ia.
Led on by faith in heav-en's star, al - le - lu - ia, al - le - lu - ia.
And bend-ing low they wor - ship him, al - le - lu - ia, al - le - lu - ia.

REFRAIN

Let grate-ful hearts now sing A song of joy

and ho - ly praise To Christ the new - born King!

Text: Puer natus, 14th c., tr. Irvin Udulutsch, O.F.M., Cap., b. 1920, ©
Music: Plainchant Mode I; acc. Irvin Udulutsch, O.F.M., Cap., b. 1920, ©

88 with Alleluias and Refrain
PUER NATUS

Puer Natus in Bethlehem 204

1. Pu - er na - tus in Béth - le - hem, al - le - lú - ia:
2. Hic ja - cet in prae - sé - pi - o, al - le - lú - ia.
3. In hoc ná - ta - li gáu - di - o, al - le - lú - ia.
4. Lau - dé - tur sanc - ta Trí - ni - tas, al - le - lú - ia.

Un - de gau - det Je - rú - sa - lem, al - le - lú - ia, al - le - lú - ia.
Qui reg - nat si - ne tér - mi - no, al - le - lú - ia, al - le - lú - ia.
Be - ne - di - cá - mus Dó - mi - no, al - le - lú - ia, al - le - lú - ia.
De - o Di - cá - mus grá - ti - as, al - le - lú - ia, al - le - lú - ia.

REFRAIN

In cor - dis jú - bi - lo Chri - stum na - tum

ad - o - ré - mus, Cum no - vo cán - ti - co.

Music: Plainchant, Mode I; acc. Rev. Bartholomew Sayles, O.S.B., b. 1918
and Sr. Cecile Gertken, O.S.B., b. 1902, ©

88 with Alleluias and Refrain
PUER NATUS

205 Wexford Carol

1. Good peo - ple all, this Christ-mas - time, Con - si - der well and bear in mind What our good God for us has done, In send-ing his be - lo - ved Son.
2. The night be - fore that hap - py tide, The no - ble Vir - gin and her guide Were long time seek - ing up and down To find a lodg - ing in the town.
3. Near Beth - le - hem did shep - herds keep Their flocks of lambs and feed - ing sheep; To whom God's an - gels did ap - pear, Which put the shep - herds in great fear.
4. With thank-ful heart and joy - ful mind, The shep-herds went the babe to find, And as God's an - gel had fore-told, They did our Sav - ior Christ be - hold.

Text: English and Irish traditional
Music: Irish traditional; harm. Martin Shaw, ©

With Ma - ry ho - ly we should pray To
But mark how all things came to pass: From
"Pre - pare and go," the an - gels said, "To
With - in a man - ger he was laid, And

God with love this Christ-mas Day; In Beth-le - hem up -
ev - 'ry door re - pell'd, a - las! As long fore - told, their
Beth-le - hem, be not a-fraid; For there you'll find, this
by his side the vir - gin maid, At - tend-ing on the

on that morn There was a bless-ed Mes - si - ah born.
re - fuge all Was but an hum - ble ox - 's stall.
hap - py morn, A prince-ly babe, sweet Je - sus born."
Lord of life, Who came on earth to end all strife.

5. There were three wise men from afar
Directed by a glorious star,
And on they wandered night and day
Until they came where Jesus lay.
And when they came unto that place
Where our beloved Messiah was,
They humbly cast them at his feet,
With gifts of gold and incense sweet.

206 Angels, from the Realms of Glory

1. An - gels, from the realms of glo - ry   Wing your flight o'er   all   the earth;
2. Shep - herds, in   the   fields a - bid - ing,   Watch-ing o'er your flocks by night,
3. Sag - es, leave your con - tem-pla-tions, Bright-er   vi - sions beam a - far;
4. Though an   in - fant now we view him,   He   shall fill   his heav'n-ly throne,

You who sang cre - a - tion's sto - ry,   Now pro-claim Mes - si - ah's birth:
God on earth is   now re - sid - ing,   Yon-der shines the   in - fant light:
Seek the great De - sire   of   na-tions, You have seen his   morn-ing star:
Ga-ther all the   na - tions to him;   Ev - 'ry knee shall   then bow down:

REFRAIN

Come and wor-ship, come and wor-ship, Wor-ship Christ, the   new-born King.

Text: James Montgomery, 1771–1854
Music: Henry Smart, 1813–1879

87 87 with Refrain
REGENT SQUARE

Children Let Your Voices Ring 207

1. Chil - dren let your voi - ces ring! To wel - come Christ, your
2. An - gels fill the skies with song, For him to whom the
3. Ma - ry sings her lull - a - by, While Jo - seph stands with
4. Chil - dren, sing with voi - ces clear, And greet your new - born

prais - es sing! He sleeps and smiles, a
skies be - long. They sing of peace on
watch - ful eye: The shep - herds kneel be -
Sav - ior dear. He is the Lord of

child so small, Yet he is King and Lord of all.
Christ - mas morn, For now the Prince of Peace is born.
fore their King. And kings from far their gifts will bring.
heav'n a - bove. Now born a child to win our love.

Text: James Quinn, S.J., b. 1919; © 1969, 1988
Music: Traditional Irish Melody; acc. Robert S. Ross

78 88
INNISKEEN

208 Joy to the World

1. Joy to the world! the Lord is come; Let earth re-ceive her King;
2. Joy to the world! the Sav-ior reigns; Let earth her songs em-ploy;
3. He rules the world with truth and grace And makes the na-tions prove
4. His name shall be the Prince of Peace, The ev-er-last-ing Lord,

Let ev-'ry heart pre-pare him room
While fields and floods, rocks, hills and plains
The glo-ries of his right-eous-ness,
The Won-der-ful, the Coun-sel-lor,

And heav'n and na-ture sing, And heav'n and na-ture
Re-peat the sound-ing joy, Re-peat the sound-ing
And won-ders of his love, And won-ders of his
The God by all a-dored, The God by all a-

sing, And heav'n, and heav'n, and na-ture sing.
joy, Re-peat, re-peat the sound-ing joy.
love, And won-ders, won-ders of his love.
dored, The God, the God by all a-dored.

Text: Isaac Watts, 1674–1748, alt.
Music: George F. Handel, 1685–1759; adapt. and arr. Lowell Mason, 1792–1872

86 86 with Repeat
ANTIOCH

5. "Glory to God," the sounding skies
    With joy their anthems ring:
    "Peace to the earth, good will to all,"
    From heav'n's eternal King.

Lully Lullay Thou Little Tiny Child 209

REFRAIN

Lul-ly, lul-lay, thou lit-tle tin-y child, bye-bye, lul-ly lul-lay.

1. O sis-ters, too, how may we do For to pre-serve this day
2. He-rod the king, in his ra-ging Charg-ed he hath this day
3. That woe is me, poor child for thee! And ev-'ry morn and day,

Repeat Refrain after verse 3

This poor young-ling For whom we sing Bye-bye, lul-ly lul-lay?
His men of might, in his own sight, All young chil-dren to slay.
For thy part-ing nor say nor sing Bye-bye, lul-ly lul-lay.

Text: Robert Croo, 1534
Music: Traditional English melody; arr. Martin Shaw, 1875–1958, ©

44 6 D with Refrain
COVENTRY CAROL

210 Stars of Glory

1. Stars of glo - ry shine more bright-ly, Pur - er be the moon-lights beam.
2. See the shep-herds quick - ly ris - ing, Hast-'ning to the hum - ble stall,
4. Hark! the swell of heav'n-ly voic - es, Peals a - long the vault-ed sky.

Glide ye hours and mo-ments light-ly, Swift-ly down time's deep-'ning stream.
And the new-born in - fant priz-ing, As the might - y Lord of all.
An - gels sing while earth re - joic - es, "Glo-ry to our God on high!

Bring the hour that ban - ished sad - ness, Brought re-demp-tion down to earth,
Low - ly now they bend be - fore him In his help - less in - fant state.
Glo - ry in the high-est heav-en Peace to low - ly ones on earth.

When the shep-herds heard with glad-ness Tid-ings of a Sav - ior's birth.
Firm - ly faith-ful we a - dore him, And his great-ness cel - e - brate.
Joy to these and bliss be giv - en In the great Re-deem-er's birth."

Text: Rev. Charles Frederick Husenbeth, 1796–1872, vv. 1–2, 4; Edward J. McKenna, b. 1939, v. 3, ©
Music: From A Daily Hymn Book, London, vv. 1–2, 4 adapt.; Edward J. McKenna, b. 1939, v. 3, ©   STELLAE GLORIAE

3. See how Ma-ry loves her boy - child in the light of Beth - le -

hem. Low - ly ox and ass breathe warm - ly on the

lit-tle Lord of all. Now the world is hushed in still - ness, in the

joy of know - ing God is near! Hope and love have come to

dwell here, driv-ing out the night of fear.

211 The First Nowell

1. The first No-well the an-gel did say Was to cer-tain poor
2. They look-ed up and saw a star Shin-ing in the
3. And by the light of that same star Three wise-men
4. This star drew nigh to the north-west, O'er Beth-le-

shep-herds in fields as they lay; In fields as they lay,
east be-yond them far, And to the earth it
came from coun-try far; To seek for a king was
hem it took its rest, And there it did both

keep-ing their sheep, On a cold win-ter's night that was so deep.
gave great light, And so it con-tin-ued both day and night.
their in-tent, And to fol-low the star wher-ev-er it went.
stop and stay Right o-ver the place where Je-sus lay.

Text: English carol, 18th c.
Music: English carol, 17th c.; harm. John Stainer, 1840–1901

Irregular with Refrain
THE FIRST NOWELL

REFRAIN

No - well, No - well, No - well, No - well,

born is the King of Is - ra - el.

5. Then entered in those wise men three
   full rev'rently upon their knee,
   and offered there in his presence
   their gold, and myrrh, and frankincense.
   Refrain

6. Then let us all with one accord
   sing praises to our heav'nly Lord;
   that hath made heav'n and earth of nought,
   and with his blood our life hath bought.
   Refrain

212 Once in Royal David's City

1. Once in roy - al Da - vid's ci - ty Stood a
2. He came down to earth from hea - ven, Who is
3. We, like Ma - ry, rest con - found - ed That a
4. For he is our life - long pat - tern; Dai - ly,

low - ly cat - tle shed, Where a mo - ther laid her
God and Lord of all, And his shel - ter was a
sta - ble should dis - play Hea-ven's Word, the world's cre -
when on earth he grew, He was tempt - ed, scorned, re -

ba - by In a man - ger for his bed: Ma - ry
sta - ble, And his cra - dle was a stall; With the
a - tor, Cra - dled there on Christ - mas Day, Yet this
ject - ed, Tears and smiles like us he knew. Thus he

was that mo - ther mild, Je - sus Christ her lit - tle child.
poor, the scorned, the low - ly, Lived on earth our Sa - vior ho - ly.
child, our Lord and bro-ther, Brought us love for one an - oth - er.
feels for all our sad-ness, And he shares in all our glad-ness.

Text: Cecil Frances Alexander, 1818–1895, alt. vv. 1–2, 4–6; James Waring McCrady, b. 1938, v. 3, ©
Music: Henry John Gauntlett, 1805–1876; harm. Arthur Henry Mann, 1850–1929, ©

87 87 77
IRBY

5. And our eyes at last shall see him,
Through his own redeeming love;
For that child who seemed so helpless
Is our Lord in heav'n above;
And he leads his children on
To the place where he is gone.

6. Not in that poor lowly stable,
With the oxen standing round,
We shall see him; but in heaven,
Where his saints his throne surround:
Christ, revealed to faithful eye,
Set at God's right hand on high.

From Heaven Above To Earth I Come 213

1. From heav'n a - bove to earth I come To bring good news to ev - 'ry - one! Glad tid - ings of great joy I bring To all the world and glad - ly sing:
2. To you this night is born a child Of Ma - ry, cho - sen vir - gin mild; This new - born child of low - ly birth Shall be the joy of all the earth.
3. This is the Christ, God's Son most high, Who hears your sad and bit - ter cry; He will him - self your Sav - ior be And from all sin will set you free.
4. The bless - ing which the Fa - ther planned The Son holds in his in - fant hand, That in his king - dom bright and fair, You may with us his glo - ry share.

Text: Martin Luther, 1483-1546; tr. Lutheran Book of Worship, 1978, ©
Music: Martin Luther, 1483-1546, attr.; harm. Hans Leo Hassler, 1564-1612

88 88
VOM HIMMEL HOCH

214 How Bright Appears The Morning Star

1. How bright ap - pears the Morn-ing Star, With mer - cy beam - ing
2. Though cir - cled by the hosts on high, He deigned to cast a
3. Re - joice, ye heav'ns; thou earth, re - ply; With praise, ye sin - ners,

from a - far; The host of heav'n re - joic - es;
pit - ying eye Up - on his help - less crea - ture;
fill the sky, For this his In - car - na - tion.

O right-eous Branch, O Jes - se's Rod! Thou Son of Man and
The whole cre - a - tion's Head and Lord, By high-est ser - a -
In - car - nate God, put forth thy power, Ride on, ride on, great

Son of God! We, too, will lift our voic - es:
phim a - dored, As - sumed our ve - ry na - ture;
Con - quer - or, Till all know thy sal - va - tion.

Text: Philipp Nicolai, 1556–1608; Wm. Mercer, 1811–1873
Music: Philipp Nicolai, 1556–1608; arr. and harm. J. S. Bach, 1685–1750

Irregular
Wie shön leuchet (FRANKFORT)

Je - sus,   Je - sus!   Ho - ly   ho - ly,   Yet most low - ly,
Je - sus,   grant us,   Through thy mer - it,   To   in - her - it
A - men,   a - men!   Al - le - lu - ia,   Al - le - lu - ia!

Draw thou near   us;   Great Em - man - uel, come and hear   us.
Thy sal - va   - tion;   Hear, O hear our sup - pli - ca - tion.
Praise be giv - en   Ev - er - more, by earth and heav - en.

215 What Child Is This?

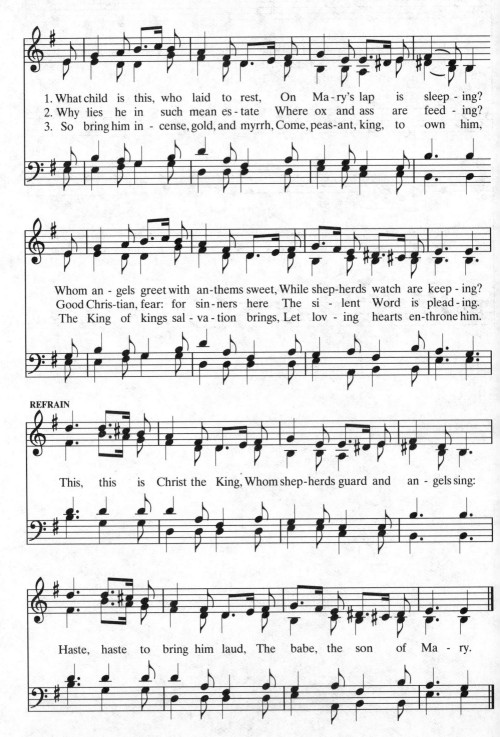

1. What child is this, who laid to rest, On Ma-ry's lap is sleep-ing?
2. Why lies he in such mean es-tate Where ox and ass are feed-ing?
3. So bring him in-cense, gold, and myrrh, Come, peas-ant, king, to own him,

Whom an-gels greet with an-thems sweet, While shep-herds watch are keep-ing?
Good Chris-tian, fear: for sin-ners here The si-lent Word is plead-ing.
The King of kings sal-va-tion brings, Let lov-ing hearts en-throne him.

REFRAIN

This, this is Christ the King, Whom shep-herds guard and an-gels sing:

Haste, haste to bring him laud, The babe, the son of Ma-ry.

Text: William Chatterton Dix, 1837–1898
Music: English melody, 1580

87 87 with Refrain
GREENSLEEVES

When Blossoms Flowered 216
'Mid the Snows

1. When blos-soms flow-'red 'mid the snows Up-on a win-ter night, Was
   - gain the heart with rap-ture glows To greet the ho-ly night, That

born the Child, the Christ-mas Rose, The King of Love and Light. The
gave the world its Christ-mas Rose, Its King of Love and Light. Let

an-gels sang, the shep-herds sang, The grate-ful earth re-joiced;
ev-'ry voice ac-claim His name, The grate-ful cho-rus swell.

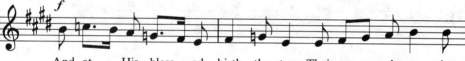

And at His bless-ed birth the stars Their ex-ul-ta-tion
From par-a-dise to earth He came That we with Him might

REFRAIN

voiced. O come let us a-dore Him, O
dwell.

come let us a-dore Him, O come let us a-

| 1. | 2. |

dore Him Christ the Lord. 2. A—

Text: Pietro Alessandro Yon, 1866–1943; tr. Frederick H. Martens, 1874–1932, ©
Music: Pietro Alessandro Yon, 1866–1943, ©

86 86 86 86 with Refrain
GESU BAMBINO

217 Go Tell It on the Mountain

REFRAIN

Go, tell it on the moun-tain, O-ver the hills and ev-'ry-where;

Go, tell it on the moun-tain That Je-sus Christ is born!

VERSES

1. While shep-herds kept their watch-ing O'er si-lent flocks by night,
2. The shep-herds feared and trem-bled When lo! A-bove the earth
3. Down in a low-ly man-ger The hum-ble Christ was born,

To Refrain

Be-hold through-out the heav-ens There shone a ho-ly light.
Rang out the an-gel cho-rus That hailed our Sav-ior's birth.
And God sent us sal-va-tion That bless-ed Christ-mas morn.

Text: Afro–American Spiritual, 19th cent.; adapt. tr. John W. Work, b. 1901, ©
Music: Afro–American Spiritual; acc. John W. Work, b. 1901, ©

76 76 with Refrain
GO TELL IT ON THE MOUNTAIN

Huron Carol 218

1. 'Twas in the moon of win - ter time, When all the birds had fled,
2. With - in a lodge of bro - ken bark, The ten - der babe was found,
3. O chil - dren of the for - est free, O sons of Man - i - tou,
4. Three Chiefs to - ge - ther made a pact, When glo - ry filled the night.

That might - y Git - chi Man - i - tou Sent an - gel choirs in - stead;
A rag - ged robe of rab - bit skin En - wrapped his beau - ty round;
The ho - ly child of earth and heav'n Is born to - day for you.
To fol - low where that glo - ry led And find the source of light.

Be - fore their light the stars grew dim, And won - d'ring hun - ters
But as the hun - ter braves drew nigh, The an - gel song rang
Come, kneel be - fore the ra - diant boy, Who brings you beau - ty,
For God to them re - vealed His plan, They hast - 'ned towards the

heard the hymn: Our Sav - ior, Christ, is there,
loud and high: Our Sav - ior, Christ, is born,
peace and joy: Our Sav - ior, Christ, is born,
God made man: And Je - sus wel - comed them.

Je - sus is there, Has - ten, then, to Beth - le - hem.
Je - sus is born. Has - ten, then, to Beth - le - hem.
Je - sus is born. Has - ten, then, to Beth - le - hem.
Je - sus the child. Wel - comed Chiefs to Beth - le - hem.

5. The time has come for each of us,   For holiness and him we'll fight:
To kneel before the Lord.   That promise now we make,
He came in answer to our prayer, Make to our Chief,
Now let Him be adored.   Jesus Christ of Bethlehem.
And as we kneel this holy night

Text: St. Jean de Brebeuf, 1593–1649; tr. J. Edgar Middleton, 1872–1960, vv. 1–3; Francis Hurley, S. J., vv. 4–5, ©
Music: French folk melody, 16th c.; arr. and harm. Sr. Mary Florian, ©

Irregular
JESOUS AHATONNIA

219 Angels We Have Heard on High

1. An - gels we have heard on high Sweet - ly sing - ing o'er the plains,
2. Shep - herds, why this ju - bi - lee? Why your joy - ous strains pro - long?
3. Come to Beth - le - hem and see Him whose birth the an - gels sing;
4. See him in a man - ger laid, Whom the choirs of an - gels praise;

And the moun - tains in re - ply Ech - o back their joy - ous strains.
Say what may the ti - dings be, Which in - spire your heav'n - ly song.
Come a - dore, on bend - ed knee, Christ, the Lord, the new - born King.
Ma - ry, Jo - seph, lend your aid, While our hearts in love we raise.

Glo - ri - a

in ex - cel - sis De - o, Glo -

Text: *Traditional French Carol, tr. anon.*
Music: *Traditional French Carol*

77 77 with Refrain
GLORIA

- ri - a   in ex-cel-sis De   -   o.

220 Of the Father's Love Begotten

1. Of the Fa - ther's love be - got - ten, Ere the worlds be -
2. Bless - ed was the day for ev - er When the Vir - gin
3. This is he whom seers in old time Chant - ed of with
4. O ye heights of heav'n, a - dore him; An - gel hosts, his

gan to be, He is Al - pha and O - me - ga,
full of grace, By the Ho - ly Ghost con - ceiv - ing,
one ac - cord, Whom the voic - es of the proph - ets
prais - es sing; All do - min - ions, bow be - fore him,

He the source the end - ing he, Of the things that
Bore the Sav - ior of our race, And the child, the
Prom - ised in their faith - ful word; Now he shines, the
And ex - tol our God and King; Let no tongue on

are, that have been, And that fu - ture years shall see,
world's Re - deem - er, First re - vealed his sa - cred face,
long ex - pect - ed; Let cre - a - tion praise the Lord,
earth be si - lent, Ev - 'ry voice in con - cert ring,

Ev - er - more and ev - er - more.
Ev - er - more and ev - er - more.
Ev - er - more and ev - er - more.
Ev - er - more and ev - er - more. A - men.

5. Glory be to God the Father,
   Glory be to God the Son,
   Glory to the Holy Spirit,
   Persons three, yet Godhead One.
   Glory be from all creation
   While eternal ages run,
   Evermore and evermore.

Text: Aurelius Clemens Prudentius, 348–413, tr. John Mason Neale, 1818–1866, et al.
Music: Didrik Pedersen of Abo, harm. Rev. Percy Jones, ©

87 87 87 with Refrain
CORDE NATUS (DIVINUM)

Winter's Snow 221

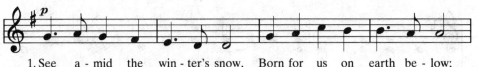

1. See a - mid the win - ter's snow, Born for us on earth be - low;
2. Lo, with - in a man - ger lies He who built the star - ry skies;
3. Say, you ho - ly shep - herds, say, Tell your joy - ful news to - day,
4. As we watched at dead of night, Lo, we saw a won - drous light:

See the ten - der Lamb ap - pears, Pro - mised from e - ter - nal years:
He who, throned in height sub - lime, Sits a - mid the cher - u - bim:
Why have you now left your sheep On the lone - ly moun - tain steep?
An - gels sing - ing "Peace on earth" Told us of the Sav - ior's birth:

REFRAIN

Hail, thou ev - er bless - ed morn; Hail, re - demp - tion's hap - py dawn;

Sing through all Je - ru - sa - lem, Christ is born in Beth - le - hem.

5. Sacred infant, all divine,
   What a tender love was thine.
   Thus to come from highest bliss
   Down to such a world as this: *Refrain*

6. Teach, O teach us, holy Child,
   By thy face so meek and mild,
   Teach us to resemble thee,
   In thy sweet humility: *Refrain*

Text: Edward Caswall, 1814–1878
Music: John Goss, 1800–1880

77 77 with Refrain
HUMILITY

222 Hark! The Herald Angels Sing

1. Hark! the her - ald an - gels sing, Glo - ry to the new-born King!
2. Christ, by high - est heav'n a - dored, Christ, the ev - er - last - ing Lord,
3. Mild he lays his glo - ry by, Born that we no more may die,
4. What good news the an - gels bring, What glad ti - dings of our King!

Peace on earth and mer - cy mild, God and sin - ners rec - on - ciled!
Late in time be - hold him come, Off - spring of the Vir-gin's womb.
Born to raise us from the earth, Born to give us sec - ond birth.
Christ the Lord is born to - day, Christ who takes our sins a - way!

Joy - ful, all ye na - tions, rise, Join the tri - umph of the skies;
Veiled in flesh the God - head see; Hail th'In-car - nate De - i - ty,
Ris'n with heal - ing in his wings, Light and life to all he brings.
He who rules both heav'n and earth Hath in Beth-le - hem his birth;

With th'an-gel - ic host pro-claim, "Christ is born in Beth-le-hem!"
Pleased as man with us to dwell, Je - sus our Em-man-u - el!
Hail, the Sun of Right-eous-ness! Hail, the heav'n - born Prince of Peace!
With th'an-gel - ic host pro-claim, "Christ is born in Beth-le-hem!"

Text: Charles Wesley, 1707–1788, alt., vv. 1–3; William Hammond, 1719–1783, v. 4
Music: Felix Mendelssohn, 1808–1847; adapt. William H. Cummings, 1831–1915

77 77 D and Refrain
MENDELSSOHN

REFRAIN

Hark! the her-ald an-gels sing, Glo-ry to the new-born King!

A Child My Choice 223

1. Let   fol - ly praise that   fan - cy loves,   I   praise and love that   child
2. I   praise him most,   I   love him best, All   praise and love are   his;
3. Love's sweet-est mark, laud's high-est theme, Our   most de - sir - ed   light,
4. He   mine by gift,   I   his by debt, Thus   each to oth - er   due;

Whose heart no thought, Whose tongue no word, Whose hand no deed de - filed.
While him I love,   In   him   I   live,   And   can - not live a - miss.
To   love him life,   to   leave him death, To   live   in him de - light.
First friend he was,   best   friend he   is,   All   times will try him   true.

5. Though young, yet wise,
Though small, yet strong
Though man, yet God he is;
As wise he knows, as strong he can,
As God he loves to bless.

6. His knowledge rules,
His strength defends,
His love doth cherish all,
His birth our joy, his life our light,
His death our end of thrall.

Text: St. Robert Southwell, S.J., 1561-1595, alt.
Music: Dan Tucker, b. 1925; arr. Edward J. McKenna, b. 1939, ©

86 86

TUCKERTON

224 God Rest You Merry, Gentlemen

1. God rest you mer - ry, gen - tle - men, let noth-ing you dis - may;
2. From God our heav'n-ly Fa - ther a bless-ed an - gel came
3. "Fear not, then," said the an - gel, "Let noth-ing you af - fright;
4. Now to the Lord sing prais - es, all you with-in this place,

Re - mem-ber Christ our Sa - vior was born on Christ-mas Day,
And un - to cer - tain shep - herds brought tid - ings of the same:
This day is born a Sa - vior of a pure vir - gin bright,
And with true love and char - i - ty each o - ther now em - brace;

To save us all from Sa - tan's pow'r when we were gone a - stray.
How that in Beth - le - hem was born the Son of God by name.
To free all those who trust in him from Sa - tan's pow'r and might."
This ho - ly tide of Christ - mas doth bring re - deem-ing grace.

Text: 18th century English carol
Music: 18th century English carol; harm. John Stainer, 1840–1901

76 76 86 with Refrain
GOD REST YOU MERRY

REFRAIN

O tid - ings of com - fort and joy, com-fort and joy; O tid - ings of com - fort and joy!

CHRISTMAS

225 O Come, All Ye Faithful/Adeste Fideles

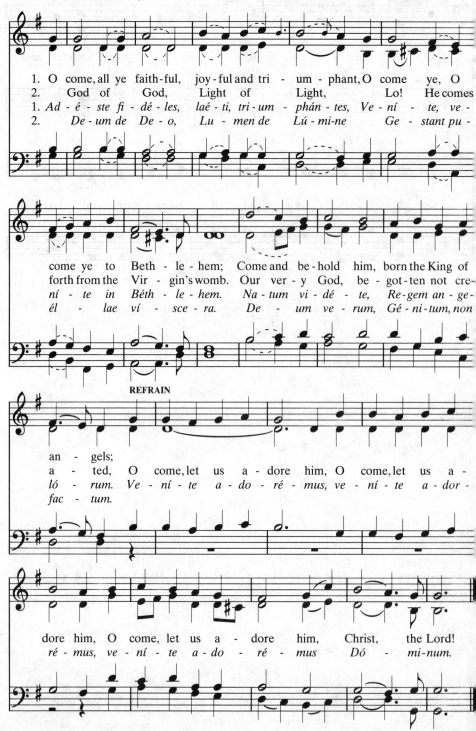

1. O come, all ye faith-ful, joy-ful and tri - um - phant, O come ye, O
2. God of God, Light of Light, Lo! He comes
1. Ad - é - ste fi - dé - les, laé - ti, tri - um - phán - tes, Ve - ní - te, ve -
2. De - um de De - o, Lu - men de Lú - mi - ne Ge - stant pu -

come ye to Beth - le - hem; Come and be - hold him, born the King of
forth from the Vir - gin's womb. Our ver - y God, be - got-ten not cre -
ní - te in Béth - le - hem. Na - tum vi - dé - te, Re - gem an - ge -
él - lae ví - sce - ra. De - um ve - rum, Gé - ni-tum, non

REFRAIN

an - gels;
a - ted, O come, let us a - dore him, O come, let us a -
ló - rum. Ve - ní - te a - do - ré - mus, ve - ní - te a - dor -
fac - tum.

dore him, O come, let us a - dore him, Christ, the Lord!
ré - mus, ve - ní - te a - do - ré - mus Dó - mi - num.

Text: John F. Wade, c. 1711–1786; tr. Frederick Oakeley, 1802–1880, alt.
Music: John F. Wade, c. 1711–1786; arr. David Willcocks, b. 1919, ©

Irregular with Refrain
ADESTE FIDELES

3. Sing, choirs of angels, sing in exultation,
   Sing, all ye citizens of heav'n above!
   Glory to God, all glory in the highest; *Refrain*

3. Cantet nunc Io! Chorus angelórum,
   Cantet nunc aula caeléstium.
   Glória, glória, in excélsis Deo. *Refrain*

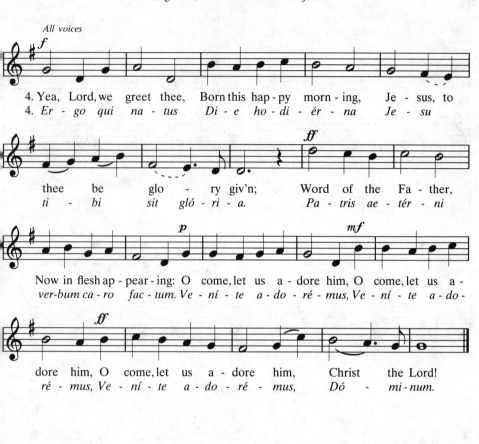

4. Yea, Lord, we greet thee, Born this hap-py morn-ing, Je - sus, to
4. *Er - go qui na - tus Di - e ho - di - ér - na Je - su*

thee be glo - ry giv'n; Word of the Fa - ther,
ti - bi sit gló - ri - a. Pa - tris ae - tér - ni

Now in flesh ap - pear-ing: O come, let us a - dore him, O come, let us a -
ver-bum ca - ro fac - tum. Ve - ní - te a - do - ré - mus, Ve - ní - te a - do -

dore him, O come, let us a - dore him, Christ the Lord!
ré - mus, Ve - ní - te a - do - ré - mus, Dó - mi - num.

226 Silent Night, Holy Night!

1. Si - lent night, ho - ly night! All is calm,
2. Si - lent night, ho - ly night! Shep - herds quake
3. Si - lent night, ho - ly night! Son of God,

all is bright Round yon Vir - gin Moth - er and Child.
at the sight! Glo - ries stream from heav - en a - far,
love's pure light, Ra - diant beams from thy ho - ly face,

Ho - ly In - fant so ten - der and mild, Sleep in
Heav'n - ly hosts sing al - le - lu - ia. Christ, the
With the dawn of re - deem - ing grace, Je - sus

heav - en - ly peace, Sleep in heav - en - ly peace.
Sav - ior, is born, Christ, the Sav - ior, is born.
Lord, at thy birth, Je - sus Lord, at thy birth.

Text: Joseph Mohr, 1792–1848; tr. John Freeman Young, 1820–1885
Music: Franz Gruber, 1787–1863

Irregular
STILLE NACHT

Away in a Manger 227

1. A - way in a man - ger, no crib for a bed,
2. The cat - tle are low - ing, the ba - by a - wakes,
3. Be near me, Lord Je - sus, I ask thee to stay

The lit - tle Lord Je - sus laid down his sweet head.
But lit - tle Lord Je - sus, no cry - ing he makes.
Close by me for - ev - er, and love me, I pray.

The stars in the sky looked down where he lay,
I love thee, Lord Je - sus, look down from the sky,
Bless all the dear chil - dren in thy ten - der care,

The lit - tle Lord Je - sus, a - sleep on the hay.
And stay by my cra - dle till morn - ing is nigh.
And fit us for heav - en to live with thee there.

Text: John Thomas McFarland, 1851–1913, v. 3; anon., vv. 1–2
Music: James R. Murray, 1841–1905

11 11 11 11
AWAY IN A MANGER

228 All My Heart This Night Rejoices

1. All my heart this night re - joic - es As I
2. Hark! a voice from yon - der man - ger, Soft and
3. Come then, let us has - ten yon - der; Here let

hear, far and near, Sweet - est an - gel voic - es;
sweet, doth en - treat, "Flee from woe and dan - ger;
all, great and small, Kneel in awe and won - der,

"Christ is born," their choirs are sing - ing, Till the
Dear ones, come; from all that grieves you You are
Love him who with love is yearn - ing; Hail the

air ev - 'ry - where Now with joy is ring - ing.
freed; all you need I will sure - ly give you."
star that from far Bright with hope is burn - ing.

Text: Paul Gerhardt, 1607–1676; tr. Catherine Winkworth, 1829–1878, alt.
Music: Johann G. Ebeling, 1637–1676

83 36 D
WARUM SOLLT ICH

As with Gladness Men of Old 229

1. As with glad-ness men of old   Did the guid-ing   star be-hold,
2. As with joy-ful steps they sped   To that low-ly   man-ger-bed,
3. As they of-fered gifts most rare   At that man-ger   rude and bare,

As with joy they hailed its light,   Lead-ing   on-ward, beam-ing bright,
There to   bend the   knee be-fore   Him whom heav'n and earth a-dore,
So   may we with ho-ly joy,   Pure and   free from sin's al-loy,

So, most   gra-cious God,   may we   Ev-er-more be   led to   thee.
So may   we with will-ing feet   Ev-er seek thy   mer-cy-seat.
All our   cost-liest treas-ures bring,   Christ, to thee our heav'n-ly   King.

4. Christ Redeemer, with us stay,
   Help us live your holy way;
   And when earthly things are past,
   Bring our ransomed souls at last
   Where they need no star to guide,
   Where no clouds your glory hide.

Lower Key: For the Beauty of the Earth, no. 562
Text: William Chatterton Dix, 1837–1898
Music: Conrad Kocher, 1786–1872; arr. William Henry Monk, 1823–1889

77 77 77
DIX

230 Earth Has Many a Noble City

1. Earth has man - y a no - ble cit - y;
2. Fair - er than the sun at morn - ing
3. East - ern sa - ges at his cra - dle
4. Sa - cred gifts of sol - emn mean - ing;

Beth - le - hem does all ex - cel; From it came the
Was the star that told his birth, To the world its
Make their off - 'rings rich and rare; See them give, in
In - cense does their God dis - close; Gold the King of

Lord from heav - en Came to rule his Is - ra - el.
God an - nounc - ing Seen in hu - man form on earth.
deep de - vo - tion Gold and frank - in - cense and myrrh.
kings pro - claim - ing; Myrrh his sep - ul - cher fore - shows.

5. Jesus, whom the Gentiles worshiped
   At your glad epiphany,
   Unto you with God the Father
   And the Spirit, glory be.

Text: Marcus Aurelius Clemens Prudentius, 348–413; tr. Edward Caswall, 1814–1878
Music: Christian Friedrich Witt, 1660–1716; adapt. John Gauntlett, 1805–1876

87 87
STUTTGART

Songs of Thankfulness and Praise 231

1. Songs of thank-ful-ness and praise, Je-sus, Lord, to you we raise,
2. Man-i-fest at Jor-dan's stream, Pro-phet, Priest, and King su-preme;
3. Grant us, Lord, your gifts of grace. Faith to see your sa-cred face,
4. Grant us grace to see you, Lord, Mir-rored in your ho-ly word;

Man-i-fest-ed by the star To the sa-ges from a-far;
And at Ca-na, wed-ding-guest, In your God-head man-i-fest;
Still re-vealed in your true Church, Giv-ing life to those who search;
May we im-i-tate you here, Live as those who know no fear;

Branch of roy-al Da-vid's stem, In your birth at Beth-le-hem.
Man-i-fest in pow'r di-vine, Chang-ing wa-ter in-to wine.
That same face which we shall see In that great E-piph-a-ny,
That we like to you may be At your great E-piph-a-ny;

An-thems be to you ad-dressed, God in flesh made man-i-fest!
An-thems be to you ad-dressed, God in flesh made man-i-fest!
An-thems be to you ad-dressed, God in flesh made man-i-fest!
God in flesh made man-i-fest! God in flesh made man-i-fest!

Higher key: At the Lamb's High Feast, no. 268

Text: Christopher Wordsworth, 1807–1885, vv. 1, 2, & 4 alt.; Irvin Udulutsch, O.F.M. Cap., b. 1920, v. 3, ©
Music: Jacob Hintze, 1622–1702; adapt. J. S. Bach, 1685–1750

77 77 77 77
SALZBURG

232 We Three Kings of Orient Are

1. We three kings of O - ri - ent are, Bear - ing
2. Born a King on Beth - le - hem's plain, Gold I
3. Frank - in - cense to of - fer have I, In - cense
4. Myrrh is mine; its bit - ter per - fume Breathes a

gifts we tra - verse a - far, Field and foun - tain,
bring to crown him a - gain, King for ev - er,
owns a De - i - ty nigh, Prayer and prais - ing,
life of gath - er - ing gloom; Sor - rowing, sigh - ing,

Moor and moun - tain, Fol - low - ing yon - der star.
Ceas - ing nev - er O - ver us all to reign.
All are rais - ing, Wor - ship him, God on high.
Bleed - ing, dy - ing, Sealed in the stone - cold tomb.

Text: John Henry Hopkins, Jr., 1820–1891
Music: John Henry Hopkins, Jr., 1820–1891

88 86 with Refrain
KINGS OF ORIENT (Hopkins)

REFRAIN

O star of won - der, star of night, Star with roy - al beau - ty bright; West - ward lead - ing, Still pro - ceed - ing, Guide us to thy per - fect light!

5. Glorious now behold him arise,
King, and God, and Sacrifice;
Heav'n sings "Alleluia;"
"Alleluia," earth replies. *Refrain*

233 Brightest and Best

1. Bright-est and best of the stars of the morn - ing, Dawn on our
2. Cold on his cra - dle the dew - drops are shin - ing, Low lies his
3. Shall we then yield him, in cost - ly de - vo - tion, O - dors of
4. Vain - ly we of - fer each am - ple o - bla - tion, Vain - ly with

dark - ness, and lend us thine aid; Star of the east, the hor -
head with the beasts of the stall; An - gels a - dore him in
E - dom, and of - f'rings di - vine, Gems of the moun - tain, and
gifts would his fa - vor se - cure, Rich - er by far is the

i - zon a - dorn - ing, Guide where our in - fant Re-deem - er is laid.
slum-ber re - clin - ing, Ma - ker and Mon-arch and Sa - vior of all.
pearls of the o - cean, Myrrh from the for - est, and gold from the mine?
heart's a - dor - a - tion, Dear - er to God are the prayers of the poor.

REFRAIN

Bright-est and best of the stars of the morn - ing, Dawn on our

dark - ness and lend us thine aid; Star of the east, the hor -

i - zon a - dorn - ing, Guide where our in - fant Re-deem-er is laid.

Text: Reginald Heber, 1783–1826, alt.
Music: The Southern Harmony, 1835; acc. Edward J. McKenna, b. 1939, ©

11 10 11 10 with Refrain
STAR IN THE EAST

Beloved Son and Daughter Dear 234

1. Be - lov - ed son and daugh-ter dear, I call you by your name.
2. O turn to me with all your heart; With joy ap-proach my hall.
3. Now blow the trum-pet, call a fast, As - sem-ble in my name,

My peo - ple, lis - ten to my voice: Your heart's love now I claim.
From far and wide I gath-er you. My peo - ple, hear my call!
And wel-come to your ban-quet hall My poor and blind and lame.

O come, let us re - turn to him, For gra - cious is the Lord.
More faith - ful than the ris - ing sun, More gen - tle than the breeze,
A - rise and let us come to him Who knows our fears and needs.

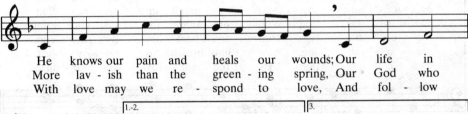

He knows our pain and heals our wounds; Our life in
More lav - ish than the green - ing spring, Our God who
With love may we re - spond to love, And fol - low

him re - stored!
saves and frees!
where he leads.

Text: Sr. Delores Dufner, O.S.B., b. 1939, ©
Music: Jay F. Hunstiger, b. 1950, ©

86 86 86 86
ST. CLOUD

235 At the Cross Her Station Keeping

1. At the cross her sta - tion keep - ing, Mar - y stood in
2. While she wait - ed in her an - guish, See - ing Christ in
3. With what pain and des - o - la - tion, With what no - ble
4. Ev - er pa - tient in her yearn - ing Though her tear - filled
5. Who, that sor - row con - tem - pla - ting, On that pas - sion
6. Christ she saw, for our sal - va - tion, Scourged with cru - el
7. Christ she saw with life - blood fail - ing, All her an - guish
8. Mar - y, fount of love's de - vo - tion, Let me share with

sor - row weep - ing When her Son was cru - ci - fied.
tor - ment lan - guish, Bit - ter sor - row pierced her heart.
re - sig - na - tion, Mar - y watched her dy - ing Son.
eyes were burn - ing, Mar - y gazed up - on her Son.
me - di - ta - ting, Would not share the Vir - gin's grief?
ac - cla - ma - tion, Bruised and beat - en by the rod.
un - a - vail - ing, Saw him breathe his ver - y last.
true e - mo - tion All the sor - row you en - dured.

9. Virgin, ever interceding,
   Hear me in my fervent pleading:
   Fire me with your love of Christ.

10. Mother, may this prayer be granted:
    That Christ's love may be implanted
    In the depths of my poor soul.

11. At the cross, your sorrow sharing,
    All your grief and torment bearing,
    Let me stand and mourn with you.

12. Fairest maid of all creation,
    Queen of hope and consolation,
    Let me feel your grief sublime.

13. Virgin, in your love befriend me,
    At the Judgment Day defend me.
    Help me by your constant prayer.

14. Savior, when my life shall leave me,
    Through your mother's prayers
        receive me
    With the fruits of victory.

15. Let me to your love be taken,
    Let my soul in death awaken
    To the joys of Paradise.

Alt. Tune: Careworn Mother Stood Attending, no. 236

Text: Jacopone da Todi, 1230–1306, attr.; tr. Anthony G. Petti, 1932–1985, abrid. ©
Music: Maintzisch Gesangbuch, 1661

88 7
STABAT MATER

Careworn Mother Stood Attending 236

May be used at Stations of the Cross

1. Care - worn moth - er stood at - tend - ing, Wit - ness to the
2. Though her soul was torn with ach - ing, Heart to heart she
3. Moth - er of the Sole Be - got - ten Grieved for him, for -
4. While she saw that great a - ton - ing, From her sad heart
5. Spring of love, I love thee, Moth - er! Help me mourn with
6. No one tru - ly o - pen - heart - ed, See - ing Mar - y
7. Ev - 'ry - one dealt Christ the scour - ging, Nailed him fast at
8. She be - held her dear Be - lov - ed Left by all, by

bit - ter end - ing, God, her Son, up - on the tree.
shared His break - ing, Pierc - ing sword of ag - on - y!
lorn, for - got - ten. Gen - tle heart all sor - row knows.
soft - ened moan - ing To that glo - rious Son a - rose.
thee my Broth - er. Share the se - crets of your woe.
bro - ken - heart - ed, But would com - fort her in woe.
e - vil's ur - ging; Mar - y saw his blood run red.
dark - ness cov - ered, Till his spir - it fell and fled.

9. May his flesh and five wounds
   bind me!
   Holy Mother, ever find me
   Near my Master crucified.

10. Christ, whose wounds I share and
    treasure,
    Willed to suffer without measure;
    Saving me in pain he died.

11. Queen of virgins, be not troubled,
    Though the weight of woe be doubled.
    Let me shoulder all your care.

12. Friend of Christ, I share his giving,
    Jesus dying in my living;
    All his precious wounds I wear.

13. With those wounds, his lifeblood
    spilling,
    Be the cross my joy fulfilling,
    Fresh as drink at break of day.

14. Virgin Mother, David's tower,
    Keep me safe from Satan's power
    On that fiery judgment Day.

15. Christ, may Mary be the portal,
    Gateway to reward immortal,
    When my soul is borne above.

16. When to earth my body's given,
    Grant my spirit light of heaven,
    There with Mary thee to love.

Alt. Tune: At The Cross Her Station Keeping, no. 235

Text: Jacopone da Todi, 1230–1306, attr.; tr. Edward J. McKenna, b. 1939, ©
Music: Adapt. and arr. Edward J. McKenna, b. 1939 ©

88 7
BURRILL

237 Create In Me

REFRAIN

Cre-ate in me a clean heart, O God, and put a new and
stead-fast spir-it in my soul. Give back to me the joy of your sal-
va - tion, and hold me al-ways with a will-ing spir - it. ____ Have

Last time to Coda ⊕   *To verses*

VERSES

(3.) For

1. mer - cy O Lord, ac cord - ing to your
2. O - pen my lips, and my mouth shall sing your
3. you will be pleased by a life ____ lived in

love; ____ cleanse me from my sin; _____ wash me in your
praise; my sac - ri - fice, O Lord, is a heart con-trite and
truth; ____ teach your wis - dom to me; ____ deep with-in my

mer - cy, and fill my heart with joy and glad - ness. ___
hum - ble; ____ this, O Lord, you will re - ceive.
heart, _ O wash me and I shall be clean.

⊕ **CODA**

and hold me al - ways with a will-ing spir - it. ____

Text: Marty Haugen, b. 1952, ©
Music: Marty Haugen, b. 1952, ©

Hear Our Entreaties Lord/Attende, Domine 238

REFRAIN

Hear our en-treat-ies, Lord, and show us mer-cy, For we are sin-ners be - fore you.
At - tén-de, Dó - mi - ne, et mi - se - ré - re, Qui-a pec-cá - vi-mus ti - bi.

VERSES

1. King high ex - alt - ed, all the world's Re - deem - er,
2. Right hand of God - head, head - stone of the cor - ner,
3. We, your e - ter - nal maj - es - ty en - treat - ing,
1. *Ad te Rex sum - me, óm - ni - um Re - dém - ptor,*
2. *Déx - te - ra Pa - tris, la - pis an - gu - lá - ris,*
3. *Ro - gá - mus, De - us, tu - am ma - jes - tá - tem:*

To you your chil - dren lift their eyes with weep - ing;
Path of sal - va - tion, gate of heav - en's king - dom,
Make lam - en - ta - tion in your ho - ly hear - ing.
Ó - cu - los nó - stros sub - le - vá - mus flen - tes;
Vi - a sa - lú - tis, já - nu - a cae - lé - stis,
Áu - ri - bus sa - cris gé - mi - tus ex - aú - di:

To Refrain

Christ, we im - plore you, hear our sup - pli - ca - tion.
Lord, cleanse your peo - ple, stained with much trans - gres - sion.
Gra - cious - ly grant, Lord, to our sins for - give - ness.
Ex - aú - di, Chri - ste, sup - pli - cán - tum pre - ces.
Áb - lu - e no - stri má - cu - las de - lí - cti.
Crí - mi - na no - stra plá - ci - dus in - dúl - ge.

4. Humbly confessing all our sins against you,
   All our misdoings, hidden now no longer;
   Lord, our Redeemer, by your love grant pardon.
   Refrain

5. Led away captive, guiltless, unresisting,
   Brought by false witness unto death for sinners,
   Christ Jesus, keep us whom your blood has ransomed.
   Refrain

4. *Tibi fatémur crímina admíssa:*
   Contríto corde pándimus occúlta:
   Tua, Redémpter, piétas ignóscat.
   Refrain

5. *Ínnocens captus, nec repúgnans ductus;*
   Téstibus falsis pro impiis damnatús;
   Quos redemísti, tu consérva, Christe.
   Refrain

Text: Ancient Mozarabic Litany; Irvin Udulutsch, O.F.M., Cap., b. 1920, ©
Music: Mode V; acc. Roger Nachtwey, b. 1930, ©

11 11 11 with Refrain
ATTENDE DOMINE

239 Jesus Sought out the Desert

1. Je - sus sought out the des - ert, for - ty long days to fast;
2. Can we with Je - sus trav - el in - to a des - ert place,
3. Christ had to face temp - ta - tion; three times did Sa - tan speak.

Climbed up the bar - ren moun - tain, reach - ing the top at last.
Fast - ing and ev - er plead - ing, seek - ing the Fa - ther's grace?
When Christ was weak and hun - gry, Sa - tan his soul did seek.

Spent all his time in pray - ing, ask - ing his Fa - ther's will;
One with him in our pray - ing, mak - ing his words our own;
Je - sus with-stood his temp - ting, strong was he, good and wise,

Soon to be - gin his mis - sion, proph - e - cies to ful - fill.
Ask - ing for bread to feed us, God will not give a stone.
Show - ing us how to con - quer, un - der the des - ert skies.

Text: Willard F. Jabusch, b. 1930, ©
Music: Old Basque Hymn; acc. David Kraehenbuehl, b. 1923, ©

Lord, Jesus, Have Pity on Us 240

REFRAIN

Lord, Je - sus, __ have pit - y on us; Our days are caught up in the whirl - wind. Lord Je - sus, __ have pit - y on us; We're scat - tered like leaves by the wind. __

VERSES

1. When Is - ra - el came out of E - gypt, A - way from an
2. Lead us from the bon - dage of E - gypt, From dread and con -
3. 'Round us __ our neigh - bors have fash - ioned Their i - dols of
4. Come, dwell in the midst of this na - tion, Where vi - o - lence

1. al - i - en race, The Lord ____ made of Ju - dah his
2. fu - sion of soul; The gods ____ of the pa - gans are
3. pow - er and lust; We turn ____ to you, Lord, for di -
4. ra - ges and kills, __ Come, make of our coun - try your

To Refrain

1. king - dom, His tem - ple and own dwell - ing place.
2. worth - less; They're made out of sil - ver and gold.
3. rec - tion, For you are the Sa - vior we trust.
4. king - dom, So peace - ful - ness ev - 'ry heart fills.

Text: Psalm 118 adapted, Willard F. Jabusch, b. 1930, ©
Music: Robert E. Kreutz, b. 1922, ©

241 Lord Jesus, as We Turn from Sin

1. Lord Jesus, as we turn from sin
With strength and hope restored,
Receive the homage that we bring
To you, our risen Lord.

2. We call on you whose living word
Has made the Father known;
O Shepherd, we have wandered far.
Find us and lead us home.

3. Your glance at Peter helped him know
The love he had desired.
Now gaze on us and heal us, Lord,
Of selfishness and pride.

4. Reach out and touch with healing pow'r
The wounds we have received,
That in forgiveness we may love
And may no longer grieve.

Text: Ralph Wright, O.S.B., b. 1938 ©
Music: Johann Cruger, 1598–1662

86 86
GRAEFENBERG

5. Then stay with us when evening comes
   And darkness makes us blind,
   O stay until the light of dawn
   May fill both heart and mind.

Forty Days and Forty Nights 242

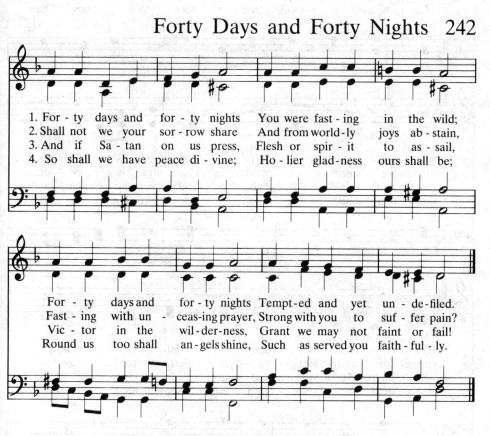

1. For - ty days and for - ty nights You were fast - ing in the wild;
2. Shall not we your sor - row share And from world - ly joys ab - stain,
3. And if Sa - tan on us press, Flesh or spir - it to as - sail,
4. So shall we have peace di - vine; Ho - lier glad - ness ours shall be;

For - ty days and for - ty nights Tempt-ed and yet un - de-filed.
Fast - ing with un - ceas-ing prayer, Strong with you to suf - fer pain?
Vic - tor in the wil - der-ness, Grant we may not faint or fail!
Round us too shall an - gels shine, Such as served you faith - ful - ly.

5. Guard and keep us, Savior dear,
   Ever constant by your side;
   That with you we may appear
   At th' eternal Eastertide.

Alt. Tune: Holy Spirit Truth Divine, no. 500

Text: George Hunt Smyttan, 1822–1870; tr. Francis Pott, 1832–1909, alt.
Music: Martin Herbst, 1654–1681, attr.

77 77
HEINLEIN

243 Come, Let Us to the Lord Our God

1. Come, let us to the Lord our God With con-trite hearts re-turn; Our God is gra-cious, nor will leave The des-o-late to mourn.

2. His voice com-mands the tem-pest forth, And stills the storm-y wave, His arm is ev-er strong to smite But al-so strong to save.

3. Long has the night of sor-row reigned, The dawn shall bring us light God shall ap-pear, and we shall rise With glad-ness in his sight.

4. Our hearts, if God we seek to know, Shall know him and re-joice; His com-ing like the morn shall be, Like morn-ing songs his voice.

5. As dew upon the tender herb,
Diffusing fragrance round;
As show'rs that usher in the spring
And cheer the thirsty ground:

6. So shall his presence bless our souls
And shed a joyful light;
That hallowed morn shall chase away
The sorrows of the night.

Text: John Morison, 1750–1798
Music: Neil Dougall, 1776–1862

86 86
KILMARNOCK

Lord, Teach Us to Pray Aright 244

1. Lord, teach us how to pray a-right With reverence and with fear;
2. God of all grace, we come to thee With broken contrite hearts;
3. Patience to watch, and wait, and weep, Though mercy long delay;

Though dust and ashes in thy sight, We may, we must draw near.
Give, what thine eye delights to see, Truth in the inward parts;
Courage our fainting souls to keep, And trust thee though thou slay.

We perish if we cease from prayer; O grant us pow'r to pray;
Faith in the only sacrifice That can for sin atone;
Give these, and then thy will be done; Thus strengthened with all might,

And when to meet thee we prepare, Lord, meet us by the way.
To cast our hopes, to fix our eyes, On Christ, on Christ alone;
We, through thy Spirit and thy Son, Shall pray, and pray aright.

Text: James Montgomery, 1771–1854
Music: Henry Bryan Hays, O.S.B., b. 1920 ©

86 86 86 86
ELKHORN TAVERN

245 O Mortal Men and Women

1. O mortal men and women, hear The
2. Great God our sin now drives us down, Our
3. My people, hear me; turn from wrong. No
4. Our days of wine and roses fade; Our

Word of God, Most High: To dust you turn. Your
greed, our guilt, our shame. O Lord on high, of
long - er fear your fate. For when you turn, I
time is come and gone. At night we kneel; we

end is near. Your world will dim and die. Your
great re - nown, We trust your ho - ly Name, We
make you strong; I o - pen heav - en's gate. I
cry for aid. We yearn to see the dawn, We

world will dim and die.
trust your ho - ly Name.
o - pen heav - en's gate.
yearn to see the dawn.

5. Remember mercy, once again.
   Your eyes will see my Son.
   Your struggle shall be over then.
   Your final race be won.
   Your final race be won.

6. Great God, we know not what to do.
   When shall we see your face?
   Your faithful Church cries out to you:
   O, save your chosen race,
   O, save your chosen race.

7. Lift up your heart and turn to me.
   Now hear what I shall give:
   Your world renewed, your soul set free.
   By faith in me, you live.
   By faith in me, you live.

Text: Michael Gilligan, ©
Music: Old English Lenten carol; acc. Helen Silvia, ©

© ACP

86 86
SUSSEX MUMMER'S CAROL

Out of the Depths We Cry 246

1. Out of the depths we cry, O Lord.
2. Your lov - ing kind - ness gives us hope
3. For with you is for - give - ness, Lord;

To you we cry for mer - cy.
Of mer - ci - ful re - demp - tion.
Your prom - ise, our sal - va - tion.

O hear us, Lord, hear now our voice
Lord, free your Church from ev - 'ry sin,
So in that Word we shall stand firm

And grant our prayer for mer - cy.
And show us your re - demp - tion.
And wait for our sal - va - tion.

Higher key: The King of Love My Shepherd Is, no. 460

Text: Psalm 130; tr. Sr. Delores Dufner, O.S.B., b. 1939 ©
Music: Traditional Irish Hymn Melody; acc. Russell Woollen, b. 1923, ©

87 87
ST. COLUMBA (ERIN)

247 Sole Hope of All the World

1. Sole hope of all the world, and Lord, Be - stow - er of the
2. And, though our con - scien - ces pro - claim Our deep trans - gres - sion
3. Our sins re - mem - ber now no more; For - give; your mer - cy
4. Ac - cept, O Lord, this Len - ten tide. This fast which you have

great re - ward, Re - ceive the prayers your ser - vants raise;
and our shame, Cleanse us, O God, we hum - bly plead,
can re - store; So, Lord, take on your - self our care,
sanc - ti - fied, That we, through sac - ra - men - tal ways,

Ac - cept our psalms and hymns of praise.
From sins of thought and word and deed.
That pure in heart we make our prayer.
May reach the joys of Pas - chal days.

Text: Sarum Breviary; tr. Alan G. McDougal, 1811–1873, alt.
Music: Mainz Gesangbuch, 1833; acc. A. Gregory Murray, O.S.B., b. 1905, ©

88 88
ST. BONIFACE

248 O Merciful Redeemer, Hear

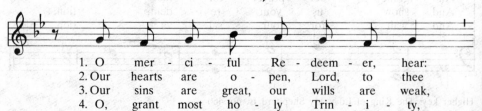

1. O mer - ci - ful Re - deem - er, hear:
2. Our hearts are o - pen, Lord, to thee
3. Our sins are great, our wills are weak,
4. O, grant most ho - ly Trin - i - ty,

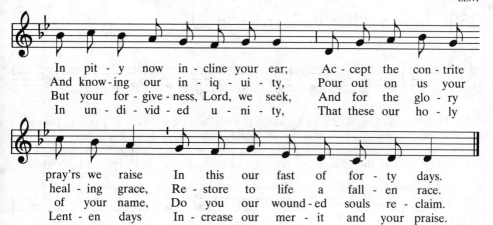

In pit - y now in - cline your ear;   Ac - cept the con - trite
And know - ing our in - iq - ui - ty,   Pour out on us your
But your for - give - ness, Lord, we seek,   And for the glo - ry
In un - di - vid - ed u - ni - ty,   That these our ho - ly

pray'rs we raise   In this our fast of for - ty days.
heal - ing grace,   Re - store to life a fall - en race.
of your name,   Do you our wound - ed souls re - claim.
Lent - en days   In - crease our mer - it and your praise.

Text: St. Gregory the Great, 540–604; tr. Irvin Udulutsch, O.S.F. Cap., b. 1920, ©
Music: Plainchant, Mode II; acc. Irvin Udulutsch, O.S.F. Cap., b. 1920, ©

88 88
AUDI REDEMPTOR

In the Cross of Christ I Glory 249

1. In the Cross of Christ I glo - ry,   Tow'r - ing o'er the
2. When the woes of life o'er - take me,   Hopes de - ceive and
3. When the sun of bliss is beam - ing   Light and love up -
4. Bane and bless - ing, pain and plea - sure,   By the Cross are

wrecks of time;   All the light of sac - red sto - ry
fears an - noy,   Nev - er shall the Cross for - sake me,
on my way,   From the Cross the ra - diance stream - ing,
sanc - ti - fied;   Peace is there that knows no mea - sure,

Ga - thers round its head sub - lime.   All the light of
Lo! it glows with peace and joy.   Nev - er shall the
Adds more lus - tre to the day.   From the Cross the
Joys that through all time a - bide.   Peace is there that

sac - red sto - ry   Ga - thers round its head sub - lime.
Cross for - sake me   Lo! it glows with peace and joy.
ra - diance stream - ing   Adds more lus - tre to the day.
knows no mea - sure   Joys that through all time a - bide.

Text: Sir. J. Bowring, 1792–1872
Music: Henry Bryan Hays. O.S.B., b. 1920, ©

87 87
RICHARD'S SHOP

250 Have Mercy, Lord, on Us

1. Have mer - cy, Lord, on us, For you are ev - er kind; Though
2. Lord, wash a - way our guilt, And cleanse us from our sin; For
3. The joy your grace can give, Let us a - gain ob - tain; And
4. To God the Fa - ther, Son, And Spir - it glo - ry be, Who

we have sinned be - fore you, Lord, Your mer - cy let us find.
we con - fess our wrongs and see How great our guilt has been.
may your Spir - it's firm sup - port Our spir - its then sus - tain.
was and is and shall be so For all e - ter - ni - ty.

Text: Nahum Tate, 1652–1715, & Nicholas Brady 1659–c. 1726
Music: William Damon, c. 1550–1593

66 86
SOUTHWELL

251 As The Sun with Longer Journey

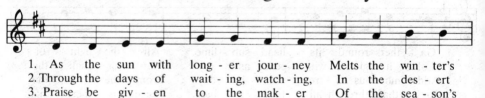

1. As the sun with long - er jour - ney Melts the win - ter's
2. Through the days of wait - ing, watch - ing, In the des - ert
3. Praise be giv - en to the mak - er Of the sea - son's

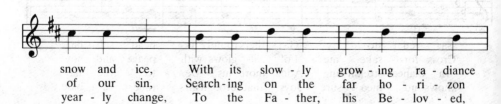

snow and ice, With its slow - ly grow - ing ra - diance
of our sin, Search - ing on the far ho - ri - zon
year - ly change, To the Fa - ther, his Be - lov - ed,

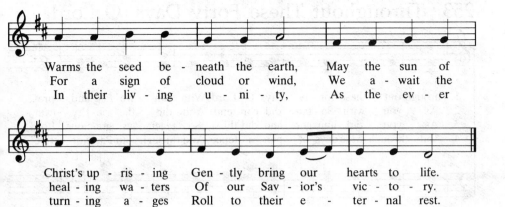

Warms the seed be - neath the earth, May the sun of
For a sign of cloud or wind, We a - wait the
In their liv - ing u - ni - ty, As the ev - er

Christ's up - ris - ing Gen - tly bring our hearts to life.
heal - ing wa - ters Of our Sav - ior's vic - to - ry.
turn - ing a - ges Roll to their e - ter - nal rest.

Text: John Patrick Earls, O.S.B., b. 1935, ©
Music: Henry Bryan Hays, O.S.B., b. 1920, ©

87 87 87
SUN JOURNEY

When From Bondage   252

1. When from bon - dage we are sum-moned Out of dark-ness in - to light,
2. When our God names us his peo - ple, Then he leads us by the hand
3. At all sta - ges of the jour - ney God is with us, night and day,

We must go in hope and pa - tience, Walk by faith and not by sight.
Through a lone - ly, bar - ren des - ert, To a great and glo-rious land.
With com - pas - sion for our weak-ness Ev - 'ry step a - long the way.

REFRAIN

Let us throw off all that hin - ders; Let us run the race to win!

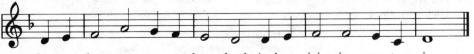

Let us has - ten to our home-land And, re - joic - ing, en - ter in.

Text: Sr. Delores Dufner, O.S.B., b. 1939, ©
Music: Jay F. Hunstiger, b. 1950, ©

253 Throughout These Forty Days, O Lord

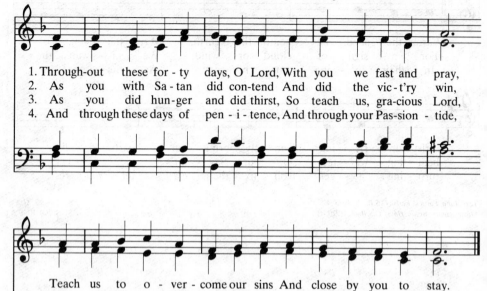

1. Through-out these for-ty days, O Lord, With you we fast and pray,
2. As you with Sa-tan did con-tend And did the vic-t'ry win,
3. As you did hun-ger and did thirst, So teach us, gra-cious Lord,
4. And through these days of pen-i-tence, And through your Pas-sion-tide,

Teach us to o-ver-come our sins And close by you to stay.
O give us strength in you to fight, In you to con-quer sin.
To die to self and so to live By your most ho-ly word.
For ev-er-more, in life and death, O Lord, with us a-bide.

5. Abide with us, that through this life
   Of suff'ring and of pain
   An Easter of unending joy
   We may at last attain.

Alt. Tune: The Head That Once Was Crowned With Thorns, no. 516
Text: Claudia F. Hernaman, 1838–1898, alt.
Music: Adapted from John Day's Psalter, 1562

86 86
ST. FLAVIAN

Alternate Text

254   O Cross Of Christ

1. O Cross of Christ, immortal tree
   On which our Savior died,
   The world is sheltered by your arms
   That bore the Crucified.

2. O faithful Cross, you stand unmoved
   While ages run their course;
   Foundation of the universe,
   Creation's binding force.

3. Give glory to the risen Christ
   And to his Cross give praise,
   The sign of God's unfathomed love,
   The hope of all our days.

Text: Benedictine Nuns of Stanbrook Abbey ©

86 86
ST. FLAVIAN

Prepare the Royal Highway 255

1. Pre - pare the roy - al high - way; The King of kings is near!
2. God's peo - ple, see him com - ing: Your own e - ter - nal king!
3. Then fling the gates wide o - pen To greet your prom - ised king!
4. His is no earth - ly king - dom; It comes from heav'n a - bove,

Let ev - 'ry hill and val - ley A lev - el road ap - pear!
Palm branch - es strew be - fore him! Spread gar - ments! Shout and sing!
Your king, yet ev - 'ry na - tion Its trib - ute too may bring.
His rule is peace and free - dom And jus - tice, truth, and love.

Then greet the King of glo - ry, Fore - told in sa - cred sto - ry:
God's prom - ise will not fail you! No more shall doubt as - sail you!
All lands will bow be - fore him; Their voic - es join your sing - ing:
So let your praise be sound - ing For kind - ness so a - bound - ing:

REFRAIN

Ho - san - na to the Lord, For he ful - fills God's Word!

Text: Frans Mikael Frazen, 1772–1847; tr. Lutheran Book of Worship, 1978 ed., ©
Music: Swedish Folk Tune, 14th c.

76 76 77 with Refrain
MESSIAH

256 All Glory, Laud and Honor

REFRAIN

All glo-ry, laud, and hon - or To thee Re-deem-er King!

To whom the lips of chil - dren Made sweet ho-san-nas ring.

1. Thou art the King of Is - ra - el, Thou Da - vid's roy - al Son.
2. The com-pa - ny of an - gels Are prais - ing thee on high;
3. The peo-ple of . the He - brews With palms be - fore thee went:
4. To thee be - fore thy pas - sion They sang their hymns of praise;

To Refrain

Who in the Lord's Name com - est, The King and Bless-ed One.
And hu - man-kind and all things Cre - a - ted make re - ply.
Our praise and prayers and an - thems Be - fore thee we pre - sent.
To thee, now high ex - alt - ed, Our mel - o - dy we raise.

5. Thou didst accept their praises;
   Accept the prayers we bring,
   Who in all good delightest,
   Thou good and gracious King. *Refrain*

Text: Theodulph of Orleans, c. 760–821; tr. John Mason Neale, 1818–1866
Music: Melchior Teschner, 1584–1635

76 76 with Refrain
VALET WILL ICH DIR GEBEN

All Glory, Praise and Honor 257

1. All glo - ry, praise, and hon - or To you, Re - deem-er King!
2. True King are you, Lord Je - sus, Of Da-vid's roy - al line!
3. The saints and an - gels praise you, While all on earth pro - claim

To whom the lips of chil - dren Made glad ho - san - nas ring!
Our King by right e - ter - nal, Both hu - man and di - vine!
Your rule of love and mer - cy In hearts that bless your name!

REFRAIN

All glo - ry, praise, and hon - or To you, Re - deem-er King!

To whom the lips of chil - dren Made glad ho - san - nas ring!

Text: Theodulph of Orleans, c. 760–821; tr. Irvin Udulutsch, O.F.M. Cap., b. 1920, ©
Music: Anon.; acc. Roger Nachtwey, ©

76 76 with Refrain
FULDA MELODY

258 My Song Is Love Unknown

1. My song is love un-known, My Sa-vior's love to me, Love
2. He came from his blest throne Sal-va-tion to be-stow, But
3. Some-times they strew his way, And his strong prais-es sing, Re-
4. Why, what hath my Lord done? What makes this rage and spite? He

to the love-less shown That they might love-ly be. O
all made strange, and none The longed-for Christ would know. But
sound-ing all the day Ho-san-nas to their King. Then
made the lame to run, He gave the blind their sight. Sweet

who am I that for my sake My Lord should take frail flesh, and die?
O my friend, my friend in-deed, Who at my need his life did spend.
"Cru-ci-fy!" is all their breath, And for his death they thirst and cry.
in-ju-ries! Yet they at these Them-selves dis-please, and 'gainst him rise.

5. They rise, and needs will have
   My dear Lord made away;
   A murderer they save,
   The Prince of Life they slay.
   Yet steadfast he to suff'ring goes,
   That he his foes from thence might free.

6. In life no house, no home
   My Lord on earth might have;
   In death no friendly tomb
   But what a stranger gave.
   What may I say? Heav'n was his home;
   But mine the tomb wherein he lay

7. Here might I stay and sing,
   No story so divine:
   Never was love, dear King,
   Never was grief like thine.
   This is my friend, in whose sweet praise
   I all my days could gladly spend.

Text: Samuel Crossman, 1624–1683, alt.
Music: John Ireland, 1879–1962, ©

66 66 88
LOVE UNKNOWN

O Sacred Head Surrounded 259

1. O Sa-cred Head, sur - round - ed By crown of pierc-ing thorn,
2. The Lord of ev - ery na - tion Was hung up - on a tree;
3. In this, your bit - ter pas - sion, Good Shep-herd, think of me

O bleed-ing Head, so wound - ed Re - viled and put to scorn.
His death was our sal - va - tion Our sins, his ag - o - ny.
With your most kind com - pas - sion, Un - wor - thy though I be:

Our sins have marred the glo - ry Of your most ho - ly face,
O Je - sus, by your pas - sion, Your Life in us in - crease;
Be - neath your cross a - bid - ing For ev - er would I rest,

Yet an - gel hosts a - dore thee, And trem-ble as they gaze.
Your death for us did fash - ion Our par - don and our peace.
In your dear love con - fid - ing, And with your pres-ence blest.

Lower key: O King of Might and Splendor, no. 383

Text: St. Bernard of Clairvaux, c. 1091–1153, attr.; tr. Henry Williams Baker, 1821–1977, v. 1;
Melvin Farrell, S.S., b. 1930, v. 2; Arthur Russell, 1806–1874, alt. v. 3
Music: Hans Leo Hassler, 1564–1612; harm. J. S. Bach, 1685–1750

76 76 D
PASSION CHORALE

Translation v. 2 © 1961, World Library Publications, Inc.

260 Savior, When in Dust to Thee

1. Sa - vior, when in dust to thee Low we bow the a - dor - ing knee;
2. By thy help-less in - fant years, By thy life of want and tears,
3. By thine hour of dire de - spair, By thine ag - o - ny of prayer,
4. By thy deep ex - pir - ing groan, By the sad sep - ul - chral stone,

When, re - pent - ant, to the skies Scarce we dare to lift our eyes;
By thy days of sore dis - tress In the sav - age wil - der - ness,
By the cross, the nail, the thorn, Pierc-ing spear and taunt and scorn;
By the vault, whose dark a - bode Held in vain the ris - ing God;

O by all thy pains and woe Suf-fer'd once for us be - low,
By the dread mys - te - rious hour Of the in-sult - ing temp-ter's pow'r;
By the gloom that veiled the skies O'er the dread-ful sac - ri - fice;
O from earth to heav'n re - stored, Might-y, re - as - cend - ed Lord,

Bend-ing from thy throne on high, Hear our sol - emn lit - a - ny!
Turn, O turn, a fa - v'ring eye, Hear our sol - emn lit - a - ny!
Lis - ten to our hum - ble cry, Hear our sol - emn lit - a - ny!
Lis - ten, lis - ten to the cry Of our sol - emn lit - a - ny!

Text: Robert Grant, 1779–1838
Music: Ancient Spanish; acc. Benjamin Carr, 1768–1831

77 77 77 77
SPANISH CHANT

To Mock Your Reign, O Dearest Lord 261

1. To mock your reign, O dear-est Lord, They made a crown of thorns;
2. In mock ac - claim, O gra-cious Lord, They snatched a pur - ple cloak,
3. A scep-tered reed, O pa - tient Lord, They thrust in - to your hand,

Set you with taunts a - long that road From which no one re - turns.
Your pas-sion turned, for all they cared, In - to a sol-dier's joke.
And act - ed out their grim cha-rade To its ap-point-ed end,

They did not know, as we do now, That glo - rious is your crown;
They did not know, as we do now, That though we mer - it blame
They did not know, as we do now, Though em - pires rise and fall,

That thorns would flow'r up-on your brow, Your sor - rows heal our own.
You will your robe of mer - cy throw A - round our na - ked shame.
Your King - dom shall not cease to grow Till love em - bra-ces all.

Alt. Tune: Saint Joseph Was A Quiet Man, no. 342

Text: Fred Pratt Green, b. 1903, alt.   86 86 86 86
Music: Thomas Tallis, 1505?–1585; arr. John Wilson, b. 1905   THIRD MODE MELODY

Text © 1973, Music arrangement © 1985, Hope Publishing Co.

262 Were You There?

1. Were you there when they cru-ci-fied my Lord?____ Were you
2. Were you there when they nailed him to the tree?____ Were you
3. Were you there when they laid him in the tomb?____ Were you
4. Were you there when he rose up from the grave?____ Were you

there when they cru-ci-fied my Lord?
there when they nailed him to the tree?
there when they laid him in the tomb?
there when he rose up from the grave?

O!____

Some-times it caus-es me to trem-ble, trem-ble, trem-ble.____

Were you there when they cru-ci-fied my Lord?____
Were you there when they nailed him to the tree?____
Were you there when they laid him in the tomb?____
Were you there when he rose up from the grave?____

Text: Afro–American Spiritual
Music: Afro–American Spiritual

Irregular
WERE YOU THERE

When I Survey the Wondrous Cross 263

1. When I sur - vey the won-drous cross On which the
2. For - bid it, Lord, that I should boast Save in the
3. See, from his head, his hands, his feet, Sor - row and
4. His dy - ing crim - son, like a robe Spreads o'er his

Prince of glo - ry died, My rich - est gain I
death of Christ, my God; All the vain things that
love flow min - gled down; Did e'er such love and
bod - y on the tree; Then am I dead to

count but loss, And pour con-tempt on all my pride.
charm me most, I sac - ri - fice them to his blood.
sor - row meet, Or thorns com-pose so rich a crown?
all the globe, And all the globe is dead to me.

5. Were the whole realm of nature mine,
That were a present far too small:
Love so amazing, so divine,
Demands my soul, my life, my all.

Text: Isaac Watts, 1674–1748
Music: Edward Miller, 1731–1807, adapt.; arr. Samuel Webb, 1740–1816

88 88
ROCKINGHAM

264 The Night Has Come

1. The night has come, the wind is still, A lone - ly
2. His friends are wear - y from the day, They do not
3. The ol - ive trees are old and gray, They cast their
4. O Chris - tians, at your fi - nal breath, Know there is

man climbs up the hill; He comes to pray be - neath the
have a word to say. He stands a - lone to face his
shad - ows on his way. "O Fa - ther, take this cup from
One who con - quered death; But first he drank the cup of

trees, His com - ing ag - o - ny and death he
fear; No kind - ly word, no strong sup - port is
me, Yet not my will, but rath - er yours must
pain, To lead the way - ward gent - ly home a -

sees; He comes to pray be - neath the trees; His com - ing
near. He stands a - lone to face his fear; No kind - ly
be!" "O Fa - ther, take this cup from me, Yet not my
gain; But first he drank the cup of pain, To lead the

ag - o - ny and death he sees.
word, no strong sup - port is near.
will, but rath - er yours must be!"
way - ward gent - ly home a - gain.

Text: Willard F. Jabusch, b. 1930, ©
Music: German Folk Melody; acc. S. R. Rudcki, b. 1928, ©

This Is the Feast of Victory 265

REFRAIN

This is the feast of vic-to-ry for our God.

Al - le - lu - ia, al - le - lu - ia, al - le - lu - ia!

VERSES

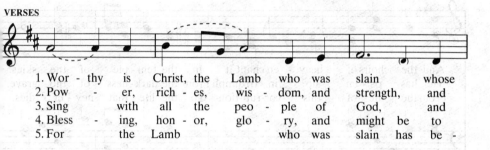

1. Wor - thy is Christ, the Lamb who was slain whose
2. Pow - er, rich - es, wis - dom, and strength, and
3. Sing with all the peo - ple of God, and
4. Bless - ing, hon - or, glo - ry, and might be to
5. For the Lamb who was slain has be -

To Refrain

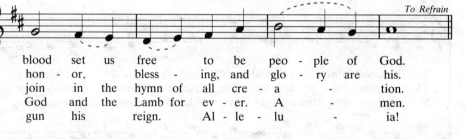

blood set us free to be peo - ple of God.
hon - or, bless - ing, and glo - ry are his.
join in the hymn of all cre - a - tion.
God and the Lamb for ev - er. A - men.
gun his reign. Al - le - lu - ia!

FINAL REFRAIN

This is the feast of vic-to-ry for our God.

Al - le - lu - ia, al - le - lu - ia, al - le - lu - ia!

Text: Revelations 5; adapted John W. Arthur, 1922–1980, ©
Music: Richard Hillert, © *1975, 1988*

FESTIVAL CANTICLE
Irregular with Refrain

266 Alleluia, Let the Holy Anthem Rise

1. Al - le - lu - ia, al - le - lu - ia, Let the ho - ly an - them rise!
2. Al - le - lu - ia, al - le - lu - ia, Like the sun from out the wave,
3. Al - le - lu - ia, al - le - lu - ia, Bless-ed Je - sus, make us rise

And the choirs of heav - en chant it In the tem - ple of the skies.
He has ris - en up in tri-umph From the dark-ness of the grave.
From the life of this cor-rup-tion To the life that nev - er dies.

Let the moun-tains skip with glad - ness And the joy - ful val-leys ring,
He, the splen - dor of the na - tions, He, the lamp of end-less day,
May we share with thee thy glo - ry When the days of time are past,

With ho - san - nas in the high - est To our Sav - ior and our King:
It is he, the Lord of glo - ry, Who is ris - en up to - day.
And the dead shall be a - wak-ened By the trum-pet's might - y blast.

Text: Edward Caswall, 1841–1878
Music: Richard R. Terry, 1865–1938, ©

87 87 87 8
ECCLESI

With ho - san - nas in the high - est To our Sav - ior and our King.
It is he, the Lord of glo - ry, Who is ris - en up to - day.
And the dead shall be a - wak-ened By the trum-pet's might-y blast.

Regina Caeli 267

Re - gí - na cae - li Lae - tá - re, al - le - lú - ia: Qui - a quem me - ru -

í - sti por - tá - re, al - le - lú - ia. Re - sur - ré - xit, sic -

ut di - xit, al - le - lú - ia. O - ra pro no - bis De - um, al - le - lú - ia.

Text: Anonymous, 14th. c.
Music: Plainchant, Mode VI; acc. Rev. Bartholomew Sayles, O.S.B., b. 1918;
Sr. Cecile Gertken, O.S.B., b. 1902, ©

268 At the Lamb's High Feast

1. At the Lamb's high feast we sing Praise to our vic-to-rious King.
2. Where the Pas-chal blood is poured, Death's dark an-gel sheathes his sword;
3. Might-y vic-tim from the sky, Pow'rs of hell be-neath you lie;
4. Eas-ter tri-umph, Eas-ter joy, Sin a-lone can these des-troy;

He has washed us in the tide Flow-ing from his o-pened side.
Is-rael's hosts tri-um-phant go Through the wave that drowns the foe.
Death is bro-ken in the fight, You have brought us life and light.
From sin's death now set us free: Souls re-born, O Lord, we'll be.

Praise we him, whose love di-vine Gives his sac-red blood for wine,
Christ the Lamb, whose blood was shed, Pas-chal vic-tim, Pas-chal bread!
Vic-t'ry's ban-ner you now wave, Con-qu'ring Sa-tan and the grave;
Hymns of glo-ry, songs of praise, Fa-ther, un-to you we raise;

Gives his bod-y for the feast, Christ the vic-tim, Christ the priest.
With sin-cer-i-ty and love Eat we man-na from a-bove.
You have o-pened par-a-dise, And in you all saints shall rise.
And to you, our ris-en King, With the Spir-it, praise we sing.

Lower Key: Songs of Thankfulness and Praise, no. 231

Text: Ad regias Agni dapes; tr. Robert Campbell, 1814–1868, alt.
Music: Jacob Hintze, 1622–1702; harm. J. S. Bach, 1685–1750

77 77 77 77
SALZBURG

Christ Is Alive 269

1. Christ is a - live! Let Chris - tians sing. His cross stands
2. Christ is a - live! No long - er bound To dis - tant
3. Not throned a - bove, re - mote - ly high, Un - touched, un -
4. In ev - 'ry in - sult, rift, and war Where co - lor,

emp - ty to the sky. Let streets and homes with
years in Pal - es - tine, He comes to claim the
moved by hu - man pains, But dai - ly, in the
scorn or wealth di - vide, He suf - fers still, yet

prais - es ring. His love in death shall nev - er die.
here and now And con - quer ev - 'ry place and time.
midst of life, Our Sa - vior with the Fa - ther reigns.
loves the more, And lives, though ev - er cru - ci - fied.

5. Christ is alive! His Spirit burns
Through this and ev'ry future age,
Till all creation lives and learns
His joy, his justice, love, and praise.

Text: Brian A. Wren, b. 1936, rev.
Music: Psalmodia Evangelica, Part II, 1789; harm. Lowell Mason, 1792–1872, alt.

Text © 1975 by Hope Publishing Co.

88 88
TRURO

270 Christians Praise the Paschal Victim /
Victimae Paschali Laudes

1. Chris-tians praise the Pas-chal Vic-tim! Of - fer thank-ful sac - ri - fice!
1. *Ví - cti - mae Pa-schá - li lau-des im-mó-lent Chri-sti - á - ni.*

2. Christ the Lamb has saved the sheep. Christ the Just One paid the price,
2. *A - gnus re - dé - mit o - ves: Chri-stus ín - no - cens Pa - tri*

Re-con-cil-ing sin-ners to the Fa-ther. 3. Death and life fought bit-ter - ly,
re-con-ci - li - á - vit pec-ca-tó - res. 3. *Mors et vi - ta du - él - lo*

For this won-drous vic - to - ry. The Lord of life who died reigns glo - ri -fied!
con - fli - xé - re mi - rán-do: dux vi - tae mór-tu - us re - gnat vi - vus.

4. O Mar - y come and say, What you saw at break of day.
4. *Dic no - bis Ma - rí - a quid vi - dí - sti in vi - a?*

5. "The emp - ty tomb of my liv-ing Lord! I saw Christ Je-sus ris-en and a - dored!
5. *Se - púl-chrum Chri-sti vi - vén - tis, et gló - ri - am vi-di re-sur-gén - tis.*

6. Bright an - gels tes - ti - fied, Shroud and grave clothes side by side!
6. *An - gé - li - cos te - stes, su - dá - ri - um, et ve - stes.*

7. Yes, Christ my hope rose glo-ri-ous-ly. He goes be-fore you in-to Ga - li-lee."
7. *Sur - ré - xit Chri-stus spes me - a: Prae-cé-det su - os in Ga-li-láe - am.*

Text: Wipo of Burgundy, c. 1048, attr.; tr. Peter J. Scagnelli, b. 1949, ©
Music: Plainchant, Tone I; acc., Theodore Marier, alt., adapt. by Edward J. McKenna, ©

8. Share the good news, sing joy-ful-ly: His death is vic-to-ry! Lord Je-sus Vic-
8. *Sci - mus Chri-stum sur - re - xís - se* *a mor-tu - is ve - re:* *tu no - bis vi -*

tor King, Show us mer - cy. A - men. Al - le - lu - ia.
ctor Rex, mi - se - ré - re. A - men. *Al - le - lú - ia.*

271 Good Christians All, Rejoice and Sing!

1. Good Christians all, rejoice and sing! Now is the tri-umph of our King! To all the world glad news we bring:
2. The Lord of life is ris'n to-day! Sing songs of praise a-long his way; Let all the earth re-joice and say:
3. Praise we in songs of vic-to-ry That love, that life which can-not die, And sing with hearts up-lift-ed high:
4. Your Name we bless, O ris-en Lord, And sing to-day with one ac-cord The life laid down, the life re-stored:

Alleluia, alleluia, alleluia!

Al-le-lu-ia, al-le-lu-ia, al-le-lu-ia!

Al-le - lu-ia, al-le - lu-ia, al-le-lu-ia!

Al-le-lu-ia, al-le-lu-ia, al-le-lu-ia!

Text: Cyril A. Arlington, 1872–1955, alt., ©
Music: Melchior Vulpius, 1560?–1616

888 with Alleluias
GELOBT SEI GOTT

Let Hymns of Grief to Joy Succeed 272

1. Let hymns of grief to joy suc-ceed. We know that Christ is ris'n in-deed.
2. The morn has spread her crim-son rays, When rang the skies with shouts of praise:
3. The days of mourn-ing now are past, The pains of death are loosed at last;
4. To God the Fa - ther let us sing; To God the Son, our ris - en King:

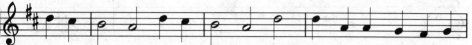

Al - le - lu - ia, Al - le - lu - ia!

We hear his white-robed an - gel's
Earth joined the joy - ful hymn to
An an - gel robed in light has
And e - qual-ly let us a -

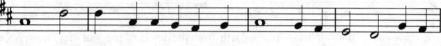

voice, And in our ris - en Lord re - joice.
swell, That brought des-pair to van-quished hell.
said: "The Lord is ris - en from the dead."
dore, The Ho - ly Spir-it ev - er - more.

Al - le - lu - ia, Al - le -

lu - ia, Al - le - lu - ia, Al - le - lu - ia, Al - le - lu - ia!

Alt. Tune: All Creatures of Our God and King, no. 555

Text: Aurora caelum purpurat; tr. R. Campbell, 1868, alt.
Music: Geistliche Kirchengesange, Cologne, 1623; harm. Ralph Vaughan Williams, 1872–1958, ©

88 44 88 with Alleluias
LASST UNS ERFREUEN

Alternate text for the Ascension

Sing We Triumphant Hymns of Praise 273

1. Sing we triumphant hymns of praise
To greet our Lord these festive days,
Alleluia, Alleluia;
Who by a road before untrod
Ascended to the throne of God,
Alleluia, Alleluia,
Alleluia, Alleluia, Alleluia!

2. In wond'ring awe his faithful band
Upon the Mount of Olives stand.
Alleluia, Alleluia!
And with the Virgin Mother see
Their Lord ascend in majesty.
Alleluia, Alleluia,
Alleluia, Alleluia, Alleluia!

3. O risen Christ, ascended Lord,
All praise to you let earth accord,
Alleluia, Alleluia!
Who are, while endless ages run,
With Father and with Spirit One.
Alleluia, Alleluia,
Alleluia, Alleluia, Alleluia.

4. To God the Father let us sing,
To God the Son, our risen King,
Alleluia, Alleluia!
And equally let us adore,
The Holy Spirit evermore,
Alleluia, Alleluia,
Alleluia, Alleluia, Alleluia.

Text: The Venerable Bede, c. 673–735; tr. John David Chambers, 1805–1893,
vv. 1, 2, & 4; Benjamin Webb, 1819–1885, v. 3

274 Hail Thee, Festival Day!

REFRAIN

(Easter) Hail thee, fes - ti - val day! Blest day to be hal-lowed for - ev - er;
(Ascension) Hail thee, fes - ti - val day! Blest day to be hal-lowed for - ev - er;
(Pentecost) Hail thee, fes - ti - val day! Blest day to be hal-lowed for - ev - er;

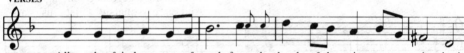

Day when our Lord was raised, break-ing the king - dom of death. death.
Day when our ris - en Lord rose in the heav - ens to reign. reign.
Day when the Ho - ly Ghost shone in the world with God's grace. grace.

VERSES

(Easter) All the fair beau-ty of earth from the death of the win - ter a - ris - ing!
(Ascension) He who was nailed to the cross is rul - er and Lord of all peo - ple.
(Pentecost) Bright and in like-ness of fire, on those who a - wait his ap-pear-ing,
3. God the Al-might-y, the Lord, the rul - er of earth and the heav-ens
5. Spir - it of life and of pow'r now flow in us, fount of our be - ing,

Repeat Refrain once after each stanza

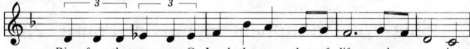

Ev - 'ry good gift of the year now with its mas-ter re - turns:
All things cre - at - ed on earth sing to the glo-ry of God:
He whom the Lord had fore-told sud - den-ly, swift-ly de-scends:
Guard us from harm with - out; cleanse us from e - vil with - in:
Light that en - light-ens us all, life that in all may a - bide:

(Easter) Rise from the grave now, O Lord, the au - thor of life and cre - a - tion.
(Ascension) Dai - ly the love - li - ness grows, a-dorned with the glo - ry of blos-som;
(Pentecost) Forth from the Fa - ther he comes with sev - en-fold mys - ti - cal of-f'ring,
4. Je - sus, the health of the world, en-light - en our minds, great Re-deem-er,
6. Praise to the giv - er of good! O Lov - er and Au - thor of con-cord,

Repeat Refrain once after each stanza

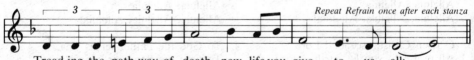

Tread-ing the path-way of death, new life you give to us all:
Heav - en her gates un-bars, fling - ing her in - crease of light:
Pour-ing on all hu-man souls in - fi-nite rich - es of God:
Son of the Fa - ther su - preme, on - ly-be-got - ten of God:
Pour out your balm on our days; or - der our ways in your peace:

Text: Venantius Fortunatus, c. 530–609; tr. English Hymnal 1906, alt. ©
Music: Ralph Vaughan Williams, 1872–1958, ©

Irregular
SALVE, FESTA DIES

Christ Jesus Lay in Death's Strong Bands 275

1. Christ Je-sus lay in death's strong bands For our of-fens-es giv-en;
2. It was a strange and dread-ful strife When life and death con-tend-ed;
3. So let us keep the fes-ti-val To which the Lord in-vites us;
4. Then let us feast this ho-ly day On the true bread of heav-en;

But now at God's right hand he stands And brings us life from heav-en;
The vic-to-ry re-mained with life, The reign of death was end-ed;
Christ is him-self the joy of all, The sun that warms and lights us;
The word of grace hath purged a-way The old and wick-ed leav-en;

There-fore let us joy-ful be, And sing to God right thank-ful-ly
Stripped of pow'r, no more he reigns, An emp-ty form a-lone re-mains;
By his grace he doth im-part E-ter-nal sun-shine to the heart;
Christ a-lone our souls will feed, He is our meat and drink in-deed;

Loud songs of al-le-lu - ia! Al-le-lu-ia!
His sting is lost for ev - er! Al-le-lu-ia!
The night of sin is end - ed! Al-le-lu-ia!
Faith lives up-on no o - ther! Al-le-lu-ia!

Text: Martin Luther, 1483–1546; tr. Richard Massie, 1800–1887, alt.

Music: Geystliche gesangk Buckleyn, 1524; harm. Hans Leo Hassler, 1564–1612, alt., ©

87 87 78 74

CHRIST LAG IN TODESBANDEN

276 The Strife Is O'er, the Battle Done

REFRAIN

Al - le - lu - ia! Al - le - lu - ia! Al - le - lu - ia!

VERSES

1. The strife is o'er, the bat - tle done. The vic - to -
2. The pow'rs of death have done their worst, But Christ their
3. On the third morn he rose a - gain Glo - rious in
4. He closed the yawn - ing gates of hell, The bars from

ry of life is won; The song of tri - umph
le - gions has dis - persed: Let shouts of praise and
maj - es - ty to reign; O let us swell the
heav'n's high por - tals fell; Let hymns of praise his

Repeat Refrain

has be - gun: Al - le - lu - ia!
joy out - burst:
joy - ful strain:
tri - umphs tell:

Text: Anon.; tr. Francis Pott, 1832–1909, alt.
Music: Giovanni Pierluigi da Palestrina, c. 1525–1594; adapt. with alleluias William Henry Monk, 1823–1889

888 with Alleluia
VICTORY

5. Lord, by your death on Calvary,
From death's dread sting your people free,
That we may live eternally: Alleluia!
Refrain

Awake, Arise, Lift Up Your Voice 277

1. A - wake, a - rise, lift up your voice, Let
2. Oh, with what glad - ness and sur - prise The
3. Those hands of lib - eral love in - deed In
4. His en - e - mies had sealed the stone As

Eas - ter mu - sic swell; Re - joice in Christ, a -
saints their Sa - vior greet; Nor will they trust their
in - fi - nite de - gree, Those feet still free to
Pi - late gave them leave, Lest dead and friend - less

gain re - joice And on his prais - es dwell.
ears and eyes But by his hands and feet,
move and bleed For mil - lions and for me.
and a - lone He should their skill de - ceive.

5. O Dead arise! O Friendless stand
By seraphim adored!
O Solitude again command
Your host from heav'n restored!

Text: Christopher Smart, 1722–1771, alt.
Music: Thomas Haweis, 1734–1820; adapt. and arr. Samuel Webbe, 1740–1816

86 86
RICHMOND

278 The Day of Resurrection

1. The day of res-ur-rec-tion! Earth, spread the news a-broad;
2. Our hearts be free from e-vil That we may see a-right
3. His love is ev-er-last-ing; His mer-cies nev-er cease;
4. Now let the heav'ns be joy-ful, And earth her song be-gin;

The Pas-chal feast of glad-ness, The Pas-chal feast of God.
The Sav-ior res-ur-rect-ed In his e-ter-nal light,
The res-ur-rect-ed Sav-ior, Will all our joys in-crease.
The whole world keep high tri-umph And all that is there-in;

From death to life e-ter-nal, From earth to heav-en's height
And hear his mes-sage plain-ly, De-liv-ered calm and clear:
He'll keep us in his fa-vor, Sup-ply-ing ho-ly grace,
Let all things in cre-a-tion Their notes of glad-ness blend,

Our Sav-ior Christ has brought us, The glo-rious Lord of Light.
"Re-joice with me in tri-umph, Be glad and do not fear."
To all his pil-grim peo-ple Who seek his heav'n-ly place,
For Christ the Lord has ris-en, Our joy that has no end.

Text: St. John of Damascus, c. 696–c. 754; tr. John Mason Neale, 1818–1866, alt. vv. 1, 2, 4; John Dunn, v. 3, ©
Music: Würtemburg Gesangbuch, 1784

76 76 76 76
ELLACOMBE

Come, You Faithful, Raise the Strain 279

1. Come, you faith - ful, raise the strain Of tri - um - phant glad - ness;
2. Now the spring of souls has come; Christ has burst his pris - on,
3. Now the bright-ness of the spring With the day of splen - dor,
4. Nei - ther might the gates of death, Nor the tomb's dark por - tal,

God has brought his Is - ra - el In - to joy from sad - ness;
And from three days' sleep in death As a sun has ris - en;
With the roy - al feast of feasts, Comes its joy to ren - der.
Nor the watch - ers, nor the seal Hold you as a mor - tal;

Loosed from Pha-roah's bit - ter yoke Ja - cob's sons and daugh - ters
All the win - ter of our sins, Long and dark is fly - ing
Comes to glad Je - ru - sa - lem, And with true af - fec - tion
But to - day a - mong the twelve You ap-peared be - stow - ing

Led them with un - mois-tened foot Through the Red Sea wa - ters.
From his light, to whom we sing Songs of praise un - dy - ing.
Wel-comes in un - wea - ried strains Je - sus' res - ur - rec - tion.
Bless-ed peace which ev - er - more Pass - es hu - man know - ing.

Text: St. John of Damascus, 8th c.; tr. John Mason Neale, 1818–1866, alt.
Music: Johann Horn, c. 1495–1547

76 76 76 76
GAUDEAMUS PARITER

280 Alleluia! Alleluia! Let the Holy Anthem Ris

1. Al - le - lu - ia Al - le - lu - ia Let the ho - ly an-them rise,
2. Al - le - lu - ia Al - le - lu - ia Like the sun from out the wave,
3. Al - le - lu - ia Al - le - lu - ia Bless-ed Je - sus make us rise,
4. Al - le - lu - ia Al - le - lu - ia Sing-ers sing, mu - si - cians play!

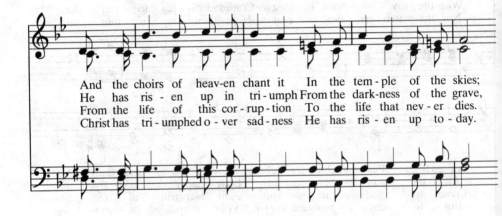

And the choirs of heav-en chant it In the tem - ple of the skies;
He has ris - en up in tri - umph From the dark-ness of the grave,
From the life of this cor - rup - tion To the life that nev - er dies.
Christ has tri - umphed o - ver sad-ness He has ris - en up to - day.

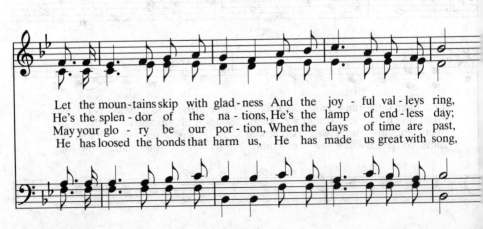

Let the moun-tains skip with glad-ness And the joy - ful val - leys ring,
He's the splen - dor of the na - tions, He's the lamp of end - less day;
May your glo - ry be our por - tion, When the days of time are past,
He has loosed the bonds that harm us, He has made us great with song,

Text: Edward Caswall, 1841–1878, vv. 1–3; Edward J. McKenna, b. 1939, v. 4, ©
Music: Traditional Melody

87 87 87 8
HOLY ANTHEM

With Ho - san - nas in the high - est To our Sav - ior and our King.
He's the ver - y Lord of glo - ry Who is ris - en up to - day.
And the dead shall be a - wak - ened By the trum - pet's might-y blast.
As he walks a - mong his peo - ple Ho - ly peo - ple, hap-py throng.

281 The Paschal Hymn

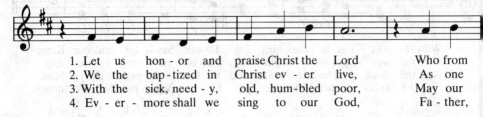

1. Let us hon-or and praise Christ the Lord   Who from
2. We the bap-tized in Christ ev-er live,   As one
3. With the sick, need-y, old, hum-bled poor,   May our
4. Ev-er-more shall we sing to our God,   Fa-ther,

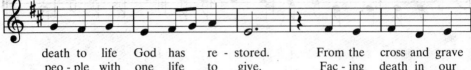

death to life God has re-stored.   From the cross and grave
peo-ple with one life to give.   Fac-ing death in our
works of love and care en-dure.   What we weak-ly per-
Son, and Ho-ly Spir-it, one!   Ev-'ry per-son on

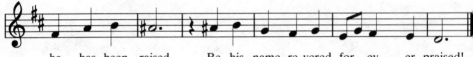

he has been raised.   Be his name re-vered, for-ev-er praised!
ser-vice to life,   We rise freed from sin, re-deemed from strife.
form in Christ's name,   He re-makes in peace as strong and pure.
earth, sound the cry: "Till the end of time, Thy will be done!"

Text: Edward J. McKenna, b. 1939, ©
Music: C. Saint-Saens; adapt. and arr. Edward J. McKenna, b. 1939, ©   NER▮

282 These Things Did Thomas Count as Real

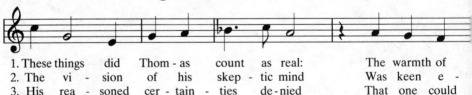

1. These things did Thom-as count as real: The warmth of
2. The vi-sion of his skep-tic mind   Was keen e-
3. His rea-soned cer-tain-ties de-nied   That one could
4. May we, O God, by grace be-lieve   And thus the

blood, the chill of steel,   The grain of wood, the
nough to make him blind   To an-y un-ex-
live when one had died,   Un-til his fin-gers
ris-en Christ re-ceive,   Whose raw im-print-ed

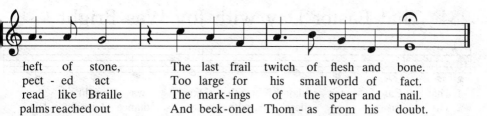

heft of stone,	The last frail	twitch of flesh and	bone.
pect - ed act	Too large for	his small world of	fact.
read like Braille	The mark-ings	of the spear and	nail.
palms reached out	And beck-oned	Thom - as from his	doubt.

Text: Thomas H. Troeger, b. 1945; John 20: 19–31, ©
Music: Carol Doran, b. 1936, ©

88 88
MERLE MARIE

We Know that Christ Is Raised 283
And Dies No More

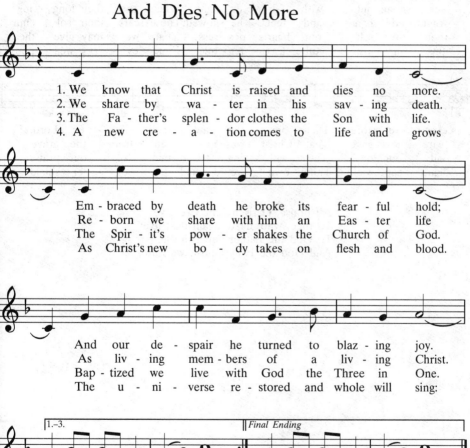

1. We know that Christ is raised and dies no more.
2. We share by wa - ter in his sav - ing death.
3. The Fa - ther's splen - dor clothes the Son with life.
4. A new cre - a - tion comes to life and grows

Em - braced by death he broke its fear - ful hold;
Re - born we share with him an Eas - ter life
The Spir - it's pow - er shakes the Church of God.
As Christ's new bo - dy takes on flesh and blood.

And our de - spair he turned to blaz - ing joy.
As liv - ing mem - bers of a liv - ing Christ.
Bap - tized we live with God the Three in One.
The u - ni - verse re - stored and whole will sing:

1.–3. ‖ *Final Ending*

Al - le - lu - ia! Al - le - lu - ia!

Text: John Brownlow Geyer, b. 1932, alt., ©
Music: Charles Villiers Stanford, 1852–1924

10 10 10 with Alleluia
ENGELBERG

284 That Easter Day with Joy Was Bright

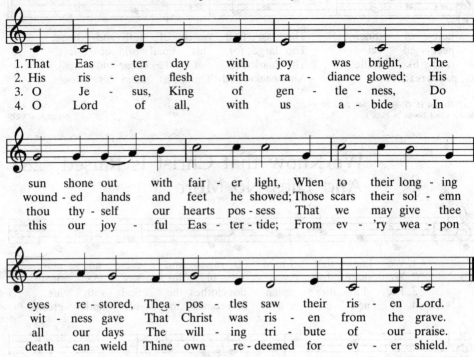

1. That Eas - ter day with joy was bright, The
2. His ris - en flesh with ra - diance glowed; His
3. O Je - sus, King of gen - tle - ness, Do
4. O Lord of all, with us a - bide In

sun shone out with fair - er light, When to their long - ing
wound - ed hands and feet he showed; Those scars their sol - emn
thou thy - self our hearts pos - sess That we may give thee
this our joy - ful Eas - ter - tide; From ev - 'ry wea - pon

eyes re - stored, The a - pos - tles saw their ris - en Lord.
wit - ness gave That Christ was ris - en from the grave.
all our days The will - ing tri - bute of our praise.
death can wield Thine own re - deemed for ev - er shield.

5. All praise, O risen Lord, we give
   To thee, who, dead, again dost live;
   To God the Father equal praise,
   And God the Holy Ghost, we raise.

Text: Latin, 5th C.; tr. John M. Neale, 1818–1866, alt.
Music: Michael Praetorius, 1571–1621, adapt.; harm. Hymns Ancient & Modern, Revised, 1950, ©

88 88
PUER NOBIS

He Is Risen, He Is Risen 285

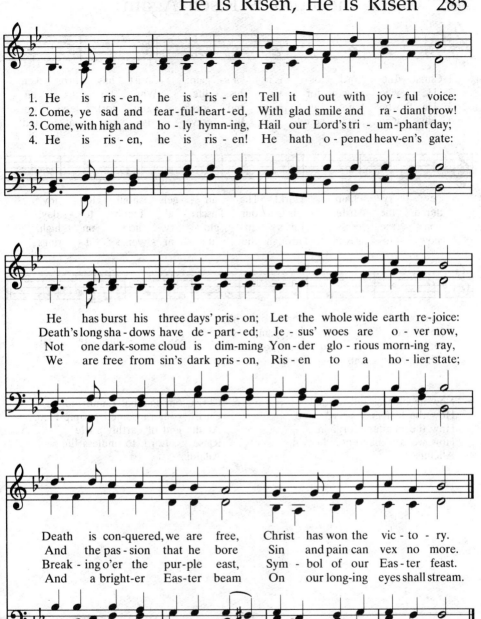

1. He is ris - en, he is ris - en! Tell it out with joy - ful voice:
2. Come, ye sad and fear - ful - heart - ed, With glad smile and ra - diant brow!
3. Come, with high and ho - ly hymn - ing, Hail our Lord's tri - um - phant day;
4. He is ris - en, he is ris - en! He hath o - pened heav - en's gate:

He has burst his three days' pris - on; Let the whole wide earth re - joice:
Death's long sha - dows have de - part - ed; Je - sus' woes are o - ver now,
Not one dark - some cloud is dim - ming Yon - der glo - rious morn - ing ray,
We are free from sin's dark pris - on, Ris - en to a ho - lier state;

Death is con - quered, we are free, Christ has won the vic - to - ry.
And the pas - sion that he bore Sin and pain can vex no more.
Break - ing o'er the pur - ple east, Sym - bol of our Eas - ter feast.
And a bright - er Eas - ter beam On our long - ing eyes shall stream.

Alt. Arr.: Open Now thy Gates of Beauty, no. 496

Text: Cecil Frances Alexander, 1818–1895, alt.
Music: Joachim Neander, 1650–1680

87 87 77
UNSER HERRSCHER

286 Christ the Lord Is Risen Again

1. Christ the Lord is ris'n a - gain; Christ has bro - ken
2. He who gave for us his life, Who for us en -
3. He who bore all pain and loss Com - fort - less up -
4. He who slum - bered in the grave Is ex - al - ted

ev - 'ry chain; Hark! The an - gels shout for joy,
dured the strife, Is our Pasch - al Lamb to - day;
on the cross, Lives in glo - ry now on high,
now to save; Through the u - ni - verse it rings

Sing - ing ev - er - more on high:
We too sing for joy, and say: Al - le - lu - ia!
Pleads for us, and hears our cry:
That the Lamb is King of kings:

5. Now he bids us tell abroad
   How the lost may be restored,
   How the penitent forgiv'n,
   How we too may enter heav'n:
   Alleluia!

6. Christ, our Paschal Lamb indeed,
   Christ, your ransomed people feed.
   At the end of earthly strife
   Raise us, Lord, to endless life.
   Alleluia!

Text: Michael Weisse, 1480–1534; tr. Catherine Winkworth, 1827–1878, alt.
Music: Medieval French Traditional Melody; harm. Ralph Vaughan Williams, 1872–1958, ©

77 77 with Alleluias
ORIENTIS PARTIBUS

Jesus Lives! Thy Terrors Now 287

1. Je - sus lives! thy ter - rors now Can no long - er,
2. Je - sus lives! for us he died; Then, a - lone to
3. Je - sus lives! our hearts know well Nought from us his
4. Je - sus lives! to him the throne O - ver all the

death, ap - pall us; Je - sus lives! by this we know
Je - sus liv - ing, Pure in heart may we a - bide,
love shall sev - er; Life, nor death, nor pow'rs of hell
world is giv - en: May we go where he has gone,

Thou, O grave, canst not en - thrall us. Al - le - lu - ia!
Glo - ry to our Sa - vior giv - ing, Al - le - lu - ia!
Tear us from his keep - ing ev - er. Al - le - lu - ia!
Rest and reign with him in hea - ven. Al - le - lu - ia!

Text: Christian Furchtegott Gellert, 1715–1769; tr. Frances Elizabeth Cox, 1812–1897, alt.
Music: Cyril Vincent Taylor, b. 1907

78 78 with Alleluia
MOWSLEY

Music © 1985, Hope Publishing Co.

288 Jesus Christ Is Ris'n Today

1. Je - sus Christ is ris'n to - day, Al - le - lu - ia!
2. Hymns of praise then let us sing, Al - le - lu - ia!
3. But the pains which he en - dured, Al - le - lu - ia!
4. Sing we to our God a - bove, Al - le - lu - ia!

Our tri - um - phant ho - ly day, Al - le - lu - ia!
Un - to Christ, our heav'n - ly King, Al - le - lu - ia!
Our sal - va - tion have pro - cured; Al - le - lu - ia!
Praise e - ter - nal as his love; Al - le - lu - ia!

Who did once up - on the cross, Al - le - lu - ia!
Who en - dured the cross and grave, Al - le - lu - ia!
Now ex - alt - ed he is king, Al - le - lu - ia!
Praise him, all you heav'n - ly host, Al - le - lu - ia!

Suf - fer to re - deem our loss. Al - le - lu - ia!
Sin - ners to re - deem and save. Al - le - lu - ia!
Where the an - gels ev - er sing. Al - le - lu - ia!
Fa - ther, Son and Ho - ly Ghost. Al - le - lu - ia!

Text: Latin carol, 14th cent. vv1–3; Charles Wesley, 1707–1788, v. 4
Music: Lyra Davidica, 1708

77 77 with Alleluias
EASTER HYMN

Christ the Lord Is Risen Today 289

1. Christ the Lord is ris'n to-day; Chris-tians, haste your vows to pay;
2. Christ, the vic-tim un-de-filed, God and sin-ners rec-on-ciled;
3. Say, O wond'ring Mar-y, say What you saw a-long the way.
4. Christ, who once for sin-ners bled, Now the first-born from the dead,

Of-fer now your prais-es meet At the Pas-chal Vic-tim's feet;
When in strange and aw-ful strife Met to-geth-er death and life;
"I be-held, where Christ had lain, Emp-ty tomb and an-gels twain;
Throned in end-less might and pow'r, Lives and reigns for ev-er-more.

For the sheep the Lamb has bled, Sin-less in the sin-ner's stead.
Chris-tians, on this hap-py day Haste with joy your vows to pay.
I be-held the glo-ry bright Of the ris-ing Lord of light.
Hail, e-ter-nal hope on high! Hail, our King of vic-to-ry!

Christ the Lord is ris'n on high; Now he lives, no more to die.
Christ the Lord is ris'n on high; Now he lives, no more to die.
Christ my hope is ris'n a-gain; Now he lives, and lives to reign."
Hail, our Prince of life a-dored! Help and save us, gra-cious Lord!

Text: Wipo of Burgundy, c. 10th century, attr.; tr. Jane Elizabeth Leeson, 1809–1881
Music: Wurth's Katholisches Gesangbuch, 1859

77 77 77 77
VICTIMAE PASCHALI

290 O Sons and Daughters

REFRAIN

Al - le - lu - ia, al - le - lu - ia, al - le - lu - ia.

VERSES

1. O sons and daugh - ters, let us sing! The King of heav'n, the
2. That Eas - ter morn, at break of day, The faith - ful wom - en
3. An an - gel clad in white they see, Who sat and spoke un -
4. That night th'a - pos - tles met in fear; A - mong them came their

Repeat Refrain

glo - rious King, O'er death to - day rose tri - umph - ing. Al-le-lu-ia!
went their way To seek the tomb where Je - sus lay. Al-le-lu-ia!
to the three, "Your Lord has gone to Gal - i - lee." Al-le-lu-ia!
Lord most dear, And said, "My peace be with you here." Al-le-lu-ia!

5. When Thomas first the tidings heard,
   How they had seen the risen Lord,
   He doubted the disciples' word. Alleluia!
   Refrain

6. "My wounded side, O Thomas, see;
   Behold my hands, my feet," said he;
   "Not faithless, but believing be." Alleluia!
   Refrain

7. No longer Thomas then denied,
   He saw the feet, the hands, the side;
   "You are my Lord and God," he cried. Alleluia!
   Refrain

8. How blest are they who have not seen,
   And yet whose faith has constant been,
   For they eternal life shall win. Alleluia!
   Refrain

9. On this most holy day of days,
   To God your hearts and voices raise,
   In laud, and jubilee, and praise. Alleluia!
   Refrain

Text: Jean Tisserand, 16th c.; tr. John Mason Neale, 1818–1866
Music: Plainchant, Mode II; acc. Rev. Percy Jones

888 with Alleluias
O FILII ET FILIAE

Now the Green Blade Riseth 291

1. Now the green blade ris - eth from the bur - ied grain,
2. In the grave they laid him, love by ha - tred slain,
3. Forth he came at Eas - ter, like the ris - en grain,
4. When our hearts are win - try, griev - ing, or in pain,

Wheat that in dark earth man - y days has lain;
Think - ing that nev - er he would wake a - gain,
He that for three days in the grave had lain;
His touch can call us back to life a - gain,

Love lives a - gain, that with the dead has been;
Laid in the earth like grain that sleeps un - seen;
Raised from the dead, my liv - ing Lord is seen;
Fields of our hearts that dead and bare have been;

Love is come a - gain like wheat that spring-eth green.

Text: John M.C. Crum, 1872–1958, ©
Music: French Carol, arr. Martin Shaw, 1875–1958, ©

11 10 10 11
NOEL NOUVELET

292 Alleluia, Alleluia, Give Thanks To the Risen Lord

REFRAIN

Al - le - lu - ia, al - le - lu - ia, give thanks to the ris - en Lord. Al - le -

lu - ia, al - le - lu - ia, give praise to his name. name.

VERSES

1. Je - sus is Lord of all the earth,
2. Spread the good news o'er all the earth,
3. We have been cru - ci - fied with Christ.
4. God has pro - claimed the just re - ward,
5. Come let us praise the liv - ing God,

He is the King of cre - a - tion.
Je - sus has died and has ris - en.
Now we shall live for - ev - er. Al - le -
Life for all, al - le - lu - ia.
Joy - ful - ly sing to our Sav - ior.

Text: Donald Fishel, b. 1950
Music: Donald Fishel, b. 1950; harm. Betty Carr Pulkingham, b. 1929

8 8 with Refrain
ALLELUIA NO. 1

I Know that My Redeemer Lives! 293

1. I know that my Re - deem - er lives! What joy the
2. He lives tri - um - phant from the grave; He lives e -
3. He lives to grant me rich sup - ply; He lives to
4. He lives to si - lence all my fears; He lives to

blest as - sur - ance gives! He lives, he lives, who
ter - nal - ly to save; He lives in maj - es -
guide me with his eye; He lives to com - fort
wipe a - way my tears; He lives to calm my

once was dead; He lives, my ev - er - liv - ing head!
ty a - bove; He lives to guide his Church in love.
me when faint; He lives to hear my soul's com - plaint.
trou - bled heart; He lives all bless - ings to im - part.

5. He lives to bless me with his love;
   He lives to plead for me above;
   He lives my hungry soul to feed;
   He lives to help in time of need.

6. He lives, my kind, wise, heav'nly friend;
   He lives and loves me to the end;
   He lives, and while he lives, I'll sing;
   He lives, my Prophet, Priest, and King!

7. He lives and grants me daily breath;
   He lives, and I shall conquer death;
   He lives my mansion to prepare;
   He lives to bring me safely there.

8. He lives, all glory to his name!
   He lives, my Savior, still the same;
   What joy this blest assurance gives;
   I know that my Redeemer lives!

Higher Key: Jesus Shall Reign, no. 508
Text: Samuel Medley, 1738–1799
Music: John Hatton, c. 1710–1793, attr.

88 88
DUKE STREET

294 Let All the Earth

REFRAIN

Melody: Let all the earth cry out in joy to the Lord;

Tenor: Al le lu ia,

Alto: Cry out in joy un - to the Lord Al - le - lu - ia,

1.–3. (To Verses)

Let all the earth cry out in joy to the Lord!

Cry out in joy un - to the Lord!

FINAL ENDING

Lord! to the Lord!

Lord! to the Lord!

rit.

VERSES

1. Cry out in joy to the Lord, all peo-ples on earth,

2. Lead-ing his peo - ple safe through fire and wa - ter,

3. Hear-ken to me as I sing my love of the Lord, he

Text: Psalm 66; tr. Marty Haugen, b. 1952, ©
Music: Marty Haugen, b. 1952, ©

sing to the praise of his name, pro-claim him for -

bring-ing their souls to life, come sing of his

an - swers the prayer of my heart, he leads me in

(To Refrain)

ev - er, tre - men-dous his deeds for us. Oh

(To Refrain)

glo - ry, his love is e - ter - nal. Oh

(To Refrain)

safe - ty, from death un - to life. Oh

295 Hail the Day That Sees Him Rise

1. Hail the day that sees him rise, Al - le - lu - ia!
2. There for him high tri - umph waits; Al - le - lu - ia!
3. High - est heav'n its Lord re - ceives, Al - le - lu - ia!
4. See, he lifts his hands a - bove; Al - le - lu - ia!

To his throne a - bove the skies; Al - le - lu - ia!
Lift your heads, e - ter - nal gates; Al - le - lu - ia!
Yet he loves the earth he leaves: Al - le - lu - ia!
See, he shows the prints of love; Al - le - lu - ia!

Christ, a - while to mor - tals giv'n, Al - le - lu - ia!
He has con - quered death and sin; Al - le - lu - ia!
Though re - turn - ing to his throne, Al - le - lu - ia!
Hark, his gra - cious lips be - stow Al - le - lu - ia!

Re - as - cends his na - tive heav'n. Al - le - lu - ia!
Take the King of glo - ry in. Al - le - lu - ia!
Still he calls us all his own. Al - le - lu - ia!
Bless - ing on his Church be - low. Al - le - lu - ia!

Text: Charles Wesley, 1707–1788
Music: Robert Williams, 1781–1821; harm. John Roberts, 1822–1877

77 77 with Alleluias
LLANFAIR

Alternate text to Hymn no. 295.

Praise Him as He Mounts the Skies 296

1. Praise him as he mounts the skies, Alleluia!
   Christ, the Lord of Paradise! Alleluia!
   Cry hosanna in the height Alleluia!
   As he rises out of sight! Alleluia!

2. Now at last he takes his throne, Alleluia!
   From all ages his alone! Alleluia!
   With his praise creation rings: Alleluia!
   "Lord of lords and King of kings!" Alleluia!

3. Hands and feet and side reveal Alleluia!
   Wounds of love, high priesthood's seal! Alleluia!
   Advocate, for us he pleads; Alleluia!
   Heav'nly Priest, he intercedes! Alleluia!

4. Christians, raise your eyes above! Alleluia!
   He will come again in love, Alleluia!
   On that great and wondrous day Alleluia!
   When this world will pass away! Alleluia!

5. At his word new heav'ns and earth Alleluia!
   Will in glory spring to birth! Alleluia!
   Joy of angels, women, men, Alleluia!
   Come, Lord Jesus, come again! Alleluia!

Text: James Quinn, S.J., b. 1919, © 1969

77 77 with Alleluias
LLANFAIR

297 Come Creator Spirit

1. Come Cre - a - tor Spi - rit high - ly blest, And in our hearts
2. O Com - fort - er to you we cry, The heav - en - ly gift
3. Your sev - en gifts in us ap - pear, Fin - ger of God beck -
4. To ev - 'ry sense your light im - part, And shed your love

take up your rest; Come with your grace and
of God most high; The fount of life and
on - ing us near; You are the prom - ise
in ev - 'ry heart. To our weak flesh, your

heav'n - ly aid, To fill the hearts which you have made.
fire of love, And sweet a - noint - ing from a - bove.
of the Fa - ther, Who touch - es tongues with ho - ly word.
strength sup - ply: Un - fail - ing cour - age from on high.

5. Drive far from us the foe we dread,
And grant us your true peace instead;
So shall we not, with you for guide,
Turn from the path of life aside.

6. O grant that we through you may come
To know the Father and the Son.
And hold with firm, unchanging faith
That you are Spirit of them both.

7. Praise we the Father and the Son,
And Holy Spirit, with them one;
And may the Son on us bestow
The gifts that from the Spirit flow.

Text: Rabanus Maurus, c. 776–856, attr.; tr. Edward Caswall, 1814–1848, alt, and others
Music: Plainchant, Mode VIII

88 88
VENI CREATOR SPIRITUS

298 Veni Creator Spiritus

1. Ve - ni, Cre - á - tor Spí - ri - tus, Men-tes tu - ó - rum ví - si - ta:
2. Qui dí - ce - ris Pa - rá - cli - tus, Al - tís - si - mi do - num De - i,
3. Tu se - pti - for - mis mú - ne - re, Dígi-tus pa - tér - nae deÿ - te - rae,
4. Ac-cén-de lu - men sén - si - bus, In fun-de a-mó - rem cór - di-bus,
5. Ho-stem re - pél - las lón - gi - us, Pa-cém-que do - nes pró - ti-nus:
6. Per te sci - á - mus da Pa-trem, No-scá-mus at - que Fí - li - um
7. De - o Pa - tri sit gló - ri - a, Et Fí - li - o qui - a mór-tu - is

Im - ple su - pér -	na grá - ti - a	Quae tu cre - á - sti	pé - cto - ra.
Fons vi - vus, i -	gnis, cá - ri - tas,	Et spi - ri - tá - lis	uń - cti - o.
Tu ri - te pro -	miś-sum Pa-tris,	Ser - mó-ne di - tans	gút - tu - ra.
In - fír - ma no -	stri cór-po-ris	Vir - tú - te fir-mans	pér - pe - ti.
Du - ctó re sic	te praé-vi - o,	Vi - té-mus o - mne	nó - xi-um.
Te-que u - tri - ús -	que Spí - ri-tum	Cre - dá-mus o - mni	tém-po-re.
Sur - ré - xit, ac	Pa - rá - cli - to,	In sae-cu - ló - rum	saé-cu-la.

Text: Rabanus Maurus, c. 776–856, attr.
Music: Plainchant, Mode VIII

88 88
VENI CREATOR SPIRITUS

Come Holy Ghost, Creator Blest 299

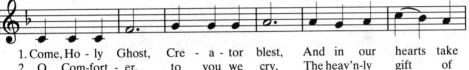

1. Come, Ho - ly Ghost,	Cre - a - tor blest,	And in our	hearts take
2. O Com-fort - er,	to you we cry,	The heav'n-ly	gift of
3. To ev - 'ry sense	your light im - part	And shed your	love in
4. O grant that we	through you may come	To know the	Fa - ther

up your rest;	Come with your grace	and heav'n - ly aid	To fill the
God most high.	The font of life	and fire of love,	And sweet a -
ev - 'ry heart.	To our weak flesh,	your strength sup - ply:	Un - fail-ing
and the Son,	And hold with firm,	un - chang - ing faith,	That you are

hearts which you have made,	To fill the hearts which	you have made.
noint - ing from a - bove,	And sweet a - noint - ing	from a - bove.
cour - age from on high,	Un - fail-ing cour - age	from on high.
Spir - it of them both,	That you are Spir - it	of them both.

5. Praise we the Father and the Son,
And Holy Spirit, with them one;
And may the Son on us bestow
The gifts that from the Spirit flow,
The gifts that from the Spirit flow.

Text: Edward Caswall, 1814–1878
Music: Louis Lambillotte, S.J., 1796–1855; acc. Sister Theophane Hytrek, O.S.F, b. 1915, ©

88 888
HOLY SPIRIT

300 Carol of the Holy Spirit

1. A might-y sound from heav - en At Pen - te - cost there came,
2. In Sa - lem's street was gath - ered A crowd from man-y a land,
3. Then come, all Chris-tian peo - ple, Keep fes - ti - val to - day,

And filled the place of meet - ing With rush-ing wind and flame;
And all in their own tongues did The Gos-pel un - der-stand:
For God the Ho - ly Spir - it Dwells with the Church al - way:

What Christ had prom-ised now oc - curred As each A - pos - tle
For by the tri - umph of the Son The curse of Ba - bel
And grieve him not, O Chris-tian soul, His grace with - in shall

spoke the word Be - neath the Spir - it's thun - der, And to the
was un - done When God did send the Spir - it; So to the
make you whole In bod - y, mind, and spir - it, Un - til you

Text: George B. Timms, b. 1910, vv. 1, 3, ©
Music: Dutch Melody; harm. Alec Wynton, b. 1921, alt., ©

76 76 887 87
SONG OF THE HOLY SPIRIT

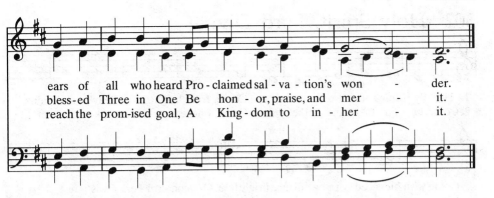

ears of all who heard Pro - claimed sal - va - tion's won - der.
bless-ed Three in One Be hon - or, praise, and mer - it.
reach the prom-ised goal, A King - dom to in - her - it.

Our Blest Redeemer, Ere He Breathed 301

1. Our blest Re - deem - er, ere he breathed His ten - der last fare -
2. He came in tongues of liv - ing flame, To teach, con - vince, sub -
3. He came sweet in - flu-ence to im - part, A gra - cious will - ing
4. And his that gen - tle voice we hear, Soft as the breath of

well, A Guide, a Com - fort - er be-queathed With us to dwell.
due; All pow - er - ful as wind he came, As view - less too.
Guest, While he can find one hum - ble heart Where-in to rest.
ev'n, That checks each fault, that calms each fear, And speaks of heav'n.

5. And ev'ry virtue we possess,
And ev'ry victory won,
And ev'ry thought of holiness,
Are his alone.

6. Spirit of purity and grace,
Our weakness, pitying, see:
O make our hearts thy dwelling-place,
And worthier thee.

Text: Harriet Auber, 1773–1862
Music: Irish Traditional (slightly adapted); acc. Owen Wynne, b. 1898

86 84
WICKLOW

302 Holy Spirit, Lord Divine

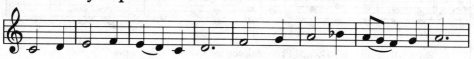

1. Ho - ly Spir - it, Lord Di - vine, Come, from heights of heav'n and shine,
2. Come, O Fa - ther of the poor, Come, whose treas-ured gifts en - dure,

Come with bless - ed ra - diance bright! 3. Of con - sol - ers wis - est, best,
Come, our heart's un - fail - ing light! 4. In our la - bor rest most sweet,

And our soul's most wel - come guest, Sweet re - fresh-ment sweet re - pose.
Pleas-ant cool - ness in the heat. Con - so - la - tion in our woes.

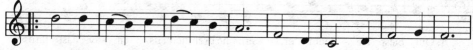

5. Light most bless - ed, shine with grace In our heart's most se - cret place,
6. Left with - out your pres - ence here, Life it - self would dis - ap - pear,

Fill your faith-ful through and through. 7. Cleanse our soil - ed hearts of sin,
Noth-ing thrives a - part from you! 8. Bend the stub-born heart and will,

Ar - id souls re - fresh with - in, Wound-ed lives to health re - store.
Melt the fro - zen, warm the chill, Guide the way-ward home once more!

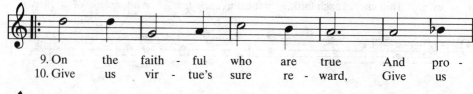

9. On the faith - ful who are true And pro -
10. Give us vir - tue's sure re - ward, Give us

fess their faith in you, In your sev'n - fold gift des - cend!
your sal - va - tion, Lord, Give us joys that nev - er end!

Text: translation by Peter J. Scagnelli, b. 1949, ©
Music: Arr. Edward J. McKenna, b. 1939, ©

777 777
VENI SANCTE SPIRITUS

Joy! Because the Circling Year   303

1. Joy! be - cause the cir - cling year
2. Like to quiv - 'ring tongues of flame
3. So the won - drous works of God
4. Hard - ened scof - fers vain - ly jeered;

Brings our day of bless - ings here,
On to each the Spir - it came,
Won - drous - ly were spread a - broad;
List - 'ning strang - ers heard and feared,

Day when first the
Tongues, that earth might
Ev - 'ry tribe's fa -
Knew the proph - et's

light di - vine On the Church be - gan to shine.
hear their call, Fire, that love might burn in all.
mil - iar tone Made the glo - rious mar - vel known.
word ful - filled, Owned the work which God had willed.

5. Still your Spirit's fullness, Lord,
On your waiting Church be poured;
Grant our burdened hearts release;
Grant us your abiding peace.

Text: Beata nobis gaudia, Latin, 8th c.; John Ellerton, 1826–1893 and F.J.A. Hort, 1828–1892
Music: Adapted from a chorale, Halle, 1704

77 77
LÜBECK

304 Holy Spirit, Come / Veni, Sancte Spiritus

1. Ho - ly Spir-it, come to us, Clasp us tight in heav - en's trust,
2. Come, O Fa-ther of the poor, Come, Giv-er of gifts most pure,
1. *Ve - ni Sanc-te Spí - ri - tus, Et e - mít - te caé - li - tus,*
2. *Ve - ni, pa - ter paú - pe - rum, Ve - ni, da - tor mú - ne - rum,*

Wrap us in your dazz - ling light. 3. Friend and trust-ed Ad - vo - cate,
Set our troub-led hearts a - right. 4. Af - ter work our pre - cious rest,
Lu - cis tu - ae rá - di - um. 3. *Con - so - lá - tor ó - pti - me,*
Ve - ni, lu - men cór - di - um. 4. *In la - bó - re ré - qui - es,*

Wel-come guest for whom we wait, Our re - fresh-ment cool and sweet.
Goal of ev - 'ry fran - tic quest, In our sor - row hope we need.
Dul - cis ho - spes á - ni-mae, Dul-ce re - fri - gé - ri - um.
In ae - stu tem-pé - ri - es, In fle-tu so - lá - ti - um.

5. O light of sur - prise di - vine, Store in mind how short our time,
6. With-out your help we are lost, Use-less fluff not worth the cost;
5. *O lux be - a - tís - si - ma, Re - ple cor - dis ín - ti - ma*
6. *Si - ne tu - o nú - mi - ne, Ni - hil est in hó - mi - ne,*

Our strength and will please re-new, 7. Heal what-ev - er may be ill,
Our on - ly hope lies in you. 8. En - er - gize what may be old,
Tu - ó - rum fi - dé - li-um. 7. *La - va quod est sór - di-dum,*
Ni - hil est in nó - xi-um. 8. *Fle - cte quod est rí - gi-dum,*

Text: Stephen Langton 13th c; tr. Andrew M. Greeley, b. 1928, ©
Music: Pope Innocent III, 1161–1216, attr.; acc. Theodore Marier, ©

77 7 77 7
VENI SANCTE SPIRITUS

Quick-en that which may be still, Sooth our rest-less, ach-ing hearts.
Warm what-ev - er may be cold, Bind us who have come a - part.
Ri - ga quod est á - ri-dum, Sa - na quod est saú - ci - um.
Fo - ve quod est frí - gi-dum, Re - ge quod est dé - vi - um.

9. Pro - tect us in love with you, Par - don all the wrong we do,
10. Give us life's last great re - ward, Bring us home to you, O Lord,
9. Da tu - is fi - dé - li - bus, In te con - fi - dén - ti - bus,
10. Da vir - tú - tis mé - ri - tum, Da sa - lú - tis é - xi - tum,

Grant us joy that does not cease.
Grant us ev - er - last-ing peace.
Sa - crum sep - te - ná - ri - um. A - men! Al - le - lu - ia!
Da per - én - ne gaú - di - um. A - men! Al - le - lú - ia!

305 I Bind unto Myself Today

1. I bind un - to my - self to - day The strong Name of The Trin - i - ty,
By in - vo - ca - tion of the same, The Three in One, and One in Three.

2. I bind this day to me for ev - er, By pow'r of
3. I bind un - to my - self the power Of the great
4. I bind un - to my - self to - day The vir - tues
5. I bind un - to my - self to - day The pow'r of

faith, Christ's In - car - na - tion; His bap - tism in the
love of cher - u - bim; The sweet "Well done" in
of the star - lit heav - en, The glo - rious sun's life -
God to hold and lead, His eye to watch, his

Jor - dan riv - er; His death on cross for my sal - va - tion;
judg - ment hour; The ser - vice of the ser - a - phim;
giv - ing ray, The white - ness of the moon at e - ven,
might to stay, His ear to hear - ken to my need;

His burst - ing from the spic - ed tomb; His rid - ing
Con - fess - ors' faith, a - pos - tles' word, The pa - triarchs'
The flash - ing of the light - ning free, The whirl - ing
The wis - dom of my God to teach, His hand to

up the heav'n - ly way; His com - ing at the
prayers, the pro - phets' scrolls; All good deeds done un -
wind's tem - pes - tuous shocks, The sta - ble earth, the
guide, his shield to ward; The word of God to

Text: St. Patrick, 372–466; tr. Cecil Frances Alexander, 1818–1895
Music: Charles V. Stanford, 1852–1924; arr. Ralph Vaughan Williams, 1872–1958

88 88 88 88
DEIRDRE

day of doom; I bind un - to my - self to - day.
to the Lord, And pu - ri - ty of vir - gin souls.
deep salt sea, A - round the old e - ter - nal rocks.
give me speech, His heav'n - ly host to be my guard.

6. Christ be with me, Christ with - in me, Christ be - hind me, Christ be - fore me,
Christ be-neath me, Christ a - bove me, Christ in qui - et, Christ in dan - ger,

Christ be-side me, Christ to win me, Christ to com-fort and re-store me,
Christ in hearts of all that love me, Christ in mouth of friend and stran-ger.

7. I bind un - to my - self the Name, The strong Name of the Trin - i -

ty, By in - vo - ca - tion of the same, The Three in One, and One in

Three. Of whom all na - ture hath cre - a-tion, E - ter - nal Fa - ther, Spir - it,

Word: Praise to the Lord of my sal-va-tion, Sal - va-tion is of Christ the Lord.

306 Holy, Holy, Holy!

1. Holy, Holy, Holy! Lord God Almighty!
2. Holy, Holy, Holy! all the saints adore thee,
3. Holy, Holy, Holy! though the darkness hide thee,
4. Holy, Holy, Holy! Lord God Almighty!

Early in the morning our song shall rise to thee:
Casting down their golden crowns around the glassy sea;
Though the eye made blind by sin thy glory may not see,
All thy works shall praise thy Name, in earth, and sky, and sea;

Holy, Holy, Holy! merciful and mighty,
Cherubim and seraphim falling down before thee,
Only thou art holy; there is none beside thee,
Holy, Holy, Holy! merciful and mighty,

God in three Persons, blessed Trinity.
God everlasting through eternity.
Perfect in pow'r, in love, and purity.
God in three Persons, blessed Trinity.

Text: Reginald Heber, 1783–1826
Music: John Bacchus Dykes, 1823–1876

11 12 12 10
NICAEA

Come, Our Almighty King 307

1. Come, our al - might - y King, Help us your name to sing;
2. Come, O in - car - nate Word, By heav'n and earth a - dored;
3. Come, ho - ly Com - fort - er, Your sa - cred wit - ness bear
4. To the great One in Three, E - ter - nal prais - es be

Help us to praise: Fa - ther, all glo - ri - ous, Ev - er vic -
Our prayer at - tend: Come and your peo - ple bless, And give your
In this glad hour! Your grace to us im - part, Now rule in
Hence ev - er - more! Your sov - 'reign maj - es - ty May we in

to - ri - ous, Come and reign o - ver us, An - cient of Days.
word suc-cess; Spir - it of ho - li-ness, On us de - scend.
ev - 'ry heart, Nev - er from us de-part, Spir - it of pow'r.
glo - ry see, And to e - ter - ni - ty Love and a - dore.

Text: Anon., c. 1757, alt.
Music: Felice de Giardini, 1716–1796

664 6664
ITALIAN HYMN

Alternate text for no. 307

308 Lord, Your Almighty Word

1. Lord, your almighty word
   Chaos and darkness heard,
   And took their flight;
   Hear us, we humbly pray,
   And where the gospel-day
   Sheds not its glorious ray,
   Let there be light!

2. Savior, you came to give
   Those who in darkness live
   Healing and sight,
   Health to the sick in mind,
   Sight to the inly blind,
   Now to all humankind
   Let there be light!

3. Spirit of truth and love,
   Life-giving, holy dove,
   Speed forth your flight!
   Move on the waters' face
   Bearing the lamp of grace,
   And in earth's darkest place
   Let there be light!

4. Holy and blessed Three,
   Glorious Trinity,
   Wisdom, love, might;
   Boundless as ocean's tide,
   Rolling in fullest pride,
   Through the world far and wide,
   Let there be light!

Text: John Marriott, 1780–1825
Music: Felice de Giardini, 1716–1796

O God Almighty Father 309

1. O God, al-might-y Fa - ther, Cre - a - tor of all things, The
2. O Je - sus, Word in - car - nate, Re - deem-er most a - dored, All
3. O God, the Ho - ly Spir - it, Who lives with-in our soul, Send

heav-ens stand in won - der, While earth your glo - ry sings.
glo - ry, praise, and hon - or Be yours, O sov-'reign Lord.
forth your light and lead us To our e - ter - nal goal.

REFRAIN

O most ho - ly Trin - i - ty, Un - di - vid - ed u - ni - ty,

Ho - ly God, might - y God, God im - mor - tal be a - dored!

Text: Anon.; tr. Irvin Udulutsch, O.F.M., Cap., b. 1920, ©
Music: Limburg Gesangbuch, 1838; acc. Sr. Mary Sylvestra, O.S.F, ©

76 76 with Refrain
GOTT VATER, SEI GEPRIESEN

310 Ave, Mary, Full of Grace

1. A - ve, Mar - y, full of grace In whose vir - gin arms' em - brace
2. God is to his tem - ple come; An - gels throng the hal - lowed dome:
3. In - cense-gales of glad-ness rise Where this morn - ing sac - ri - fice
4. There be - hold th'Ob-la - tion wrought, By whose pre - cious ran - som bought,

God to God him - self doth vow: Al - le - lu - i - a, al - le - lu - i - a!
What be - yond hath heav'n in store? Al - le - lu - i - a, al - le - lu - i - a!
'Mid re - echo-ing shouts is made: Al - le - lu - i - a, al - le - lu - i - a!
We are all to God made nigh: Al - le - lu - i - a, al - le - lu - i - a!

Let me in the tem - ple wait, Je - su, for mine all art thou.
God him - self our flesh doth wear; This than heav'n it - self is more.
Eve-ning's rite in tears shall end, On the dark-'ning cross dis - played.
Now no long - er, Lord, our own, Thine we live and thine we die.

5. Let thy servants now depart;
May we see thee as thou art;
Nought of earth arrest our eyes!
Alleluia, alleluia!
Let us here with Jesus grow,
And in him hereafter rise.

Text: translation by William John, 1804–1885
Music: Burgundian tune; harm. the Dominican Nuns of Summit, New Jersey, ©

77 7 10 7
PAT–A–PAN

A Litany to Our Lady 311

Cantor: Mother of the budding earth, All: pray for us. Cantor: Mother of the flourishing field,

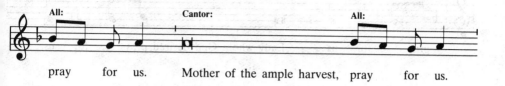

All: pray for us. Cantor: Mother of the ample harvest, All: pray for us.

Cantor: Mother of the family meal, All: pray for us. Cantor: Mother of the poor and sick,

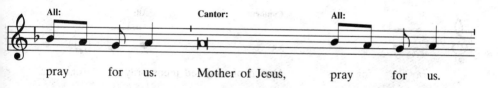

All: pray for us. Cantor: Mother of Jesus, All: pray for us.

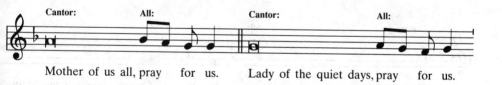

Cantor: Mother of us all, All: pray for us. Cantor: Lady of the quiet days, All: pray for us.

Cantor: Lady of the peaceful nights, All: pray for us. Cantor: Lady of song and dance,

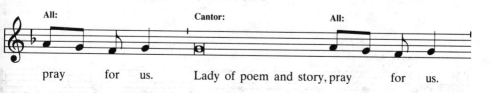

All: pray for us. Cantor: Lady of poem and story, All: pray for us.

Text: Andrew M. Greeley, b. 1928, ©
Music: Edward J. McKenna, b. 1939, ©

SOLANO

BLESSED VIRGIN MARY

Lady of burning love, pray for us. Lady of the broken heart,

pray for us. Lady whom God desired, pray for us.

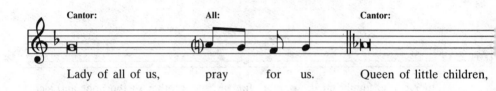

Lady of all of us, pray for us. Queen of little children,

pray for us. Queen of troubled teens, pray for us.

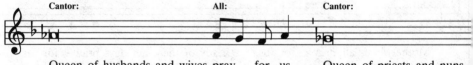

Queen of husbands and wives, pray for us. Queen of priests and nuns,

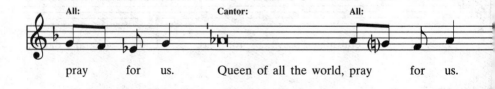

pray for us. Queen of all the world, pray for us.

Queen of peace, pray for us.

Hail, Holy Queen Enthroned Above 312

1. Hail, ho-ly Queen en-throned a-bove, O Ma-ri-a!
2. Our life, our sweet-ness here be-low, O Ma-ri-a!
3. As ex-iles all to you we cry, O Ma-ri-a!
4. Turn then, most gra-cious ad-vo-cate, O Ma-ri-a!

Hail, Queen of mer-cy and of love, O Ma-ri-a!
Our hope in sor-row and in woe, O Ma-ri-a!
Come, soothe with hope our mis-er-y, O Ma-ri-a!
Towards us your eyes com-pas-sion-ate, O Ma-ri-a!

REFRAIN

Tri-umph all ye Cher-u-bim, Sing with us ye Ser-a-phim, Heav'n and

earth re-sound the hymn: Sal-ve, Sal-ve, Sal-ve, Re-gi-na!

5. O gentle, loving, holy one, O Maria!
   Make us each day more like your Son, O Maria! *Refrain*

6. And when from death to life we passed, O Maria!
   Show us your Son, our Lord, at last, O Maria! *Refrain*

Text: Hermanus Contractus, 1013–1054, attr.; vv. 1, 2, 5, and refrain tr. anon.,
ca. 1884, alt., vv. 3, 4, 6 para. by editors, ©
Music: German Melody, Hildesheim, 1736, alt.

8 4 8 4 777 4 5
SALVE REGINA COELITUM

313 Daily, Daily Sing to Mary

1. Dai-ly, dai-ly sing to Mar-y, Sing with joy her prais-es due!
2. She is might-y in her plead-ing, Ten-der in her lov-ing care;
3. Sing my tongue, the Vir-gin's hon-ors, Who for us her mak-er bore,
4. All my sens-es, heart, af-fec-tions, Strive to sound her glo-ry forth.

All her feasts, her ac-tions hon-or, With the heart's de-vo-tion true.
Ev-er watch-ful, un-der-stand-ing, All our sor-rows she will share.
For the curse of old in-flict-ed, Peace and bless-ing to re-store,
Spread a-broad the sweet me-mo-rials Of the Vir-gin's price-less worth.

Lost in won-d'ring con-tem-pla-tion, Be her maj-es-ty con-fessed!
Ad-vo-cate and lov-ing Moth-er, Me-di-a-trix of all grace!
Sing in songs of praise un-end-ing, Sing the world's ma-jes-tic Queen;
Where the voice of mu-sic thrill-ing, Where the tongues of el-o-quence,

Call her Moth-er, call her Vir-gin, Hap-py Moth-er Vir-gin blest!
Heav-en's bless-ings she dis-pens-es On our sin-ful hu-man race.
Wea-ry not nor faint in tell-ing All the gifts that earth has seen.
That can ut-ter hymns be-fit-ting All her match-less ex-cel-lence?

Text: St. Bernard of Cluny, c. 1150, attr.; Henry Bittleston, 1818–1886;
alt. Irvin Udulutsch, O.F.M., Cap. b. 1920, ©
Music: Traditional German Melody; acc. Sr. Mary Teresine, O.S.F., ©

87 87 87 8
ALLE TAGE SING UND SAG

5. All our joys do flow from Mary
All then join her praise to sing.
Trembling sing the Virgin Mother,
Mother of our Lord and King.
While we sing her awesome glory,
Far above our fancy's reach,
Let our hearts be quick to offer
Love the heart alone can teach.

Hail Blessed Virgin Full of Grace 314

1. Hail bless-ed Vir - gin, full of grace, Splen-dor of
2. Hail Star of o - cean, shin - ing bright, For the op -
3. Hail Queen of heav - en, high a - bove, Grant that we

all the hu - man race, We hon - or you for
pressed a guid - ing light, We ask your aid to
all may share your love, And pray that heav - en

Christ your Son, Who has for us re - demp - tion won.
in - ter - cede With God to help us in our need.
we may see, To live with God e - ter - nal - ly.

Text: Anthony G. Petti, 1932–1985
Music: Josquin des Pres, c. 1445–1521; arr. Anthony G. Petti, 1932–1985, ©

88 88
AVE VERA VIRGINITAS

315 Hail, Queen of Heaven, the Ocean Star

1. Hail, Queen of heav'n, the o - cean star, Guide of the wan - d'rer here be - low; Thrown on life's surge, we claim thy care: Save us from per - il and from woe. Moth - er of Christ, star of the sea, Pray for the wan - d'rer, pray for me.

2. O gen - tle, chaste, and spot - less maid, We sin - ners make our prayers through thee; Re - mind thy son that he has paid The price of our in - i - qui - ty. Vir - gin most pure, star of the sea, Pray for the sin - ner, pray for me.

3. So - journ - ers in this vale of tears, To thee, blest ad - vo - cate, we cry; Pit - y our sor - rows, calm our fears, And soothe with hope our mis - er - y. Ref - uge in grief, star of the sea, Pray for the mourn - er, pray for me.

4. And while to him who reigns a - bove, In God-head One, in Per - sons Three, The source of life, of grace, of love, Hom - age we pay on bend - ed knee, Do thou, bright Queen, star of the sea, Pray for thy chil - dren, pray for me.

Text: John Lindgard, 1771–1851
Music: Henri Friedrich Hemy, 1818–1888

88 88 88
STELLA

Immaculate Mary 316

1. Im - mac - u - late Mar - y, your prais - es we sing. You
2. In heav - en the bless - ed your glo - ry pro - claim, On
3. We pray for the Church, our true moth - er on earth, And

reign now in splen - dor with Je - sus our King.
earth we your chil - dren in - voke your sweet name.
beg you to watch o'er the land of our birth.

REFRAIN

A - ve, A - ve, A - ve, Ma - ri - a!

A - ve, A - ve, Ma - ri - a!

Text: Anonymous, tr. by Irwin Udulutsch, O.F.M., Cap., b. 1920, ©
Music: Grenoble, 1882; acc. Irwin Udulutsch, O.F.M., Cap., b. 1920, alt., ©

65 65 with Refrain
LOURDES (MASSABIELLE)

317 O Mary, Our Mother

1. O Mar - y, our moth - er, to you do we come;
2. O Mar - y, our moth - er, be gra - cious to all;
3. O Mar - y, our moth - er, so lov - ing, so mild;

In all our af - flic - tions, your love is our home.
When bur - dened with sad - ness, to you do we call.
You love us as dear - ly as you loved your Child.

Your heart is so gen - tle, so lov - ing, so mild;
In sor - row, in dark - ness, O be at our side;
In life let us ev - er be faith - ful and true,

You will not re - ject an - y sup - pli - ant child.
For you are our moth - er, our com - fort and guide.
That death may but lead us to Je - sus and you.

Text: *Maria zu lieben*; Desmond A. Schmal, S.J., 1897–1958, alt.
Music: *Gesangbuch*, 1765

11 11 11 11
PADERBORN (MARIA ZU LIEBEN)

O Most Holy One/O Sanctissima 318

1. O most ho-ly one, O most low-ly one,
2. Vir-gin ev-er fair, Moth-er, hear our prayer,
1. *O sanc-tís-si-ma, O pi-ís-si-ma,*
2. *Vir-go, ré-spi-ce, Ma-ter, á-spi-ce,*

Lov-ing Vir-gin, Ma-ri - a!
Look up-on us, Ma-ri - a!
Dul-cis Vir-go, Ma-rí - a!
Au-di nos, O Ma-rí - a!

Moth-er, Maid of fair-est love, La-dy, Queen of all a-bove,
Bring to us your treas-ure, Grace be-yond all meas-ure;
Ma-ter a-má-ta, In-te-me-rá-ta,
Tu me-di-cí-nam Por-tas di-ví-nam,

O - ra, o - ra pro no - bis!

Text: Anonymous; tr. Charles W. Leland, C.S.B., ©
Music: Sicilian Traditional Melody, 18th. c; acc. Healey Willian, 1880–1968

10 7 10 7
SICILIAN MARINER'S

319 Remember, Holy Mary

1. Re-mem-ber, ho-ly Mar-y, As moth-er of us all,
2. Be pleased O Vir-gin Mar-y, To give your Son to us,
3. Be pleased O Vir-gin Mar-y, Sent from our God a-bove,

To ev-er show your car-ing And lis-ten to our call.
To help us as we jour-ney, Come back to God with trust.
To be for us a sym-bol Of God's ma-ter-nal love.

La-dy Wis-dom, al-ways help us, In trou-bles great and small,
For from his cross Christ told us, His sis-ter and his broth-er,
To be for us a ref-uge, In times when we're dis-tressed,

For you are God's own moth-er, Be our help-er lest we fall.
In words to his dis-ci-ple, "My Son, here is your moth-er."
That we may one day come home, And find e-ter-nal rest.

Text: St. Bernard, +1153, attr.; tr. Rev. Thomas C. Meyer, b. 1928, vv 2-3, ©
Music: Slovak Hymnal; arr. Nicola A. Montani

Hail, Our Queen and Mother Blest 320

1. Hail, our Queen and Moth-er blest! Joy when all was sad - ness,
2. Pray for us, O Pa-tron-ess, Be our con-so-la - tion!

Life and hope you brought to birth, Moth - er of our glad - ness!
Lead us home to see your Son, Je - sus, our sal - va - tion!

Chil - dren of the sin-ful Eve, Sin - less Eve, be-friend us,
Gra - cious are you, full of grace, Lov - ing as none oth - er,

Ex-iled in this vale of tears: Strength and com - fort send us!
Joy of heav'n and joy of earth, Mar - y God's own Moth - er!

Text: Hermannus Contractus, 1013–1054, attr.; tr. James Quinn, S.J., b. 1919, © 1969, 1988
Music: Johann Leisentritt, 1527–1586

76 76 76 76
AVE VIRGO VIRGINUM

321 All Who Keep the Faith of Jesus

1. All who keep the faith of Je-sus,
Sing the won-ders that were done,
When the love of God the Fa-ther
O'er our sin the vic-t'ry won,
When he made the Vir-gin Mar-y
Moth-er of his on-ly Son.
Hail Mar-y, full of grace!

2. Bless-ed were the cho-sen peo-ple
Out of whom the Lord did come,
Bless-ed was the land of prom-ise
Fash-ioned for this earth-ly home;
But more bless-ed far the Moth-er,
She who bore him in her womb.
Hail Mar-y, full of grace!

3. There-fore let all faith-ful peo-ple
Tell the hon-or of her name,
Let the Church in her fore-shad-owed
Part in her thanks-giv-ing claim;
What Christ's Moth-er sang in glad-ness
Let Christ's peo-ple sing the same.
Hail Mar-y, full of grace!

4. May the Moth-er's in-ter-ces-sions
On our homes a bless-ing win,
That the chil-dren all be pros-pered,
Strong and fair and pure with-in,
Fol-low-ing our Lord's own foot-steps,
Firm in faith and free from sin.
Hail Mar-y, full of grace!

Text: Vincent Coles, S.S., 1845–1929
Music: J.A. Freylinghausen, 1670–1739; harm. Conrad Kocher, 1786–1872

87 87 87 with Refrain
DEN DES VATERS SINN GEBOREN

5. For the sick and for the aged,
   For our dear ones far away,
   For the hearts that mourn in secret,
   All who need our prayers today,
   For the faithful gone before us,
   May the holy Virgin pray.
   Hail Mary, full of grace!

Who Is She Ascends So High 322

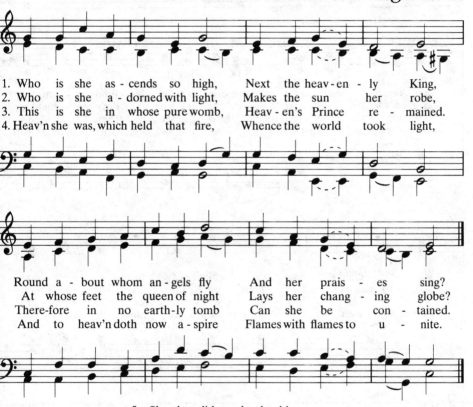

1. Who is she as-cends so high, Next the heav-en-ly King,
2. Who is she a-dorned with light, Makes the sun her robe,
3. This is she in whose pure womb, Heav-en's Prince re-mained.
4. Heav'n she was, which held that fire, Whence the world took light,

Round a-bout whom an-gels fly And her prais-es sing?
At whose feet the queen of night Lays her chang-ing globe?
There-fore in no earth-ly tomb Can she be con-tained.
And to heav'n doth now a-spire Flames with flames to u-nite.

5. She that did so clearly shine
   When our day begun,
   See how bright her beams decline:
   Now she sits with the Sun.

Text: Sir John Beaumont, 1583–1627
Music: A. Gregory Murray, b. 1905

75 75 Slightly Irregular
ASSUMPTA EST

323 Sing of Mary, Pure and Lowly

1. Sing of Mary, pure and lowly, Virgin mother undefiled,
Sing of God's own Son most holy, Who became her little child.
Fairest child of fairest mother, God the Lord who came to earth,
Word made flesh, our very God.

2. Sing of Jesus, Son of Mary, In the home at Nazareth.
Toil and labor cannot weary Love enduring unto death.
Constant was the love he gave her, Though he went forth from her side,
Forth to preach, and heal and suffer, Till on Calvary he died.

3. Sing of Mary, sing of Jesus, Holy mother's holier Son.
From his throne in heav'n he sees us, There he calls us every one.
Where he welcomes home his mother To a place at his right hand,
There his faithful servants gather, There the crowned victors stand.

4. Joyful Mother, full of gladness, In your arms your Lord was borne.
Mournful Mother, full of sadness, All your heart with pain was torn.
Glorious Mother, now rewarded With a crown at Jesus' hand,
Age to age your name recorded shall be blest in every land.

Text: Rev. Roland F. Palmer, S.S.J.E., b. 1891–1985, ©
Music: Acc. Plymouth Collection, New York, 1855

87 87 87 87
PLEADING SAVIOR (SALTASH)

ver - y broth - er, Takes our na - ture by his birth.
heal, and suf - fer, Till on Cal - va - ry he died.
ser - vants gath - er, There the bless - ed vic - tors stand.
name re - cord - ed Shall be blest in ev - 'ry land.

5. Glory be to God the Father,
   Glory be to God the Son;
   Glory be to God the Spirit;
   Glory to the Three in One.

From the heart of blessed Mary,
From all saints the song ascends,
And the Church the strain re-echoes
Unto earth's remotest ends.

Hymn to the Sorrowful Mother 324

1. God, in whom all gra - ces dwell, Grant us grace to pon - der well
2. May the tears which Mar - y poured Gain us par - don of the Lord;
3. May our con - tem - pla - tion, too, Of the sor - rows Je - sus knew,

Mar - y's sor - rows sev - en - fold, Which the high priest had fore-told.
Tears ex - cel - ling in their worth All the pen - an - ces of earth.
Source to us of bless - ing be Through-out all e - ter - ni - ty.

Text: Palunabella; tr. Edward Caswall, 1814–1878, alt.
Music: Plainchant adapt. Erfurt, 1524;
*   acc. Seth Calvisius, 1594, adapt. Sr. Mary Teresine, O.S.F., ©*

77 77
NUN KOMM DER HEIDEN HEILAND

325 Alma Redemptoris Mater

Al - ma * Re-dem-ptó-ris Ma-ter, quae pér-vi - a cae-li Por-ta ma-nes,

Et stel-la ma-ris, suc-cúr-re ca-dén-ti súr-ge-re qui cu-rat pó-pu-lo:

Tu quae ge-nu-í-sti, na-tú-ra mi-rán-te, tu-um san-ctum Ge-ni-tó - rem:

Vir - go pri - us ac po-sté-ri-us, Ga-bri-é-lis ab o - re:

su - mens il - lud A - ve, pec-ca-tó-rum mi-se-ré - re.

Text: Hermanus Contractus, fl. 1054, attr.
Music: Plainchant, Mode V; acc. Rev. Bartholomew Sayles, O.S.B., b. 1918; Sr. Cecile Gertken, O.S.B., b. 1902, ©

326 Ave Maria

A - ve Ma-rí - a, * grá-ti-a ple-na, Dó-mi-nus te-cum,

be - ne - dí - cta tu in mu-li - é - ri - bus,

et be - ne - dí - ctus fru-ctus ven-tris tu - i, Je - sus.

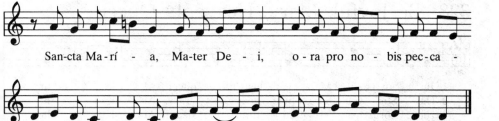

San-cta Ma - rí - a, Ma-ter De - i, o - ra pro no - bis pec-ca -

tó - ri-bus, nunc et in ho - ra mor-tis no - strae. A - men.

Text: Luke 1:26–37
Music: Plainchant, Mode I; acc. Rev. Batholomew Sayles, O.S.B., b. 1918; Sr. Cecile Gertken, O.S.B., b. 1902, ©

Irregular
AVE MARIA

Ave Regina Caelorum 327

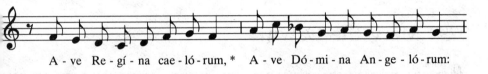

A - ve Re - gí - na cae - ló - rum, * A - ve Dó - mi - na An - ge - ló - rum:

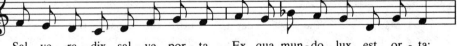

Sal - ve ra - dix, sal - ve por - ta, Ex qua mun-do lux est or - ta:

Gau - de Vir - go glo - ri - ó - sa, Su - per om - nes spe - ci - ó - sa:

Va - le, o val-de de - có - ra, Et pro no - bis Chri-stum ex - ó - ra.

Text: Anonymous, 12th c.
Music: Plainchant, Mode VI; acc. Rev. Bartholomew Sayles, O.S.B., b. 1918; Sr. Cecile Gertken, O.S.B., b. 1902, ©

328 Be Joyful, Mary, Heavenly Queen

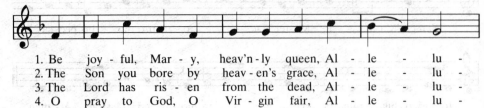

1. Be joy - ful, Mar - y, heav'n - ly queen, Al - le - lu -
2. The Son you bore by heav - en's grace, Al - le - lu -
3. The Lord has ris - en from the dead, Al - le - lu -
4. O pray to God, O Vir - gin fair, Al - le - lu -

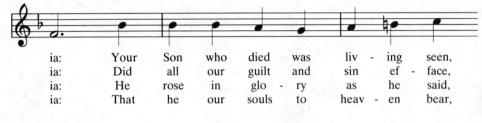

ia: Your Son who died was liv - ing seen,
ia: Did all our guilt and sin ef - face,
ia: He rose in glo - ry as he said,
ia: That he our souls to heav - en bear,

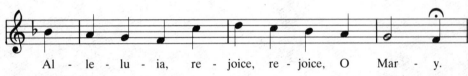

Al - le - lu - ia, re - joice, re - joice, O Mar - y.

Text: Anon.
Music: Johann Leisentritt, 1527–1586; acc. Sr. Luanne Durst, O.S.F., ©

Irregular
REGINA CAELI

329 Mary the Dawn

Choir / All

1. Mar - y the dawn, Christ the per - fect day;
2. Mar - y the root, Christ the mys - tic vine;
3. Mar - y the wheat, Christ the liv - ing bread;
4. Mar - y the font, Christ the cleans - ing flood;
5. Mar - y the tem - ple, Christ the tem - ple's lord;
6. Mar - y the bea - con, Christ the ha - ven's rest;

Choir / All

Mar - y the gate, Christ the heav'n - ly way!
Mar - y the grape, Christ the sa - cred wine!
Mar - y the stem, Christ the rose blood - red!
Mar - y the cup, Christ the sav - ing blood!
Mar - y the shrine, Christ the God a - dored!
Mar - y the mir - ror, Christ the vi - sion blest!

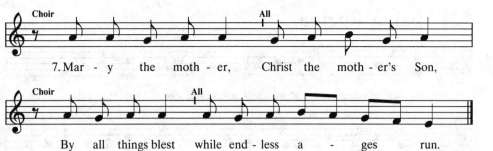

Choir / **All**

7. Mar - y the moth - er, Christ the moth - er's Son,

Choir / **All**

By all things blest while end - less a - ges run.

Text: Paul Cross, ©
Music: Paul Cross; arr. Sr. Luanne Durst, O.S.F., ©

Irregular
MARY THE DAWN

Holy Light 330

1. Ho - ly light on earth's ho - ri - zon, Star of hope to those who fall,
2. Moth - er of the world's Re - deem - er, Prom-ised from the dawn of time:
3. Earth be - low and high - est heav - en Praise the splen - dor of your state,

Light a - mid a world of shad - ows, Dawn of God's de - sign for all.
How could one so high - ly fa - vored Share the guilt of A-dam's crime?
You who now are crowned in glo - ry Were con-ceived im-mac-u - late.

Cho-sen from e - ter - nal a - ges, You a - lone of all our race,
Sun and moon and stars a - dorn you, Sin - less Eve, tri - um - phant sign;
Hail, be - lov - ed of the Fa - ther, Moth-er of his on - ly Son,

By your Son's a - ton - ing mer - its Were con-ceived in per-fect grace.
You it is who crushed the ser - pent, Mar - y, pledge of life di - vine.
Mys-tic bride of Love e - ter - nal, Hail, O fair and spot-less one!

Text: Anon.
Music: Robert LeBlanc, b. 1948, ©

331 Salve Regina

Sal - ve, Re - gí - na, ma - ter mi - se - ri - cór - di - ae; vi - ta, dul - cé - do,

et spes no-stra, sal - ve. Ad te cla-má-mus, ex - su - les fí - li - li E-vae.

Ad te su-spi-rá-mus, ge-mén-tes et flen-tes in hac la - cri-má-rum val -le.

E - ia er - go, ad - vo - cá - ta no - stra, il - los tu - os

mi - se - ri - cór - des ó - cu - los ad nos con - vér - te.

Et Je - sum, be - ne - dí - ctum fru - ctum ven - tris tu - i,

no - bis post hoc ex - si - li - um os - tén - de. O cle - mens,

O pi - a, O dul - cis Vir-go Ma - rí - a.

Text: Hermanus Contractus, 1013–1054, attr.
Music: Plainchant, Mode V; acc. John Patrick Earls, O.S.B., ©

O Mary of Graces 332

1. O Mar-y of gra-ces and moth-er of Christ, O may you di-
2. O may you pro-tect me by land and by sea, And may you pro-

rect me and guide me a-right. O may you pro-tect me from
tect me from sor-rows to be; A strong guard of an-gels a-

Sa-tan's con-trol, And may you pro-tect me in bod-y and soul.
bove me pro-vide; May God be be-fore me and God at my side.

Text: Traditional Gaelic; tr. J. Rafferty, ©
Music: Michael Dawney, ©

11 11 11 11

333 Stainless the Maiden

1. Stain-less the maid-en whom he chose for moth-er; Nine months she
2. Lan-tern in dark-ness, when the sick are sigh-ing, Thresh-old of
3. Je-sus has con-quered; to his side he raised her; Queen of the
4. Sons, come and daugh-ters, through the a-ges sing-ing, Prais-ing the

wait-ed, bear-ing Christ our broth-er; Think of her glad-ness
bright-ness, com-fort for the dy-ing, High she is hold-ing
an-gels, ev-'ry saint has praised her. Yet, in her splen-dor,
Vir-gin, joys and sor-rows bring-ing. Clothed with the sun-shine,

when at last she saw him God in a man-ger, Beth-le-hem a heav-en!
for a world a-dor-ing, Hope of the na-tions, Je-sus Christ our broth-er.
Mar-y goes on draw-ing Sin-ners and ex-iles to their prom-ised glo-ry.
Si-on's fair-est flow-er, Spouse of the Spir-it, be to us a moth-er.

Text: Willard F. Jabusch, b. 1930, ©
Music: Traditional Polish Hymn Tune; acc. David Kraehenbuehl, b. 1923, ©

11 11 11 11
SERDECZNA MATKO

The God Whom Earth and Sea and Sky   334

1. The God whom earth and sea and sky A-dore and laud and mag-ni-fy, Whose might they own, whose praise they tell, In Mar-y's bod-y deigned to dwell.

2. O Moth-er blest! the cho-sen shrine Where-in the Ar-chi-tect di-vine, Whose hand con-tains the earth and sky, Vouch-safed in hid-den guise to lie:

3. Blest in the mes-sage Ga-briel brought; Blest in the work the Spir-it wrought; Most blest, to bring to hu-man birth The long de-sired of all the earth.

4. O Lord, the Vir-gin-born, to thee E-ter-nal praise and glo-ry be, Whom with the Fa-ther we a-dore And Ho-ly Ghost for ev-er-more.

Text: Anon., Latin, 11th c.; tr. John Mason Neale, 1818–1866
Music: Johann H. Schein, 1586–1630; harm. J.S. Bach, 1685–1750

88 88
EISENACH

335 Around the Throne, a Glorious Band

1. A - round the throne, a glo - rious band, The saints in
2. Through trib - u - la - tion great they came; They bore the
3. They see their Sav - ior face to face, And sing the
4. "Wor - thy the Lamb, for sin - ners slain, Through end - less

count - less num - bers stand, Of ev - 'ry tongue, re - deemed to
cross, de - spised the shame; From all their la - bors now they
tri - umphs of his grace; Each day and night they sing his
years to live and reign; You have re - deemed us by your

God, Ar - rayed in gar - ments washed in blood. Al - le - lu - ia!
rest In God's e - ter - nal glo - ry blest. Al - le - lu - ia!
praise, To him the loud thanks - giv - ing raise: Al - le - lu - ia!
blood, And made us kings and priests to God." Al - le - lu - ia!

5. O may we tread the sacred road
   That saints and holy martyrs trod;
   Wage to the end the glorious strife
   And win, like them, a crown of life.
   Alleluia!

Text: Rowland Hill, 1744–1833 and others
Music: Nikolaus Hermann, c. 1485–1561;
arr. Australian Hymn Book Committee, 1977, ©

88 88 with Alleluia
ERSCHIENEN IST DER HERRLICHE TAG (HERMANN)

For All the Saints 336

1. For all the saints who from their la - bors rest, Who
2. Thou wast their rock, their for - tress and their might;
3. O may thy sol - diers, faith - ful, true and bold,
4. O blest com - mu - nion, fel - low - ship di - vine!
5. But lo! there breaks a yet more glo - rious day;
6. From earth's wide bounds, from o - cean's far - thest coast,

thee by faith be - fore the world con - fessed, Thy
Thou, Lord, their cap - tain in the well - fought fight:
Fight as the saints who no - bly fought of old, And
We fee - bly strug - gle, they in glo - ry shine; Yet
The saints tri - um - phant rise in bright ar - ray; The
Through gates of pearl streams in the count - less host,

name, O Je - sus, be for - ev - er blest.
Thou, in the dark - ness drear, their one true light.
win, with them, the vic - tor's crown of gold.
all are one in thee, for all are thine.
King of glo - ry pass - es on his way.
Sing - ing to Fa - ther, Son and Ho - ly Ghost.

Al - le - lu - ia! Al - le - lu - ia!

Text: William Walsham How, 1823–1897
Music: Ralph Vaughan Williams, 1872–1958, ©

10 10 10 with Alleluias
SINE NOMINE

337 Hail, Redeemer, King Most Blest!

(Opening verse) Hail, Re-deem-er, King most blest! Sav-ior whom the saints con-fessed!
(Closing verse) Come, you ho-ly ones of old, Rich with gifts so man-i-fold!

With our hon-ored saint(s) we pray: Be your peo-ple's hope, their stay!
Join our hon-ored saint(s) to-day: As we now our love dis-play!

REFRAIN

An-gels, saints and na-tions sing: "Praised be Je-sus Christ, our King,

Lord of life, earth, sky and sea, King of saints e-ter-nal-ly.

Text: Michael Kwatera, O.S.B., b. 1950; Refrain: Patrick Brennan, C.S.S.R., 1877–1951, alt, ©
Music: George Job Elvey, 1816–1893

77 77 77 77
ST. GEORGE'S WINDSOR

(Blessed Virgin Mary)
Come, dear Mary, Mother, Queen,
Full of grace and joy serene!
Join with all God's saints today,
Praising him whom worlds obey!

(Apostles)
Come, apostles, Christ's dear friends,
Preachers at earth's farthest ends,
Join our honored saint(s) today,
Close to Christ along life's way!

(Martyrs)
Come, you martyrs, mighty throng,
Help us sing your vict'ry song!
Join our honored saint(s) today
As we now our homage pay!

(Monks and Nuns)
Come, you holy monks and nuns,
Faithful daughters, loving sons!
Join our honored saint(s) today:
In your hearts Christ's love held sway!

(Pastors)
Come, you pastors of the Church,
Called to serve, correct and teach!
Join our honored saint(s) today:
Guide us on salvation's way!

(Angels)
Come, you angels, spirits bright,
Messengers from endless light!
Join with all God's saints today:
Praise your Lord without delay!

(Evangelists)
Come, you writers of God's Word,
Great the things you saw and heard!
Join our honored saint(s) today,
Glorious in the Gospel ray!

(Virgins)
Come, you virgins, strong and pure,
Victors over sin's allure!
Join our honored saint(s) today
As triumphantly we say:

(Popes and Bishops)
Come, you leaders of the flock,
Strong as iron, firm as rock!
Join our honored saint(s) today:
Guide us on our pilgrim way!

(Doctors and Educators)
Come, you teachers of God's truth,
Guides for seekers, friends of youth!
Join our honored saint(s) today:
In your hearts Christ's Word held sway!

338 Let All the World with Songs Rejoice

1. Let all the world with songs re - joice; Let heav'n re - sound with joy - ful voice; All mind - ful of th'a - pos - tles' fame, Let heav'n and earth their praise pro - claim.

2. These ser - vants once had borne the light Of gos - pel truth o'er hea - then night. Still may their work that light im - part, To glad our eyes and cheer our heart.

3. Lord, by your word to them was giv'n The key that shuts and o - pens heav'n. Our chains un - bind, our wrongs re - pair, And grant us grace to en - ter there.

4. You sent them, Lord, to preach the word Which cured dis - ease and health con - ferred: O may that heal - ing pow'r once more Our souls to grace and health re - store:

5. That when the Lord again shall come
To call and lead his people home,
We may with his apostles blest
Be asked to share his endless rest.

Text: Exultet caelum laudibus, anon. Latin, 11th c.; tr. Richard Mant, 1776–1848
Music: Katholische Geistliche Gesange, Andernach, 1608

88 88
REX GLORIOSE MARTYRUM

Now Let the Earth with Joy Resound 339

1. Now let the earth with joy re - sound And
2. Sick - ness and health your voice o - bey, At
3. So when the world is at its end And
4. All hon - or, praise and glo - ry be, O

heav'n the chant re - ech - o round; Nor heav'n nor earth too
your com - mand they go or stay; From sin's dis - ease our
Christ to judg - ment shall de - scend, May we be called those
Je - sus, Vir - gin - born, to thee; All glo - ry, as is

high can raise The great a - pos - tles' glo - rious praise!
souls re - store, In good con - firm us more and more.
joys to see Pre - pared from all e - ter - ni - ty.
ev - er meet, To Fa - ther and to Par - a - clete.

Text: Anonymous, 10th century; tr. Edward Caswall, 1814–1878, alt.
Music: John Patrick Earls, O.S.B., b. 1935, ©

88 88

340 O Blessed by God

1. E - ter - nal Fa - ther, God of love,
2. In God a - lone the no - ble youth,
3. Ob - tain for us a vi - sion clear
4. To you be praise e - ter - nal - ly,

Look kind - ly on us from a - bove,
Saint Be - ne - dict, sought af - ter truth:
And save us from all hu - man fear,
Most bless - ed Ho - ly Trin - i - ty,

And grant that we may nev - er stray
He fled the world's al - lur - ing sham
That by your guid - ance we may reach
Whose lov - ing grace did strength im - part

From paths marked out by you each day.
To share the tri - umph of the Lamb.
Per - fec - tion's goal which you did teach.
And filled our Saint's en - rap - tured heart.

Alternate Tune: Glory to Thee My God This Night, No. 438
Text: Monte Cassino Hymn to St. Benedict; tr. Roger Schoenbechler, O.S.B., 1900–1986, ©
Music: Innocent Gertken, O.S.B., 1877–1953, ©

O Blessed Saint Joseph 341

1. O blessed Saint Joseph, how great was your worth, The
2. For you to the pilgrim are father and guide, And

one chosen shadow of God upon earth, The
Jesus and Mary felt safe by your side; Ah,

father of Jesus! I wish you would be, Dear
blessed Saint Joseph, how safe I should be, Dear

spouse of our Lady, a father to me.
spouse of our Lady, if you were with me!

Text: Frederick W. Faber, 1814–1863, alt.
Music: Gesangbuch, 1765; arr. Nicola A. Montani

10 10 11 11
PADERBORN (MARIA ZU LIEBEN)

342 Saint Joseph was a Quiet Man

1. Saint Jo-seph was a qui-et man Who made things out of wood;
2. A car-pen-ter to guard the Son Who set the stars so high,

He worked with love to guide his hand And what he made was good.
A car-pen-ter made chairs for one Who made the earth and sky.

He lived with God, a lit-tle boy, From whom all things have come;
He lived with God, a lit-tle boy, From whom all things have come;

He worked for him, in peace and joy, Who made the stars and sun.
He worked for him, in peace and joy, Who made the stars and sun.

Text: David Riley, b. 1923, ©
Music: English Traditional Melody; adapt. and harm. Ralph Vaughan Williams, 1872–1958, ©

86 86 86 86
KINGSFOLD

The Eternal Gifts of Christ the King 343

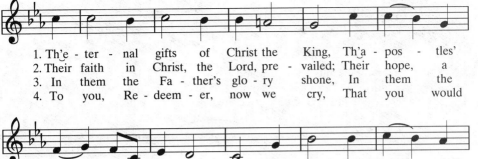

1. Th'e - ter - nal gifts of Christ the King, Th'a - pos - tles'
2. Their faith in Christ, the Lord, pre - vailed; Their hope, a
3. In them the Fa - ther's glo - ry shone, In them the
4. To you, Re - deem - er, now we cry, That you would

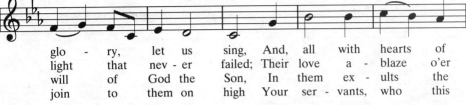

glo - ry, let us sing, And, all with hearts of
light that nev - er failed; Their love a - blaze o'er
will of God the Son, In them ex - ults the
join to them on high Your ser - vants, who this

glad-ness, raise Due hymns of thank - ful love and praise.
path-ways trod To lead them to th'e - ter - nal God.
Ho - ly Ghost, Through them re - joice the heav'n-ly host.
grace im - plore, For - ev - er and for - ev - er - more.

Text: St. Ambrose of Milan, 340–397, attr.; tr. John Mason Neale, 1818–1866
Music: Medieval English Ballad; acc. Russell Woollen, b. 1923, ©

88 88
DEO GRACIAS (AGINCOURT)

344 The Martyrs, Saints of God

1. The mar-tyrs, saints of God, in last-ing peace a-bide; Through suf-fer-ing and lone-ly death their lives were pur-i-fied.
2. In death they shed their blood and preached Christ cru-ci-fied; They wit-nessed that in suf-fer-ing fi-del-i-ty is tried.
3. Who has be-held God's face? Who knows his heart and mind? Yet those who seek him till the end, e-ter-nal life will find.

Text: Becket Senchur, O.S.B., b. 1946, ©
Music: Becket Senchur, O.S.B., b. 1946, ©

Two Noble Saints 345

1. Two no - ble saints both root - ed In
2. One on a cross is mar - tyred, One
3. The words of Paul as - sure us Of
4. So praise we the Cre - a - tor, And

faith and ho - ly love, By hope of God u -
by the sword is slain; Both tri - umph in their
Christ's re-deem - ing word; The works of Pe - ter
praise we Christ the Son, Who with the Ho - ly

nit - ed They reach to heav'n a - bove.
dy - ing, Both glo - rious saint - hood gain.
show us How we may serve the Lord.
Spir - it, Now reign, blest Three in One.

Text: Anne K. LeCroy, b. 1930, ©
Music: Frits Mehrtens, 1922–1975, ©

76 76
DE EERSTEN ZIJN LAATSTEN

346 Who Are These like Stars Appearing

1. Who are these like stars ap-pear-ing, These, be-fore God's
2. Who are these of daz-zling bright-ness, These in God's own
3. These are they who have con-tend-ed For their Sav-ior's
4. These are they whose hearts were riv-en, Sore with woe and

throne who stand? Each a gold-en crown is wear-ing;
truth ar-rayed, Clad in robes of pur-est white-ness,
hon-or long, Wres-tling on till life was end-ed,
an-guish tried, Who in prayer have ful-ly striv-en

Who are all this glo-rious band? Al-le-lu-ia!
Robes whose lus-ter ne'er shall fade, Ne'er be touched by
Fol-l'wing not the sin-ful throng; These, who well the
With the God they glo-ri-fied: Now, their pain-ful

hark, they sing, Prais-ing loud, their heav'n-ly King.
time's rude hand? Whence comes all this glo-rious band?
fight sus-tained, Tri-umph by the Lamb have gained.
con-flict o'er, God has bid them weep no more.

Text: Theobald Heinrich Schenck, 1656–1727; tr. Frances Elizabeth Cox, 1812–1897, alt.
Music: Geistreiches Gesangbuch, 1698; arr. William Henry Monk, 1823–1889. alt.

87 87 77
ZEUCH MICH, ZEUCH MICH

This Is the Spirit's Entry Now   347

1. This is the Spir - it's en - try now: The wa - ter and the Word, The cross of Je - sus on your brow, The seal both felt and heard.
2. This mir - a - cle of life re - born Comes from the Lord of breath; The per - fect man life was torn; Our life comes through his death.
3. Let wa - ter be the sa - cred sign That we must die each day To rise a - gain by his de - sign As fol - l'wers of his way.
4. Re - new - ing Spir - it, hear our praise For your bap - tis - mal pow'r That wash - es us through all our days. Lord, cleanse a - gain this hour.

Text: Thomas E. Herbranson, b. 1933, alt, ©
Music: Leo Sowerby, 1895–1968, ©

86 86
PERRY

Copyright © 1964, Abingdon Press. From THE BOOK OF HYMNS

348 You Have Put on Christ

Cantor/Choir

You have put on Christ, in him you have been bap - tized.

Al - le - lu - ia, al - le - lu - ia.

All

You have put on Christ, in him you have been bap - tized.

Al - le - lu - ia, al - le - lu - ia.

Text: Rite of Baptism, ©
Music: Howard Hughes, S.M., b. 1930, ©

*This piece may be performed as a two–part canon, with the voices entering as indicated by these numbers.

When to the Sacred Font We Came 349

1. When to the sa - cred font we came, Did
not the rite pro - claim, That, washed from sin and
all its stains, New crea - tures we be - came?

2. Too long en - slaved by sin - ful - ness, We
now are slaves no more; For Christ has van - quished
death and sin, Our free - dom to re - store.

3. With Christ the Lord we died to sin, With
him to life we rise; In Christ's new life we
now shall walk, In him at - tain the prize.

Lower Key: O Holy Spirit, Come to Us, no. 501
Text: Scottish, 1781, alt.
Music: Thomas Tallis, c. 1510–1585

86 86
TALLIS' ORDINAL

350 Springs of Water

REFRAIN
All

Springs of wa - ter, Bless the Lord,

Give God glo - ry, glo - ry and praise. For ev - er and ev - er,

1.–4. *(to Verses)* | Last Time

Al - le - lu - ia! Al - le - lu - ia! ia!

VERSE 1
Cantor

I saw wa - ter flow - ing from the tem - ple,

Al - le - lu - ia! It brought God's life and sal -

D.S.

va - tion, and the peo-ple sang in joy - ful praise. Springs of

VERSE 2
Cantor

Give thanks for the good-ness of the Lord whose

mer - cy en-dures for - ev - er. Let Is - ra - el now pro-claim,

D.S.

"The mer - cy of the Lord is for - ev - er!" Springs of

Text: Vidi Aquam and Psalm 118; tr. Eric Holland, b. 1960, ©
Music: Eric Holland, b. 1960, ©

VERSE 3

The right hand of the Lord has tri-umphed, the Lord's right hand is ex - al - ted. I shall not die, I shall live, de - clar-ing the works of the Lord! Springs of

VERSE 4

That stone which was re - ject - ed, has be - come the cor - ner - stone. It is the Lord's own work, It is won - der - ful in our eyes. Springs of

351 Come and Let Us Drink of That New River

1. Come and let us drink of that new riv - er, Not from barren
rock di - vine - ly poured, But the fount of life that springs for -
ev - er From the sa - cred bod - y of our Lord.

2. Now the world has bright il - lu - mi - na - tion, Heav-en and all
things up - on the earth: Ris - en is the God of all cre -
a - tion, Christ the Lord who gave cre - a - tion birth.

3. Yes - ter - day with you in bur - ial ly - ing, Now with you in
tri - umph I a - rise, Yes - ter - day the part - ner of your
dy - ing, Raise me with you far be - yond the skies.

Text: John of Damascus, c. 675–746; tr. John Mason Neale, 1818–1866; adapt. Anthony G. Petti, 1932–1985, ©
Music: Kenneth D. Smith, b. 1928, ©

10 9 10 9
NEW RIVER

Holy Spirit, Lord of Love   352

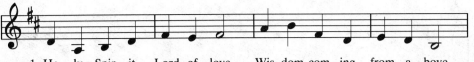

1. Ho - ly Spir - it, Lord of love,   Wis-dom com - ing from a - bove,
2. You have been our con - stant guide,   Ev - er watch-ing by our side.

Gifts of bless-ing to be - stow,   On your wait - ing Church be - low.
May we now till life shall end,   Choose and know you as our friend.

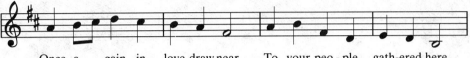

Once a - gain in love draw near,   To your peo - ple gath-ered here,
Give us life to live for you;   Give us love, for - ev - er new,

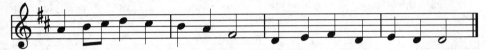

Since our great bap - tis - mal day,   You have led us on our way.
Come then, Ho - ly Spir - it, come;   Make each heart your hap - py home.

Text: William D. MacLagan, 1826–1910, alt.
Music: Patrick DeVine

77 77 77 77
MISNEACH

353 Come, O Come, Life Giving Spirit

1. Come, O come, life-giving Spir-it, God be-fore the dawn of time! Fire our hearts with ho-ly ar-dor, Bless-ed Com-for-ter sub-lime! Let thy ra-diance fill our night, Turn-ing dark-ness in-to light.

2. Grant our hearts in full-est meas-ure Wis-dom, coun-sel, pu-ri-ty, That they ev-er may be seek-ing On-ly that which pleas-eth thee. Let thy know-ledge spread and grow, Work-ing er-ror's o-ver-throw.

3. Ho-ly Spir-it, strong and might-y, Thou who mak-est all things new, Make thy work with-in us per-fect And the e-vil foe sub-due. Grant us weap-ons for the strife And with vic-t'ry crown our life.

Text: Heinrich Held, c. 1659; tr. Edward T. Horn III, b. 1909, alt. v.1;
   Charles W. Schaeffer, 1813–1896, alt. v. 2, 3
Music: Neu–vermehrtes Gesangbuch, Meiningen, 1693

87 87 77
KOMM, O KOMM, DU GEIST DES LEBENS

Creator Spirit, by Whose Aid   354

1. Cre - a - tor Spir - it, by whose aid The world's foun - da - tions first were laid, Come, vis - it ev - 'ry hum - ble mind; Come, pour thy joys on hu - man-kind; From sin and sor - row set us free, And make thy tem - ples wor - thy thee.

2. O Source of un - cre - at - ed light, The Fa - ther's prom - ised Par - a - clete, Thrice ho - ly fount, thrice ho - ly fire, Our hearts with heav'n - ly love in - spire; Come, and thy sa - cred unc - tion bring To sanc - ti - fy us while we sing.

3. O full of grace, come from on high, Rich in thy seven - fold en - er - gy; Make us e - ter - nal truth re - ceive, And prac - tice all that we be - lieve; Give us thy - self, that we may see The Fa - ther and the Son by thee.

Text: John Dryden, 1631–1700
Music: Henry Carey, 1690?–1743

88 88 88
SURREY

YOU HAVE NOT CHOSEN ME⧾ I HAVE CHOSEN YOU⧾

A Prayer for the Elect 355

REFRAIN

We praise and thank you, Lord, this day. Now
with our cat - e - chu - mens stay. With - in their hearts, O
Lord, a - bide, And their bap - tis - mal jour - ney guide.

VERSES

1. Your Spir - it send, whose breeze has blown On
2. You call them now to love you more; On
3. Their new life will be re - a - lized

these whom you have al - ways known. You ev - er call them
them your gra - ces you out - pour. You num - ber them with
When in you, Lord, they are bap - tized With wa - ter and the

To Refrain

each by name That they your glo - ry may pro - claim.
your e - lect; What you be - gan in them per - fect.
Spir - it, too. They shed their old selves, take on new.

Text: Omer Westendorf, b. 1916 ©
Music: Eugene E. Englert, b. 1931 ©

88 88 with Refrain
ENGLERT

356 A Prayer for the First Scrutiny

REFRAIN

O lov - ing Shep - herd of us all, Your

Spir - it gives us each a call. Bless these e - lect, now

cat - e - chized, A - long their way to be bap - tized.

VERSES

1. You dwell with - in our midst in - deed; You
2. Your drink comes not from na - ture's wells; All
3. Lord, may these cat - e - chu - mens live By

Text: Omer Westendorf, b. 1916 ©
Music: Eugene E. Englert, b. 1931 ©

88 88 with Refrain
ENGLERT

give   us   ev - 'ry - thing we need.   You tend us, shep - herd
oth - er   wa - ters   it   ex - cels.   Your liv - ing wa - ter
pre - cious wa - ter   that you give.   Come nour-ish us   and

To Refrain

us,   your   flock.   You bring forth   wa - ter   from   the   rock.
our wound heals;   E - ter - nal   life   this   wa - ter   seals.
for - ti - fy;   Who drinks your   wa - ter   can - not   die.

357 A Prayer for the Second Scrutiny

1. Come o - pen, Lord, the heart and ear Of these e - lect and all who hear! Then may they learn your truth, the way Which leads to their bap - tis - mal day.
2. With o - pen hearts we hear your voice; We dwell up - on it, all then re - joice. How nour - ish - ing your ho - ly Word! It gives new life when - ev - er heard.
3. A - noint - ed once with mud and spit A blind man's eyes with vi - sion lit. He looked to Christ with faith and awe Through eyes of Chris - tian faith he saw!
4. A - wak - en, sleep - ers, wake and see, And chil - dren of the light now be! To dark - ness Christ is truth and light; To all the blind - ed he gives sight.

Alt. tunes: no. 358, or nos. 355, 356 with the first verse as the refrain

Text: Omer Westendorf, b. 1916, ©

Music: Johann H. Schein, 1586–1630; arr. J.S. Bach, 1685–1750

88 88
EISENACH

A Prayer for the Third Scrutiny 358

1. Come out from tombs of death and sin;
2. When Laz - arus left the dark - ened tomb,
3. From graves the Lord will have you rise;
4. Let faith and hope be our one song.

Sal - va - tion now is yours to win.
Just like an in - fant from the womb,
Be - lieve him now with o - pen eyes.
To Christ a - lone do we be - long.

Bap - tized, all sins will wash a - way,
He saw the light of Christ that day.
His peo - ple he will take by hand
We are no long - er in - fi - dels;

When you a - rise on Eas - ter Day.
Christ is the light, the truth, the way.
And lead them to the prom - ised land.
In us the Ho - ly Spir - it dwells.

Alt. tunes: no. 357, or nos. 355, 356 with the first verse as the refrain

Text: Omer Westendorf, b. 1916
Music: Melody from Psaumes octante trois de David, 1551; harm. Louis Bourgeois. 1510?–1561?

88 88
OLD HUNDREDTH

359 A Gracious Guide the Lord

3rd verse – Choir: Congregation Optional

1. A gra - cious guide the Lord, the Shep-herd strong who came
2. His flock a wan-der-er's race, who thirst and hun - ger still
3. He knows the des - ert well, its si - lence and its dread,
4. O Shep - herd of our souls be there where we can hear

To walk in val - leys dark and call us each by name.
For what they hard - ly dream to find be - yond the hill,
The hope of hu - man - kind to turn its stones to bread.
Your strong and con - stant voice that casts a - way our fear.

A Shep-herd al - ways there, whose voice and ac - cent known
They look for one who knows where ver - dant pas - tures lie
A des - ert man him - self who knew the stars at sight,
And in that fold where you shall make your flocks be one.

Brings out all that are his and claims them for his own.
And ta - bles spread, and cup, where gen - tle streams run by.
The lone - ly Shep - herd he an *Ab - ba* cry by night.
Then time shall be no more and all our work be done.

Text: Thomas P. O'Malley, S.J., b. 1930, ©
Music: Old Dutch Melody, acc. Edward J. McKenna, b. 1939, ©

12 12 12 12
GELUKKIG

*For the Ordination of John S. Rogers, III

Long Night A–Sea 360

1. Long night a– sea, long night a– row - ing, cast - ing, and drift - ing,
*2. Fresh is the dawn, new the be - gin - ning, known is the voice and

emp - ty hands. Comes then the dawn, light - ing the shore - land,
calm the sea. Floun - der to shore, hur - ry to greet him,

calm and in - vit - ing, Je - sus stands. Stands at the shore and
hear the com - pel - ling: "Fol - low me." Com - pel - ling voice

names us each, the One that draws us yet who has our ta - ble set.
cries in the wind our name and self with - in and draws the self to him.

VERSE 3

New seas to row, new nights to puz - zle, brave be our mu - sic,

hearts that sing. Deft be our casts, fruit - ful our tak - ing,

ears cocked to hear the Fish - er King. King wound-ed once who

makes us whole, the Mas - ter Fish - er he still call-ing: "Fol-low me."

Text: Thomas P. O'Malley, S.J., b. 1930, ©
Music: Dutch tune, 1572; arr. Edward J. McKenna, b. 1939, ©

KOMT NU MET ZANG

Composed for the Ordination of Robert Power, S.J.

Instrumental interlude may precede second verse.

361 Hail Our Savior's Glorious Body/ Pange Lingua

1. Hail our Sav - ior's glo-rious Bod - y, Which his Vir - gin
2. To the Vir - gin, for our heal - ing, His own Son the
3. On that pas - chal eve-ning see him With the cho-sen
1. *Pan - ge lín - gua glo - ri - ó - si Cór - po - ris my-*
2. *No - bis da - tus, no - bis na - tus Ex in - tá - cta*
3. *In su - pré - mae no - cte coe - nae, Re - cúm-bens cum*

Moth - er bore; Hail the Blood which, shed for sin - ners,
Fa - ther sends; From the Fa - ther's love pro - ceed-ing
twelve re - cline, To the old law still o - be - dient
sté - ri - um, San - gui - nís - que pre - ti - ó - si,
Vír - gi - ne, Et in mun - do con - ver - sá - tus,
frá - tri - bus, Ob - ser - vá - ta le - ge ple - ne

Did a bro-ken world re - store; Hail the sac - ra-ment most ho - ly,
Sow - er, seed and word de - scends; Won-drous life of Word in - car-nate
In its feast of love di - vine; Love di - vine, the new law giv-ing,
Quem in mun - di pré - ti - um Fru - ctus ven-tris ge - ne - ró - si
Spar - so ver - bi sé - mi - ne, Su - i mo - ras in - co - lá - tus
Ci - bis in le - gá - li - bus, Ci - bum tur - bae du - o - dé-nae

After last Verse

Flesh and Blood of Christ a - dore!
With his great - est won - der ends.
Gives him-self as bread and wine.
Rex ef - fú - dit gén - ti - um.
Mi - ro clau - sit ór - di - ne.
Se dat su - is má - ni - bus. A - men.

4. By his word the Word almighty
   Makes of bread his flesh indeed;
   Wine becomes his very life-blood;
   Faith God's living Word must heed!
   Faith alone may safely guide us
   Where the senses cannot lead!

4. *Verbum caro, panem verum*
   Verbo carnem éfficit:
   Fitque sanguis Christi merum,
   Et si sensus déficit,
   Ad firmándum cor sincérum
   Sola fides súfficit.

Text: St. Thomas Aquinas, 1227–1274; tr. James D. Quinn, S.J., b. 1919, ©1969
Music: Plainchant, Mode III; acc. Eugene Lapierre, ©

87 87 87
PANGE LINGUA GLORIOSI

5. Come, adore this wondrous presence;
   Bow to Christ, the source of grace!
   Here is kept the ancient promise
   Of God's earthly dwelling place!
   Sight is blind before God's glory,
   Faith alone may see his face!

6. Glory be to God the Father,
   Praise to his coequal Son,
   Adoration to the Spirit,
   Bond of love, in Godhead one!
   Blest be God by all creation
   Joyously while ages run! Amen.

5. Tantum ergo Sacraméntum
   Venerémur cérnui:
   Et antíquum documéntum
   Novo cedat rítui:
   Praestet fides suppleméntum
   Sénsuum deféctui.

6. Genitóri, Genitóque
   Laus et jubilátio,
   Salus, honor, virtus quoque
   Sit et benedíctio:
   Procedénti ab utróque
   Compar sit laudátio. Amen.

362 O Saving Victim/O Salutaris

1. O Sav-ing Vic-tim, o-p'ning wide The gate of
2. To your great name be end-less praise, Im-mor-tal
1. *O sa-lu-tá-ris hó-sti-a, Quae cae-li*
2. *U-ni tri-nó-que Dó-mi-no Sit sem-pi-*

heav'n to us be-low! Our foes press on from
God-head, One in Three; O grant us end-less
pan-dis ó-sti-um: Bel-la pre-munt ho-
ter-na gló-ri-a: Qui vi-tam si-ne

ev-'ry side: Your aid sup-ply, your strength be-stow.
length of days When our true na-tive land we see.
stí-li-a, Da ro-bur fer au-xí-li-um.
tér-mi-no No-bis do-net in pá-tri-a.

Alt. Tune: We Praise You, Father, no. 440

Text: St. Thomas Aquinas, 1227–1274; tr. Edward Caswall, 1814–1878
Music: Abbe Duguet, c. 1767

88 88
DUGUET

Panis Angelicus 363

1. Pa - nis An - gé - li - cus fit pa - nis hó - mi-num,
2. Te tri - na Dé - i - tas, ú - na - que pó - sci-mus,

Dat pa - nis cóe - li - cus fi - gú - ris tér - mi -
Sic nos tu ví - si - ta, si - cut te có - li -

num; O res mi - rá - bi - lis man - dú - cat
mus; Per tu - as sé - mi-tas duc nos quo

Dó - mi-num Pau - per, ser - vus et hú - mi - lis.
tén - di-mus, Ad lu - cem quám in há - bi - tas.

Text: St. Thomas Aquinas, O.P., 1227–1274
Music: Louis Lambillotte, S.J., 1796–1885

364 Sing, My Tongue, the Savior's Glory

1. Sing, my tongue, the Sav-ior's glo-ry, Of his flesh the mys-t'ry sing:
2. Of a pure and spot-less vir-gin Born for us on earth be-low,
3. On the night of that last sup-per Seat-ed with his cho-sen band,
4. Word made flesh, the bread of na-ture By his word to flesh he turns;

Of the blood, all price ex-ceed-ing, Shed by our im-mor-tal King,
He, as man, with us con-vers-ing, Stayed, the seeds of truth to sow;
He, the Pas-chal vic-tim eat-ing, First ful-fills the law's com-mand;
Wine in-to his blood he chang-es: What though sense no change dis-cerns?

Des-tined for the world's re-demp-tion, From a no-ble womb to spring.
Then he closed in sol-emn or-der Won-drous-ly his life of woe.
Then as food to his a-pos-tles Gives him-self with his own hand.
On-ly be the heart in earn-est, Faith her les-son quick-ly learns.

5. Down in adoration falling,
   Lo! the sacred host we hail;
   Lo! o'er ancient forms departing,
   Newer rites of grace prevail,
   Faith, for all defects supplying,
   Where the feeble senses fail.

6. To the everlasting Father,
   And the Son who reigns on high
   With the Holy Ghost proceeding
   Forth from each eternally,
   Be salvation, honor, blessing,
   Might and endless majesty.

Text: St. Thomas Aquinas, 1225–1274; tr. Edward Caswall, 1814–1878
Music: John Francis Wade, c. 1711–1786, attr.

87 87 87
ST. THOMAS (WEBBE)

Tantum Ergo 365

1. Tan-tum er - go Sac-ra - mén - tum Ve - ne - ré-mur cér-nu - i:
2. Ge - ni - tó - ri Ge - ni - tó - que Laus et ju - bi - lá - ti - o,

Et an - tí-quam do - cu - mén-tum, No - vo ce - dat ri - tu - i:
Sa - lus, ho - nor, vir - tus quo-que Sit et be - ne - dí - cti - o:

Prae-stet fi-des sup-ple-mén-tum Sén - su-um de - féc - tu - i.
Pro - ce-dén-ti ab u - tró - que Com-par sit lau - dá - ti - o. A - men.

Alternate tune: Sing, My Tongue, no. 364

Text: St. Thomas Aquinas, 1227–1274
Music: Plainchant, Mode III; acc. Rev. Bartholomew Sayles, O.S.B., b. 1918, Sr. Cecile Gertken, O.S.B., b. 1902, ©

366 At that First Eucharist

VERSES

1. At that first Eucharist before you died,
O Lord, you prayed that all be one in you;
At this our Eucharist again preside,
And in our hearts your law of love renew.

2. For all your Church, O Lord, we intercede;
O make our lack of charity to cease;
Draw us the nearer each to each, we plead,
By drawing all to you, O Prince of peace.

3. We pray for those who wander from the fold;
O bring them back, Good Shepherd of the sheep,
Back to the faith which saints believed of old,
Back to the Church which still that faith does keep.

4. So, Lord, at length when sacraments shall cease,
May we be one with all your Church above,
One with your saints in one unending peace,
One with your saints in one unbounded love.

Text: William Harry Turton, 1856–1938, alt.
Music: William Henry Monk, 1823–1889, alt.

10 10 10 10 with Refrain
UNDE ET MEMORES

REFRAIN

Thus may we all one bread, one bod - y be,

Through this blest sac - ra - ment of u - ni - ty.

367 Come to the Banquet

REFRAIN

This is the bread of life, This is the cup of joy;
If you will eat from this ta - ble, Then you will nev - er
die, then you will nev - er die.

VERSES

1. Come to the ban - quet of Je - sus; Come, eat the food that he
2. Long in the past they ate man - na, Man - na that fell on the
3. Christ showed the depth of his mer - cy, Christ showed the depth of his
4. I am the Bread from the heav - ens; My blood is of - fered for

gives: Bread that will nour - ish the spir - it,
ground, Giv - ing them strength in the des - ert,
love, Giv - ing far bet - ter than man - na,
you; Mine is a heart full of mer - cy,

To Refrain

Wine that will bright - en your soul.
Giv - ing great joy all a - round.
Giv - ing us bread from a - bove.
Mine are the words that are true.

Text: Willard F. Jabusch, b. 1930, ©
Music: Robert E. Kreutz, b. 1922, ©

Godhead Here is Hiding 368

1. God - head here in hid - ing whom I do a -
2. See - ing, touch - ing, tast - ing are in thee de -
3. On the cross thy God - head made no sign to
4. I am not like Thom - as, wounds I can - not

dore Masked by these bare shad - ows,
ceived; How says trust - y hear - ing?
men; Here thy ver - y man - hood
see, But I plain - ly call thee

shape and noth - ing more, See, Lord, at thy
that shall be be - lieved; What God's Son has
steals from hu - man ken: Both are my con -
Lord and God as he: This faith each day

ser - vice low lies here a heart Lost, all lost in
told me, take for truth I do; Truth him - self speaks
fes - sion, both are my be - lief, And I pray the
deep - er be my hold - ing of, Dai - ly make me

won - der at the God thou art.
tru - ly or there's noth - ing true.
pray - er of the dy - ing thief.
hard - er hope and dear - er love.

5. O thou, our reminder of the Crucified,
   Living Bread, the life of us for whom he died,
   Lend this life to me, then; feed and feast my mind,
   There be thou the sweetness I was meant to find.

6. Like what tender tales tell of the Pelican,
   Bathe me, Jesus Lord, in what thy bosom ran
   Blood that but one drop of has the pow'r to win
   All the world forgiveness of its world of sin.

7. Jesus, whom I look at shrouded here below,
   I beseech thee, send me what I thirst for so,
   Some day to gaze on thee face to face in light
   And be blest forever with thy glory's sight.

Text: St. Thomas Aquinas, O.P., 1227–1274, attr.; tr. Gerard M. Hopkins, S.J., 1844–1889
Music: Edward J. McKenna, b. 1939, ©

11 11 11 11
WINDHOVER

369 Humbly We Adore Thee

VERSES

1. Hum - bly we a - dore thee, Christ Re - deem - er King;
2. God, the Might - y, thou hast come, Bear - ing gifts of grace;
3. Je - sus, Lord, we thank thee For this won - drous Bread;
4. We who share this mys - t'ry, In thee are made one;
5. Thou who died to save us, Live on as our light;
6. Christ, do thou be mer - ci - ful, Lamb for sin - ners slain;
7. Make us one in lov - ing thee, One in mind and heart;

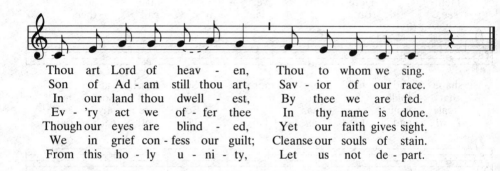

Thou art Lord of heav - en, Thou to whom we sing.
Son of Ad - am still thou art, Sav - ior of our race.
In our land thou dwell - est, By thee we are fed.
Ev - 'ry act we of - fer thee In thy name is done.
Though our eyes are blind - ed, Yet our faith gives sight.
We in grief con - fess our guilt; Cleanse our souls of stain.
From this ho - ly u - ni - ty, Let us not de - part.

REFRAIN

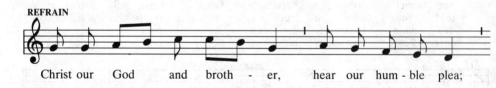

Christ our God and broth - er, hear our hum - ble plea;

By this ho - ly ban - quet keep us joined to thee.

Text: St. Thomas Aquinas, 1227–1274; tr. Melvin L. Farrell, S.S., 1930–1987
Music: Plainchant, Mode V; acc. Irvin Udulutsch, O.F.M., Cap., ©

65 65 with Refrain
ADOROTE

Alternative Text
Adoro Te Devote 370

1. Adóro te devóte, latens Déitas,
Quae sub his figúris vere látitas:
Tibi se cor meum totum súbicit,
Quia te contémplans totum déficit.

2. Visus, tactus, gustus in te fállitur;
Sed audítu solo tuto créditur.
Credo quidquid dixit Dei Fílius:
Nil hoc verbo veritátis vérius.

3. In cruce latébat solo Déitas;
At hic latet simul et humánitas.
Ambo tamen credens atque cónfitens
Peto quod petívit latro paénitens.

4. Plagas, sicut Thomas, non intúeor;
Deum tamen meum te confíteor.
Fac me tibi semper magis crédere,
In te spem habére, te diligere.

5. O memoriále mortis Dómini,
Panis vius vitam praestans hómini,
Praesta meae menti de te vívere,
Et te illi semper dulce sápere.

6. Pie pelicáne, Iesu Dómine,
Me immúndum munda tuo sánguine,
Cuius una stilla salvum fácere
Totum múndum quit ab omni scélere.

7. Iesu, quem velátum nunc aspício,
Oro fiat illud quod tam sítio:
Ut, te revelata cernens fácie,
Visu sim beátus tuae glóriae. Amen.

Text: St. Thomas Aquinas, 1227–1274, alt.

11 11 11 11
ADORO TE DEVOTE

Alternative Text
Let the Hungry Come to Me 371

1. Let the hungry come to me,
Let the poor be fed.
Let the thirsty come and drink,
Share my wine and bread.
Though you have no money,
Come to me and eat.
Drink the cup I offer;
Feed on finest wheat!

2. I myself am living bread;
Feed on me and live.
In this cup my blood for you;
Drink the wine I give.
All who eat my body,
All who drink my blood,
Shall have joy forever,
Share the life of God.

3. Here among you shall I dwell,
Making all things new.
You shall be my very own,
I, your God with you.
Blest are you invited
To my wedding feast.
You shall live forever,
All your joys increased.

4. Nourished by the Word of God,
Now we eat the bread.
With the gift of God's own life
Hungry hearts are fed.
Manna in the desert,
In our darkest night!
Food for pilgrim people,
Pledge of glory bright!

5. Many grains become one loaf,
Many grapes, the wine.
So shall we one body be
Who together dine.
As the bread is broken
As the wine is shared:
So must we be given,
Caring as Christ cared.

6. Risen Savior, walk with us,
Lead us by the hand.
Heal our blinded eyes and hearts
Help us understand.
Lord, make known your presence
At this table blest.
Stay with us forever,
God, our host and guest!

Text: Sr. Delores Dufner, O.S.B., b. 1939, ©
Music: Adoro te devote

11 11 11 11
ADORO TE DEVOTE

372 Rich in Kindness, Rich in Mercy

1. Rich in kind-ness, rich in mer-cy, Won-drous in your lov-ing
2. Lord, as once you fed the He-brews, Send-ing man-na from a-
3. We as wear-y pil-grims wan-der, Fal-t'ring in our earth-ly

ways, Lord, your gifts and wor-thy bless-ings Fol-low
bove, Now you feed us bread from heav-en In your
strife, Seek-ing food for hearts that hun-ger, Come to

us through-out our days. Gift of fin-est wheat you
per - fect gift of love. Loaves and fish-es, few in
you the bread of life. "Take and eat, this is my

give us, Fruit of vine in cup out-poured; Great-er gift could not be
num-ber, Mul-ti-plied to feed the throng, But pre-fig-ure here the
bod-y," Were the mys-tic words you said. O - pen then your hand of

of - fered Than your gift, your gift of self, O Lord. Than your
Eu-cha-rist, Heav'n-ly food, for which our spir - its long. Heav'n-ly
mer - cy; Give to us, O Lord, the liv-ing bread. Give to

gift, your gift of self, O Lord.
food, for which our spir - its long.
us, O Lord, the liv - ing bread.

After last verse

Give us, Lord, the liv - ing bread.

Text: Omer Westendorf, b. 1916, ©
Music: Robert E. Kreutz, b. 1922, ©

All that I Am 373

VERSES

1. All that I am, all that I do, All that I'll ev-er have, I of-fer now to you.
2. All that I dream, all that I pray, All that I'll ev-er make, I give to you to-day.
3. All that I am, all that I do, All that I'll ev-er have, I of-fer now to you.
4. All that I dream, all that I pray, All that I'll ev-er make, I give to you to-day.

REFRAIN

Take and sanc-ti-fy these gifts for your hon-or, Lord.

To Verse 3
To Verse 4

Know-ing that I love and serve you is e-nough re-ward.

Text: Sebastian Temple, b. 1928, ©
Music: Sebastian Temple, b. 1928; arr. Mark G. Rachelski, b. 1957, ©
Music arrangemnt © 1986, J.S. Paluch Co.

374 Father, We Thank Thee Who Hast Planted

1. Fa - ther, we thank thee who hast plant - ed Thy ho - ly
2. Watch o'er thy Church, O Lord, in mer - cy, Save it from

name with - in our hearts. Know - ledge and faith and life im -
e - vil, guard it still, Per - fect it in thy love, u -

mor - tal Je - sus thy Son to us im - parts. Thou, Lord, didst
nite it, Cleansed and con - formed un - to thy will. As grain, once

make all for thy plea - sure, Didst give us food for
scat - tered on the hill - sides, Was in this bro - ken

Text: Greek, ca. 110, tr. F. Bland Tucker, 1895–1984, rev., ©
Music: Louis Bourgeois, c. 1510–1561, attr.

98 98 98 98
RENDEZ A DIEU

all our days. Giv - ing in Christ the Bread e -
bread made one, So from all lands thy Church be

ter - nal; Thine is the pow'r, be thine the praise.
gath - ered In - to thy king - dom by thy Son.

Alternative Text

Bread of the World, in Mercy Broken   375

Bread of the world, in mercy broken,
Wine of the soul, in mercy shed,
By whom the words of life were spoken,
And in whose death our sins are dead:
Look on the heart by sorrow broken,
Look on the tears by sinners shed;
And be thy feast to us the token
That by thy grace our souls are fed.

Text: Reginald Heber, 1783–1826

98 98 98 98
RENDEZ A DIEU

376 O Lord, I Am Not Worthy

1. O Lord, I am not wor - thy That thou should'st come to me, But speak the words of com - fort, My spir - it healed shall be.

2. Oh, come, all you who la - bor In sor - row and in pain, Come, eat this Bread from heav - en; Thy peace and strength re - gain.

3. O Je - sus, we a - dore thee, Our Vic - tim and our Priest, Whose pre - cious Blood and Bod - y Be - come our sa - cred feast.

4. O sac - ra - ment most ho - ly, O sac - ra - ment di - vine! All praise and all thanks - giv - ing Be ev - 'ry mo - ment thine.

Text: vv 1 & 4, anon.; vv 2 & 3, Irvin Udulutsch, O.F.M., Cap., ©
Music: "Burns" traditional melody; inst. desc. Sr. Maurita Bernet, O.S.F., ©

76 76
NON DIGNUS (CLARIBEL)

Let All Mortal Flesh Keep Silence 377

1. Let all mor-tal flesh keep si - lence, And with fear and
2. King of kings, yet born of Mar - y, As of old on
3. Rank on rank the host of heav - en Spreads its van-guard
4. At his feet the six - winged ser - aph; Cher - u - bim with

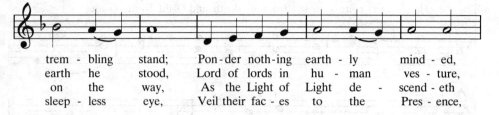

trem - bling stand; Pon-der noth-ing earth - ly mind - ed,
earth he stood, Lord of lords in hu - man ves - ture,
on the way, As the Light of Light de - scend-eth
sleep - less eye, Veil their fac - es to the Pres - ence,

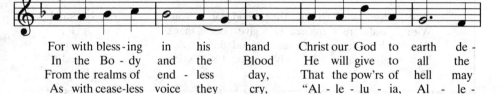

For with bless-ing in his hand Christ our God to earth de -
In the Bo - dy and the Blood He will give to all the
From the realms of end - less day, That the pow'rs of hell may
As with cease-less voice they cry, "Al - le - lu - ia, Al - le -

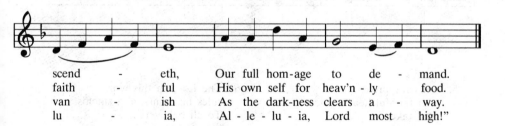

scend - eth, Our full hom-age to de - mand.
faith - ful His own self for heav'n - ly food.
van - ish As the dark-ness clears a - way.
lu - ia, Al - le - lu - ia, Lord most high!"

Text: Liturgy of St. James; tr. Gerard Moultrie, 1829–1885
Music: French Carol, 17th c.

87 87 87
PICARDY

378 Draw Near and Take the Body of Your Lord

1. Draw near and take the bod-y of your Lord,
2. Saved by his bod-y hal-lowed by his blood,
3. Sal-va-tion's giv-er, Christ, the on-ly Son,
4. He, ran-som-er from death and light from shade,

And drink with faith the blood for you out-poured.
With souls re-freshed we give our thanks to God.
By his dear cross and blood the vic-t'ry won.
Now gives his ho-ly grace his saints to aid.

5. Let us approach
   with faithful hearts sincere,
   And take the pledges
   of salvation here.

6. The Lord in this world
   rules his saints, and shields,
   To all believers
   life eternal yields:

7. With heav'nly bread makes
   those who hunger whole,
   Gives living waters
   to the thirsting soul.

8. Before your presence, Lord,
   all people bow.
   In this your feast of love
   be with us now.

Text: Latin hymn, 7th c.; tr. John M. Neale, 1818–1866. alt.
Music: Arthur S. Sullivan, 1842–1900

10 10
COENA DOMINI

Lord, Accept the Gifts 379

1. Lord, ac - cept the gifts we of - fer At this Eu - cha -
2. May our souls be pure and spot - less As the host of
3. Take our gifts, al - might - y Fa - ther, Liv - ing God, e -

ris - tic feast. Bread and wine to be trans - formed now
wheat so fine, May all stain of sin be crushed out,
ter - nal, true, Which we give through Christ, our Sav - ior,

Through the work of Christ our priest. Take us, too, O
Like the grape that forms the wine, As we, too, be -
Plead - ing here for us a - new. Grant sal - va - tion

Lord, trans - form us; Be your grace in us in - creased.
come par - tak - ers In this sac - ri - fice di - vine.
to all pres - ent And our faith and love re - new.

Alt. Tune: Tantum Ergo, no. 365

Text: Sr. Mary Teresine Hytrek, O.S.F., ©
Music: John F. Wade, 1711–1786; acc. Sr. Mary Teresine, O.S.F., ©

87 87 87
ST. THOMAS

380 O Food of Exiles Lowly

1. O Food of ex - iles low - ly, O Bread of
2. O cleans - ing wa - ter, stream - ing From Je - sus'
3. O Lord, we kneel be - fore you And fer - vent -

an - gels ho - ly, O Man - na from on high! We
side, re - deem - ing All those of A - dam's race! O
ly a - dore you, All hid be - neath this bread. But

hun - ger for your bless - ing, All good in you pos -
quench-ing foun - tain flow - ing, Our ev - 'ry want be -
make to us this prom - ise: To see you in your

sess - ing, With fa - vor hear our heart's out - cry.
stow - ing, O come and fill our souls with grace.
full - ness, The sa - cred bo - dy's mys - tic head.

Text: O Esca Viatorum, 1661; tr. Owen M. Lee, b. 1930, ©
Music: Heinrich Isaac, c. 1450–1527; arr. J.S. Bach, 1685–1750

77 6 77 8
INNSBRUCK

O Esca Viatorum 381

1. O e - sca vi - a - tó - rum, O pa - nis an - ge -
2. O lym - pha, fons a - mó - ris, Qui pu - ro Sal - va -
3. O Je - su, tu - um vul - tum Quem có - li - mus oc -

ló - rum, O man-na caé - li - tum! E - su - ri - én - tes
tó - ris E cor - de pró - flu - is! Te si - ti - én - tes
cúl-tum Sub pa - nis spé - ci - e, Fac, ut re - mó - to

ci - ba, Dul - cé - di - ne non pri - va Cor -
po - ta, Haec so - la no - stra vo - ta, His
ve - lo, A - pér - ta nos in cae - lo Cer -

da quae - rén - ti - um, Cor - da quae - rén - ti - um.
u - na súf - fi - cis, His u - na súf - fi - cis.
ná - mus á - ci - e, Cer - ná - mus á - ci - e.

Text: Anon., c. 1661
Music: Johann M. Haydn, 1737–1806; harm, Thomas Kelly, ©

382 O Jesus, We Adore Thee

VERSES

1. O Je - sus, we a - dore thee, Who in thy love di - vine,
2. O Je - sus, we a - dore thee, Our Vic - tim and our Priest,
3. O Je - sus, we a - dore thee, Our Sav - ior and our King,
4. O Je - sus, we a - dore thee, Come, live in us, we pray,

Con - ceal thy might - y God - head In forms of bread and wine.
Whose pre - cious blood and bod - y Be - come our sa - cred feast.
And with the saints and an - gels A hum - ble hom - age bring.
That all our thoughts and ac - tions Be thine a - lone to - day.

REFRAIN

O Sac - ra - ment most ho - ly, O Sac - ra - ment di - vine,

All praise and all thanks - giv - ing Be ev - 'ry mo - ment thine!

5. O come, all you who labor
In sorrow and in pain;
Come, eat this bread from heaven,
Your peace and strength regain. *Refrain*

Text: Irvin Udulutsch, O.F.M., Cap., b. 1920, ©
Music: Fulda melody; adapt. and arr. Roger Nachtwey, b. 1930, ©

76 76 with Refrain
FULDA MELODY

O King of Might and Splendor 383

1. O King of might and splen - dor, Cre - a - tor most a - dored,
2. Thy bod - y thou hast giv - en, Thy blood thou hast out - poured

This sac - ri - fice we ren - der To thee as sov - 'reign Lord.
That sin might be for - giv - en, O Je - sus, lov - ing Lord.

May these our gifts be pleas - ing Un - to thy maj - es - ty,
As now with love most ten - der Thy death we cel - e - brate,

Man - kind from sin re - leas - ing Who have of - fend-ed thee.
Our lives in self - sur - ren - der To thee we con - se - crate.

Higher Key: O Sacred Head, no. 259

Text: Tr. by A. Gregory Murray, O.S.B., b. 1905, ©
Music: Hans Leo Hassler, 1564–1612; acc. J.S. Bach, 1685–1750;
adapt. Sr. Mary Teresine Hytrek, O.S.F., ©

76 76 76 76
PASSION CHORALE

384 O Lord, with Wondrous Mystery

1. O Lord, with won-drous mys - ter - y You take our bread and wine,
2. You are the same, our Christ and Lord, Who blessed the sup - per room;

And make of these two hum - ble things Your - self, our Lord di - vine.
You are the God who died and rose Tri - um - phant from the tomb.

Our wheat and drink be - come our light, Our al - tar bears your aw-ful might;
This host bears your di - vin - i - ty, This cup con-tains in - fin - i - ty;

O Lord, we thank you for the gift That lies be - fore our sight.
The mys - t'ry fills our souls with love, O Ho - ly Maj - es - ty.

Text: Michael Valentine Gannon, b. 1927, alt.
Music: Hendrik Franciscus Andriessen, 1892–1981, ©

86 86 88 86
ANDRIESSEN

Soul of My Savior 385

1. Soul of my Sav - ior, sanc - ti - fy my breast;
2. Strength and pro - tec - tion may thy pas - sion be;
3. Guard and de - fend me from the foe ma - lign;

Bod - y of Christ, be thou my sav - ing guest;
O bless - ed Je - sus, hear and an - swer me;
In death's dread mo - ments make me on - ly thine;

Blood of my Sav - ior, bathe me in thy tide,
Deep in thy wounds, Lord, hide and shel - ter me,
Call me and bid me come to thee on high,

Wash me with wa - ter flow - ing from thy side.
So I shall nev - er, nev - er part from thee.
Where I may praise thee with thy saints for aye.

Text: Pope John XXII, 1249–1334, attr.; tr. Edward Caswall, 1814–1878
Music: William J. Maher, S.J., 1823–1877

10 10 10 10
ANIMA CHRISTI

386 Ubi Caritas

REFRAIN

U - bi cá - ri - tas et a - mor De - us i - bi est.

VERSES

1. Con-gre-gá - vit nos in u - num Chri-sti a-mor. Ex-ul-té - mus et in
2. Si-mul er - go cum in u - num con-gre-gá-mur: Ne nos men - te di - vi-
3. Si-mul quo-que cum be-á - tis vi - de-á-mus Glo-ri-án - ter vul-tum

ip - so ju-cun-dé-mur. Ti - me-á - mus et a-mé - mus De-um vi - vum.
dá - mur, ca - ve - á - mus. Ces-sent júr-gi - a ma-lí - gna, ces-sent li - tes.
tu - um, Chri-ste De - us. Gáu-di-um, quod est im-mén-sum at-que pro-bum,

To Refrain

Et ex cor-de di - li - gá - mus nos sin - cé - ro.
Et in mé-di - o no-stri sit Chri-stus De - us.
Saé-cu-la per in - fi - ní - ta sae-cu - ló - rum. A - men.

Text: Anon.
Music: Plainchant, Mode VI; acc. Sr. Luanne Durst, O.S.F., ©

12 12 12 12 with Refrain
UBI CARITAS

387 Where Charity and Love Prevail

1. Where char - i - ty and love pre - vail   There God is ev - er found;
2. With grate-ful joy and ho - ly fear   His char - i - ty we learn;
3. For - give we now each o - ther's faults   As we our faults con-fess;
4. Let strife a - mong us be un - known,   Let all con-ten-tion cease;

Brought here to - geth - er by Christ's love   By love are we thus bound.
Let us with heart and mind and strength   Now love him in re - turn.
And let us love each o - ther well   In Chris-tian ho - li - ness.
Be his the glo - ry that we seek,   Be ours his ho - ly peace.

5. Let us recall that in our midst
   Dwells God's begotten Son;
   As members of his body joined
   We are in him made one.

6. Love can exclude no race or creed
   If honored be God's name;
   Our common life embraces all
   Whose Father is the same.

Text: Ubi Caritas, Latin 9th c.; tr. Omer Westendorf, b. 1916
Music: Paul Benoit, O.S.B., 1893–1979

86 86
CHRISTIAN LOVE

The Disciples Knew the Lord Jesus 388

Music: Plainchant, Mode VI, adapt; acc. Mason Martens, b. 1933, ©

389 Gift of Finest Wheat

REFRAIN

You sat-is-fy the hun-gry heart with gift of fin-est wheat; come
give to us, O sav-ing Lord, the bread of life to eat.

VERSES

1. As when the shep - herd calls his sheep, They
2. With joy - ful lips we sing to you Our
3. Is not the cup we bless and share The
4. The mys - t'ry of your pre - sence, Lord, No

know and heed his voice, So when you call your
praise and grat - i - tude, That you should count us
blood of Christ out - poured? Do not one cup, one
mor - tal tongue can tell: Whom all the world can -

To Refrain

fam - 'ly, Lord, We fol - low and re - joice.
wor - thy, Lord, To share this heav'n - ly food.
loaf, de - clare Our one - ness in the Lord?
not con - tain Comes in our hearts to dwell.

5. You give yourself to us, O Lord;
   Then selfless let us be,
   To serve each other in your name
   In truth and charity. *Refrain*

Text: Omer Westendorf, b. 1916
Music: Robert E. Kreutz, b. 1922

86 86 with Refrain
EUCHARISTIC CONGRESS

Shepherd of Souls 390

1. Shep-herd of souls, re - fresh and bless Your cho - sen
2. We would not live by bread a - lone, But by your
3. Be known to us in break - ing bread, But do not
4. Lord, sup with us in love di - vine; Your Bod - y

pil - grim flock With man - na in the
word of grace, In strength of which we
then de - part; Sav - ior, a - bide with
and your Blood, That liv - ing bread, that

wil - der - ness, With wa - ter from the rock.
trav - el on To our a - bid - ing place.
us, and spread Your ta - ble in our heart.
heav'n - ly wine, Be our im - mor - tal food.

Text: Vv. 1 & 2, James Montgomery, 1771–1854; vv. 3 & 4, anon.
Music: John Bacchus Dykes, 1823–1876

86 86
ST. AGNES

391 On This Day of Sharing

1. On this day of shar - ing   Glad - ly do we come,
2. See the ta - ble lad - en,   With the bread and wine,
3. Food and drink sym - bol - ic   Of his life on earth:
4. In the bread that's bro - ken, In the wine that's poured,

To the Lord's own ta - ble,   Gath-ered here as one.
Sign of Christ's own pres - ence, Pledge of love di - vine!
Peace, good will to all earth,   Prom-ised from his birth.
Be the name of Je - sus   Ev - er - more a - dored!

REFRAIN

Christ, our broth - er, make us one in thee,

One in hope e - ter - nal, One in char - i - ty.

5. May our will be pleasing
   To thy majesty;
   Keep our love most faithful,
   Lord, we ask of thee. *Refrain*

6. Daily may we serve you;
   Worship you as God;
   Follow as you lead us
   In the way you trod. *Refrain*

7. Praise be to the Father,
   Honor to the Son;
   To the Holy Spirit,
   Be the glory one! *Refrain*

Text: Polish Hymnal; tr. Br. Gerard Wojchowski, O.S.B., b. 1925, ©
Music: John Siedlecki, 1878

65 65 with Refrain
BGDZIC POZDNOWIONA

See Us, Lord, About Your Altar 392

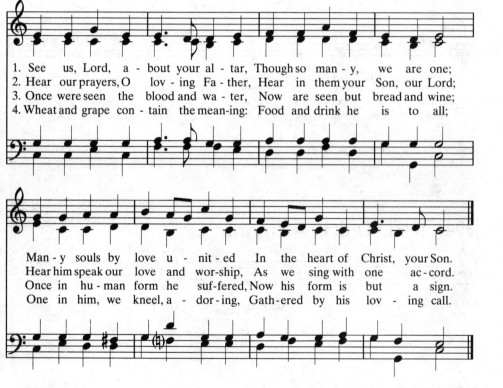

1. See us, Lord, a - bout your al - tar, Though so man - y, we are one;
   Man - y souls by love u - nit - ed In the heart of Christ, your Son.
2. Hear our prayers, O lov - ing Fa - ther, Hear in them your Son, our Lord;
   Hear him speak our love and wor-ship, As we sing with one ac - cord.
3. Once were seen the blood and wa - ter, Now are seen but bread and wine;
   Once in hu - man form he suf-fered, Now his form is but a sign.
4. Wheat and grape con - tain the mean-ing: Food and drink he is to all;
   One in him, we kneel, a - dor-ing, Gath-ered by his lov - ing call.

5. Hear us yet: so much is needful
   In our frail, disordered life;
   Stay with us and tend our weakness,
   Till that day of no more strife.

6. Members of his Mystic Body
   Now we know our prayer is heard,
   Heard by you because your children
   Have received the eternal Word.

Alt. Tune: Firmly I Believe and Truly, no. 505
Text: John Greally, b. 1934, alt., ©
Music: Edward William Elgar, 1857–1934, ©

87 87
DRAKES BOUGHTON

393 An Upper Room Did Our Lord Prepare

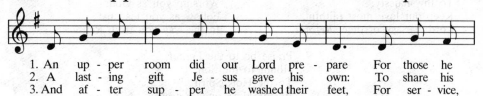

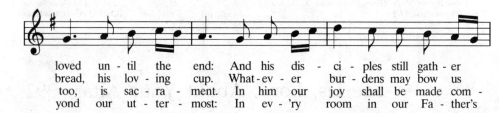

1. An up - per room did our Lord pre - pare For those he
2. A last - ing gift Je - sus gave his own: To share his
3. And af - ter sup - per he washed their feet, For ser - vice,
4. No end there is! We de - part in peace. He loves be -

loved un - til the end: And his dis - ci - ples still gath - er
bread, his lov - ing cup. What - ev - er bur - dens may bow us
too, is sac - ra - ment. In him our joy shall be made com -
yond our ut - ter - most: In ev - 'ry room in our Fa - ther's

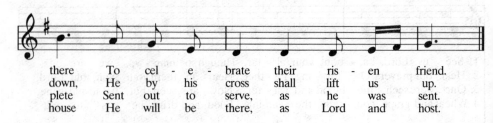

there To cel - e - brate their ris - en friend.
down, He by his cross shall lift us up.
plete Sent out to serve, as he was sent.
house He will be there, as Lord and host.

Text: Fred Pratt Green, b. 1903
Music: English Traditional Melody; arr. The Church Hymnary, 3rd ed., ©

98 98
O WALY, WALY

Text © 1974, Hope Publishing Company

394 Jesu, Dulcis Memoria

1. Je - su, dul - cis me - mó - ri - a, Dans ve - ra
2. Nil cá - ni - tur su - á - vi - us, Nil au - dí -
3. Je - su, spes pae - ni - tén - ti - bus, Quam pi - us
4. Nec lin - gua va - let dí - ce - re, Nec lít - te -

cor - dis gaú - di - a: Sed su - per mel et ó - mni - a,
tur ju - cún - di - us, Nil co - gi - tá - tur dúl - ci - us,
es pe - tén - ti - bus! Quam bo - nus te quae - rén - ti - bus!
ra ex - prí - me - re: Ex - pér - tus po - test cré - de - re,

After Final Verse

E - jus dul - cis prae - sén - ti - a.
Quam Je - sus De - i Fí - li - us.
Sed quid in - ve - ni - én - ti - bus?
Quid sit Je - sum di - lí - ge - re. A - men.

5. Sis Jesu nostrum gaúdium,
Qui es futúrus praémium:
Sit nostra in te glória,
Per cuncta semper saécula.

Alt. Acc.: O Radiant Light, no. 442
Text: St. Bernard of Clairvaux, 1091–1153, attr.
Music: Plainchant Mode I; acc. Jean–Hebert Desrocquettes, O.S.B., ©

88 88
JESU DULCIS MEMORIA

We Long for You, O Lord 395

1. We long for you, O Lord; We long for you, O Lord;
2. We can - not rest, O Lord; We can - not rest, O Lord;
3. We hun - ger for you, Lord; We hun - ger for you, Lord;
4. Your flesh is strength, O Lord; Your flesh is strength, O Lord;

Come, make us one with you in love; We long for you, O Lord.
Come, Lamb of God, and give us peace; We can - not rest, O Lord.
Come feed us now with liv - ing bread; We hun - ger for you, Lord.
Come, ho - ly strong One, make us strong; Your flesh is strength, O Lord.

5. You live in us, O Lord;
You live in us, O Lord;
To be our Way and Truth and Life;
You live in us, O Lord.

6. You live in others, Lord;
You live in others, Lord;
Our love of them is love of you;
You live in others, Lord.

7. You love through us, O Lord;
You love through us, O Lord;
We are your heart and hands and voice;
You love through us, O Lord.

8. You want one flock, O Lord;
You want one flock, O Lord;
Your word and bread can make us one;
You want one flock, O Lord.

9. We sing your wonders, Lord;
We sing your wonders, Lord;
For love shines out in all you do;
We sing your wonders, Lord.

10. We wait in joy, O Lord;
We wait in joy, O Lord;
Till you return to take us home,
We wait in joy, O Lord.

Text: Rev. Cyril A. Reilly, ©
Music: Rev. Cyril A. Reilly; acc. Roger Nachtwey, b. 1930, ©

396 Gift Bread

REFRAIN

O lov-ing Fa-ther, we thank you for the food you give

That through life's jour-ney we might live.

For our health of soul and mind The bread we need is of a diff-'rent kind

Liv-ing bread of your Son That when life's pil-grim-age is done,

We shall die not ev-er, But live, and live for-ev-er.

Text: Omer Westendorf, b. 1916, ©
Music: Edward J. McKenna, ©

88 88 88 with Refrain
BEVERLY SHORES

VERSES

Cantor

1. E - li - jah sat be - neath a tree,
2. When Mo - ses' peo - ple went un - fed
3. E - li - jah, Mo - ses had their bread,

Dis - cour - aged, hun - gry, sad was he.
God rained down heav - en's man - na bread.
By scones and man - na they were fed.

An an - gel, with a gen - tle tap,
This food then gave them need - ed strength
From God their sav - ing man - na came;

A - roused E - li - jah from his nap.
To jour - ney through the des - ert's length.
The source of our bread is the same.

And there be - side him lay some scones
Their food had come from God on high.
Our dai - ly bread is from a - bove.

To Refrain

Which he then warmed on heat - ed stones.
They ate, lived out their lives to die.
All man - na comes from God in love.

397 O Living Bread from Heaven

1. O liv-ing bread from heav-en, How well you fed your guest!
2. Lord Je-sus, here you led me With-in your ho-liest place,
3. You gave me all I want-ed This food can death de-stroy;
4. Lord, grant me that, thus strength-ened With heav'n-ly food, while here

The gifts that you have giv-en Have filled my heart with rest.
And here your-self have fed me With treas-ures of your grace,
And you have free-ly grant-ed The cup of end-less joy.
My course on earth is length-ened, I serve with ho-ly fear,

O won-drous food of bless-ing, O cup that heals our woes,
And you have free-ly giv-en What earth could nev-er buy,
O Lord, I do not mer-it The fa-vor you have shown,
And when you call my spir-it To leave this world be-low,

Higher Key: The Chruch's One Foundation, no. 489

Text: Johann Rist, 1607–1667, tr. Catherine Winkworth, 1827–1878, alt.
Music: Samuel Sebastian Wesley, 1810–1877

76 76 76 76
AURELIA

My   heart, this gift   pos - sess - ing, With prais - es   o - ver - flows!
The   bread of life   from heav - en, That   I   may nev - er   die.
And   all   my   soul   and   spir - it Bow   down be - fore your throne.
I   en - ter, through your   mer -   it, Where joys un - min - gled flow.

398 Wondrous Gift

1. Won-drous gift! The Word who fash - ioned All things by his
2. He who once to die a vic - tim On the cross did
3. While the peo - ple all u - nit - ing In the sac - ri -

might di - vine, Bread in - to his bod - y chang - es,
not re - fuse, Day by day up - on our al - tars
fice sub - lime, Of - fer Christ to his high Fa - ther,

In - to his own blood the wine; What though sense no
That same sac - ri - fice re - news; Through his ho - ly
Of - fer up them - selves with him, Join to - geth - er

change per - ceives? Faith ad - mires, a - dores, be - lieves!
priest - hood's hands, Faith - ful to his last com - mands.
with the priest In this Eu - cha - ris - tic feast.

Text: Hoste dum victo triumphanes, 1886; tr. Edward Caswall, 1814–1878, alt.
Music: Joachim Neander Bremen, 1680; acc. Arthur Hutchings, b. 1906, ©

87 87 77
COBLENZ

Litany of Comfort 399

REFRAIN

Taste and see how good is the Lord.

VERSES

1. Come unto me, all who are weary and heav - y lad - en,
2. God so loved the world that he gave his on - ly Son,
3. Know that the Lord is God: he made us, we be - long to him.
4. I am the resur - - - - - rec - tion and life.
5. Blest is the one who fears the Lord;
6. The Lord will give you rest forever and fill your soul with splen - dor.
7. You shall eat and drink at my table in the king - dom,
8. My spirit is sweet - - - - er than hon - ey,

To Refrain

1. and I will re - fresh you.
2. that whoever believes in him shall have e - ter - nal life.
3. We are his people, the sheep of his flock.
4. Whoever believes in me shall nev - er die.
5. that house shall be favored with glo - ry and wealth.
6. He will make you like a spring of water whose wa - ters do not fail.
7. and you shall be seated on thrones to judge the twelve tribes.
8. and my reward sweeter than hon - ey and the hon - ey - comb.

Text: Francis Eugene Pellegrini, 1936–1984
Music: Francis Eugene Pellegrini, 1936–1984

Irregular with Refrain
COMFORT

400 O God of Great Compassion

1. O God of great com-pas-sion, your mer-cy knows no
2. In Je-sus' name we ask it, for Je-sus is your
3. The Lord would break our shack-les, would lift us from the
4. New light up-on us dawn-ing, new hope for us is

bounds; How slow you are to an-ger with
Son. His blood and bit-ter pas-sion for
dust, From mon-ey, plea-sure, pow-er, what-
here, For Sa-tan's pow'r is bro-ken, his

sin-ners all a-round! We ask for full for-give-ness, for
us re-demp-tion won. O Fa-ther, now for-give us; we
ev-er is our lust. He o-pens up our pris-on, from
reign of hate and fear. The ris-en Lord is com-ing to

par-don is our plea; We kiss the cross of
know not what we do; From self-ish-ness and
slav-'ry gives re-lease; To trou-bled hearts and
o-pen blind-ed eyes, To help us walk in

Je-sus who died to make us free.
fight-ing we'll turn a-gain to you!
guil-ty, he brings a Chris-tian peace.
jus-tice be-neath the o-pen skies.

Text: Willard F. Jabusch, b. 1930, ©
Music: Burgundian Tune; acc. David Kraehenbuehl, b. 1923, ©

Our Father, We Have Wandered 401

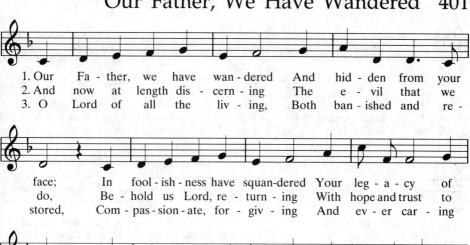

1. Our Fa - ther, we have wan - dered And hid - den from your
2. And now at length dis - cern - ing The e - vil that we
3. O Lord of all the liv - ing, Both ban - ished and re -

face; In fool - ish - ness have squan-dered Your leg - a - cy of
do, Be - hold us Lord, re - turn - ing With hope and trust to
stored, Com - pas - sion - ate, for - giv - ing And ev - er car - ing

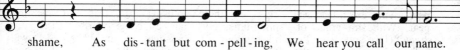

grace. But now, in ex - ile dwell-ing, We rise with fear and
you. In haste you come to meet us And home re - joic - ing
Lord, Grant now that our trans - gres-sing, Our faith-less-ness may

shame, As dis - tant but com - pell - ing, We hear you call our name.
bring, In glad-ness there to greet us With calf and robe and ring.
cease. Stretch out your hand in bless-ing In par - don and in peace.

Text: Msgr. Kevin Nichols, b. 1929, ©
Music: Erik Routley, 1917–1982, ©

76 76 76 76
NESHANIC

402 Come, My Love, the Spring is Budding

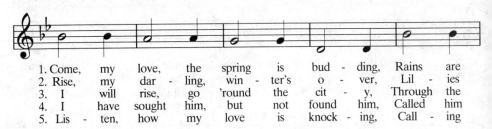

1. Come, my love, the spring is bud - ding, Rains are
2. Rise, my dar - ling, win - ter's o - ver, Lil - ies
3. I will rise, go 'round the cit - y, Through the
4. I have sought him, but not found him, Called him
5. Lis - ten, how my love is knock - ing, Call - ing

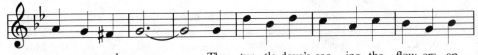

o - ver and gone. The tur - tle-dove's coo - ing, the flow-ers ap -
give forth their scent. The coun-try-side bright-ens as flow-ers ap -
streets and the squares. I'll ask ev - 'ry watch-man I see on the
with - out re - ply. Je - ru - sa-lem's daugh-ters, I beg you to
in at the door. His as - pect like ce - dar on Leb - a - non

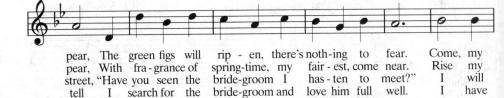

pear, The green figs will rip - en, there's noth-ing to fear. Come, my
pear, With fra - grance of spring-time, my fair - est, come near. Rise my
street, "Have you seen the bride-groom I has - ten to meet?" I will
tell I search for the bride-groom and love him full well. I have
hills, Like bal - sam, his pres - ence the coun-try - side fills. Lis - ten,

D.S.

love, the spring is bud - ding, Rains are o - ver and gone.
dar - ling, win - ter's o - ver, Lil - ies give forth their scent.
rise, go 'round the cit - y, Through the streets and the squares.
sought him, but not found him, Called him with - out re - ply.
how my love is knock-ing, Call - ing in at the door.

Text: Song of Songs; adapt. Willard F. Jabusch, b. 1930, ©
Music: Breton Folk Melody; acc. David Kraehenbuehl, b. 1923, ©

403 When Love Is Found

1. When love is found and hope comes home, Sing and be
2. When love has flow'red in trust and care, Build both each
3. When love is tried as loved - ones change, Hold still to
4. When love is torn and trust be - trayed, Pray strength to

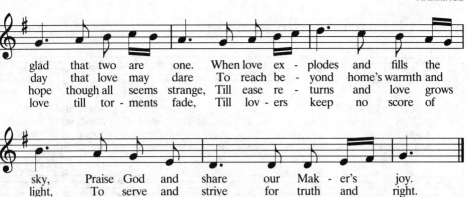

glad   that two   are   one.   When love   ex - plodes   and   fills   the
day   that love   may   dare   To   reach be - yond   home's warmth and
hope   though all   seems strange,   Till   ease re - turns   and   love   grows
love   till   tor - ments   fade,   Till   lov - ers   keep   no   score   of

sky,   Praise God   and   share   our   Mak - er's   joy.
light,   To   serve   and   strive   for   truth   and   right.
wise   Through list - 'ning   ears   and   o - pened   eyes.
wrong   But   hear through pain   love's   Eas - ter   song.

5. Praise God for love, praise God for life,
In age or youth, in husband, wife.
Lift up your hearts, let love be fed
Through death and life in broken bread.

Text: Brian Wren, b. 1936   88 88
Music: Traditional English Melody; arr. Martin West, b. 1929   O WALY WALY

May the Grace of Christ   404

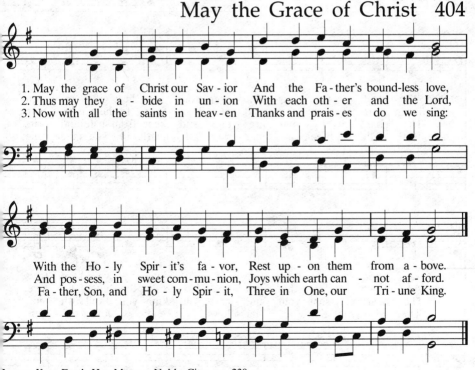

1. May the grace of   Christ our   Sav - ior   And   the   Fa - ther's bound-less love,
2. Thus may they a - bide in   un - ion   With   each oth - er   and   the   Lord,
3. Now with all   the   saints in heav - en   Thanks and prais - es   do   we   sing:

With the Ho - ly   Spir - it's   fa - vor,   Rest up - on them   from a - bove.
And pos - sess, in   sweet com - mu - nion,   Joys which earth can - not af - ford.
Fa - ther, Son, and   Ho - ly   Spir - it,   Three in   One, our   Tri - une King.

Lower Key: Earth Has Many a Noble City, no. 230

Text: John Newton, 1725–1807, alt. vv. 1 & 2; v. 3 adapt. Carroll T. Andrews, b. 1918, ©   87 87
Music: Christian Frederick Witt, 1660–1716   STUTTGART

405 O Father, All-creating

1. O Father, all-creating, Whose wisdom, love, and pow'r
2. With good wine, Lord, at Cana The wedding feast you blessed.
3. O Spirit of the Father, Breathe on them from above,
4. Unless you build it, Father, The house is built in vain;

First bound two lives together In Eden's primal hour,
Grant also these your presence, And be their dearest guest.
So mighty in your pureness, So tender in your love
Unless you, Savior, bless it, The joy will turn to pain.

Today to these your children Your earliest gifts renew:
Their store of earthly gladness Transform to heav'nly wine,
That, guarded by your presence And kept from strife and sin,
But nothing breaks a marriage Of hearts in you made one;

A home by you made happy, A love by you kept true.
And teach them, in the testing, To know the gift divine.
Their hearts may sense your guidance And know you dwell within.
The love your Spirit hallows Is endless love begun.

Lower Key: O Living Bread from Heaven, no. 397

Text: John Ellerton, 1826–1893, alt.
Music: Samuel Sebastian Wesley, 1810–1876

76 76 76 7
AURELIA

O Christ, the Healer 406

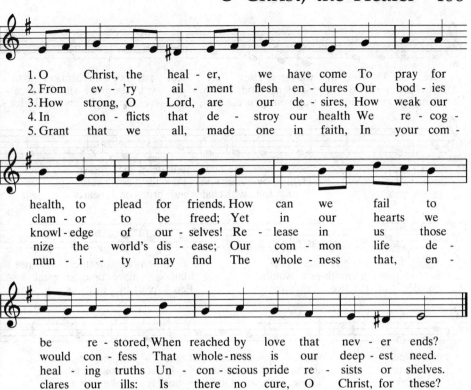

1. O Christ, the heal - er, we have come To pray for
2. From ev - 'ry ail - ment flesh en - dures Our bod - ies
3. How strong, O Lord, are our de - sires, How weak our
4. In con - flicts that de - stroy our health We re - cog -
5. Grant that we all, made one in faith, In your com -

health, to plead for friends. How can we fail to
clam - or to be freed; Yet in our hearts we
knowl - edge of our - selves! Re - lease in us those
nize the world's dis - ease; Our com - mon life de -
mun - i - ty may find The whole - ness that, en -

be re - stored, When reached by love that nev - er ends?
would con - fess That whole - ness is our deep - est need.
heal - ing truths Un - con - scious pride re - sists or shelves.
clares our ills: Is there no cure, O Christ, for these?
rich - ing us, Shall reach the whole of hu - man - kind.

Text: Fred Pratt Green, b. 1903
Music: Klug's Geistliche Lieder, 1543; acc. J.S. Bach, 1685–1750

88 88
ERHALT UNS HERR

407 Save Me, O God

1. Save me, O God the wa-ters rise, my feet can-not find firm ground to
2. Help me, don't be a si-lent God; with-out you the grave will close a-
3. When I'm in pain I'll sing your praise, no tor-ment can make my soul for-

stand on; See, how the cur-rent drags me down, no
bove me; Held by your love I'd be se-cure, as
get you. Poor folk with chains and brok-en hearts will

friend to give sup-port. E-ven my broth-ers do not
in a moth-er's womb; Man-y have come to speak a-
come to live in joy; Peo-ple in mis-er-y and

know me, mocked as an out-cast and a strang-er;
gainst me; shame does its work and I am brok-en;
an-guish, know that your God does not for-sake you;

Lord, will your love give me an an-swer?
See how they tram-ple on your ser-vant
Soon he will come to save his peo-ple,

Pull me from this mud and mis-er-y!
Hur-ry to my side and bring re-lief.
Pour-ing out his mer-cy and his peace.

Text: Willard F. Jabusch, b. 1930
Music: Willard F. Jabusch, b. 1930; acc. S.R. Rudcki, b. 1928, ©

408 O Son of God, in Galilee

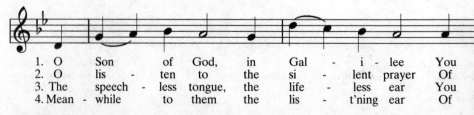

1. O Son of God, in Gal-i-lee You
2. O lis-ten to the si-lent prayer Of
3. The speech-less tongue, the life-less ear You
4. Mean-while to them the lis-t'ning ear Of

made the deaf to hear, The mute to speak, the
your af - flict - ed ones. O bid them cast on
can re - store, O Lord; Your "Eph - phe - tha," O
stead - fast faith im - part, And let your word bring

blind to see; O bless - ed Lord, be near.
you their care; Your grace to them make known.
Sav - ior dear, Can in - stant help af - ford.
light and cheer To ev - 'ry trou - bled heart.

Text: Anna Hoppe, 1889–1941, alt., ©
Music: William Billings 1746–1800; arr. Donald Busarow, b. 1934, ©

86 86
LEWIS–TOWN

Father of Mercy 409

1. Fa - ther of mer - cy, God of con - so - la - tion,
2. Son of the Fa - ther, Lord of all cre - a - tion,
3. Joy – giv - ing Spir - it, be our light in dark - ness,
4. God in three Per - sons, Fa - ther, Son, and Spir - it,

Look on your peo - ple, gath - ered here to praise you:
Come as our Sav - ior, Je - sus, friend of sin - ners:
Come to be - friend us, help us bear our bur - dens:
Come to re - new us, fill your Church with glo - ry:

Pit - y our weak - ness, come in pow'r to
Grant us for - give - ness, lift our down - cast
Give us true cour - age, breathe your peace a -
Grant us your heal - ing, pledge of res - ur -

aid us, Source of all bless - ing.
spir - it, Heal us and save us.
round us, Stay with us al - ways.
rec - tion, Fore - taste of heav - en.

Text: James Quinn, S.J., b. 1919, ©
Music: Arthur Hutchings, b. 1906, ©

11 11 11 5
COLYTON

410 Funeral Hymn

1. Je - sus, Lord, your res - ur - rec - tion
(1.) We with sin and im - per - fec - tion

gives the prom - ise to us all.
seek for - give - ness by your call.

2. Come con - sole us in our griev - ing;
(2.) She (he) was lov - ing and be - liev - ing;

Pit - y our de - part - ed friend.
On your mer - cy we de - pend.

3. Sin you van - quished, Lord most glo - rious;
(3.) You are lov - ing, most for - giv - ing

Note: Optional repeat

O - ver death you were vic - to - rious.
To the dy - ing and the liv - ing.

4. Grant to her (him) e - ter - nal rest. Let her (him)
(4.) On that day bid her (him) a - rise. Join - ing

be a - mong the blest.
you in par - a - dise.

Text: Omer Westendorf, b. 1916, ©
Music: J.S. Bach, 1685–1750, abridg. and arr. Omer Westendorf, b. 1916, ©

Irregular
JESU, JOY

In Paradisum 411

In pa - ra - dí - sum *de - dú - cant te án - ge - li:

in tu - o ad - vén - tu su - scí - pi - ant te már - ty - res,

et per-dú-cant te in ci - vi - tá-tem san - ctam Je - rú - sa-lem.

Cho - rus an - ge - ló - rum te su - scí - pi - at,

et cum Lá - za - ro quon - dam páu - pe - re,

ae - tér - nam há - be - as ré - qui - em.

Text: Ordo Exsequiarum
Music: Plainchant, Mode VIII; acc. Rev. Bartholomew Sayles, O.S.B., b. 1918,
and Sr. Cecile Gertken, O.S.B., b. 1902, ©

412 May the Angels

Gently (♩ = 72)

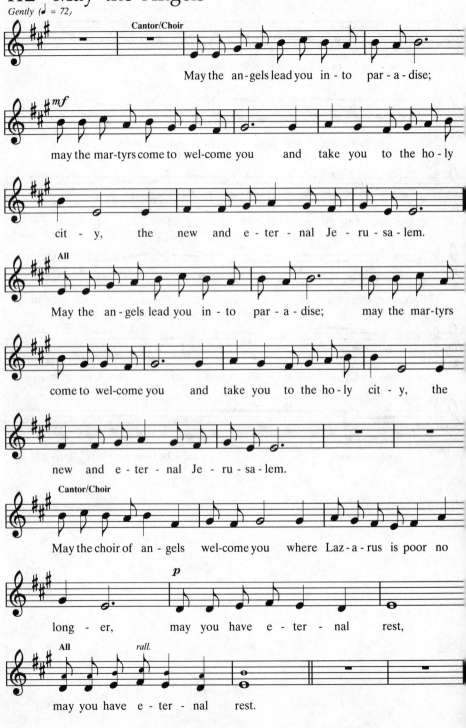

Cantor/Choir

May the an-gels lead you in - to par - a - dise;

mf

may the mar-tyrs come to wel-come you and take you to the ho - ly

cit - y, the new and e - ter - nal Je - ru - sa - lem.

All

May the an - gels lead you in - to par - a - dise; may the mar-tyrs

come to wel-come you and take you to the ho - ly cit - y, the

new and e - ter - nal Je - ru - sa - lem.

Cantor/Choir

May the choir of an - gels wel-come you where Laz - a - rus is poor no

p

long - er, may you have e - ter - nal rest,

All *rall.*

may you have e - ter - nal rest.

Text: *Rite of Funerals, 1970,* ©
Music: *Howard Hughes, S.M., b. 1930,* ©

Irregula
MAY THE ANGEL

413 I Call You to My Father's House

1. I call you to my Fa - ther's house, A
2. Lay down your sor - row, calm your fear; The
3. Al - though the way be hard and long In -
4. I have pre - pared a wed - ding feast Of
5. I call you to my Fa - ther's house, A

love - ly dwell - ing place. He comes to meet you
Fa - ther bids you come. With o - pen arms he
to the prom - ised land, Be not a - fraid to
fin - est food and wine. O join us at this
love - ly dwell - ing place. Be not a - fraid to

on the road, Arms read - y to em - brace.
wel - comes you To your e - ter - nal home.
walk with me: I hold you by the hand.
ban - quet where My friends, the saints, now dine.
trav - el there And meet him face to face.

Text: Sr. Delores Dufner, O.S.B, b. 1939, ©
Music: Jay F. Hunstiger, b. 1950, ©

Saints of God 414

Saints of God, come to her aid! Come to meet her, an-gels of the Lord! Re-ceive her soul(s) and pre-sent her to God the Most High. May Christ, who called you, take you to him-self; may an-gels lead them to A-bra-ham's side. Re-ceive her soul(s) and pre-sent her to God the Most High. Give her e-ter-nal rest, O Lord, and may your light shine on her for-ev-er. Re-ceive her soul(s) and pre-sent her to God the Most High.

Text: Rite of Funerals, 1970, ©
Music: Philip Duffy, ©

Irregular with Response
SANCTI DEI

415 A Blessing for the Fourth of July

Cantor or Celebrant

While the red flame of sun-set warms each of you And
snow-white clouds point to heav-en's door May you be wrapped in Mar-y's
man-tle blue That your land be free for-ev-er-
more. May God grant you long years of life And
li-ber-ty to serve each oth-er's need May hap-pi-ness chase all
fool-ish strife. May you seek his peace in each word and deed.

(Optional) All respond:

A-men

Text: Andrew M. Greeley, b. 1928, ©
Music: Edward J. McKenna, b. 1939, ©

MEEGAN

A Blessing for Christmastime 416

Cantor or Celebrant
sustained

May your eyes be a-lert for the sight of his face And your

ears read-y for the sound of his voice May your feet catch fire to run

in his race The song on your lips tell all the world "Re-joice."

And may you clap and leap and shout and dance Know-ing that the

Lord has come to set you free And run down the road as a per-son en-tranced

Af-ter the One who said come fol-low me. May God bless you the Fa-ther who

made you free the Son who freed you once a-

gain and the Spir-it who keeps you for-ev-er free.

(Optional) All respond:

A-men

Text: Andrew M. Greeley, b. 1928, ©
Music: Edward J. McKenna, b. 1939, ©

MORAN

417 A Blessing for Easter Eve

Cantor or Celebrant

1. As our bap - tis - mal vows we all
2. May you this ho - ly time be born

re - new, May the pas - chal can - dle ex - pel the dark.
a - gain, May you raise your head and clear your eyes,

While Chris - tians joy - ous - ly sing al - le - lu,
And when at last your life must end,

To Verse 3

May the Eas - ter wa - ter heal your heart.
A - long with Je - sus may you then a - rise.

3. May the ris - en Sav - ior flood you with life

And flame you with love of the Fa - ther and Spir - it.

(Optional) All respond:

A-men

Text: Andrew M. Greeley, b. 1928, ©
Music: Irish Traditional; harm. Marion Doherty; arr. Edward J. McKenna ©

10 9 8 10
AG AN BPOSADH

A Blessing for a Dancing God 418

Cantor or Celebrant

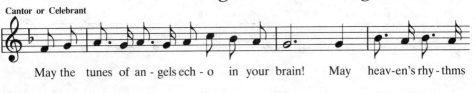

May the tunes of an-gels ech-o in your brain! May heav-en's rhy-thms

tap your twitch-ing feet! May you sing a - long with Mar-y's

sweet re - frain! And may you sway to the Lord's de-mand-ing beat!

Dance with all the lov-ers he has taught your song! And, sure, spin with him-self at

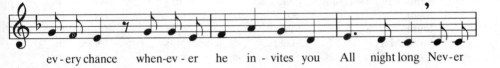

ev - ery chance when-ev - er he in - vites you All night long Nev-er

say no to the Lord of the dance! May the Lord of the dance bless you

and lead you in the dance, Fa - ther, Son, and Ho - ly Spir-it.

(Optional) All respond:

A-men

Text: Andrew M. Greeley, b. 1928, ©
Music: Edward J. McKenna, b. 1939, ©

HUGHES-CARR

419 Litany of Saints

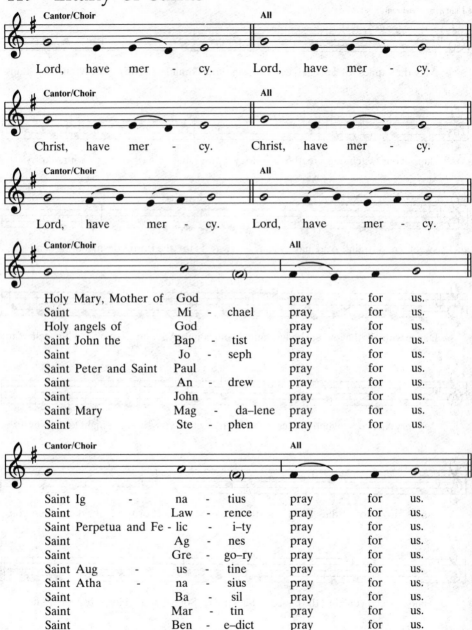

Cantor/Choir   All

Lord, have mer - cy.   Lord, have mer - cy.

Cantor/Choir   All

Christ, have mer - cy.   Christ, have mer - cy.

Cantor/Choir   All

Lord, have mer - cy.   Lord, have mer - cy.

Cantor/Choir   All

		pray	for	us.
Holy Mary, Mother of	God	pray	for	us.
Saint	Mi - chael	pray	for	us.
Holy angels of	God	pray	for	us.
Saint John the	Bap - tist	pray	for	us.
Saint	Jo - seph	pray	for	us.
Saint Peter and Saint	Paul	pray	for	us.
Saint	An - drew	pray	for	us.
Saint	John	pray	for	us.
Saint Mary	Mag - da–lene	pray	for	us.
Saint	Ste - phen	pray	for	us.

Cantor/Choir   All

		pray	for	us.
Saint Ig -	na - tius	pray	for	us.
Saint	Law - rence	pray	for	us.
Saint Perpetua and Fe - lic -	i–ty	pray	for	us.
Saint	Ag - nes	pray	for	us.
Saint	Gre - go–ry	pray	for	us.
Saint Aug -	us - tine	pray	for	us.
Saint Atha -	na - sius	pray	for	us.
Saint	Ba - sil	pray	for	us.
Saint	Mar - tin	pray	for	us.
Saint	Ben - e–dict	pray	for	us.

Music: Plainchant

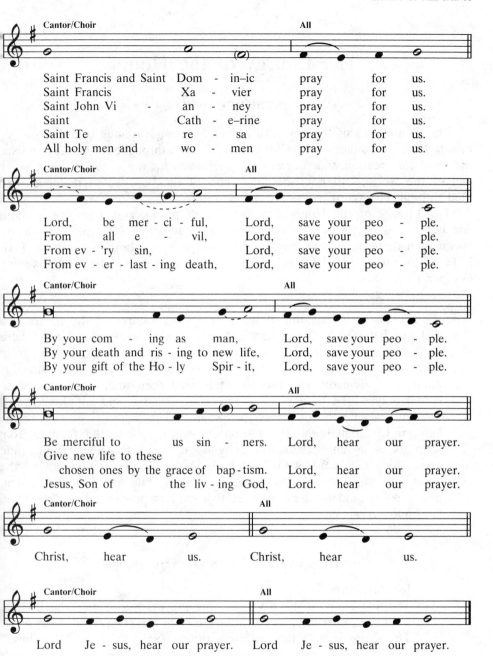

Cantor/Choir   **All**

Saint Francis and Saint Dom - in–ic   pray   for   us.
Saint Francis   Xa - vier   pray   for   us.
Saint John Vi - an - ney   pray   for   us.
Saint   Cath - e–rine   pray   for   us.
Saint Te - re - sa   pray   for   us.
All holy men and   wo - men   pray   for   us.

Cantor/Choir   **All**

Lord,   be   mer - ci - ful,   Lord,   save your peo - ple.
From   all   e - vil,   Lord,   save your peo - ple.
From ev - 'ry   sin,   Lord,   save your peo - ple.
From ev - er - last - ing death,   Lord,   save your peo - ple.

Cantor/Choir   **All**

By your com - ing as   man,   Lord,   save your peo - ple.
By your death and ris - ing to new life,   Lord,   save your peo - ple.
By your gift of the Ho - ly   Spir - it,   Lord,   save your peo - ple.

Cantor/Choir   **All**

Be merciful to   us sin - ners. Lord,   hear   our   prayer.
Give new life to these
    chosen ones by the grace of bap - tism. Lord,   hear   our   prayer.
Jesus, Son of   the liv - ing God,   Lord.   hear   our   prayer.

Cantor/Choir   **All**

Christ,   hear   us.   Christ,   hear   us.

Cantor/Choir   **All**

Lord   Je - sus, hear our prayer.   Lord   Je - sus, hear our prayer.

The Liturgy of the Hours

INTRODUCTION

The Church begins the day with prayer following the long tradition of prayer both of Judaism and Christianity. Prayer throughout the day praised the Lord for creation and redemption, interceded for the needs of the Church and of the world, and nourished the faith of the baptized in dialogue with God through His Word in Psalms and Scripture.

The Liturgy of the Hours is a sacrifice of praise, and a service of faith and hope. This prayer belongs to the whole body of the Church. Thus all are encouraged to recite or sing the Church's Office by celebrating a part of THE LITURGY OF THE HOURS, especially Morning (Lauds) and Evening (Vespers) Prayer.

The essential structure of the parts of the Liturgy of the Hours is a dialogue between God and human beings. After the opening hymn, there is always a psalm or psalms, followed by a long or short reading from holy scripture. Prayers of praise and petition form the conclusion. A number of elements are also included to deepen understanding and to enrich prayer. The psalms are accompanied by titles and antiphons which serve to indicate the theme of the psalm and to guide its praying in the light of Christian faith. The responsory which follows the reading from scripture is as an acclamation designed to assist in understanding and assimilating the Word of God. In both Morning and Evening Prayer, the psalms are supplemented by canticles from the Old and New Testament, highly poetic and rhythmic prayers that express praise and confidence in God and his works.

THE CELEBRATION OF THE HOURS

INTRODUCTION

The first Hour of the day (Morning Prayer) begins with the Invitatory
> *Lord, open my lips* (without *Glory to the Father* and *Alleluia*)

The antiphon with the invitatory psalms (95, 100, 67 or 24) follows. The antiphon may be said first and then repeated after each strophe of the psalm.

The *Glory to the Father* concludes the invitatory psalm.

The rest of Hours begin with the verse:
> *God, come to my assistance. Lord, make haste to help me.*
> *Glory to the Father, Alleluia.*

The *Alleluia* is omitted during Lent.

Introduction as above
Hymn–from the Four Week Psalter or from the Proper of Seasons.

Morning Prayer: psalm, Old Testament canticle, psalm, with their
antiphons

Evening Prayer: two psalms and New Testament canticle, with their
antiphons
Reading
Responsory
Canticle (Benedictus or Magnificat) with Antiphon
Intercessions
Lord's Prayer
Concluding Prayer (without *Let us pray* and with long conclusion)
is proper except on weekdays in Ordinary Time. If a priest or
deacon is presiding, he dismisses the people; otherwise the hour
concludes with: *May the Lord bless us.*
from the Introduction to *CHRISTIAN PRAYER*

The proper antiphons, reading intercessions and prayers for each day
are in THE LITURGY OF HOURS or CHRISTIAN PRAYER.

*A selection of hymns and canticles for Morning and Evening Prayer is
given on the following pages.*

420 Awake, My Soul, and with the Sun

1. A - wake, my soul, and with the sun Thy
2. All praise to thee, who safe hast kept And
3. Lord, I my vows to thee re - new. Dis -
4. Di - rect, con - trol, sug - gest, this day, All

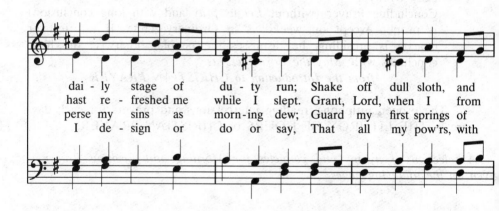

dai - ly stage of du - ty run; Shake off dull sloth, and
hast re - freshed me while I slept. Grant, Lord, when I from
perse my sins as morn - ing dew; Guard my first springs of
I de - sign or do or say, That all my pow'rs, with

joy - ful rise To pay thy morn - ing sac - ri - fice.
death shall wake, I may of end - less light par - take.
thought and will; And with thy - self my spir - it fill.
all their might, In thy sole glo - ry may u - nite.

5. Praise God, from whom all blessings flow;
Praise him, all creatures here below;
Praise him above, ye heav'nly host;
Praise Father, Son, and Holy Ghost.

Text: Thomas Ken 1637–1711
Music: Francois H. Barthelemon, 1741–1808; arr. The Church Hymnal for the Church Year, 1917

88 88
MORNING HYMN

Canticle of Zechariah (Benedictus) 421

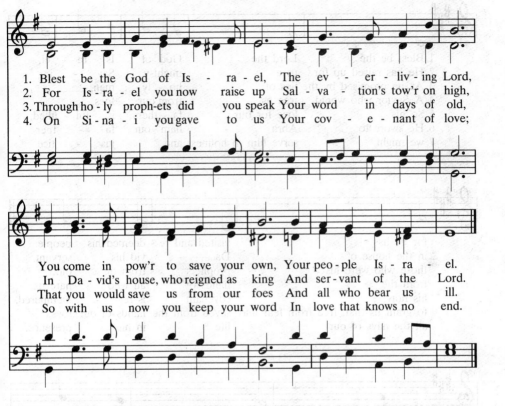

1. Blest be the God of Is - ra - el, The ev - er - liv - ing Lord,
2. For Is - ra - el you now raise up Sal - va - tion's tow'r on high,
3. Through ho - ly proph-ets did you speak Your word in days of old,
4. On Si - na - i you gave to us Your cov - e - nant of love;

You come in pow'r to save your own, Your peo - ple Is - ra - el.
In Da - vid's house, who reigned as king And ser - vant of the Lord.
That you would save us from our foes And all who bear us ill.
So with us now you keep your word In love that knows no end.

5. Of old you gave your solemn oath
   To father Abraham;
   Whose seed a mighty race should be,
   And blest forevermore.

6. You vowed to set your people free
   From fear of ev'ry foe,
   That we might serve you all our days
   In goodness, love, and peace.

7. O tiny child, your name shall be
   The prophet of the Lord;
   The way of God you will prepare
   To make God's coming known.

8. You shall proclaim to Israel
   Salvation's dawning day,
   When God shall wipe away all sins
   With mercy and with love.

9. The rising sun shall shine on us
   To bring the light of day,
   To all who sit in darkest night
   And shadow of the grave.

10. Our footsteps God shall safely guide
    To walk the ways of peace,
    Whose name forevermore be blest
    Who lives and loves and saves.

Text: James D. Quinn, S.J., b. 1919, © 1969
Music: Este's Psalter, 1592

86 86
CHESHIRE

422 Benedictus

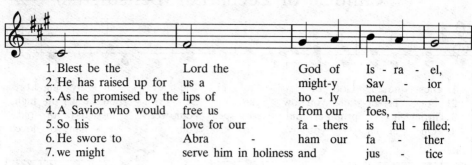

1. Blest be the Lord the God of Is - ra - el,
2. He has raised up for us a might-y Sav - ior
3. As he promised by the lips of ho - ly men,_____
4. A Savior who would free us from our foes,
5. So his love for our fa - thers is ful - filled;
6. He swore to Abra - ham our fa - ther
7. we might serve him in holiness and jus - tice

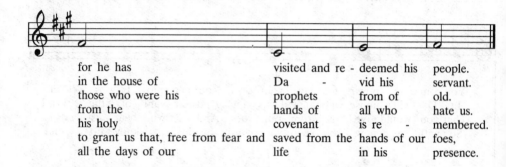

for he has visited and re - deemed his people.
in the house of Da - vid his servant.
those who were his prophets from of old.
from the hands of all who hate us.
his holy covenant is re - membered.
to grant us that, free from fear and saved from the hands of our foes,
all the days of our life in his presence.

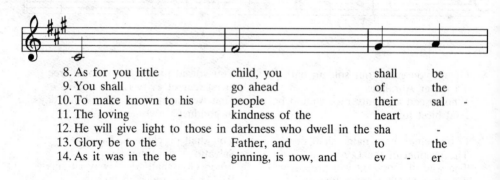

8. As for you little child, you shall be
9. You shall go ahead of the
10. To make known to his people their sal -
11. The loving - kindness of the heart
12. He will give light to those in darkness who dwell in the sha -
13. Glory be to the Father, and to the
14. As it was in the be - ginning, is now, and ev - er

called _____ a prophet of
Lord _____ to pre -
va - tion through the for -
of our God who visits us like the
dow of death, and into the way of
Son, _____ and
shall _____ be, world with -

Text: Luke 1:68–79, tr. The Grail, ©
Music: Vernon Kroening, 1948–1980, ©

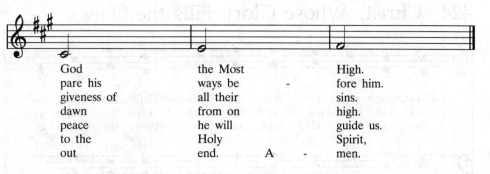

God   the Most   High.
pare his   ways be -   fore him.
giveness of all their   sins.
dawn   from on   high.
peace   he will   guide us.
to the   Holy   Spirit,
out   end.   A -   men.

Now as New Light Reveals the Sky 423

1. Now as new light re-veals the sky, An-nounc-ing
2. May we pre-serve our souls from sin And keep our
3. All praise be to the Tri-ni-ty, To Fa-ther,

God's cre-a-tive work; We turn to him with con-fi-dence,
thoughts and works in peace; May wis-dom be our con-stant guide
Son and Par-a-clete; Who live in ev-er-last-ing day,

That he will work in us to-day.
In or-der and in ho-li-ness.
In un-di-vid-ed u-ni-ty.   A -   men.

Text: Ambrosian, 5th c.; tr. Sr. Cecile Gertken, O.S.B., b. 1902, ©
Music: Benedictine Antiphonal; acc. Sr. Cecile Gertken, O.S.B., b. 1902, ©

88 88
JAM LUCIS ORTO SIDERE

424 Christ, Whose Glory Fills the Skies

1. Christ, whose glo - ry fills the skies, Christ, the true, the
2. Dark and cheer - less is the morn Un - ac - com - pa -
3. Vis - it then this soul of mine! Pierce the gloom of

on - ly Light, Sun of Right - eous - ness, a - rise!
nied by thee; Joy - less is the day's re - turn,
sin and grief! Fill me, ra - dian - cy di - vine;

Tri - umph o'er the shades of night; Day - spring from on
Till thy mer - cy's rays I see; Till they in - ward
Scat - ter all my un - be - lief; More and more thy -

high be near; Day - star, in my heart ap - pear.
light im - part, Glad my eyes and warm my heart.
self dis - play, Shin - ing to the per - fect day.

Text: Charles Wesley, 1707–1788
Music: Choralbuch, 1815; arr. William Henry Havergal, 1793–1870

77 77 77
RATISBON

Morning Has Broken   425

1. Morn-ing has bro - ken like the first morn - ing, Black-bird has
2. Sweet the rain's new fall sun - lit from heav - en, Like the first
3. Mine is the sun - light! Mine is the morn - ing Born of the

spo - ken like the first bird. Praise for the sing - ing! Praise for the
dew - fall on the first grass. Praise for the sweet - ness of the wet
one light E - den saw play! Praise with e - la - tion, praise ev - 'ry

morn - ing! Praise for them, spring - ing Fresh from the Word!
gar - den, Sprung in com - plete - ness Where his feet pass.
morn - ing, God's re - cre - a - tion Of the new day!

Text: Eleanor Farjeon, 1881–1965, © 1957
Music: Scots Gaelic Melody

55 54 55 54
BUNESSAN

Alternative Text

This Day God Gives Me   426

1. This day God gives me
   Strength of high heaven,
   Sun and moon shining,
   Flame in my hearth,
   Flashing of lightning,
   Wind in its swiftness,
   Deeps of the ocean,
   Firmness of earth.

2. This day God sends me
   Strength as my steersman,
   Might to uphold me,
   Wisdom as guide.
   Your eyes are watchful,
   Your ears are list'ning,
   Your lips are speaking,
   Friend at my side.

3. God's way is my way,
   God's shield is round me,
   God's host defends me,
   Saving from ill.
   Angels of heaven,
   Drive from me always
   All that would harm me,
   Stand by me still.

4. Rising, I thank you
   Mighty and strong One,
   King of creation,
   Giver of rest,
   Firmly confessing
   Threeness of Persons,
   Oneness of Godhead,
   Trinity blest.

Text: St. Patrick, 372–466, attr.; tr. James Quinn, S.J., b. 1919, © 1969

55 54 55 54
BUNESSAN

427 Lord God of Morning and of Night

1. Lord God of morn - ing and of night,
We thank you for your gifts of light; As
in the dawn the shad - ows fly, We
seem to find you now more nigh.

2. Fresh hopes have wak - ened in the heart,
Fresh force to do our dai - ly part; In
peace - ful sleep our strength re - store, Through-
out the day to serve you more.

3. O Lord of light, your love a - lone
Can make our hu - man hearts your own; Be
ev - er with us, Lord, that we
bless - ed face one day may see.

4. Praise God, our mak - er and our friend;
Praise him through time, till time shall end; Till
psalm and song his name a - dore, Through
heav'n's great day of ev - er - more.

Lower Key: O Jesus Joy of Loving Hearts, no. 510
Text: Francis Turner Palgrave, 1824–1897
Music: William Gardiner, 1770–1853, attr.

88 88
FULDA (WALTON)

When Morning Gilds the Skies 428

1. When morn-ing gilds the skies, My heart, a-wak-ing cries,
2. The night be-comes as day When from the heart we say,
3. Let all of hu-man-kind, In this their con-cord find,
4. Be this, while life is mine, My can-ti-cle di-vine,

May Je-sus Christ be praised! A-like at work and prayer
May Je-sus Christ be praised! The pow'rs of dark-ness fear
May Je-sus Christ be praised! Let all the earth a-round
May Je-sus Christ be praised! Be this th'e-ter-nal song,

To Je-sus I re-pair; May Je-sus Christ be praised!
When this sweet chant they hear, May Je-sus Christ be praised!
Ring joy-ous with the sound, May Je-sus Christ be praised!
Through all the a-ges long, May Je-sus Christ be praised!

Text: German hymn, 19th c; tr. Edward Caswall, 1814–1878, alt.
Music: Joseph Barnby, 1838–1896

666 666
LAUDES DOMINI

429 Darkness Has Faded

1. Dark - ness has fad - ed, night gives way to morn - ing: Sleep has re - freshed us, now we thank our mak - er Sing - ing his prais - es, lift - ing up to heav - en Hearts, minds and voic - es.

2. Fa - ther of mer - cies, bless the hours be - fore us; While there is day - light may we work to please you, Build - ing a ci - ty fit to be your dwell - ing, Home for all na - tions.

3. Day - star of heav - en, dawn that ends our dark - ness, Sun of sal - va - tion, Lord en-throned in splen - dor, Stay with us, Je - sus: let your Eas - ter glo - ry Fill all cre - a - tion.

4. Flame of the Spir - it, fire with love's de - vo - tion Hearts love cre - at - ed, make us true a - pos - tles; Give us a vi - sion wide as heav'n's hor - i - zon, Bright with your prom - ise.

Text: James Quinn, S.J., b. 1919, © 1969
Music: Ralph Vaughan Williams, 1872–1958, ©

11 11 11 5
CHRISTE SANCTORUM

5. Father in heaven, guide your children homewards;
   Jesus, our brother, walk beside us always;
   Joy-giving Spirit, make the world one people,
   Sign of God's kingdom.

The King Shall Come 430

1. The King shall come when morn-ing dawns And light tri - um-phant breaks,
2. Not as of old a lit - tle child, To bear and fight and die,
3. Oh, bright-er than the ris - ing morn When Christ, vic - to - rious, rose
4. Oh, bright-er than that glo - rious morn Shall dawn up - on our race

When beau - ty gilds the east - ern hills And life to joy a-wakes.
But crowned with glo - ry like the sun That lights the morn-ing sky.
And left the lone-some place of death, De - spite the rage of foes.
The day when Christ in splen-dor comes, And we shall see his face.

5. The King shall come when morning dawns
   And light and beauty brings.
   Hail, Christ the Lord! Your people pray:
   Come quickly, King of kings.

Text: John Brownlie, 1859–1925, alt., ©
Music: Kentucky Harmony, 1816; acc. A. Davisson, ©

86 86
MORNING SONG (CONSOLATION)

431 Abide with Me!

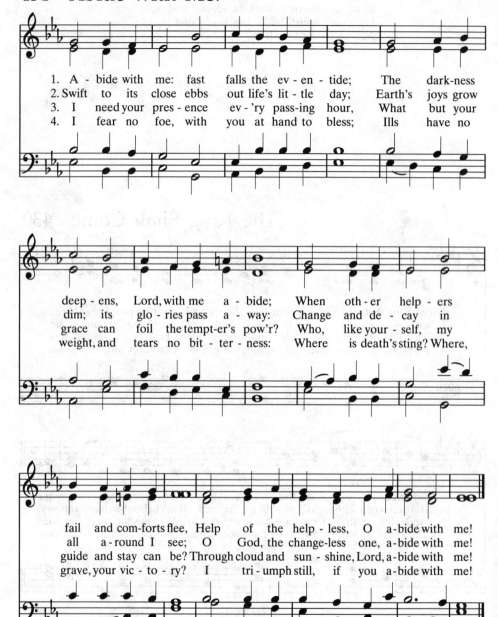

1. A - bide with me: fast falls the ev - en - tide; The dark-ness
2. Swift to its close ebbs out life's lit - tle day; Earth's joys grow
3. I need your pres - ence ev - 'ry pass-ing hour, What but your
4. I fear no foe, with you at hand to bless; Ills have no

deep - ens, Lord, with me a - bide; When oth - er help - ers
dim; its glo - ries pass a - way: Change and de - cay in
grace can foil the tempt-er's pow'r? Who, like your - self, my
weight, and tears no bit - ter - ness: Where is death's sting? Where,

fail and com-forts flee, Help of the help - less, O a-bide with me!
all a - round I see; O God, the change-less one, a-bide with me!
guide and stay can be? Through cloud and sun - shine, Lord, a-bide with me!
grave, your vic - to - ry? I tri - umph still, if you a-bide with me!

5. Hold then your cross before my closing eyes;
   Shine through the gloom, and point me to the skies:
   Heav'n's morning breaks, and earth's vain shadows flee;
   In life, in death, O Lord, abide with me!

Text: Henry Francis Lyte, 1793–1847
Music: William Henry Monk, 1823–1889

10 10 10 10
EVENTIDE

My Soul Magnifies the Lord 432

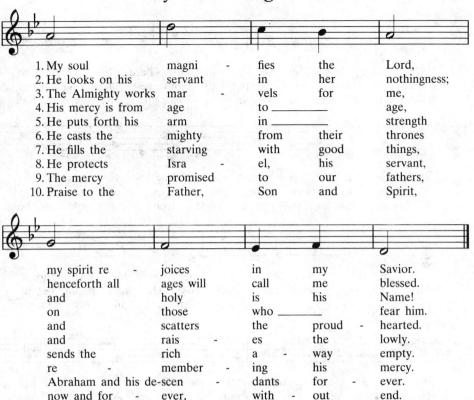

1. My soul magni - fies the Lord,
2. He looks on his servant in her nothingness;
3. The Almighty works mar - vels for me,
4. His mercy is from age to _____ age,
5. He puts forth his arm in _____ strength
6. He casts the mighty from their thrones
7. He fills the starving with good things,
8. He protects Isra - el, his servant,
9. The mercy promised to our fathers,
10. Praise to the Father, Son and Spirit,

my spirit re - joices in my Savior.
henceforth all ages will call me blessed.
and holy is his Name!
on those who _____ fear him.
and scatters the proud - hearted.
and rais - es the lowly.
sends the rich a - way empty.
re - member - ing his mercy.
Abraham and his de-scen - dants for - ever.
now and for - ever, with - out end.

Text: Luke 1:46–55; tr. The Grail, alt., ©
Music: Vernon Kroening, 1948–1980, ©

433 Canticle of Mary (Magnificat)

1. My soul gives glo - ry to the Lord, In God my
2. His mer - cy goes to all who fear, From age to
3. He raised his ser - vant Is - ra - el, Re - mem - b'ring

Sav - ior I re - joice. My low - li - ness he
age and to all parts. His arm of strength to
his e - ter - nal grace, As from of old he

did re - gard, Ex - alt - ing me by his own choice.
all is near; He scat - ters those who have proud hearts.
did fore - tell To A - bra - ham and all his race.

From this day all shall call me blest, For he has
He casts the might - y from their thrones And rais - es
O Fa - ther, Son and Spir - it blest, In three - fold

done great things for me, Of all great names his
those of low de - gree; He feeds the hun - gry
Name are you a - dored, To you be ev - 'ry

is the best, For it is ho - ly; strong is he.
as his own, The rich de - part in pov - er - ty.
prayer ad - drest, From age to age the on - ly Lord.

Text: Anon., 1535, Mein Seel, O Gott, muss loben dich; tr. John T. Mueller, 1940, alt., ©
Music: Michael Joncas, b. 1951; harm. Mark Smith, b. 1956, ©

88 88 88 88
MAGNIFICAT

Magnificat 434

Lively

1. My heart ex-tols the Lord, my God. My joy is God my
2. His name the Ho - ly, great his love Through count-less gen - er -
3. He fills the hun - gry, and the poor He lav - ish - es with

Sav - ior. He looks up - on his hum - ble maid,
a - tions. His mer - cy is from age to age
plen - ty. But rich and greed - y ones are doomed,

with love and gen - tle fa - vor. Now all the earth from
on all God-fear - ing na - tions. With might - y arm he
for these he ex - iles emp - ty. God's mer - cy comes to

this great day will call me hap - py daugh - ter:
shows his pow'r, he strikes the proud, they crum - ble.
Is - ra - el and A - bra - ham's great na - tion.

The might - y God his ser - vant found,
The rul - ers of the land de - posed,
From prom - ise made in an - cient days

and won - drous gra - ces brought her.
the Lord en - thrones the hum - ble.
to end - less gen - er - a - tions.

Text: Luke 1:46–55; tr. Aelred Rosser, O.S.B., ©
Music: Hugh Tasch, O.S.B., ©

435 Now All the Woods Are Sleeping

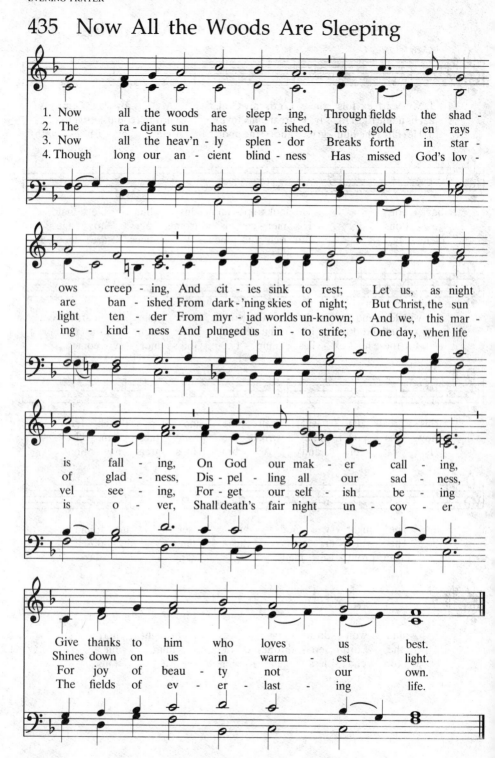

1. Now all the woods are sleep - ing, Through fields the shad - ows creep - ing, And cit - ies sink to rest; Let us, as night is fall - ing, On God our mak - er call - ing, Give thanks to him who loves us best.

2. The ra - diant sun has van - ished, Its gold - en rays are ban - ished From dark - 'ning skies of night; But Christ, the sun of glad - ness, Dis - pel - ling all our sad - ness, Shines down on us in warm - est light.

3. Now all the heav'n - ly splen - dor Breaks forth in star - light ten - der From myr - iad worlds un-known; And we, this mar - vel see - ing, For - get our self - ish be - ing For joy of beau - ty not our own.

4. Though long our an - cient blind - ness Has missed God's lov - ing - kind - ness And plunged us in - to strife; One day, when life is o - ver, Shall death's fair night un - cov - er The fields of ev - er - last - ing life.

Text: Paul Gerhardt, 1607–1676; tr. Lutheran Book of Worship, 1978 ed., ©
Music: Heinrich Isaac, ca. 1450–1517

776 778
INNSBRUCK

O Gladsome Light, O Grace   436

1. O glad-some Light, O grace Of God the Fa-ther's face,
2. Now, ere day fad - eth quite, We see the eve-ning light,
3. To thee of right be - longs All praise of ho - ly songs,

Th'e - ter - nal splen-dor wear - ing: Ce - les - tial, ho - ly blest,
Our wont-ed hymn out - pour - ing, Fa - ther of might un - known,
O Son of God, Life - giv - er; Thee, there-fore, O Most High,

Our Sav - ior Je - sus Christ, Joy - ful in thine ap - pear - ing!
Thee, his in - car-nate Son, And Ho - ly Ghost a - dor - ing.
The world doth glo - ri - fy And shall ex - alt for - ev - er.

Text: Greek, 3rd c.; tr. Robert Seymour Bridges, 1844–1930
Music: Louis Bourgeois, 1510?–1561?; arr. Claude Goudimel, 1514–1572

667 667
NUNC DIMITTIS

437 Day Is Done, But Love Unfailing

1. Day is done, but love un-fail-ing Dwells e - ver here;
2. Dark des-cends, but light un-end-ing Shines through our night;
3. Eyes will close, but you un-sleep-ing Watch by our side;

Sha - dows fall, but hope, pre-vail-ing, Calms ev - 'ry fear.
You are with us, ev - er lend-ing New strength to sight.
Death may come, in love's safe keep-ing Still we a - bide.

Lov-ing Fa - ther, none for-sak-ing, Take our hearts, of love's own mak-ing,
One in love, your truth con-fess-ing, One in hope of heav-en's bless-ing,
God of love, all e - vil quell-ing, Sin for-giv - ing, fear dis-pel-ling,

Watch our sleep-ing, guard our wak-ing, Be al - ways near.
May we see, in love's pos-sess-ing, Love's end - less light!
Stay with us, our hearts in-dwell-ing, This e - ven-tide.

Text: James Quinn, S.J., b. 1919, © 1969
Music: Ralph Vaughan Williams, 1872–1958, ©

8 4 8 4 888 4
AR HYD NOS

Glory to Thee, My God, This Night 438

1. Glo - ry to thee, my God, this night, For all the bless - ings of the light; Keep me, O keep me, King of kings, Be - neath thine own al - might - y wings.

2. For - give me, Lord, for thy dear Son, The sin that I this day have done, That with the world, my - self, and thee, I, be - fore sleep, at peace may be.

3. Teach me to live, that I may dread The grave as lit - tle as my bed; Teach me to die, that so I may Rise glo - rious on the fi - nal day.

4. O may my soul on thee re - pose, And with deep sleep my eye - lids close, The gift of rest I glad - ly take To serve my God when I a - wake.

5. Praise God, from whom all blessings flow;
   Praise him, all creatures here below;
   Praise him above, ye heav'nly host;
   Praise Father, Son, and Holy Ghost.

Alt. arr.: O God of Love, O King of Peace, no. 599
Alt. tune: O Blessed by God, no. 340

Text: Thomas Ken, 1637–1711
Music: Thomas Tallis, ca. 1510–1585

88 88
TALLIS' CANON

439 Lord Bid Your Servant Go in Peace

1. Lord, bid your ser - vant go in peace. Your
2. This is the Sav - ior of the world, The
3. This child shall see the rise, the fall, Of
4. His moth - er's soul a sword shall pierce, Of

word is now ful - filled. These eyes have seen sal -
Gen - tiles' prom-ised light, God's glo - ry dwell - ing
those in Is - ra - el, God's sign raised high for
sor - row keen and deep: And se - cret thoughts of

va - tion's dawn, This child so long fore - told.
in our midst, The joy of Is - ra - el.
all to see, Whom some shall yet de - ny.
man - y hearts Through him shall be re - vealed.

5. Blest be the Father, who has giv'n
   His Son to be our Lord;
   Blest, too, that Son, and with them both
   The Spirit of their love.

Alt. arr.: The King Shall Come, no. 430

Text: Nunc Dimittis, tr. James Quinn, S.J., b. 1919, alt., © 1969
Music: Elkanah Kelsay Dare, 1782–1826, attr.

86 86
MORNING SONG (CONSOLATION)

We Praise You, Father   440

1. We praise you, Father, for your gift Of dusk and
2. Within your hands we rest secure; In quiet
3. Your glory may we ever seek In rest, as

night - fall o - ver earth, Fore-shad-ow - ing the
sleep our strength re - new; Yet give your peo - ple
in ac - tiv - i - ty, Un - til its full - ness

mys - ter - y Of death that leads to end - less day.
hearts that wake In love to you, un - sleep - ing Lord.
is re - vealed, O Source of life, O Trin - i - ty.

Alt. tune: O Saving Victim, no. 362

Text: Benedictine Nuns of St. Mary's Abbey, West Malling, Kent, ©
Music: Anthony Werner, fl. 1863

88 88
WERNER

441 Before the Close of Day

1. Be - fore the close of day we come To you Cre - a - tor
2. Pro - tect this house and calm our fears, Pre - serve us from dis -
3. To you the Fa - ther of us all, We pray through Je - sus

of the world; In mer - cy guard us through the night
tur - bing dreams. Send far from us the e - vil one,
Christ our Lord; Who with the Spir - it and with you

As dark - ness cov - ers things from sight.
And keep us faith - ful to your Son.
Are Tri - ni - ty e - ter - nal - ly. A - men.

Text: Ambrosian, 7th c.; tr. Sr. Cecile Gertken, O.S.B., b. 1902, ©
Music: Benedictine Antiphonal; acc. Sr. Cecile Gertken, O.S.B., b. 1902, ©

88 88
TE LUCIS ANTE TERMINUM

442 O Radiant Light

1. O ra - diant Light, O Sun di - vine Of God the
2. O Son of God, the source of life, Praise is your
3. Lord Je - sus Christ, as day - light fades, As shine the

Fa - ther's death - less face, O im - age of the Light sub -
due by night and day. Our hap - py lips must raise the
lights of e - ven - tide, We praise the Fa - ther with the

lime That fills the heav'n - ly dwell - ing place.
strain Of your es - teem and splen - did name.
Son, The Spir - it blest, and with them one.

Alt. arr.: Jesu Dulcis Memoria, no. 394

Text: Greek, ca. 200; tr. William Storey, b. 1923, ©
Music: Plainchant, Tone I; acc. Richard Proulx, b. 1937, ©

88 88
JESU DULCIS MEMORIA

As a Chalice Cast of Gold 443

1. As a chal - ice cast of gold,
2. Save me from the sooth - ing sin
3. When I bend up - on my knees,
4. When I dance or chant your praise,

Burn - ished, bright and brimmed with wine,
Of the emp - ty cul - tic deed
Clasp my hands, or bow my head,
When I sing a psalm or hymn,

Make me, Lord, as fit to hold Grace and
And the pi - ous, bab - bling din Of the
Let my spo - ken, pub - lic pleas Be di -
When I preach your lov - ing ways, Let my

truth and love di - vine.
claimed but un - lived creed.
rect - ly, sim - ply said,
heart add its A - men.

Let my praise and wor - ship start With the
Let my ac - tions, Lord, ex - press What my
Free of tan - gled words that mask What my
Let each cher - ished, out - ward rite Thus re -

cleans - ing of my heart.
tongue and lips pro - fess.
soul would plain - ly ask.
flect your in - ward light.

Text: Thomas H. Troeger, b. 1945, ©
Music: Carol Doran, b. 1936, ©

77 77 77 77
INWARD LIGHT

444 As Those Who Serve

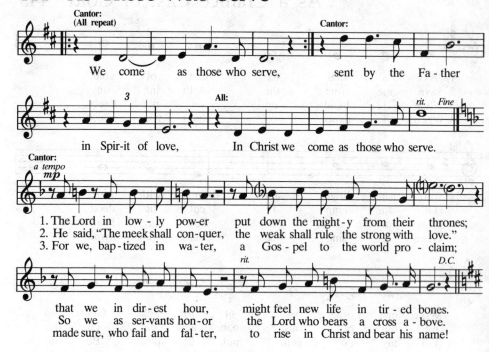

We come as those who serve, sent by the Fa-ther in Spir-it of love, In Christ we come as those who serve.

1. The Lord in low-ly pow-er put down the might-y from their thrones;
2. He said, "The meek shall con-quer, the weak shall rule the strong with love."
3. For we, bap-tized in wa-ter, a Gos-pel to the world pro-claim;

that we in dir-est hour, might feel new life in tir-ed bones.
So we as ser-vants hon-or the Lord who bears a cross a-bove.
made sure, who fail and fal-ter, to rise in Christ and bear his name!

Text: Edward J. McKenna, b. 1939, ©
Music: Edward J. McKenna, b. 1939, ©

BERNARDIN

445 Before the Fruit Is Ripened by the Sun

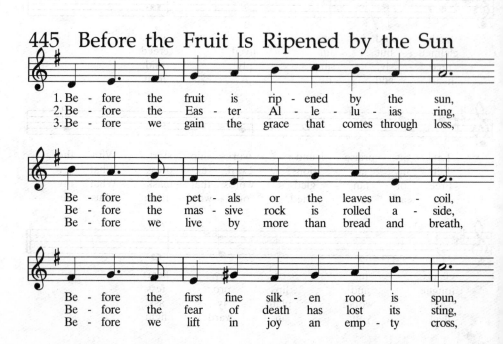

1. Be - fore the fruit is rip - ened by the sun,
2. Be - fore the Eas - ter Al - le - lu - ias ring,
3. Be - fore we gain the grace that comes through loss,

Be - fore the pet - als or the leaves un - coil,
Be - fore the mas - sive rock is rolled a - side,
Be - fore we live by more than bread and breath,

Be - fore the first fine silk - en root is spun,
Be - fore the fear of death has lost its sting,
Be - fore we lift in joy an emp - ty cross,

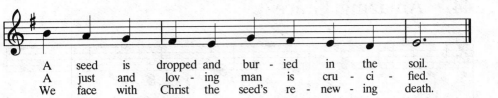

A   seed   is   dropped and   bur - ied   in   the   soil.
A   just   and   lov - ing   man   is   cru - ci - fied.
We   face   with   Christ   the   seed's   re - new - ing   death.

Text: John 12:20–23; adapt. Thomas H. Troeger, b. 1945, ©
Music: Carol Doran, b. 1936, ©

10 10 10 10
RENEWING DEATH

Come Thou Fount of Every Blessing 446

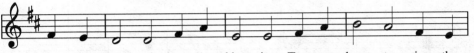

1. Come, thou   fount   of   ev - 'ry   bless - ing, Tune my   heart   to   sing thy
2. Here   I   find   my   great-est   trea - sure; Hith - er,   by   thy   help, I've
3. Oh,   to   grace how   great a   debt - or   Dai - ly   I'm   con - strained to

grace! Streams of   mer - cy   nev - er   ceas - ing, Call for songs of   loud-est praise.
come; And   I   hope, by   thy good plea-sure, Safe - ly   to   ar - rive at   home.
be!   Let   thy good-ness, like a   fet - ter, Bind my   wan-d'ring heart to   thee:

Teach me   some   me - lo - dious   son - net,   Sung by   flam - ing tongues a -
Je - sus   sought me when   a   stran - ger   Wan - d'ring from the fold of
Prone to   wan - der, Lord, I   feel   it,   Prone to   leave the   God I

bove. Praise the mount! Oh,   fix me   on   it, Mount of   God's un - chang-ing   love.
God; He,   to   res - cue me from dan-ger, In - ter-posed his   pre - cious blood.
love; Here's my heart,   oh, take and seal it, Seal   it   for   thy courts a - bove.

Text: Robert Robinson, 1735–1790, alt.
Music: John Wyeth, 1770–1858; harm. Gerre Hancock, b. 1934, ©

87 87 87 87
NETTLETON

447 Amazing Grace

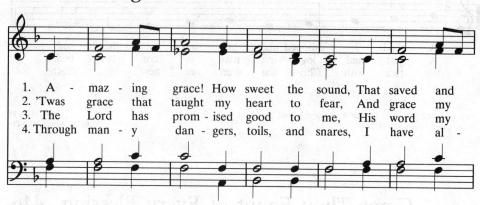

1. A - maz - ing grace! How sweet the sound, That saved and
2. 'Twas grace that taught my heart to fear, And grace my
3. The Lord has prom - ised good to me, His word my
4. Through man - y dan - gers, toils, and snares, I have al -

strength - ened me! I once was lost, but
fears re - lieved; How pre - cious did that
hope se - cures; He will my shield and
read - y come; 'Tis grace that brought me

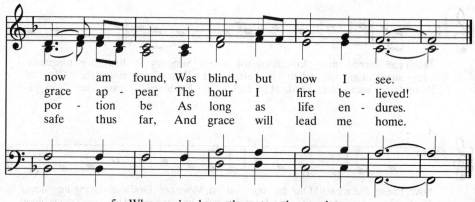

now am found, Was blind, but now I see.
grace ap - pear The hour I first be - lieved!
por - tion be As long as life en - dures.
safe thus far, And grace will lead me home.

5. When we've been there ten thousand years,
   Bright shining as the sun,
   We've no less days to sing God's praise
   Than when we'd first begun.

Text: John Newton, 1725–1807, alt., vv. 1–4; John Rees, fl. 1859, v. 5
Music: Early American Melody, 1831; adapt. Edwin Othello Excell, 1851–1921

86 86
NEW BRITAIN

Christian, Do You Hear the Lord? 448

1. Chris - tian, do you hear the Lord? Je - sus
2. "I de - liv - ered you when bound, And when
3. "Can a moth - er's ten - der - ness For her
4. "Mine is an un - chang - ing love, High - er

speaks his gra - cious word. Gent - ly sounds the Sav - ior's call,
bleed - ing healed your wound. Saw you wan - d'ring, set you right,
own dear child grow less? Though she may for - get - ful be,
than the heights a - bove, Deep - er than the depths be - neath,

"Do you love me best of all?
Turned your dark - ness in - to light.
You are al - ways dear to me. Al - le - lu - ia.
Free and faith - ful, strong as death.

5. "You shall see my glory soon,
   When the work of grace is done;
   Crowned with splendor you shall be:
   Christian, come and follow me!"
   Alleluia.

6. Lord, it is my chief complaint
   That my love is weak and faint;
   Yet I love you, and adore—
   O for grace to love you more!
   Alleluia.

Text: William Cowper, 1731–1800
Music: Medieval Traditional French Melody

77 77 with Alleluia
ORIENTIS PARTIBUS

Text © (Jubilate Hymns), alt., 1982, by Hope Publishing Co.,

449 God of Mercy and Compassion

1. God of mer - cy and com - pas - sion, Lord of life and blind-ing light. Truth whom crea - tures would re - fash - ion, Place on us the gift of sight.
2. God most ho - ly and for - giv - ing, Pe - ne - trate our pride and sloth; On a peo - ple part - ly liv - ing, Place the gift of life and growth.
3. Lord, who out of love con - sent - ed To the worst that we could do; Lord, a - ban - doned and tor - ment - ed, Let us love and suf - fer too.

REFRAIN

Truth in - sis - tent and de - mand-ing, Love re - sent - ed and ig - nored, Life be-

Text: Michael Hodgetts, alt., ©
Music: Traditional French Melody; arr. Percy Jones, ©

87 87 87 87
AU SANG QU'UN DIEU

yond all un-der-stand-ing, Give us peace and par-don, Lord.

Blest Are the Pure in Heart 450

1. Blest are the pure in heart, For they shall see our God; The
2. The Lord, who left the heav'ns Our life and peace to bring, To
3. Still to the low-ly soul He does him-self im - part, And
4. We seek your pres-ence, Lord; This grace to us im - part: Make

se - cret of the Lord is theirs, Their soul is Christ's a - bode.
dwell in low - li - ness on earth, Our pat - tern and our King.
for his dwell-ing and his throne Choos-es the pure in heart.
us a tem - ple fit for you, A pure and low - ly heart.

Higher Key: The Advent of Our God, no. 187

Text: John Keble, 1792–1866, vv. 1 & 3; Wm. John Hall, 1793–1861, vv. 2 & 4
Music: Johann B. Konig, 1691–1758, from his Chorale; adapt. and harm. Wm. Henry Havergal, 1793–1870

66 86
FRANCONIA

451 How Lovely is Your Dwelling Place

REFRAIN *(obligatory before Vs. 1 and after Vs. 4)*

How love-ly is your dwell-ing place, O Lord, God of hosts,

Hap-py are they who live in your house, For - ev - er sing-ing your praise.

VERSES

1. Long-ing and yearn - ing is my soul, Long-ing for
2. Hap - py are they who dwell in your courts, Sing - ing for -
3. Lord God of hosts, O hear my pray'r. God of
4. God, our Lord, is a ram - part, a shield; His fa - vor and

God's a - bode;
ev - er your praise.
Ja - cob, give ear.
glo - ry he gives.

All my be - ing rings out its
Hap-py are they whose strength is in
Turn your eyes, O God our
He will not re - fuse an - y

Text: Ps. 84: 2–13; Henry Bryan Hays, O.S.B., b. 1920, ©
Music: Henry Bryan Hays, O.S.B., b. 1920, ©

Irregular with Refrain
MALVERN HILL

joy   To God, the liv - ing   God.   Ev - en the
you; Your high-ways are in their mind.   As through the
shield.   Be - hold your serv - ant's face.   Bet - ter is
good   To those who walk with - out blame.   Lord God of

spar-row has   found   a   home,   The swal-low a   nest for her
bit - ter val - ley they go,   They make it a   re - gion of
one day with - in   your court Than a   thou-sand else - where,   O
hosts, how   great   you are,   Blest be   your name for -

brood;   She   lays   her young by your   al - tar, O
springs.   With   ev - er   grow - ing   strength they
God.   The   thresh - old of   the   house of the
ev - er!   O   hap - py the   one   who   trusts   in

God,   My   King, Lord of   hosts, and my   God.
walk; They will   see   the   God   of Zi - on.
Lord I   pre - fer to   the tents of the   wick - ed.
you,   Who   walks   the paths of your   love.

452 How Firm a Foundation

1. How firm a foun - da - tion, you saints of the
Lord, Is laid for your faith in his ex - cel - lent
word; What more can he say than to you he has
said, To all who for ref - uge to Je - sus have fled?

2. Fear not, he is with you, O be not dis -
mayed, For he is your God, and will still give you
aid: He'll strength - en you, help you, and cause you to
stand, Up - held by his right - eous, om - ni - po - tent hand.

3. When through the deep wa - ters he calls you to
go, The riv - ers of grief shall not you o - ver -
flow; The Lord will be with you in trou - ble to
bless, And sanc - ti - fy you in your deep - est dis - tress.

4. When through fi - 'ry tri - als your path - way shall
lie His grace all - suf - fi - cient shall be your sup -
ply; The flame shall not hurt you, his on - ly de -
sign Your dross to con - sume and your gold to re - fine.

Text: Richard Keen, c. 1787, attr.
Music: The Sacred Harp, 1844; arr. Russell Woollen, b. 1923

11 11 11 11
FOUNDATION

I Heard the Voice of Jesus Say 453

1. I heard the voice of Je-sus say, "Come un-to me and rest;
2. I heard the voice of Je-sus say, "Be-hold, I free-ly give
3. I heard the voice of Je-sus say, "I am this dark world's light;

And in your wea-ri-ness lay down Your head up-on my breast."
The liv-ing wa-ter; thirst-y one, Stoop down and drink, and live."
Look un-to me, your morn shall rise, And all your day be bright."

I came to Je-sus as I was, So wea-ry, worn, and sad;
I came to Je-sus, and I drank Of that life-giv-ing stream;
I looked to Je-sus, and I found In him my Star, my Sun;

I found in him a rest-ing place, And he has made me glad.
My thirst was quenched, my soul re-vived, And now I live in him.
And in that light of life I'll walk Till pil-grim days are done.

Alt. Tune: All You Who Seek a Comfort Sure, no. 503

Text: Horatius Bonar, 1808–1889
Music: Thomas Tallis, c. 1505–1585; harm. John Wilson, b. 1905

86 86 86 86
THIRD MODE MELODY

454 Love Divine All Loves Excelling

1. Love di - vine, all loves ex - cell - ing, Joy of
2. Breathe, oh, breathe thy lov - ing Spir - it In - to
3. Come, al - might - y to de - liv - er, Let us
4. Fin - ish then thy new cre - a - tion; Pure and

heav'n, to earth come down, Fix in us thy
ev - 'ry trou - bled breast; Let us all in
all thy life re - ceive; Sud - den - ly re -
spot - less let us be; Let us see thy

hum - ble dwell - ing, All thy faith - ful mer - cies crown.
thee in - her - it; Let us find thy prom - ised rest.
turn, and nev - er, Nev - er - more thy tem - ples leave.
great sal - va - tion Per - fect - ly re - stored in thee:

Je - sus, thou art all com - pas - sion, Pure, un -
Take a - way the love of sin - ning; Al - pha
Thee we would be al - ways bless - ing, Serve thee
Changed from glo - ry in - to glo - ry, Till in

Text: Charles Wesley, 1707–1788
Music: Rowland H. Prichard, 1811–1887

87 87 87 87
HYFRYDOL

bound - ed love thou art; Vis - it us with
and O - me - ga be; End of faith, as
as thy hosts a - bove, Pray, and praise thee
heav'n we take our place, Till we cast our

thy sal - va - tion, En - ter ev - 'ry trem-bling heart.
its be - gin - ning, Set our hearts at lib - er - ty.
with - out ceas - ing, Glo - ry in thy per - fect love.
crowns be - fore thee, Lost in won - der, love, and praise.

455 Lead Kindly Light

1. Lead, kind-ly light, a-mid the en-cir-cling gloom, Lead thou me on; The night is dark, and I am far from home, Lead thou me on. Keep thou my feet; I do not ask to see The dis-tant scene; one step e-nough for me.

2. I was not ev-er thus, nor prayed that thou Shouldst lead me on; I loved to choose and see my path; but now Lead thou me on. I loved the gar-ish day, and, spite of fears, Pride ruled my will: re-mem-ber not past years.

3. So long thy pow'r hath blest me, sure it still Will lead me on, O'er moor and fen, o'er crag and tor-rent, till The night is gone; And with the morn those an-gel fa-ces smile Which I have loved long since and lost a-while.

Text: John Henry Newman, 1801–1890
Music: W.H. Harris, 1883–1973, ©

10 4 10 4 10 1

ALBERT/

O Christ Our True and Only Light 456

1. O Christ our true and on - ly light, Il -
2. And all those who have strayed from thee O
3. O make the deaf to hear thy word, And
4. Shine on the dark - ened and the cold, Re -

lu - mine those who sit in night; Let those a - far now
gent - ly seek; thy heal - ing be, To ev - 'ry wound - ed
teach the dumb to speak, dear Lord, Who dare not yet the
call the wan - d'rers from thy fold, Those now u - nite who

hear thy voice, And in thy fold with us re - joice.
con - science giv'n, And let them al - so share thy heav'n.
faith a - vow, Though se - cret - ly they hold it now.
walk a - part, Con - firm the weak and doubt - ing heart.

5. So they with us may evermore
   Such grace with wond'ring thanks adore;
   And endless praise to thee be giv'n
   By all thy Church in earth and heav'n.

Alt. Tune: Take Up Your Cross, no. 651

Text: Johann Heermann, 1585–1647; tr. Catherine Winkworth, 1827–1878
Music: Henry Lawes, 1595–1662

88 88
WHITEHALL

457 O God, Our Help in Ages Past

1. O God, our help in a - ges past, Our
2. Be - neath the shad - ow of your throne Your
3. Be - fore the hills in or - der stood, Or
4. A thou - sand a - ges in your sight Are

hope for years to come, Our shel - ter from the
saints have dwelt se - cure; Suf - fi - cient is your
earth re - ceived her frame, From ev - er - last - ing
like an eve - ning gone, Short as the watch that

storm - y blast, And our e - ter - nal home;
arm a - lone, And our de - fense is sure.
you are God, To end - less years the same.
ends the night Be - fore the ris - ing sun.

5. Time, like an ever-rolling stream,
   Bears all our lives away;
   They fly forgotten, as a dream
   Dies at the op'ning day.

6. O God, our help in ages past,
   Our hope for years to come,
   Be now our guard while troubles last,
   And our eternal home.

Text: Isaac Watts, 1674–1748, alt.
Music: William Croft, 1678–1727, alt.; harm. William Henry Monk, 1823–1889

86 86
ST. ANNE

My Shepherd Will Supply My Need 458

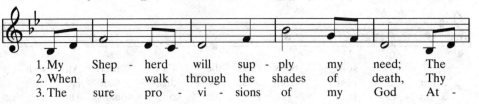

1. My Shep - herd will sup - ply my need; The
2. When I walk through the shades of death, Thy
3. The sure pro - vi - sions of my God At -

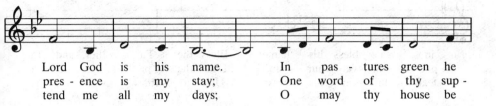

Lord God is his name. In pas - tures green he
pres - ence is my stay; One word of thy sup -
tend me all my days; O may thy house be

makes me feed, Be - side the liv - ing stream. He
port - ing breath Drives all my fears a - way. Thy
my a - bode, And all my work be praise! There

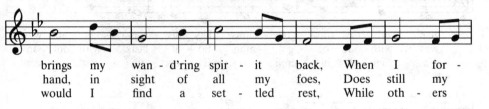

brings my wan - d'ring spir - it back, When I for -
hand, in sight of all my foes, Does still my
would I find a set - tled rest, While oth - ers

sake his ways; And leads me for his
ta - ble spread; My cup with bless - ings
go and come, No more a stran - ger

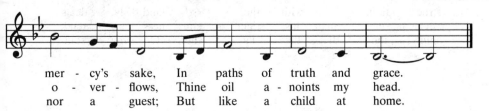

mer - cy's sake, In paths of truth and grace.
o - ver - flows, Thine oil a - noints my head.
nor a guest; But like a child at home.

Text: Isaac Watts, 1674–1748, alt.
Music: Southern Harmony, 1835

86 86 86 86
RESIGNATION

459 O My Soul, Bless God the Father

1. O my soul, bless God the Fa - ther; All with -
2. Far as east from west is dis - tant, He hath
3. Un - to such as keep his cove - nant, And are

in me bless his name; Bless the Fa - ther, and for -
put a - way our sin; Like the pi - ty of a
stead - fast in his way; Un - to those who still re -

get not All his mer - cies to pro - claim. Who for -
fa - ther Hath the Lord's com - pas - sion been. As it
mem - ber His com - mand - ments, and o - bey. Bless the

give - eth thy trans - gres - sions, Thy dis - eas - es all who
was with - out be - gin - ning, So it lasts with - out an
Fa - ther, all his crea - tures, Ev - er un - der his con -

heals; Who re - deems thee from de -
end; To their chil - dren's chil - dren
trol; All through - out his vast do -

struc - tion, Who with thee so kind - ly deals.
ev - er Shall his right - eous - ness ex - tend;
min - ion Bless the Fa - ther, O my soul.

Text: Adapt. in *Hymns Ancient & Modern,* 1861.
Music: Henry Bryan Hays, O.S.B., b. 1920, ©

SABINE CROSSROADS

The King of Love My Shepherd Is 460

1. The King of love my Shep - herd is, Whose good-ness
2. Where streams of liv - ing wa - ter flow, My ran - somed
3. Con - fused and fool - ish oft I strayed, But yet in
4. In death's dark vale I fear no ill With you, dear

fails me nev - er; I noth - ing lack if I am
soul he's lead - ing, And where the ver - dant pas - tures
love he sought me, And on his shoul - der gent - ly
Lord, be - side me; Your rod and staff my com - fort

his, And he is mine for - ev - er.
grow, With food ce - les - tial feed - ing.
laid, And home re - joic - ing, brought me.
still, Your cross be - fore to guide me.

5. You spread a table in my sight;
   Your grace so rich bestowing;
   And, oh, what transport of delight,
   From your pure cup is flowing.

6. And so through all the length of days
   Your goodness fails me never;
   Good Shepherd, may I sing your praise
   Within your house forever.

Lower Key: Out of the Depths We Cry, no. 246

Text: Henry W. Baker, 1821–1877
Music: Ancient Irish Melody

87 87
ST.COLUMBA

461 The Thirsty Deer Will Yearn and Dream

1. The thirst-y deer will yearn and dream To
   foes look on; they laugh at me: "Where
   Lord, my life is filled with woe; My

find the cool-ing, run-ning stream. So too, my God, you
is your God: yes where is he?" Now I re-call those
heart is crushed, my spir-it low. But morn-ing, noon, and

still come first; And like the deer, for you I thirst.
times of prayer When songs of joy would fill the air.
night I share Your liv-ing pres-ence, found in prayer.

REFRAIN

Why should I be sad, trou-bled or in pain? My

hope is in my God, my hope is not in vain.   2. My not in vain.
                                               3. O

Text: Psalm 42; tr. Robert Brennan, b. 1943, ©
Music: Robert LeBlanc, b. 1948, ©

© 1987, ACP

88 88 without (iambic) Refrain

Bring Judgment, Lord, Upon the Earth   462

1. Bring judg - ment, Lord, up - on the earth; And
   Lord, send out your truth and light; Now
   in your Church, I'll sing your praise With

show my foes what I am worth, The peo - ple who do
take my side and fight my fight. Your praise is ev - er
saints and an - gels all my days. Your truth will guide me

not be - lieve, Whose clev - er, cut - ting words de - ceive.
on my tongue, Since I was born, since I was young.
clear - ly, then; Your light will lead me home a - gain.

REFRAIN

Why should I be sad, trou - bled or in pain? My

1.–2. **3.**

hope is in my God, my hope is not in vain. 2. O not in vain.
3. With-

Text: Psalm 43; tr. Robert Brennan, b. 1943, ©
Music: Robert LeBlanc, b. 1948, ©
1987, ACP

88 88 without (iambic) Refrain

463 To You, O Lord, I Lift My Soul

1. To you, O Lord, I lift my soul, In
2. The Lord is right - eous, the Lord is good, He
3. My eyes, O Lord, are turned toward you. O

you, I place my trust. Let me nev - er for -
teach - es the way to the sin - ners, He guides the
Lord, my God, I love you. Look with mer - cy on

get that you are my Sav - ior. For you, I wait all the
low - ly in ho - li - ness, He teach - es his way to the
me, your hum - ble ser - vant, For I am a - lone and af -

day. For no one who hopes in you will be con -
meek. All the paths of the Lord are mer - cy and
flict - ed. Re - lieve all the an - guish and grief of my

found - ed, No one who loves you will fall in - to shame. O
kind - ness. Jus - tice re - wards those who keep all his laws. O
heart. Strength - en my faith as I wait for you. O

REFRAIN

Lord show me your ways, teach me your paths, guide me in

1.–2. 3.

good - ness for ev - er.

Text: Psalm 25; Robert E. Kreutz, b. 1922, ©
Music: Robert E. Kreutz, b. 1922, ©

We Walk by Faith 464

1. We walk by faith, and not by sight; No
2. We may not touch his hands and side, Nor
3. Help then, O Lord, our un - be - lief; And
4. That, when our life of faith is done, In

gra - cious words we hear From him who spoke as
fol - low where he trod; But in his prom - ise
may our faith a - bound, To call on you when
realms of clear - er light We may be - hold you

none e'er spoke; But we be - lieve him near.
we re - joice; And cry, "My Lord and God!"
you are near, And seek where you are found:
as you are, With full and end - less sight.

Text: Henry Alford, 1810–1871, alt.
Music: Gordon Slater, 1896–1979, ©

86 86
ST. BOTOLPH

465 Grant to Us, O Lord

REFRAIN

Grant to us, O Lord, a heart re - newed;

Re - cre - ate in us your own Spir - it, Lord!

VERSES

1. Be - hold, the days are com-ing, says the Lord our God, When I will

To Refrain

make a new cov - e - nant with the house of Is - ra - el.

2. Deep with - in their be - ing I will im - plant my Law;

To Refrain

I will write it in their hearts. 3. I will be their God, and

To Refrain

they shall be my peo - ple. 4. And for all their faults I will

To Refrain

grant for - give-ness; Nev - er - more will I re - mem - ber their sins.

Text: Lucien Deiss, C.S., b. 1929
Music: Lucien Deiss, C.S., b. 1929

Irregular with Refrain
GRANT TO US

Father, Lord of All Creation 466

1. Fa - ther, Lord of all cre - a - tion,
2. Je - sus Christ the man for oth - ers,
3. Ho - ly Spir - it, rush - ing, burn - ing

Ground of be - ing, life and love; Height and depth be -
We, your peo - ple, make our prayer: Give us grace to
Wind and flame of Pen - te - cost, Fire our hearts a -

yond de - scrip - tion On - ly life in you can prove:
love all oth - ers, Those whose bur - dens we can share.
fresh with yearn - ing To re - gain what we have lost.

You are mor - tal life's de - pen - dence:
Where your name binds us to - geth - er
May your love u - nite our ac - tion,

Thought, speech, sight are ours by grace; Yours is ev - 'ry
You, Lord Christ, will sure - ly be; Where no self - ish -
Nev - er - more to speak a - lone: God, in us a -

hour's ex - ist - ence, Sov - 'reign Lord of time and space.
ness can sev - er, There your love we all may see.
bol - ish fac - tion, God, through us your love make known.

Text: Steward Cross, b. 1928, ©
Music: George H. Day, 1883–1966, ©

87 87 87 87
GENEVA

467 All Who Love and Serve Your City

1. All who love and serve your ci - ty,
   All who bear its dai - ly stress,
   All who cry for peace and jus - tice,
   All who curse and all who bless,

2. In your day of loss and sor - row,
   In your day of help - less strife,
   Hon - or, peace, and
   Seek the Lord, who is your life.

3. In your day of wealth and plen - ty,
   Wast - ed work and wast - ed play,
   Call to mind the
   word of Je - sus, "I must work while it is day."

4. For all days are days of judg - ment,
   And the Lord is wait - ing still,
   Draw - ing near a
   world that spurns him, Of - f'ring peace from Cal - vary's hill.

5. Risen Lord! Shall yet the city
   Be the city of despair?
   Come today, our Judge, our Glory;
   Be its name, "The Lord is there!"

Text: Erik Routley, 1917–1982, rev., ©
Music: The Southern Harmony, 1835; harm. Alastair Cassels–Brown, b. 1927, ©

87 87
CHARLESTOWN

468 I Love You, O My Lord Most High

1. I love you, O my Lord most high,
   For first your love has cap-tured me; I seek no oth - er

2. May mem - o - ry no thought sug - gest
   But shall to your pure glo - ry tend, May un - der-stand - ing

3. All mine is yours: say but the word,
   Say what you will it shall be done; I know your love, most

4. A - part from you, no - thing can be,
   So grant me this, my on - ly wish, To love you, Lord, e -

lib - er - ty: Bound   by   your   love,   I   shall   be   free.
find   no   rest,   Ex - cept   in   you,   its   on - ly   end.
gra - cious Lord,   I   know you   seek   my   good   a - lone.
ter - nal - ly,   You   give   me   all   in   giv - ing   this.

Text: St. Ignatius Loyola, 1491–1556; tr. Edward Caswall, 1814–1878, adapt.
Music: Traditional Irish Melody; arr. Percy Jones, ©

88 88
DANIEL

Jerusalem, My Happy Home 469

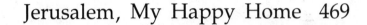

1. Je - ru - sa - lem,   my   hap - py   home,   When
2. O   hap - py   har - bor   of   the   saints,   O
3. Thy   gar - dens   and   thy   gal - lant   walks   Con -
4. There   trees   for   ev - er - more   bear   fruit   And

shall   I   come   to   thee?   When   shall   my   sor - rows
sweet   and   pleas - ant   soil!   In   thee   no   sor - row
tin - ual - ly   are   green;   There   grow   such   sweet   and
ev - er - more   do   spring;   There   ev - er - more   the

have   an   end?   Thy   joys   when   shall   I   see?
may   be   found,   No   grief,   no   care,   no   toil.
pleas - ant   flow'rs   As   no - where   else   are   seen.
an - gels   sit   And   ev - er - more   do   sing.

5. Jerusalem, Jerusalem,
   God grant that I may see
   Thine endless joy, and of the same
   Partaker ever be!

Text: Joseph Bromehead, 1747–1826, alt.; F.P.B. (c. 16th c.), v.2
Music: Scottish–American Folk Melody; adapt. and arr. Annabel Morris Buchanan, 1889–1983, ©

86 86
LAND OF REST

470 My God, Accept My Heart

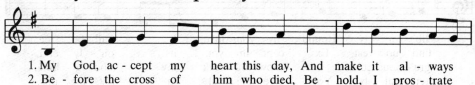

1. My God, ac - cept my heart this day, And make it al - ways
2. Be - fore the cross of him who died, Be - hold, I pros - trate
3. A - noint me with thy heav'n-ly grace, And seal me for thine
4. Let ev - 'ry thought, and work and word To thee be ev - er

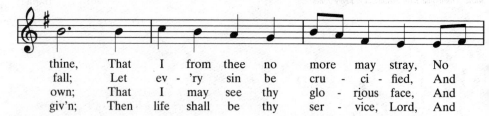

thine, That I from thee no more may stray, No
fall; Let ev - 'ry sin be cru - ci - fied, And
own; That I may see thy glo - rious face, And
giv'n; Then life shall be thy ser - vice, Lord, And

After Verse 5

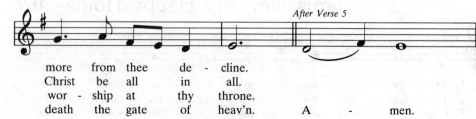

more from thee de - cline.
Christ be all in all.
wor - ship at thy throne.
death the gate of heav'n. A - men.

5. All glory to the Father be,
   All glory to the Son,
   All glory, Holy Ghost, to thee,
   While endless ages run.

Text: Matthew Bridges, 1800–1894
Music: Henry Bryan Hays, O.S.B., b. 1920, ©

86 86
SEVEN PINES

471 Stand Firm in Faith

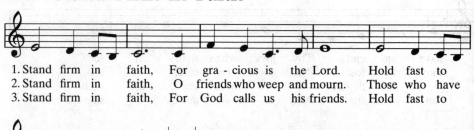

1. Stand firm in faith, For gra - cious is the Lord. Hold fast to
2. Stand firm in faith, O friends who weep and mourn. Those who have
3. Stand firm in faith, For God calls us his friends. Hold fast to

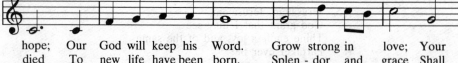

hope; Our God will keep his Word. Grow strong in love; Your
died To new life have been born. Splen - dor and grace Shall
hope; His ten - der care he sends. Grow strong in love; God's

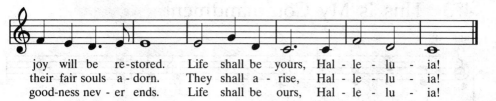

joy will be re-stored.	Life shall be yours,	Hal - le - lu - ia!
their fair souls a - dorn.	They shall a - rise,	Hal - le - lu - ia!
good-ness nev - er ends.	Life shall be ours,	Hal - le - lu - ia!

Text: Sr. Delores Dufner, O.S.B., b. 1939, ©
Music: Jay F. Hunstiger, b. 1950, ©

46 46 46 44
DUFNER

There Is a Balm in Gilead 472

REFRAIN

There is a balm in Gil-e-ad To make the wound-ed whole,

There is a balm in Gil-e-ad To heal the sin-sick soul.

VERSES

1. Some - times I feel dis - cour-aged And think my work's in vain,
2. If you can - not preach like Pe - ter, If you can - not pray like Paul,
3. Don't ev - er feel dis - cour-aged, For Je - sus is your friend;

To Refrain

But then the Ho - ly Spir - it Re - vives my soul a - gain.
You can tell the love of Je - sus, And say, "He died for all!"
And if you lack for knowl-edge He'll ne'er re - fuse to lend.

Text: Jeremiah 8:22
Music: Spiritual

Irregular with Refrain
BALM IN GILEAD

473 This Is My Commandment

REFRAIN

This is my com - mand-ment, that you love one an - oth - er as I have loved you.

VERSES

1. Greater love has no one than this, than to lay down one's life for one's friends. You are my
2. No longer do I call you servants, but I have called you friends; for the servant does not
3. You did not choose me, but I have chosen you, that you should bear
4. What - ever you ask in my name the Father will give to you. This I com-

Text: John 15:12–17; Revised Standard Version, alt., ©
Music: Erik Routley, 1917–1982, ©

Irregular
OF LOVE DIVINE

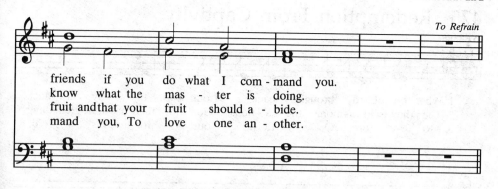

To Refrain

friends if you do what I com - mand you.
know what the mas - ter is doing.
fruit and that your fruit should a - bide.
mand you, To love one an - other.

O Lord, Our Fathers Oft Have Told 474

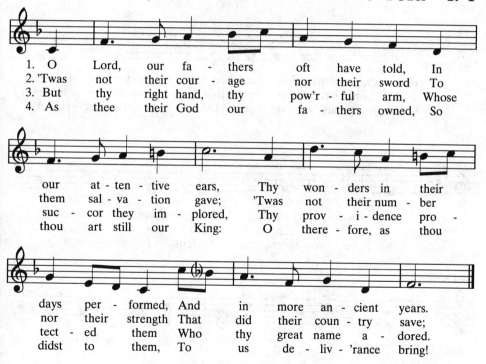

1. O Lord, our fa - thers oft have told, In
2. 'Twas not their cour - age nor their sword To
3. But thy right hand, thy pow'r - ful arm, Whose
4. As thee their God our fa - thers owned, So

our at - ten - tive ears, Thy won - ders in their
them sal - va - tion gave; 'Twas not their num - ber
suc - cor they im - plored, Thy prov - i - dence pro -
thou art still our King: O there - fore, as thou

days per - formed, And in more an - cient years.
nor their strength That did their coun - try save;
tect - ed them Who thy great name a - dored.
didst to them, To us de - liv - 'rance bring!

5. To thee the glory we ascribe,
From whom salvation came;
In God our shield, we will rejoice
And ever bless thy name.

Text: Nahum Tate, 1652–1715; Nicholas Brady, 1659–1726
Music: Henry Bryan Hays, O.S.B., b. 1920, ©

86 86
KINSTON

475 Redemption From Captivity

1. When the Lord brought back from cap - ti - vi - ty his flock,
2. Then they said a - mong the na - tions "God for them has done great things;
3. Re - store, O Lord, our for-tunes as of old,

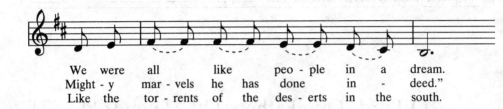

We were all like peo - ple in a dream.
Might - y mar - vels he has done in - deed."
Like the tor - rents of the des - erts in the south.

Then our throats with laugh-ter rang, And our tongues burst out in song;
Yes, the Lord has won-ders done, End-less pow - er he has shown,
Those who weep - ing sow the seed Shall in joy the har - vest reap.

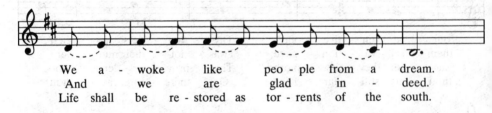

We a - woke like peo - ple from a dream.
And we are glad in - deed.
Life shall be re - stored as tor - rents of the south.

REFRAIN

Though with tears we set out sad - ly in the ear - ly morn, Bear-ing

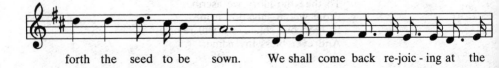

forth the seed to be sown. We shall come back re-joic - ing at the

Text: Psalm 126; adapt. Henry Bryan Hays, O.S.B., b. 1920, ©
Music: Henry Bryan Hays, O.S.B., b. 1920, ©

Irregular with Refrain
LOOKOUT MOUNTAIN

set-ting   of   the sun,   We   shall come   back   car - ry-ing   the

sheaves.   We shall come back re-joic - ing,   car - ry-ing the sheaves, We shall

come back re-joic-ing all the way.   Though we left   in   the morn-ing with a

bit-ter seed to sow,   We shall come back re-joic - ing all   the   way.

CODA (to be sung after last chorus)   *rall.*

We shall come back re-joic-ing   all   the   way.

476 Happy Are They

1. Hap - py those who shy from e - vil coun - sel,
2. Their de - light the sta - tutes of the Lord; they
3. Like the trees whose leaves shall nev - er fade, pros -
4. Come to judg - ment, they will sure - ly fall; no
5. Praise to God our Fa - ther and Cre - a - tor,

those who lin - ger not in sin - ners' ways;
pon - der on them ev - 'ry day and night.
per - i - ty shall show in all their deeds.
room is theirs a - mong those count - ed just.
to our Sav - ior Je - sus Christ the Lord,

those who will not sit a - mong the scorn - ers.
They are like the trees near flow - ing wa - ters
Not so are the with - ered wick - ed ones; like
For the Lord pro - tects the ho - ly path; but
to their Spir - it dwell - ing in our hearts, both

1.–4.

Hap - py will they be and blest their name.
bring - ing forth their fruit at sea - son's height.
win - nowed chaff they're dri - ven by the breeze.
e - vil ways he turns to doom and dust.

5.

now and for e - ter - ni - ty. A- men.

Text: Psalm 1; adapt. Jerome Coller, O.S.B., b. 1929
Music: Jerome Coller, O.S.B., b. 1929

In My Name 477

1. Wher - ev - er two or three have come, And gath - ered
2. I'll walk with you down through the years, A - long the
3. No eye has seen, no ear has heard, Nor an - y
4. You see me now in a dark - ened glass, But lat - er

in my name, There I am in the midst of them,
dust - y road, I'll speak to you a word of hope,
heart con - ceived, What God has wait - ing for his friends
face to face, And all will come to praise their God

For Christ as Lord they claim. There I am in the
And share your heav - y load. I'll speak to you a
Who love and have be - lieved. What God has wait - ing
From ev - 'ry tribe and race. And all will come to

midst of them, For Christ as Lord they claim.
word of hope, And share your heav - y load.
for his friends Who love and have be - lieved.
praise their God From ev - 'ry tribe and race.

Text: Willard F. Jabusch, b. 1930, ©
Music: Russian Folk Melody; arr. Francis E. Pellegrini, 1936–1984
Music Arr. © 1970, J.S. Paluch Co., Inc..

478 O For A Closer Walk With God

1. O for a clos-er walk with God, A calm and heav'n-ly
frame, A light to shine up-on the road That
leads me to the Lamb. Where is the bless-ed-
ness I knew When first I saw the Lord? Where

2. What peace-ful hours I once en-joyed! How sweet their mem-ory
still! But they have left an ach-ing void The
world can nev-er fill. Re-turn, O ho-ly
Dove, re-turn, Sweet mess-en-ger of rest! I

3. The dear-est i-dol I have known, What-e'er that i-dol
be, Help me to tear it from thy throne, And
wor-ship on-ly thee. So shall my walk be
close with God, Calm and se-rene my frame; So

Text: William Cowper, 1731–1800
Music: Henry Bryan Hays, O.S.B., b. 1920, ©

86 86 86 86
MANASSAS

is the soul - re - fresh-ing view Of Je - sus and his
hate the sins that made thee mourn, And drove thee from my
pur - er light shall mark the road That leads me to the

word? Of Je - sus and his word?
breast. And drove thee from my breast.
Lamb. That leads me to the Lamb.

479 The Lord's My Shepherd

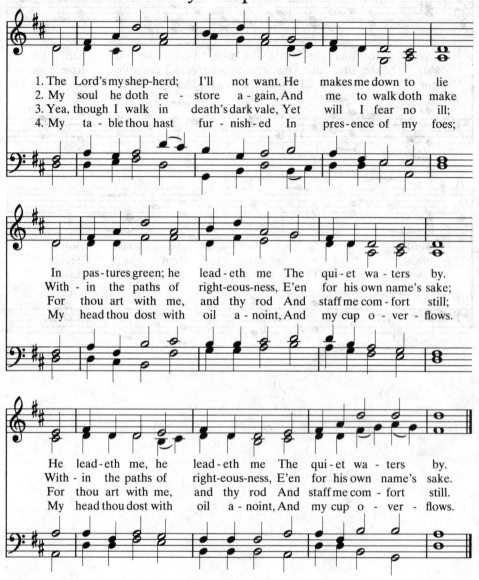

1. The Lord's my shep-herd; I'll not want. He makes me down to lie
2. My soul he doth re - store a - gain, And me to walk doth make
3. Yea, though I walk in death's dark vale, Yet will I fear no ill;
4. My ta - ble thou hast fur - nish-ed In pres-ence of my foes;

In pas-tures green; he lead-eth me The qui-et wa-ters by.
With - in the paths of right-eous-ness, E'en for his own name's sake;
For thou art with me, and thy rod And staff me com-fort still;
My head thou dost with oil a - noint, And my cup o - ver - flows.

He lead-eth me, he lead-eth me The qui-et wa-ters by.
With - in the paths of right-eous-ness, E'en for his own name's sake.
For thou art with me, and thy rod And staff me com-fort still.
My head thou dost with oil a - noint, And my cup o - ver - flows.

5. Goodness and mercy all my life
   Shall surely follow me,
   And in God's house forevermore
   My dwelling-place shall be.
   And in God's house forevermore
   My dwelling-place shall be.

Text: Ps. 23; adapt. J. Driscoll, S.J., ©
Music: J.L. Macbeth Bain, c. 1840–1985, adapt.; arr. Gordon Jacob, 1895–1984, ©

86 86 86
BROTHER JAMES' AIR

This Is My Will 480

1. This is my will, my one com - mand, That
2. No great - er love that one can have, Than
3. I call you now no long - er slaves; No
4. You chose not me, but I chose you, That

love should dwell a - mong you all. This is my will, that
that one die to save one's friends. You are my friends if
slave knows all the mas - ter does. I call you friends, for
you should go and bear much fruit. I chose you out that

you should love As I have shown that I love you.
you o - bey What I com - mand that you should do.
all I hear My Fa - ther say, you hear from me.
you in me Should bear much fruit that will a - bide.

5. All that you ask my Father dear,
For my name's sake you shall receive.
This is my will, my one command,
That love should dwell in each, in all.

Text: James Quinn, S.J., b. 1919, © 1969
Music: Musikalisches Handbuch; adapt., Hamburg, 1690

88 88
WINCHESTER NEW

481 Those Who Love and Those Who Labor

1. Those who love and those who la - bor Fol - low in the way of Christ; Thus the first dis - ci - ples found him, Thus the gift of love suf - ficed. Je - sus says to those who seek him, I will ne - ver pass you by; Raise the

2. Where the man - y work to - geth - er They with Christ him - self a - bide, But the lone - ly work-ers al - so Find him ev - er at their side. Lo, the Prince of com - mon wel - fare Dwells with - in the mar - ket strife; Lo, the

3. Let the seek - er ne - ver fal - ter Till the truth is found a - far With the wis - dom of the a - ges un - der - neath a gi - ant star. With the rich - est and the poor - est, Of the sum of things pos - sessed. Like a

Text: Geoffrey Dearmer, b. 1893, ©
Music: Gaelic; acc. Edward Currie

87 87 87 87
DOMHNACH TRIONOIDE

stone and you shall find me; Cleave the wood and there am I.
bread of heav'n is bro - ken In the sac - ra - ment of life.
child at first to won - der, Like a king at last to rest.

482 Hosea

VERSES

1. Come back to me with all your heart.
2. wil-der-ness will lead you
3. You shall sleep se-cure with peace;

v. 3 go to Refrain

Don't let fear keep us a-part.
to your heart where I will speak. In-
faith-ful-ness will be your joy.

Trees do bend, though straight and tall:
te-gri-ty and jus-tice with
ten-der-ness you shall know.

so must we to oth-ers' call

REFRAIN

Long have I wait-ed for your com-ing home to me and

1.–2.

liv-ing deep-ly our new life.

After v. 3 if Interlude is used

2. The
3. life.

Text: Gregory Norbet, O.S.B., b. 1940, ©
Music: Gregory Norbet, O.S.B., b. 1940; acc. Sr. Mary David Callahan, O.S.B., b. 1923, ©

Father of Heaven, Whose Love Profound 483

1. Fa - ther of heav'n, whose love pro - found
2. Al - might - y Son, in - car - nate Word,
3. E - ter - nal Spir - it, by whose breath
4. Thrice Ho - ly! Fa - ther, Spir - it, Son;

A ran - som for our souls has found,
Our Proph - et, Priest, Re - deem - er, Lord,
The soul is raised from sin and death,
Mys - te - rious God - head, Three in One,

Be - fore your throne we sin - ners bend,
Be - fore your throne we sin - ners bend,
Be - fore your throne we sin - ners bend,
Be - fore your throne we sin - ners bend,

To us your par - d'ning love ex - tend.
To us your sav - ing grace ex - tend.
To us your quick - 'ning pow'r ex - tend.
Grace, par - don, life to us ex - tend.

Text: Edward Cooper, 1770–1833
Music: Orlando Gibbons, 1583–1625 (Melody and Bass adapted)

88 88
SONG 5

Living Stones 484

REFRAIN

As liv-ing stones, as bricks of clay, We come, O God, to you to-day. Please use us as you will To build the tem-ple you have planned.

You are our Fa - ther, build - er, pot - ter;

We are the work of your own hand.

VERSES

1. In Zi - on God will lay the stones. True jus - tice is the line of
2. Christ is the rare and pre-cious stone, A might-y Lord, yet meek and
3. Place us, O God, up - on that stone, Re - ject - ed once in con - dem-

mea - sure; The plumb-line will be hon - es - ty, And
hum - ble: For us the stone on which to build; For
na - tion: The on - ly one, true cor - ner - stone, Our

To Refrain

Christ, our Lord, the on - ly trea - sure.
some a stone on which to stum - ble.
Lord, the Church's firm foun - da - tion.

Text: Omer Westendorf, b. 1916, ©
Music: Jerry Brubaker, b. 1946, ©

485 Christ Is Made the Sure Foundation

1. Christ is made the sure foun-da-tion, Christ the head and
   cor - ner - stone; Cho - sen of the Lord, and pre - cious,
   Bind - ing all the Church in one; Ho - ly Zi - on's
   help for - ev - er, And her con - fi - dence a - lone.

2. To this tem - ple, where we call you, Come, O Lord of
   hosts, to - day; With your wont - ed lov - ing - kind - ness
   Hear your ser - vants as they pray, And your full - est
   ben - e - dic - tion Shed in all its bright ar - ray.

3. Grant, we pray, to all your peo - ple, All the grace they
   ask to gain; What they gain from you for - ev - er
   With the bless - ed to re - tain, And here - af - ter
   in your glo - ry Ev - er - more with you to reign.

Text: Latin, 7th c.; tr. John Mason Neale, 1818–1866, alt.
Music: Henry Purcell, 1659–1695, adapt.; instrumental descant, James Gillespie, b. 1929, ©

87 87 87
WESTMINSTER ABBEY

We Love Your Temple, Lord 486

1. We love your tem - ple, Lord, For there your hon - or ev - er dwells;
2. We love the sa - cred font, Whose sav - ing wa - ters o - ver - flow
3. We love your words of life, The words that grant us your own peace,
4. Lord Je - sus, give us grace On earth to love and praise you more,

The joy of your a - bode All earth - ly joy for us ex - cels.
And pour as ev - er wont Your bless - ing on us here be - low.
Of com - fort in the strife, And won-drous joys that nev - er cease.
In heav'n to see your face, And with your lov - ing saints a - dore.

It is the house of prayer, Where - in your ser - vants meet;
We love your ta - ble, Lord, Where nour-ished here on earth
We love to sing be - low For mer - cies free - ly giv'n;
Be - fore you, Lord, we bow, E - ter - nal One in Three;

And you, O Lord, are there Your cho - sen ones to greet.
Our lives are new re - stored, Our souls find new re - birth.
But oh, we long to know The tri - umph song of heav'n.
For thus it was, is now, And ev - er - more shall be.

Text: William Bullock, 1797–1874; H.W. Baker, 1821–1877; tr. alt. John Dunn, ©
Music: Ahasuerus Fritsch, 1629–1701; harm. J.S. Bach, 1685–1750

67 67 66 66
DARMSTADT

487 Christ's Church Shall Glory in His Power

1. Christ's Church shall glo - ry in his pow'r
2. Christ's peo - ple serve his way - ward world
3. Christ's liv - ing lamp shall bright - ly burn,

And grow to his per - fec - tion;
To whom he seems a stran - ger;
And to our earth - ly cit - y

He is our rock, our might - y tow'r
He knows its wel - come from of old,
For - got - ten beau - ty shall re - turn,

Our life, our res - ur - rec - tion:
He shares our joy, our dan - ger:
And pu - ri - ty and pit - y:

Text: Christopher Idle, b. 1938
Music: Martin Luther, 1483–1546; harm. J.S. Bach, 1685–1750

Text © 1982, Hope Publishing Co.

87 87 66 66 7
EIN FESTE BURG

So by his skill - ful hand The Church of
So strong, and yet so weak, The Church of
To give the op - pressed their right The Church of

Christ shall stand; The mas - ter - build - er's plan
Christ shall speak; His cross our great - est need,
Christ shall fight; And though the years seem long

He works, as he be - gan,
His word the vi - tal seed
He is our strength and song,

And soon will crown with splen - dor.
That brings a fruit - ful har - vest.
And he is our sal - va - tion.

488 O Christ the Great Foundation

1. O Christ the great foun-da-tion On which your peo-ple stand
2. Bap-tized in one con-fes-sion, One Church in all the earth,
3. Where ty-rants' hold is tight-ened, Where strong de-vour the weak,
4. This is the mo-ment glo-rious When he who once was dead

To preach your true sal-va-tion In ev-'ry age and land:
We bear our Lord's im-pres-sion, The sign of sec-ond birth:
Where in-no-cents are fright-ened The righ-teous fear to speak,
Shall lead his Church vic-to-rious, Their cham-pion and their head.

Pour out your Ho-ly Spir-it To make us strong and pure,
One ho-ly peo-ple gath-ered In love be-yond our own,
There let your Church a-wak-ing At-tack the pow'rs of sin
The Lord of all cre-a-tion His heav'n-ly king-dom brings

To keep the faith un-bro-ken As long as worlds en-dure.
By grace we were in-vit-ed, By grace we make you known.
And, all their ram-parts break-ing, With you the vic-t'ry win.
The fi-nal con-sum-ma-tion, The glo-ry of all things.

Lower Key: O Living Bread from Heaven, no. 397
Text: Timothy T'ingfang Lew, 1891–1947, alt.
Music: Samuel S. Wesley, 1810–1876

76 76 76 76
AURELIA

Alternative Text

The Church's One Foundation 489

1. The Church's one foundation
   Is Jesus Christ her Lord:
   She is his new creation
   By water and the word;
   From heav'n he came and sought her
   To be his holy bride;
   With his own blood he bought her,
   And for her life he died.

2. Elect from ev'ry nation
   Yet one o'er all the earth,
   Her charter of salvation
   One Lord, one faith, one birth,
   One holy name she blesses,
   Partakes one holy food,
   And to one hope she presses,
   With ev'ry grace endued.

3. Through toil and tribulation
   And tumult of her war
   She waits the consummation
   Of peace for evermore,
   Till with the vision glorious
   Her longing eyes are blest,
   And the great Church victorious
   Shall be the Church at rest.

4. Yet she on earth has union
   With God, the Three in One,
   And mystic sweet communion
   With those whose rest is won.
   O happy ones and holy!
   Lord, give us grace that we
   Like them, the meek and lowly,
   On high may dwell with thee.

Text: Samuel John Stone, 1839–1900

76 76 76 76
AURELIA

490 Who Are We That Stand Together?

1. Who are we that stand to-geth-er, Rock in strength up-on the Rock? Like some ci-ty crowned with tur-rets, Brav-ing storm and earth-quake shock! Peo-ple stand with arms u-ni-ted, Christ our head, a world re-stored,

2. As the moon its splen-dor bor-rows From a sun un-seen all night, So from Christ the sun of jus-tice, Ev-er-more we draw our light. Touched by his, our hands have heal-ing, Bread of life, ab-solv-ing key:

3. Em-pires rise and sink like bil-lows Things we know are seen no more; Stea-dy as the star of morn-ing, We are firm a-gainst all war. Ours the house-hold all—em-brac-ing, Ours the vine that shad-ows earth:

Text: Aubrey DeVere, 1814–1902; Edward J. McKenna, b. 1939, alt., ©
Music: Richard R. Terry, 1865–1938, ©

87 87 87 87 with Refrain
ECCLESIA

CHURCH

All the an-thems of cre-a-tion Lift-ing to cre-a-tion's Lord.
Christ in-car-nate is our bro-ther, God is ours, his tem-ple we.
Blest our chil-dren, fa-ther, mo-ther; Safe the strang-er at the door.
REFRAIN
We the king-dom, we the peo-ple of all na-tions in God's sight;
This the truth whose fruit is free-dom; eas-y yoke and bur-den light.

491 There Comes a Time

VERSES

1. There comes a time when an - ger melts in
2. The air is fresh, God's wind will blow a -
3. Though "all be one" was Je - sus' great and

peace - ful - ness; There comes a time when mem - o - ries are
way the past; New vig - or comes when sing - ing with one
ur - gent prayer, Di - vi - sions came and hate - ful things were

healed; There comes a time, a time to leave our
voice; One Lord, one faith, one faith, and wash - ing
done; What joy to know, to know that Je - sus'

stuf - fy nar - row rooms; There comes a time to
from our com - mon sins. One sup - per shared, is
voice is be - ing heard, What joy to know re -

walk, to walk in o - pen fields.
al - so is al - so our firm choice.
un - ion, re - un - ion has be - gun!

REFRAIN

We all be - lieve in the same good God, We all are

res-cued from death by his Son, We all are bap-tized by wa-ter and the

Spir-it Is it not time that we all were one?

Text: Willard F. Jabusch, b. 1930, ©
Music: Robert E. Kreutz, b. 1922, ©

O Love, Who Drew from Jesus' Side 492

1. O Love, who drew from Jesus' side, One body freed from Adam's shame, One Church sent forth to serve and guide, One faith confirmed by gifts of flame; When worldly schemes our hopes assail, Your kingdom come, your truth prevail.

2. Round Peter's chair may all unite; From blinded eyes the veil withdraw; The minds of rulers set aright Who bind your Church beneath their law; Where faith grows dim and hearts are frail, Your kingdom come, your truth prevail.

3. While Christians pray for unity, Pour forth the light your saints have seen; Dispel the dark of enmity: Make known to all what love can mean, Where brooding minds old wounds bewail, Your kingdom come, your truth prevail.

4. Spoiled children, we, so blest with sight, Redeemed by love surpassing all; Lest we who glory in your light Share not our gift, heed not your call, In Christian hearts that faint and fail, Your kingdom come, your truth prevail.

Text: Richard J. Wojcik, b. 1923, ©
Music: Georg Neumark, 1621–1681; arr. J.S. Bach, 1685–1750

88 88 88 (alt)
NEUMARK (ALT)

493 Jesus Renews the Parish

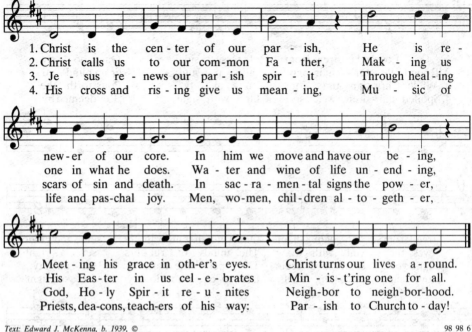

1. Christ is the cen-ter of our par-ish, He is re-
new-er of our core. In him we move and have our be-ing,
Meet-ing his grace in oth-er's eyes. Christ turns our lives a-round.

2. Christ calls us to our com-mon Fa-ther, Mak-ing us
one in what he does. Wa-ter and wine of life un-end-ing,
His Eas-ter in us cel-e-brates Min-is-t'ring one for all.

3. Je-sus re-news our par-ish spir-it Through heal-ing
scars of sin and death. In sac-ra-men-tal signs the pow-er,
God, Ho-ly Spir-it re-u-nites Neigh-bor to neigh-bor-hood.

4. His cross and ris-ing give us mean-ing, Mu-sic of
life and pas-chal joy. Men, wo-men, chil-dren al-to-geth-er,
Priests, dea-cons, teach-ers of his way: Par-ish to Church to-day!

Text: Edward J. McKenna, b. 1939, ©
Music: Edward J. McKenna, b. 1939, ©

98 98 6
MARYHAVEN

494 There Is a Prayer

1. There is a prayer that ris-es in the dark through-
out this world where Chris-tians live a-part:
May we be one, O Fa-ther, mind and heart.

2. Our wounds of scorn, of en-vy, fear and pride
Harsh-ly pro-claim how false-hood can di-vide;
Truth is our hope and truth must be our guide.

3. Lord, we im-plore with all our gath-'ring might
Give us that wis-dom which a-lone gives light.
Stay with us, Mas-ter, through the dark-'ning night.

4. Ful-fill our prayer for this di-vid-ed land:
Lead us u-nit-ed by your pow'r-ful hand;
Give us a love that seeks to un-der-stand.

Al - le - lu - ia, al - le - lu - ia.

5. As one great people serving humankind,
   One in your Spirit, one in heart and mind,
   May we proclaim that all who seek will find.
   Alleluia, alleluia.

Text: Ralph Wright, O.S.B., b. 1938, ©
Music: Robert E. Kreutz, b. 1922, ©

Only Begotten, Word of God Eternal 495

1. On - ly be - got - ten, Word of God e -
2. Ho - ly this tem - ple where our Lord is
3. Lord, we be - seech you, as we throng your
4. God in Three Per - sons, Fa - ther ev - er -

ter - nal, Lord of cre - a - tion, mer - ci - ful and
dwell - ing, This is none oth - er than the gate of
tem - ple, By your past bless - ings, by your pres - ent
liv - ing, Son co - e - ter - nal, ev - er - bless - ed

might - y, Hear now your ser - vants, when their tune - ful
heav - en; Stran - gers and pil - grims, seek - ing homes e -
boun - ty, Smile on your chil - dren, and with ten - der
Spir - it, Yours be the glo - ry, praise and ad - or -

voic - es Rise to your pres - ence.
ter - nal, Pass through its por - tals.
mer - cy Hear our pe - ti - tions.
a - tion, Now and for - ev - er.

Text: Anon. Latin, 9th c.; tr. Maxwell J. Blacker, 1822–1888
Music: Rouen Church Melody, Processionale, 1763; arr. Carl Schalk, b. 1929, ©

11 11 11 5
ISTE CONFESSOR

496 Open Now Thy Gates of Beauty

1. O - pen now thy gates of beau - ty, Zi - on, let me en - ter there,
2. Gra - cious God, I come be - fore thee; Come thou al - so un - to me;
3. Here thy praise is glad - ly chant - ed, Here thy seed is du - ly sown;
4. Thou my faith in - crease and quick - en, Let me keep thy gift di - vine;

Where my soul in joy - ful du - ty Waits for God who an - swers prayer.
Where we find thee and a - dore thee, There a heav'n on earth must be.
Let my soul, where it is plant - ed, Bring forth pre - cious sheaves a - lone,
How - so - e'er temp - ta - tions thick - en, May thy Word still o'er me shine

Oh, how bless - ed is this place, Filled with sol - ace, light, and grace!
To my heart, oh, en - ter thou, Let it be thy tem - ple now!
So that all I hear may be Fruit - ful un - to life in me.
As my guid - ing star through life, As my com - fort in all strife.

5. Speak, O God, and I will hear thee,
Let thy will be done indeed;
May I undisturbed draw near thee
While thou dost thy people feed.
Here of life the fountain flows;
Here is balm for all our woes.

Alt. Arr.: He Is Risen, He Is Risen, no. 285

Text: Benjamin Schmolck, 1672–1737; tr. Catherine Winkworth, 1829–1878, alt.
Music: Joachim Neander 1650–1680

87 87 77
UNSER HERRSCHER

Breathe on Me, Breath of God 497

1. Breathe on me, breath of God, Fill me with life a-new, That I may love the things you love, And do what you would do.
2. Breathe on me, breath of God, Un-til my heart is pure; Un-til with you I will one will, To do and to en-dure.
3. Breathe on me, breath of God, My will to yours in-cline, Un-til this self-ish part of me Glows with your fire di-vine.
4. Breathe on me, breath of God, So shall I nev-er die, But live with you the per-fect life Of your e-ter-ni-ty.

Text: Edwin Hatch, 1835–1889
Music: Charles Lockhart, 1745–1815

66 86
CARLISLE

498 Come Down, O Love Divine

1. Come down, O Love divine, Seek thou this soul of mine,
2. O let it freely burn, Till earthly passions turn
3. And so the yearning strong, With which the soul will long,

And visit it with thine own ardor glowing;
To dust and ashes in its heat consuming;
Shall far outpass the pow'r of human telling;

O Comforter, draw near, Within my heart appear,
And let thy glorious light Shine ever on my sight,
For none can guess its grace, Till Love create a place

And kindle it, thy holy flame bestowing.
And clothe me round, the while my path illuming.
Wherein the Holy Spirit makes a dwelling.

Text: Bianco da Siena, +1434?; tr. Richard Frederick Littledale, 1833–1890, alt.
Music: Ralph Vaughan Williams, 1872–1958, ©

66 11 66 11
DOWN AMPNEY

Come, Gracious Spirit, Heavenly Dove 499

1. Come, gra - cious Spir - it, heav'n - ly dove, With light and
com - fort from a - bove. Come, be our guard - ian
and our guide; O'er ev - 'ry thought and step pre - side.

2. The light of truth to us dis - play And make us
know and choose your way; Plant ho - ly fear in
ev - 'ry heart, That we from God may ne'er de - part.

3. Lead us to Christ, the liv - ing way, Nor let us
from his pas - tures stray; Lead us to ho - li -
ness, the road That we must take to dwell with God.

4. Lead us to heav'n, that we may share Full - ness of
joy for - ev - er there; Lead us to our e -
ter - nal rest, To be with God for - ev - er blest.

Text: Simon Browne, 1680–1732, alt.
Music: William Knapp, 1698–1768

88 88
WAREHAM

500 Holy Spirit, Truth Divine

1. Ho-ly Spir-it, truth di-vine, Dawn up-on this
2. Ho-ly Spir-it, love di-vine, Glow with-in this
3. Ho-ly Spir-it, pow'r di-vine, Strength-en this weak
4. Ho-ly Spir-it, law di-vine, Reign with-in this

soul of mine; Breath of God and in-ward light,
heart of mine; Kin-dle ev-'ry high de-sire;
will of mine; May your sure sup-port pre-cede
soul of mine: Be my law and I shall be

Wake my spir-it, clear my sight.
Con-quer me in your pure fire.
Ev-'ry thought and word and deed.
Firm-ly bound, for ev-er free.

5. Holy Spirit, peace divine,
   Still this restless heart of mine:
   Speak and calm this tossing sea,
   Bring it to tranquility.

6. Holy Spirit, joy divine,
   Gladden now this heart of mine.
   Help me now to sing and pray,
   Praising God by night and day.

Alt. Tune: Forty Days and Forty Nights, no. 242
Text: Samuel Longfellow, 1819–1892
Music: Orlando Gibbons, 1583–1625

77 77
SONG 13

O Holy Spirit, Come to Us 501

1. O Holy Spirit, come to us The
2. You are our source of strength and might, Great
3. We thank you for your gifts of grace, O
4. Then come, great Spirit, to your own; Our

chil - dren you have made; In - flame our hearts and
gift from God a - bove; You are the font of
Prom - ised One of God; Your won - drous life be -
hearts make pure and strong. Di - rect our wea - ry

rule our minds With your un - fail - ing aid.
truth and light, The flame of hope and love.
comes our own, Your strength, our staff and rod.
steps to you, And turn our wills from wrong.

5. O highest wisdom fill us all
   With light to truly see,
   That in your love alone in hope
   To live eternally.

6. Show us the Father and the Son,
   O Spirit, we implore,
   That in the Godhead we may live
   Both now and evermore.

Higher Key: When to the Sacred Font We Came, no. 349

Text: Anon.; tr. Melvin L. Farrell, S.S., b. 1930
Music: Thomas Tallis, c. 1505–1585

86 86
TALLIS' ORDINAL

502 Spirit Divine, Attend Our Prayers

1. Spir - it di - vine, at - tend our prayers, And make this
house your home; De - scend with all your gra - cious pow'rs
O come, great Spir - it, come!

2. Come as the light; to us re - veal Our emp - ti -
ness and woe, And lead us in those paths of life
Where all the right - eous go.

3. Come as the fire, and purge our hearts Like sac - ri -
fi - cial flame; Let our whole soul and of - f'ring be
To our Re - deem - er's Name.

4. Come as the dove, and spread your wings, The wings of
peace - ful love; And let your Church on earth be - come
Blest as the Church a - bove.

5. Spirit divine, accept our prayers;
Make a lost world your home;
Descend with all your gracious pow'rs;
O come, great Spirit, come!

Text: Andrew Reed, 1788–1862, alt.
Music: Johann Crüger, 1598–1662

86 86
GRAEFENBERG

All You Who Seek a Comfort Sure 503

1. All you who seek a com-fort sure In trou-ble and dis-tress,
2. You hear how kind-ly he in-vites; You hear his words so blest:

What-ev-er sor-row vex the mind, Or guilt the soul op-press,
"All you that la-bor come to me, And I will give you rest."

Je-sus, who gave him-self for you Up-on the cross to die,
Christ Je-sus, joy of saints on high, The hope of sin-ners here,

O-pens to you his sa-cred heart; Oh, to that heart draw nigh.
At-tract-ed by those lov-ing words To you we lift our prayer.

Text: tr. Edward Caswall, 1814–1878
Music: English folk melody; adapt. and harm. Ralph Vaughan Williams, 1872–1958, ©

86 86 86 86
KINGSFOLD

504 Alleluia! Sing to Jesus

1. Al - le - lu - ia! Sing to Je - sus! His the
2. Al - le - lu - ia! Not as or - phans Are we
3. Al - le - lu - ia! Bread of heav - en, Here on
4. Al - le - lu - ia! King e - ter - nal, You the

scep - ter, his the throne; Al - le - lu - ia! his the
left in sor - row now; Al - le - lu - ia! he is
earth our food, our stay! Al - le - lu - ia! here the
Lord of lords we own: Al - le - lu - ia! born of

tri - umph, His the vic - to - ry a - lone; Hark! The
near us, Faith be - lieves, nor ques - tions how; Though the
sin - ful Flee to you from day to day; In - ter -
Mar - y, Earth your foot - stool, heav'n your throne: You with -

songs of peace - ful Zi - on Thun - der like a
cloud from sight re - ceived him, When the for - ty
ces - sor, friend of sin - ners, Earth's Re - deem - er,
in the veil have en - tered, Robed in flesh, our

Alt. Tune: Lord of Light, no. 638
Text: William Chatterton Dix, 1837–1898, alt.
Music: Rowland H. Prichard, 1811–1887

87 87 87 87
HYFRYDOL

might - y flood; Je - sus out of ev - 'ry
days were o'er, Shall our hearts for - get his
plead for me, Where the songs of all the
great High Priest: Here on earth both Priest and

na - tion Has re - deemed us by his blood.
prom - ise, "I am with you ev - er - more"?
sin - less Sweep a - cross the crys - tal sea.
Vic - tim In the eu - cha - ris - tic feast.

505 Firmly I Believe and Truly

1. Firm - ly I be - lieve and tru - ly God is
2. And I trust and hope most ful - ly In that
3. Simp - ly to his grace and whol - ly Light and
4. And I hold in ven - er - a - tion, For the

Three, and God is One; And I next ac -
Man - hood cru - ci - fied; And each thought and
life and strength be - long, And I love su -
love of him a - lone, Ho - ly Church as

know - ledge du - ly Man - hood tak - en by the Son.
deed un - rul - y Do to death, as he has died.
preme - ly, sole - ly, Him the ho - ly, him the strong.
his cre - a - tion, And her teach-ings as his own.

5. Adoration ay be given,
   With and through th'angelic host,
   To the God of earth and heaven,
   Father, Son, and Holy Ghost.

Alt. Tune: See Us, Lord, About Your Altar, no. 392
Text: John Henry Newman, 1801–1890
Music: Henry Bryan Hays, O.S.B., b. 1920, ©

87 87
CREDO

God Unseen Is Seen In Christ 506

1. God un-seen is seen in Christ, First-born son a-
2. Through him, for him, God has made Thrones, do-min-ions,
3. Christ gives life to all that live, Christ is head, the
4. God has cho-sen that the Son, Ful-ly God in

bove all crea-tures. God cre-a-ted all through him,
princ-es, pow-ers. He was first be-fore all things;
Church his bod-y. First-born of the dead he reigns
his own na-ture, Buy with blood shed on the cross

Seen and un-seen, earth and heav-en.
In him all things hold to-geth-er.
First be-fore all God's cre-a-tion.
Peace and rec-on-cil-i-a-tion.

Text: Bro. Louis Blenkner, O.S.B., b. 1922, ©
Music: Henry Bryan Hays, O.S.B., b. 1920, ©

78 78
INDIAN MOUND

507 Hail, Jesus, Hail

1. Hail, Je - sus, hail, who for my sake Sweet blood from
2. To end - less a - ges let us praise The pre - cious
3. O no - blest blood, that can im - plore Par - don of

Mar - y's veins did take And shed it all for me;
blood, whose price could raise The world from wrath and sin;
God, and heav'n re - store, The heav'n which sin had lost;

Oh, bless - ed be my Sav - ior's blood, My life, my
Whose streams our in - ward thirst ap - pease And heal the
While A - bel's blood for ven - geance pleads, The blood of

light, my on - ly good, To all e - ter - ni - ty.
sin - ner's worst dis - ease, If he but bathe there - in.
Christ still in - ter - cedes For those who trust there - in.

Text: Anon.; tr. Frederick W. Faber, 1814–1863, alt.
Music: Orlando Gibbons, 1583–1625; David Fetler, alt., ©

886 886
SONG 18

Jesus Shall Reign 508

1. Je - sus shall reign wher - e'er the sun Does his suc -
2. To him shall end - less prayers be made, And all our
3. Peo - ple and realms of ev - 'ry tongue Dwell on his
4. Bless - ings a - bound wher - e'er he reigns: The pris-'ners

ces - sive jour - neys run; His king-dom stretch from
songs de - clare him head; His Name like sweet per -
love with cheer - ful song; And chil-dren's voic - es
leap to lose their chains, The wea - ry find e -

shore to shore, Till moons shall wax and wane no more.
fume shall rise With ev - 'ry morn - ing sac - ri - fice.
shall pro - claim Their ear - ly bless - ings on his name.
ter - nal rest, And all who suf - fer want are blest.

5. Let ev'ry creature rise and sing
   Their joyful praises to their King;
   Angels descend with songs again,
   And earth repeat the loud Amen.

Lower Key: I Know That My Redeemer Lives, no. 293
Text: Isaac Watts, 1674–1748
Music: John Hatton, c. 1710–1793, attr.

88 88
DUKE STREET

509 O Christ, Our Hope

1. O Christ, our hope, our hearts' de-sire, Re-demp-tion's on-ly
spring; Cre-a-tor of the world are you, Its
Sav-ior and its King, Its Sav-ior and its King.

2. How vast the mer-cy and the love Which led you to the
tree, And on this cross you died for us To
set your peo-ple free, To set your peo-ple free.

3. But now the bonds of death are burst, The ran-som has been
paid; And you are on your Fa-ther's throne In
maj-es-ty ar-rayed, In maj-es-ty ar-rayed.

4. O may your might-y love pre-vail Our sin-ful souls to
spare, O may we come be-fore your throne And
find ac-cep-tance there, And find ac-cep-tance there!

5. Christ Jesus, be our present joy,
Our future great reward;
Our only glory may it be
To glory in the Lord,
To glory in the Lord!

6. All praise to you, ascended Lord;
All glory ever be
To Father, Son and Holy Ghost
Through all eternity,
Through all eternity.

Text: tr. John Chandler, 1806–1876
Music: Nikolaus Hermann, 1480–1561

86 866
HERMAN (LOBT GOTT)

O Jesus, Joy of Loving Hearts 510

1. O Je - sus, joy of lov - ing hearts, The fount of
2. Your truth un - changed has ev - er stood; You save all
3. We taste you, Lord, our liv - ing bread, And long to
4. For you our rest - less spir - its yearn Wher-e'er our

life and our true light, We seek the peace your
those who heed your call; To those who seek you,
feast up - on you still; We drink of you, the
chang - ing lot is cast; Glad, when your pres - ence

love im - parts And stand re - joic - ing in your sight.
you are good, To those who find you all in all.
foun - tain - head, Our thirst - ing souls to quench and fill.
we dis - cern, Blest, when our faith can hold you fast.

5. O Jesus, ever with us stay;
   Make all our moments calm and bright;
   Oh, chase the night of sin away,
   Shed o'er the world your holy light.

Higher Key: Lord God of Morning and of Night, no. 427
Text: St. Bernard Clairvaux, 1091–1153, attr.; tr. Ray Palmer, 1808–1887, alt.
Music: William Gardiner, 1770–1853, attr.

88 88
FULDA (WALTON)

511 O Sacred Heart All Holy

1. O Sacred Heart all ho - ly, That heart so meek and low - ly, Our hard-ened hearts re - fine, For in your heart is trea - sure, Of good - ness with - out mea - sure, Of mer - cy, grace, and love di - vine.

2. Your heart for love is yearn - ing, While we to sin are turn - ing, Un - mind-ful of your love, But in your gra - cious kind - ness, Lord, cure us of our blind - ness, And lead us to your throne a - bove.

Text: Eugene M. Lindusky, b. 1924, ©
Music: Heinrich Isaac, c. 1450–1517; harm. J.S. Bach, 1685–1750

776 778
INNSBRUCK

O Wondrous Type! O Vision Fair 512

1. O won - drous type! O vi - sion fair Of glo - ry
2. With Mo - ses and E - li - jah nigh The in - car - nate
3. With shin - ing face and bright ar - ray, Christ deigns to
4. And faith - ful hearts are raised on high By this great

that the Church may share, Which Christ up - on the
Lord holds con - verse high; And from the cloud, the
man - i - fest to - day What glo - ry shall be
vi - sion's mys - te - ry; For which in joy - ful

moun - tain shows, Where bright - er than the sun he glows!
Ho - ly One Bears re - cord to the on - ly Son.
theirs a - bove Who joy in God with per - fect love.
strains we raise The voice of prayer, the hymn of praise.

5. O Father, with the eternal Son,
And Holy Spirit, ever One,
Vouchsafe to bring us by thy grace
To see thy glory face to face.

Text: Mason's Hymnal Noted, 1851; tr. John Mason Neale, 1818–1866, alt.
Music: William Knapp, 1698–1768; acc. James Turle, 1802–1882

88 88
WAREHAM

513 Praise Christ Jesus, King of Heaven

1. Praise Christ Jesus, King of heaven; To his throne due tribute bring; Ransomed, healed, restored, forgiven, Gratefully your love now sing: Alleluia! Alleluia! Praise the everlasting King.

2. Praise him for his grace and favor To our forebears in distress; Praise him truly who is ever, Slow to chide and swift to bless: Alleluia! Alleluia! Glorious in his faithfulness.

3. Father-like he tends and spares us; Well our weaknesses he knows; In his hands he gently bears us, Rescues us from all our foes. Alleluia! Alleluia! Widely yet his mercy flows.

4. Angels, help us to adore him; You behold him face to face; Sun and moon, bow down before him, Dwellers all in time and space. Alleluia! Alleluia! Praise with us the God of grace.

Text: Henry F. Lyte, 1793–1847, alt.
Music: John Goss, 1800–1880

87 87 87
LAUDA ANIMA

Praise to the Holiest in the Height 514

1. Praise to the Ho - liest in the height, And in the
2. O lov - ing wis - dom of our God! When all was
3. O wis - est love! that flesh and blood, Which did in
4. And that a high - er gift than grace Should flesh and

depth be praise; In all his words most
sin and shame, A sec - ond A - dam
A - dam fail, Should strive a - fresh a -
blood re - fine: God's pres - ence and his

won - der - ful, Most sure in all his ways!
to the fight And to the res - cue came.
gainst the foe, Should strive, and should pre - vail;
ver - y self, And es - sence all - di - vine.

5. And in the garden secretly,
And on the cross on high,
Should teach his brethren, and inspire
To suffer and to die.

Text: John Henry Newman, 1801–1890, alt.
Music: Richard Runciman Terry, 1865–1938,

86 86
NEWMAN

515 Rejoice, The Lord Is King

1. Re - joice, the Lord is King! Your Lord and King a - dore!
2. The Lord, our Sav - ior, reigns, The God of truth and love;
3. His king - dom can - not fail, He rules o'er earth and heav'n;
4. Re - joice in glo - rious hope! Our Lord the judge shall come

Re - joice, give thanks, and sing, And tri - umph ev - er - more:
When he had purged our stains, He took his seat a - bove:
The keys of death and hell Are to our Je - sus giv'n:
And take his ser - vants up To their e - ter - nal home:

REFRAIN

Lift up your heart, lift up your voice! Re -

joice, a - gain I say, re - joice!

Text: Charles Wesley, 1707–1788
Music: John Darwall, 1731–1789, (Melody and Bass); acc. William Henry Monk, 1823–1889, alt.

66 66 88
DARWALL'S 148TH

The Head That Once Was 516
Crowned with Thorns

1. The head that once was crowned with thorns Is
2. The high-est place that heav'n af-fords Be-
3. The joy of all who dwell a-bove, The
4. To them the cross with all its shame, With

crowned with glo-ry now; A roy-al di-a-
longs to him by right; The King of kings, and
joy of all be-low, To whom he man-i-
all its grace is giv'n; Their name an ev-er-

dem a-dorns The might-y vic-tor's brow.
Lord of lords, And heav'n's e-ter-nal light.
fests his love, And grants his name to know.
last-ing name; Their joy the joy of heav'n.

5. They suffer with their Lord below;
They reign with him above;
Their profit and their joy to know
The myst'ry of his love.

6. The cross he bore is life and health,
Though shame and death to him,
His people's hope, his people's wealth,
Their everlasting theme.

Alt. Tune: Throughout These Forty Days, no. 253

Text: Thomas Kelly, 1769–1855
Music: Jeremiah Clark, c. 1670–1707, attr.

86 86
ST. MAGNUS

517 The Lord Is King! Lift Up Your Voice

1. The Lord is King! lift up your voice,
2. He reigns! ye saints, ex - alt your strains;
3. Come, make your wants, your bur - dens, known;
4. One Lord, one em - pire all se - cures;

O earth, and all ye heav'ns, re - joice;
Your God is King, your Sav - ior reigns;
He will pre - sent them at the throne;
He reigns, and life and death are yours:

From world to world the joy shall ring,
And he is at the Fa - ther's side,
And an - gel bands are wait - ing there
Through earth and heav'n one song shall ring,

"The Lord Om - ni - po - tent is King!"
The Man of love, the Cru - ci - fied.
His mes - sa - ges of love to bear.
"The Lord Om - ni - po - tent is King!"

Text: Josiah Conder, 1789–1855
Music: Grenoble Antiphoner, 1753

88 88
DEUS TUORUM MILITUM

'Tis Good, Lord, to Be Here 518

1. 'Tis good, Lord, to be here! Your
2. 'Tis good, Lord, to be here, Your
3. Ful - fill - er of the past! Prom -
4. Be - fore we taste of death, We

glo - ry fills the night; Your face and gar - ments,
beau - ty to be - hold, Where Mo - ses and E -
ise of things to be! We hail your bod - y
see your king - dom come; We long to hold the

like the sun, Shine with un - bor - rowed light.
li - jah stand, Your mes - sen - gers of old.
glo - ri - fied, And our re - demp - tion see.
vi - sion bright, And make this hill our home.

5. 'Tis good, Lord, to be here!
Yet we may not remain;
But since you bid us leave the mount,
Come with us to the plain.

Text: Joseph A. Robinson, 1858–1933
Music: Johann J. Speiss, 1715–1772; adapt. William H. Havergal, 1793–1870

66 86
SWABIA

519 Ye Servants of God, Your Master Proclaim

1. Ye ser-vants of God, your Mas-ter pro-claim,
2. God rul-eth on high, al-might-y to save;
3. "Sal - va - tion to God, who sits on the throne!"
4. Then let us a - dore and give him his right,

And pub-lish a - broad his won-der-ful name;
And still he is nigh, his pres-ence we have.
Let all cry a - loud and hon-or the Son:
All glo-ry and pow'r, all wis-dom and might,

The name all vic - to - rious of Je-sus ex - tol;
The great con-gre - ga - tion his tri-umph shall sing,
The prais-es of Je - sus the an-gels pro - claim,
All hon-or and bless-ing, with an-gels a - bove,

His king-dom is glo-rious, he rules o - ver all.
As - crib-ing sal - va - tion to Je - sus, our King.
With joy-ful ho - san-nas they wor-ship the Lamb.
And thanks nev - er ceas-ing, and in - fi - nite love.

Lower Key: The Kingdom of God, no. 550
Text: Charles Wesley, 1707–1788, alt.
Music: Charles H. H. Parry, 1840–1918

10 10 11 11
LAUDATE DOMINUM

You Are the Way 520

1. You are the way; to you a - lone From
2. You are the truth; your word a - lone True
3. You are the life; the rend - ing tomb Pro -
4. You are the way, the truth, the life; Grant

sin and death we flee; And all who would the
wis - dom can im - part; You on - ly can in -
claims your con - qu'ring arm; And those who put their
us that way to know, That truth to keep, that

Fa - ther seek, Must seek you faith - ful - ly.
form the mind And pu - ri - fy the heart.
trust in you Not death nor hell shall harm.
life to win, Whose joys e - ter - nal flow.

Text: George Washington Doane, 1799–1859, alt.
Music: Scottish Psalter, Edinburgh, 1615; acc. Thomas Ravenscroft, c. 1590–1633

86 86
DUNDEE

521 All Hail the Power of Jesus' Name

1. All hail the pow'r of Je-sus' name! Let an-gels pros-trate
2. Crown him, you mar-tyrs of our God, Who from his al-tar
3. Hail him, you heirs of Da-vid's line, Whom Da-vid Lord did
4. You cho-sen seed of Is-rael's race, A rem-nant weak and

fall; Bring forth the roy-al di-a-dem, And
call: Praise him whose way of pain you trod, And
call, The God in-car-nate, Man di-vine, And
small, Hail him who saved you by his grace, And

crown him Lord of all, Bring forth the roy-al
crown him Lord of all, Praise him whose way of
crown him Lord of all, The God in-car-nate,
crown him Lord of all, Hail him who saved you

di-a-dem, And crown him Lord of all.
pain you trod, And crown him Lord of all.
Man di-vine, And crown him Lord of all.
by his grace, And crown him Lord of all.

Text: Edward Perronet, 1726–1792; tr. John Rippon, 1751–1836, alt.
Music: Oliver Holden, 1765–1844

86 86 86
CORONATION

5. As sinners let us not forget,
   The wormwood and the gall;
   We spread our trophies at his feet,
   And crown him Lord of all,
   We spread our trophies at his feet,
   And crown him Lord of all.

6. Let ev'ry tribe and ev'ry tongue
   Respond to Jesus' call,
   Lift high the universal song,
   And crown him Lord of all,
   Lift high the universal song,
   And crown him Lord of all.

In the Midst of Work or Pain 522

1. In the midst of work or pain, Je-sus, be for ev-er near;
2. Kind-est Lord, my tru-est friend, Be my aid in ev-'ry care;
3. Work-ing for your reign of love, Let me walk the way you trod;
4. When the path seems hard to me, Deign to watch with lov-ing care;

Let your grace my soul sus-tain, May I trust and nev-er fear.
What your love is pleased to send, All with will-ing heart I bear.
Guide me to your home a-bove, Fol-low-ing the will of God.
Your own grace my strength will be, Till your heav'n-ly joys I share.

Text: Slovak Hymnal; tr. L.G. Lovasik, S.V.D., ©
Music: Slovak Hymnal; adapt. and arr. L.G. Lovasik, S.V.D., ©

523 Born of the Father, Image Pure and Bright

Vigorously

1. Born of the Fa - ther, Im - age pure and bright,
2. A - pex and Cen - ter e'er the world be - gan
3. Flow'r of the Vir - gin, Moth - er un - de - filed
4. Sub - ject to Sa - tan, all our fal - len race,

True God of God, and light of ver - y light:
Of time and God's all - wise cre - a - tive plan:
The head of A - dam's race and yet his child;
Had lost the strength of God's re - deem - ing grace;

To you, Re - deem - er, pow'r and hon - or be,
To you the Fa - ther gave su - preme do - main;
O rock with mys - t'ry carved from moun - tain height
Through you we break the chains that bind us fast;

Who reigns as King of kings e - ter - nal - ly.
To you be - longs by right the pow'r to reign.
To fill the dark - ened world with dazz - ling light!
And find the way to heav - en's peace at last.

Text: *Aeterna Imago Altissimi*, 1623; tr. Desmond A. Schmal, S.J., 1897–1958, ©
Music: Orlando Gibbons, 1583–1625

10 10 10 10
SONG 22

5. High Priest and Prophet, King by ev'ry right:
   Your grateful people come before your sight,
   And offer you our lives and all we own;
   Within our hearts, O Christ, set up your throne.

Lord of All Hopefulness 524

1. Lord of all hope-ful-ness, Lord of all joy, Whose trust, ev - er
2. Lord of all ea - ger-ness, Lord of all faith, Whose strong hands were
3. Lord of all kind - li - ness, Lord of all grace, Your hands swift to
4. Lord of all gen - tle-ness, Lord of all calm, Whose voice is con -

child-like, no care could de - stroy: Be there at our wak-ing, and
skilled at the plane and the lathe: Be there at our la - bors, and
wel-come, your arms to em - brace: Be there at our hom-ing, and
tent-ment, whose pres-ence is balm: Be there at our sleep-ing, and

give us, we pray, Your bliss in our hearts, Lord, at the break of the day.
give us, we pray, Your strength in our hearts, Lord, at the noon of the day.
give us, we pray, Your love in our hearts, Lord, at the eve of the day.
give us, we pray, Your peace in our hearts, Lord, at the end of the day.

Text: Jan Struther, 1901–1953, ©
Music: Irish Folk Tune; acc. Erik Routley, 1917–1982

10 11 11 12
SLANE

Music accompaniment © Hope Publishing Co.

525 Crown Him With Many Crowns

1. Crown him with man - y crowns, The Lamb up - on his throne;
2. Crown him the Lord of life, Who tri - umphed o'er the grave,
3. Crown him the Lord of love, Be - hold his hands and side,
4. Crown him the Lord of peace, Whose pow'r a scep - ter sways

Hark! How the heav'n-ly an - them drowns All mu - sic but its own.
And rose vic - to - rious in the strife For those he came to save.
Rich wounds yet vis - i - ble a - bove In beau - ty glo - ri - fied.
From pole to pole, that wars may cease, Ab - sorbed in prayer and praise.

A - wake, my soul, and sing Of him who set us free,
His glo - ries now we sing, Who died and rose on high,
No an - gel in the sky Can ful - ly bear that sight,
His reign shall know no end, And round his pierc - ed feet

And hail him as your heav'n-ly King Through all e - ter - ni - ty.
Who died, e - ter - nal life to bring, And lives that death may die.
But down - ward bends his burn - ing eye At mys - ter - ies so bright.
Fair flow'rs of par - a - dise ex - tend Their fra - grance ev - er sweet.

Text: Matthew Bridges, 1800–1894, vv. 1,3–5; Godfrey Thring, 1823–1903, v. 2
Music: George Job Elvey, 1816–1893

66 86 66 86
DIADEMATA

5. Crown him the Lord of years,
   The risen Lord sublime,
   Creator of the rolling spheres,
   The Master of all time.
   All hail, Redeemer, hail!
   For you have died for me;
   Your praise and glory shall not fail
   Throughout eternity.

To Christ, the Prince of Peace 526

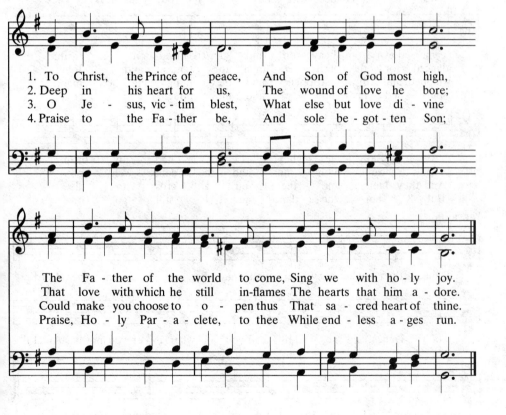

1. To Christ, the Prince of peace, And Son of God most high,
2. Deep in his heart for us, The wound of love he bore;
3. O Jesus, victim blest, What else but love divine
4. Praise to the Father be, And sole begotten Son;

The Father of the world to come, Sing we with holy joy.
That love with which he still inflames The hearts that him adore.
Could make you choose to open thus That sacred heart of thine.
Praise, Holy Paraclete, to thee While endless ages run.

Text: Summi parentis filis, Paris Breviary, 1736; tr. Edward Caswall, 1814–1876, alt.
Music: Otto A. Singenberger, 1944; arr. Richard W. Hillert, b. 1923

66 86
SINGENBERGER

Music arrangement © 1978, J.S. Paluch, Inc.

527 Lord of the Dance

1. I danced in the morn-ing when the world was be-gun, And I
2. I danced for the scribe and the phar-i - see, But they
3. I danced on the Sab-bath and I cured the lame; The
4. I danced on a Fri-day when the sky turned black; It's

danced in the moon and the stars and the sun, And I
would not dance and they would-n't fol-low me; I
ho-ly peo-ple said it was a shame. They
hard to dance with the dev-il on your back. They

came down from heav-en and I danced on the earth;
danced for the fish-er-men, for James and John;
whipped and they stripped and they hung me on high,
bur-ied my bod-y and they thought I'd gone;

At Beth-le-hem I had my birth:
They came with me and the dance went on:
And they left me there on a cross to die:
But I am the dance and I still go on:

REFRAIN

Dance, then wher-ev-er you may be; I am the Lord

of the Dance, said he, And I'll lead you all, wher-ev-er you may be, And I'll

|1.-4.|

lead you all in the dance, said he.

|5.|

dance, said he.

5. They cut me down and I leap up high;
I am the life that'll never, never die;
I'll live in you if you'll live in me:
I am the Lord of the Dance, said he:
Refrain

Text: Sydney Carter, b. 1915
Music: American Shaker Melody; acc. Sydney Carter, b. 1915

May the Mind of Christ My Savior 528

1. May the mind of Christ my Sav-ior Live in me from day to day,
2. May the peace of God my Fa-ther Rule my life in ev-'ry-thing,
3. May I run the race be-fore me, Strong and brave to face the foe,

By his love and pow'r con-trol-ling All I do and say.
That I may be calm to com-fort Sick and sor-row-ing.
Look-ing on-ly un-to Je-sus As I on-ward go.

May the Word of God dwell rich-ly In my heart from hour to hour
May the love of Je-sus fill me, As the wa-ters fill the sea;
May his beau-ty rest up-on me As I seek the lost to win,

So that all may see I tri-umph On-ly through his pow'r.
Him ex-alt-ing, self a-bas-ing, This is vic-to-ry.
And may they for-get the chan-nel, See-ing on-ly him.

Text: K.B. Wilkinson
Music: Henry Bryan Hays, O.S.B., b. 1920, ©

87 85 87 85
CROCKETT'S COVE

529 O Praise the Gracious Power

1. O praise the gra - cious pow'r That tum - bles
2. O praise per - sis - tent truth That o - pens
3. O praise in - clu - sive love, En - cir - cling
4. O praise the word of faith That claims us

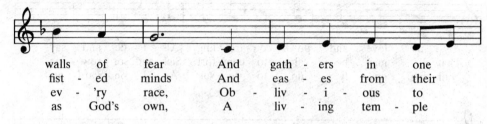

walls of fear And gath - ers in one
fist - ed minds And eas - es from their
ev - 'ry race, Ob - liv - i - ous to
as God's own, A liv - ing tem - ple

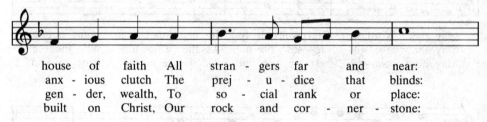

house of faith All stran - gers far and near:
anx - ious clutch The prej - u - dice that blinds:
gen - der, wealth, To so - cial rank or place:
built on Christ, Our rock and cor - ner - stone:

REFRAIN

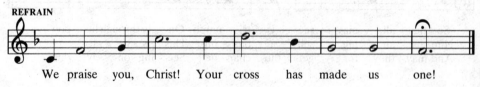

We praise you, Christ! Your cross has made us one!

5. O praise the tide of grace
   That laps at ev'ry shore
   With visions of a world at peace,
   No longer bled by war:
   Refrain

6. O praise the pow'r, the truth,
   The love, the word, the tide.
   Yet more than these, O praise their source,
   Praise Christ the crucified:
   Refrain

7. O praise the living Christ
   With faith's bright songful voice!
   Announce the gospel to the world
   And with these words rejoice:
   Refrain

Text: Thomas H. Troeger, b. 1945, ©
Music: Carol Doran, b. 1936, ©

66 86 with Refrain
CHRISTPRAISE RAY

What Wondrous Love Is This?   530

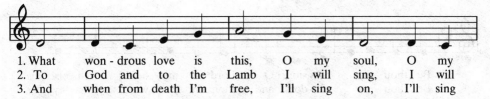

1. What won-drous love is this, O my soul, O my
2. To God and to the Lamb I will sing, I will
3. And when from death I'm free, I'll sing on, I'll sing

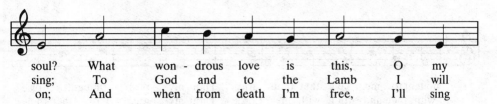

soul? What won-drous love is this, O my
sing; To God and to the Lamb I will
on; And when from death I'm free, I'll sing

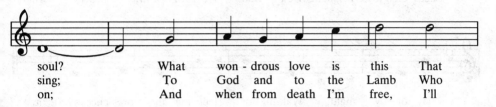

soul? What won-drous love is this That
sing; To God and to the Lamb Who
on; And when from death I'm free, I'll

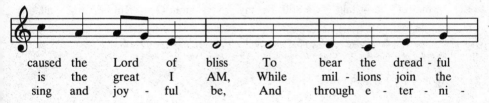

caused the Lord of bliss To bear the dread-ful
is the great I AM, While mil-lions join the
sing and joy-ful be, And through e-ter-ni-

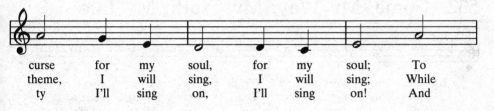

curse for my soul, for my soul; To
theme, I will sing, I will sing; While
ty I'll sing on, I'll sing on! And

bear the dread-ful curse for my soul?
mil-lions join the theme, I will sing.
through e-ter-ni-ty, I'll sing on.

Text: Rev. Alexander Means, 1801–1853
Music: American Folk Hymn, c. 1835; arr. Sr. Theophane Hytrek, O.S.F., b. 1915, ©

12 9 12 12 9
WONDROUS LOVE

531 Be Thou My Vision

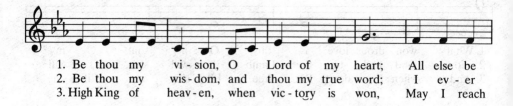

1. Be thou my vi - sion, O Lord of my heart; All else be
2. Be thou my wis - dom, and thou my true word; I ev - er
3. High King of heav - en, when vic - tory is won, May I reach

nought to me, save that thou art. Thou my best thought, by
with thee and thou with me, Lord; Thou my great Fa - ther; thine
heav - en's joys, bright heav - en's Sun! Heart of my heart, what -

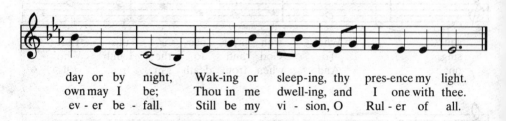

day or by night, Wak-ing or sleep-ing, thy pres-ence my light.
own may I be; Thou in me dwell-ing, and I one with thee.
ev - er be - fall, Still be my vi - sion, O Rul - er of all.

Text: Irish, ca. 700, versified by Mary Elizabeth Byrne, 1880–1931; tr. Eleanor H. Hull, 1860–1935, alt.,
Music: Irish Ballad Melody; adapt. The Church Hymnary, 1927; harm. David Evans, 1874–1948, ©

10 10 9 10
SLANE

532 Come, My Way, My Truth, My Life

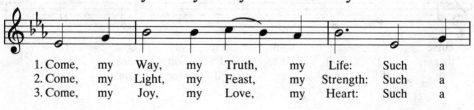

1. Come, my Way, my Truth, my Life: Such a
2. Come, my Light, my Feast, my Strength: Such a
3. Come, my Joy, my Love, my Heart: Such a

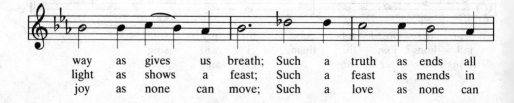

way as gives us breath; Such a truth as ends all
light as shows a feast; Such a feast as mends in
joy as none can move; Such a love as none can

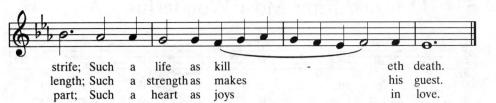

strife; Such a life as kill - eth death.
length; Such a strength as makes his guest.
part; Such a heart as joys in love.

Text: George Herbert, 1593–1632
Music: Ralph Vaughan Williams, 1872–1958, ©

77 77
THE CALL

He Walks Among the Golden Lamps 533

1. He walks a - mong the gol - den lamps On feet like bur - nished
2. And in his hand the sev - en stars, And from his mouth a
3. More ra - diant than the sun at noon, Who was, and is to

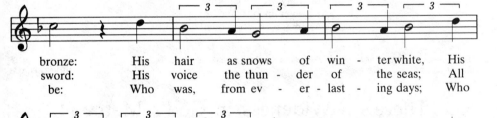

bronze: His hair as snows of win - ter white, His
sword: His voice the thun - der of the seas; All
be: Who was, from ev - er - last - ing days; Who

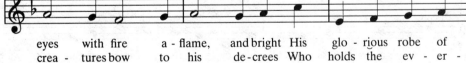

eyes with fire a - flame, and bright His glo - rious robe of
crea - tures bow to his de - crees Who holds the ev - er -
lives, the Lord of all our ways To him be maj - es -

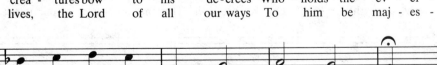

seam - less light Sur - pass - ing Sol - o - mon's.
last - ing keys And reigns as sov - 'reign Lord.
ty and praise For all e - ter - ni - ty.

Text: Timothy Dudley-Smith, b. 1926
Music: Edward J. McKenna, b. 1939, ©

86 88 86
GOLDEN LAMPS

Text © 1973, Hope Publishing Co.

534 O Jesus, King Most Wonderful!

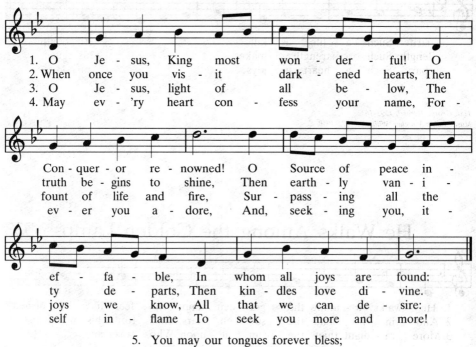

1. O Je - sus, King most won - der - ful! O
2. When once you vis - it dark - ened hearts, Then
3. O Je - sus, light of all be - low, The
4. May ev - 'ry heart con - fess your name, For -

Con - quer - or re - nowned! O Source of peace in -
truth be - gins to shine, Then earth - ly van - i -
fount of life and fire, Sur - pass - ing all the
ev - er you a - dore, And, seek - ing you, it -

ef - fa - ble, In whom all joys are found:
ty de - parts, Then kin - dles love di - vine.
joys we know, All that we can de - sire:
self in - flame To seek you more and more!

5. You may our tongues forever bless;
   You may we love alone
   And ever in our lives express
   The image of your own!

Text: St. Bernard Clairvaux, 1091–1153, attr.; tr. Edward Caswall, 1814–1878, alt.
Music: Joshua Leavitt, 1794–1837

86 86
HIDING PLACE

535 There's a Wideness in God's Mercy

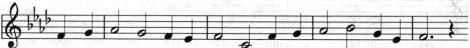

1. There's a wide-ness in God's mer - cy, Like the wide-ness of the sea;
2. For the love of God is broad-er Than the mea-sure of our mind;

There's a kind-ness in his jus - tice, Which is more than lib - er - ty.
And the heart of the E - ter - nal Is most won - der - ful - ly kind.

There is wel-come for the sin - ner, And more bless-ings for the good;
There is plen - ti - ful re - demp-tion In the blood that has been shed;

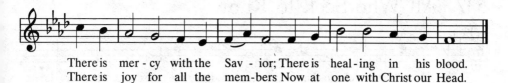

There is mer - cy with the Sav - ior; There is heal - ing in his blood.
There is joy for all the mem - bers Now at one with Christ our Head.

Text: Frederick William Faber, 1814–1863, alt.
Music: Gerard Wojchowski, O.S.B., b. 1925, ©

87 87 87 87

When You Speak 536

REFRAIN

When you speak or act, do ev - 'ry-thing in the name of Je - sus Christ,

Giv-ing thanks to God the Fa - ther through our good Lord Je - sus Christ.

VERSES

1. Were	you	not	raised	to	life	with	him,	with
2. He	was	be -	fore	all	things	be -	gan,	and
3. He	is	the	first	to	rise	a -	gain,	a -
4. Now	Christ	is	in	you;	he's	the	hope	of

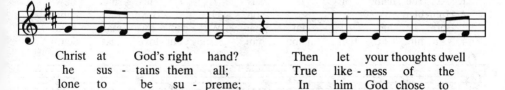

Christ	at	God's	right	hand?	Then	let	your thoughts dwell
he	sus -	tains	them	all;	True	like - ness	of	the
lone	to	be	su -	preme;	In	him	God chose	to
glo -	ry	yet	to	come;	God's	treas - ures	lie	in

To Refrain

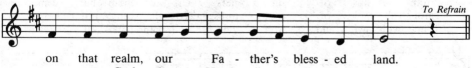

on	that	realm,	our	Fa - ther's	bless - ed	land.
un - seen	God,	the	Head	of	all	that	is!
rec - on - cile	the	whole	world	to	him - self.
him,	all	wis - dom,	knowl - edge,	peace	and	love.

Text: Willard F. Jabusch, b. 1930, ©
Music: Willard F. Jabusch, b. 1930, ©

537 All Who Seek to Know

1. All who seek to know and serve God, See the past and un-der-stand:
2. If our God does not con-demn us, Who a-gainst us then will stand?
3. Al-le-lu-ia, al-le-lu-ia! Joy a-waits all those who mourn.

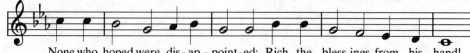

None who hoped were dis-ap-point-ed; Rich the bless-ings from his hand!
Will the Lord, who died for sin-ners, Who sits now at God's right hand?
Al-le-lu-ia, al-le-lu-ia! Death has died and life is born.

None who wait-ed were for-sa-ken; None who trust-ed were de-ceived.
What could take us from Christ Je-sus? Nei-ther hun-ger, sword, nor pain!
Al-le-lu-ia, al-le-lu-ia! Our re-deem-er, Je-sus, lives!

All who asked his gra-cious par-don, Gen-tle mer-cy have re-ceived.
Nei-ther life nor death shall part us From the Lamb for us once slain.
Al-le-lu-ia, al-le-lu-ia! Grace and glo-ry Je-sus gives!

Text: Delores Dufner, O.S.B., b. 1939, ©
Music: Jay F. Hunstiger, b. 1950, ©

87 87 87 87

538 At the Name of Jesus

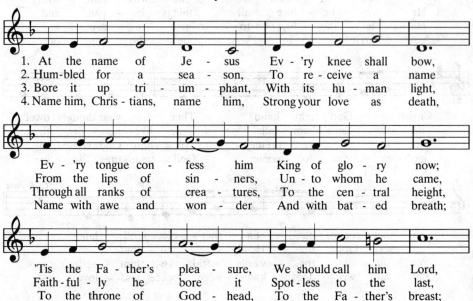

1. At the name of Je-sus Ev-'ry knee shall bow,
2. Hum-bled for a sea-son, To re-ceive a name
3. Bore it up tri-um-phant, With its hu-man light,
4. Name him, Chris-tians, name him, Strong your love as death,

Ev-'ry tongue con-fess him King of glo-ry now;
From the lips of sin-ners, Un-to whom he came,
Through all ranks of crea-tures, To the cen-tral height,
Name with awe and won-der And with bat-ed breath;

'Tis the Fa-ther's plea-sure, We should call him Lord,
Faith-ful-ly he bore it Spot-less to the last,
To the throne of God-head, To the Fa-ther's breast;
He is God the Sa-vior, He is Christ the Lord,

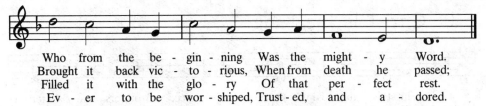

Who from the be - gin - ning Was the might - y Word.
Brought it back vic - to - rious, When from death he passed;
Filled it with the glo - ry Of that per - fect rest.
Ev - er to be wor - shiped, Trust - ed, and a - dored.

5. In your hearts enthrone him;
There let him subdue
All that is not holy,
All that is not true;
Crown him as your Captain
In temptation's hour;
Let his will enfold you
In its light and pow'r.

6. Christians, this Lord Jesus
Shall return again,
With his Father's glory
O'er the earth to reign;
For all wreaths of empire
Meet upon his brow,
And our hearts confess him
King of glory now.

Text: Caroline Maria Noel, 1817–1877, alt.
Music: Ralph Vaughan Williams, 1872–1958, ©

65 65 65 65
KING'S WESTON

O Merciful Redeemer 539

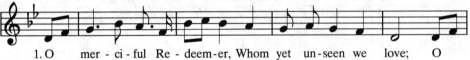

1. O mer - ci - ful Re - deem - er, Whom yet un - seen we love; O
2. In thee all full-ness dwell-eth, All grace and pow'r di - vine; The

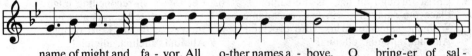

name of might and fa - vor, All o-ther names a - bove. O bring-er of sal -
glo - ry that ex - cel-leth, O Son of God is thine. O grant the con-sum-

va - tion, Who won-drous-ly hast wrought, Thy - self the rev - e - la - tion Of
ma - tion Of this our song a - bove, In end-less ad - o - ra - tion And

love be-yond all thought: We wor-ship thee and bless thee; To thee a - lone we
ev - er - last-ing love; Then shall we praise and bless thee; Where per-fect prais-es

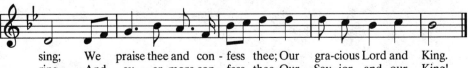

sing; We praise thee and con - fess thee; Our gra-cious Lord and King.
ring, And ev - er more con - fess thee, Our Sav-ior and our King!

Text: Frances R. Havergal, 1836–1879, alt.
Music: Gustav Holst, 1874–1934, alt., ©

13 13 13 13 13 13
THAXTED

540 Christ Is the King!

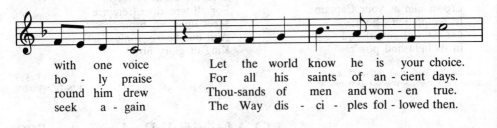

1. Christ is the King! O friends, re - joice; Broth-ers and sis - ters,
2. O mag - ni - fy the Lord, and raise An - thems of joy and
3. They with a faith for ev - er new Fol - lowed the King, and
4. O Chris-tian wom - en, Chris - tian men, All the world o - ver

with one voice Let the world know he is your choice.
ho - ly praise For all his saints of an - cient days.
round him drew Thou-sands of men and wom - en true.
seek a - gain The Way dis - ci - ples fol - lowed then.

Al - le - lu - ia, al - le - lu - ia, al - le - lu - ia!

5. Christ through all ages is the same:
Place the same hope in his great name,
With the same faith his word proclaim.
Alleluia, alleluia, alleluia!

6. Let love's all-reconciling might
Your scattered companies unite
In service to the Lord of light.
Alleluia, alleluia, alleluia!

7. So shall God's will on earth be done,
New lamps be lit, new tasks begun,
And the whole Church at last be one.
Alleluia, alleluia, alleluia!

Alt. Tune: Good Christians All Rejoice and Sing!, no. 271
Text: George K.A. Bell, 1883-1958, alt., ©
Music: Charles R. Anders, b. 1929, ©

888 with Alleluias
BEVERLY

The King of Glory 541

REFRAIN

The King of glo - ry comes, the na - tion re - joic - es;

O - pen the gates be - fore him; lift up your voic - es.

VERSES

1. Who is the King of glo - ry; how shall we call him?
2. In all of Gal - i - lee, in cit - y and vil - lage,
3. Sing then of Da - vid's Son, our Sav - ior and broth - er;
4. He gave his life for us, the Lamb of sal - va - tion;
5. He con - quered sin and death; he tru - ly has ris - en.

To Refrain

He is Em - man - u - el, the prom-ised of a - ges.
He goes a - mong his peo - ple cur - ing their ill - ness.
In all of Gal - i - lee was nev - er an - oth - er.
He took up - on him - self the sins of the na - tion.
And he will share with us his heav - en - ly vi - sion.

Text: Willard F. Jabusch, b. 1930, ©
Music: Willard F. Jabusch, b. 1930, ©

75 75 with Refrain
KING OF GLORY

542 Lift High the Cross

REFRAIN

Lift high the cross, the love of Christ pro - claim
till all the world a - dore his sa - cred name.

VERSES

1. Led on their way by this tri - um - phant sign,
2. Each new - born ser - vant of the Cru - ci - fied
3. O Lord, once lift - ed on the glo - rious tree,
4. So shall our song of tri - umph ev - er be:

To Refrain

The hosts of God in con quering ranks com - bine.
Bears on the brow the seal of him who died.
As thou hast prom - ised, draw the world to thee.
Praise to the Cru - ci - fied for vic - to - ry.

Text: Geo. W. Kitchin, 1827–1912; M.R. Newbolt, 1874–1956, alt., ©
Music: Sydney H. Nicholson, 1875–1947; descant Richard Proulx, b. 1937, ©

10 10 with Refrain
CRUCIFER

543 Jesus Come! For We Invite You

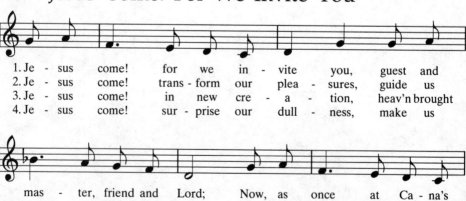

1. Je - sus come! for we in - vite you, guest and
2. Je - sus come! trans - form our plea - sures, guide us
3. Je - sus come! in new cre - a - tion, heav'n brought
4. Je - sus come! sur - prise our dull - ness, make us

mas - ter, friend and Lord; Now, as once at Ca - na's
in - to paths un - known; Bring your gifts, com - mand your
near in pow'r di - vine; Give your un - ex - pec - ted
will - ing to re - ceive More than we can yet im -

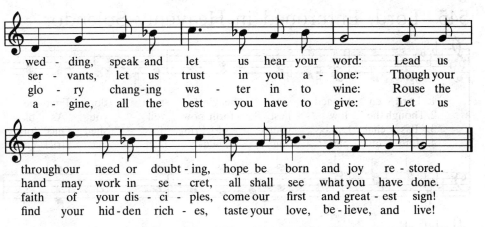

wed - ding, speak and let us hear your word: Lead us
ser - vants, let us trust in you a - lone: Though your
glo - ry chang-ing wa - ter in - to wine: Rouse the
a - gine, all the best you have to give: Let us

through our need or doubt - ing, hope be born and joy re - stored.
hand may work in se - cret, all shall see what you have done.
faith of your dis - ci - ples, come our first and great - est sign!
find your hid - den rich - es, taste your love, be - lieve, and live!

Text: Christopher Idle, b. 1938
Music: Robert LeBlanc, b. 1948, ©

Text © 1982, Hope Publishing Co.

Jesus, My Lord, My God, My All 544

VERSES

1. Je - sus, my Lord, my God, my all, How can I
2. Had I but Mar - y's sin - less heart, How I would

love you as I ought? And how re - vere this
love you, dear - est King! O with what bursts of

won - drous gift So far sur - pass - ing hope or thought?
fer - vent praise Your good-ness, Je - sus, would I sing!

REFRAIN

O God of love, whom we a - dore, O make us love you

more and more; O make us love you more and more!

Text: Frederick William Faber, 1814–1863; adapt., ©
Music: Anon.; arr. Rev. Percy Jones, ©

88 88 with Refrain
SWEET SACRAMENT

545 Lord, Enthroned in Heavenly Splendor

1. Lord, en - throned in heav'n - ly splen - dor, First - be -
2. Though the low - liest form now veil you As of
3. Pas - chal Lamb, your of - f'ring, fin - ished Once for
4. Life - im - part - ing heav'n - ly man - na, Strick - en

got - ten from the dead, You a - lone, our strong de -
old in Beth - le - hem, Here as there your an - gels
all when you were slain, In its full - ness un - di -
rock with stream - ing side, Heav'n and earth with loud ho -

fend - er, Lift - ing up your peo - ple's head. Al - le -
hail you, Branch and flow'r of Jes - se's stem. Al - le -
min - ished Shall for - ev - er - more re - main. Al - le -
san - na Wor - ship you, the Lamb who died, Al - le -

lu - ia, al - le - lu - ia, al - le - lu - ia! Je - sus, true and
lu - ia, al - le - lu - ia, al - le - lu - ia! We in wor - ship
lu - ia, al - le - lu - ia, al - le - lu - ia! Cleans - ing souls from
lu - ia, al - le - lu - ia, al - le - lu - ia! Ris'n, as - cend - ed,

Text: George H. Bourne, 1840–1925
Music: William Owen, 1814–1893, ©

87 87 444 77
BRYN CALFARIA

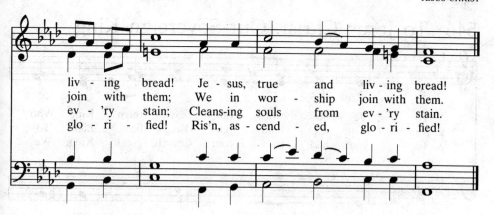

liv - ing bread! Je - sus, true and liv - ing bread!
join with them; We in wor - ship join with them.
ev - 'ry stain; Cleans-ing souls from ev - 'ry stain.
glo - ri - fied! Ris'n, as - cend - ed, glo - ri - fied!

546 To Jesus Christ, Our Sovereign King

1. To Jesus Christ, our sov - 'reign King Who
2. Your reign ex - tend, O King be - nign, To
3. To you and to your Church, great King, We

is the world's sal - va - tion, All praise and hom - age
ev - 'ry land and na - tion; For in your king - dom,
pledge our hearts' ob - la - tion; Un - til be - fore your

do we bring And thanks and ad - o - ra - tion.
Lord di - vine, A - lone we find sal - va - tion.
throne we sing In end - less ju - bi - la - tion.

REFRAIN

Christ Je - sus, Vic - tor! Christ Je - sus, Rul - er!

Text: Martin B. Hellriegel, 1890–1981, ©
Music: Godfrey Ridout, b. 1918; instrumental descant, Sr. Maurita Bernet, O.S.F., ©

87 87 with Refrain
ICH GLAUB AN GOTT

Christ Je - sus, Lord and Re - deem - er!

All Praise to Thee 547

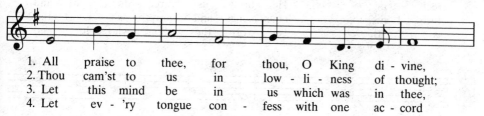

1. All praise to thee, for thou, O King di - vine,
2. Thou cam'st to us in low - li - ness of thought;
3. Let this mind be in us which was in thee,
4. Let ev - 'ry tongue con - fess with one ac - cord

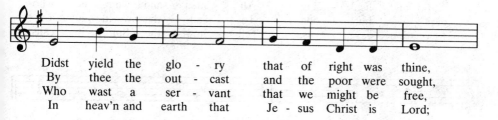

Didst yield the glo - ry that of right was thine,
By thee the out - cast and the poor were sought,
Who wast a ser - vant that we might be free,
In heav'n and earth that Je - sus Christ is Lord;

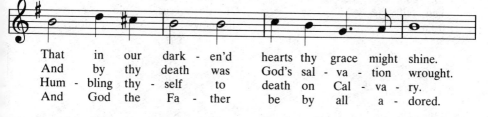

That in our dark - en'd hearts thy grace might shine.
And by thy death was God's sal - va - tion wrought.
Hum - bling thy - self to death on Cal - va - ry.
And God the Fa - ther be by all a - dored.

Al - le - lu - ia, al - le - lu - ia!

Text: F. Bland Tucker, 1895–1984, ©
Music: Francis Muench, O.S.B., b. 1952, ©

10 10 10 with Alleluias
O'LEARY

548 Rise, Shine, You People!

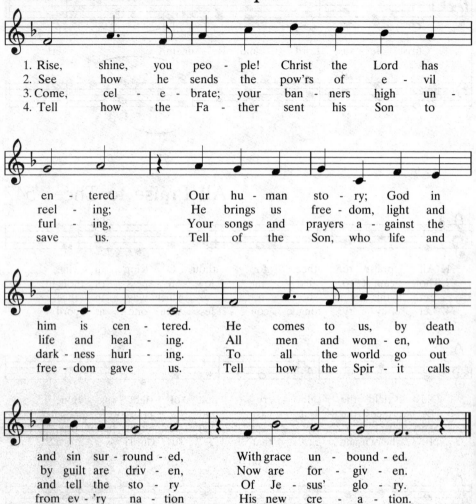

1. Rise, shine, you peo - ple! Christ the Lord has
2. See how he sends the pow'rs of e - vil
3. Come, cel - e - brate; your ban - ners high un -
4. Tell how the Fa - ther sent his Son to

en - tered Our hu - man sto - ry; God in
reel - ing; He brings us free - dom, light and
furl - ing, Your songs and prayers a - gainst the
save us. Tell of the Son, who life and

him is cen - tered. He comes to us, by death
life and heal - ing. All men and wom - en, who
dark - ness hurl - ing. To all the world go out
free - dom gave us. Tell how the Spir - it calls

and sin sur - round - ed, With grace un - bound - ed.
by guilt are driv - en, Now are for - giv - en.
and tell the sto - ry Of Je - sus' glo - ry.
from ev - 'ry na - tion His new cre - a - tion.

Text: Ronald A. Klug, b. 1939, ©
Music: Dale Wood, b. 1934, ©

11 11 11 5
WOJTKIEWIECZ

O God, You Are the Father 549

1. O God, you are the Father Of all who have be - lieved;
2. O God you are the Mak - er Of all cre - a - ted things;

From whom all choirs of an - gels Have life and pow'r re - ceived.
The u - ni - verse is in your hands, O might - y King of kings.

Now to the meek and low - ly, Your king - dom you un - fold.
I walk se - cure and bless - ed In him who strength - ens me.

Your sav - ing plan u - nites in Christ All things both new and old.
The Fa - ther, Son and Spir - it, One God e - ter - nal - ly.

Text: St. Columba; tr. anon.
Music: Gaelic Melody

76 76 76 86
DURROW

550 The Kingdom of God

1. The king-dom of God is jus-tice and joy;
2. The king-dom of God is mer-cy and grace;
3. The king-dom of God is chal-lenge and choice:
4. God's king-dom is come, the gift and the goal;

For Je-sus re-stores what sin would de-stroy.
The cap-tives are freed, the sin-ners find place,
Be-lieve the good news, re-pent and re-joice!
In Je-sus be-gun, in heav-en made whole.

God's pow-er and glo-ry in Je-sus we know;
The out-cast are wel-comed God's ban-quet to share;
God's love for us sin-ners brought Christ to his cross:
The heirs of the king-dom shall an-swer his call;

And here and here-af-ter the king-dom shall grow.
And hope is a-wak-ened in place of de-spair.
Our cri-sis of judge-ment for gain or for loss.
And all things cry "Glo-ry!" to God all in all.

Higher Key: Ye Servants of God, no. 519

Text: Bryn A. Rees, 1911–1983, ©
Music: Charles H.H. Parry, 1848–1918

10 10 11 11
LAUDATE DOMINUM

Your Kingdom Come 551

1. Your king - dom come! O Fa - ther, hear our prayer; Shine through the
2. Stum - bling and blind, we strive to do your will, Trust - ing the
3. Come through the faith where - by the Church must live; Come through the
4. Your king - dom come; come too, God's glo - rious Son! Oh, may our

clouds that threat-en ev - 'ry - where; Light from a - bove, our
word you sure - ly will ful - fill, That all are yours, how -
Word and Sac - ra-ments you give; Come through your teach - ing,
task for you be no - bly done! Faith - ful let all your

on - ly life and joy. Show us the hope that noth-ing can de -
ev - er far they roam; That love shall tri-umph, and your king-dom
and your heal-ing too; Come through the work en - light-ened hearts can
ser-vants be, and true, Un - til they bring all na - tions home to

stroy; Show us the hope that noth-ing can de - stroy.
come; That love shall tri - umph, and your king - dom come.
do; Come through the work en - light-ened hearts can do.
you; Un - til they bring all na - tions home to you.

Text: Margaret R. Seebach, 1875–1948, alt.
Music: Louis Bourgeois, c. 1510–1561

10 10 10 10 10
OLD 124TH

552 Thy Kingdom Come! On Bended Knee

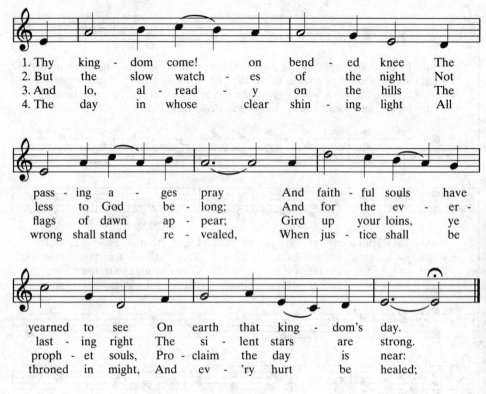

1. Thy king - dom come! on bend - ed knee The
2. But the slow watch - es of the night Not
3. And lo, al - read - y on the hills The
4. The day in whose clear shin - ing light All

pass - ing a - ges pray And faith - ful souls have
less to God be - long; And for the ev - er-
flags of dawn ap - pear; Gird up your loins, ye
wrong shall stand re - vealed, When jus - tice shall be

yearned to see On earth that king - dom's day.
last - ing right The si - lent stars are strong.
proph - et souls, Pro - claim the day is near:
throned in might, And ev - 'ry hurt be healed;

5. When knowledge, hand in hand with peace,
   Shall walk the earth abroad;
   The day of perfect righteousness,
   The promised day of God.

Text: Frederick L. Hosmer, 1840–1929
Music: Henry Bryan Hays, O.S.B., b. 1920, ©

86 86
LACY FARMHOUSE

Be As Children 553

1. Be as chil-dren who come run-ning, don't be proud and don't be
2. Let your eyes be wide with won-der, with a lit-tle child's
3. Let your heart re-gain its glad-ness, put a-way your grief and
4. God him-self has set a ta-ble such as on-ly he is

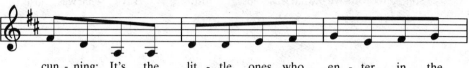

cun-ning; It's the lit-tle ones who en-ter in the
won-der, As you come to know the splen-dor of the
sad-ness, For you're called to eat a sup-per in the
a-ble, Food to sat-is-fy the hun-gry in the

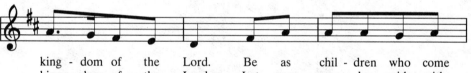

king-dom of the Lord. Be as chil-dren who come
king-dom of the Lord. Let your eyes be wide with
king-dom of the Lord. Let your heart re-gain its
king-dom of the Lord. God him-self has set a

run-ning, don't be proud and don't be cun-ning; It's the
won-der, with a lit-tle child's won-der, As you
glad-ness, put a-way your grief and sad-ness, For you're
ta-ble such as on-ly he is a-ble, food to

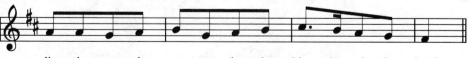

lit-tle ones who en-ter in the king-dom of the Lord.
come to know the splen-dor of the king-dom of the Lord.
called to eat a sup-per in the king-dom of the Lord.
sat-is-fy the hun-gry in the king-dom of the Lord.

Text: Willard F. Jabusch
Music: Andalusian melody; acc. David Kraehenbuehl, b. 1923

REFRAIN

For God sent his Son to save what was lost, For God sent his

Son to save what was lost. lost, save what was lost.

Give Thanks to God on High 554

1. Give thanks to God on high   For saints of oth - er
2. Their vi - sion long - ful - filled,   Our prayer is still the
3. New tasks to - day are ours   Who serve a world in
4. Give thanks to God on high   For all the fu - ture

days,   Whose hope it was to live and die   In
same;   Up - on their work of faith to build, Their
pain,   New calls to chal - lenge all our pow'rs Of
sends,   In praise of Christ to live and die   Who

love's con - sum - ing blaze,   For Christ and his
word of truth pro - claim,   For Christ and his
heart and hand and brain,   For Christ and his
calls his ser - vants friends,   For Christ and his

king - dom,   His glo - ry and his praise.
king - dom,   And for his ho - ly Name.
king - dom,   While life and breath re - main.
king - dom,   Whose glo - ry nev - er ends!

1.   2.   Fine

Text: Timothy Dudley–Smith, b. 1926
Music: Edward J. McKenna, b. 1939, ©

66 86 66
CEOLA

Text © 1985, Hope Publishing Company, Carol Stream, IL 60188

555 All Creatures of Our God and King

1. All crea - tures of our God and King, Lift
2. O rush - ing wind and breez - es soft, O
3. O flow - ing wa - ters, pure and clear, Make
4. Dear moth - er earth, who day by day Un -

up your voice and with us sing: Al - le -
clouds that ride the winds a - loft: O
mu - sic for your Lord to hear. O
folds rich bless - ings on our way, O

lu - ia! Al - le - lu - ia! O
praise him! Al - le - lu - ia! O
praise him! Al - le - lu - ia! O
praise him! Al - le - lu - ia! The

burn - ing sun with gold - en beam, And
ris - ing morn, in praise re - joice, O
fire so mas - ter - ful and bright, Pro -
fruits and flow'rs that ver - dant grow, Let

sil - ver moon with soft - er gleam:
lights of eve - ning, find a voice.
vid - ing us with warmth and light. O
them his praise a - bun - dant show.

praise him! O praise him! Al - le - lu - ia, al - le -

lu - ia, al - le - lu - ia!

Text: St. Francis of Assisi, 1182–1226; tr. William Henry Draper, 1855–1933, ©
Music: Ralph Vaughan Williams, 1872–1958

88 44 88 with Refrain
LASST UNS ERFREUEN

5. O ev'ry one of tender heart,
Forgiving others, take your part,
O praise him! Alleluia!
All you who pain and sorrow bear,
Praise God and lay on him your care.
O praise him! O praise him!
Alleluia, alleluia, alleluia!

6. And you, most kind and gentle death,
Waiting to hush our final breath,
O praise him! Alleluia!
You lead to heav'n the child of God,
Where Christ our Lord the way has trod.
O praise him! O praise him!
Alleluia, alleluia, alleluia!

7. Let all things their Creator bless,
And worship him in humbleness,
O praise him! Alleluia!
O praise the Father, praise the Son,
And praise the Spirit, Three in One!
O praise him! O praise him!
Alleluia, alleluia, alleluia!

God Made the Birds 556

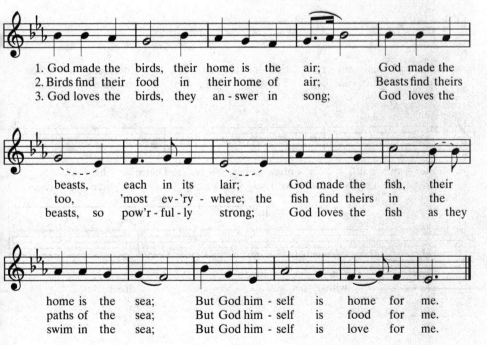

1. God made the birds, their home is the air; God made the beasts, each in its lair; God made the fish, their home is the sea; But God him-self is home for me.
2. Birds find their food in their home of air; Beasts find theirs 'most ev-'ry-where; the fish find theirs in the paths of the sea; But God him-self is food for me.
3. God loves the birds, they an-swer in song; God loves the beasts, so pow'r-ful-ly strong; God loves the fish as they swim in the sea; But God him-self is love for me.

Text: Magnus Wenninger, O.S.B., b. 1919, ©
Music: John S.B. Hodges, 1830–1915

98 98
EUCHARISTIC HYMN

557 Nature's Praise

1. Praise the Lord, o - cean and riv - er, Surge and de - liv - er
2. Praise the Lord, fal - con and swal - low, Cir - cle and fol - low

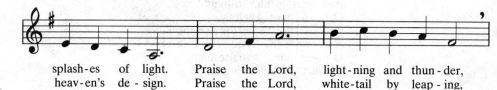

splash - es of light. Praise the Lord, light - ning and thun - der,
heav - en's de - sign. Praise the Lord, white - tail by leap - ing,

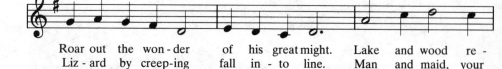

Roar out the won - der of his great might. Lake and wood re -
Liz - ard by creep-ing fall in - to line. Man and maid, your

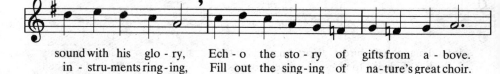

sound with his glo - ry, Ech - o the sto - ry of gifts from a - bove.
in - stru-ments ring-ing, Fill out the sing-ing of na - ture's great choir.

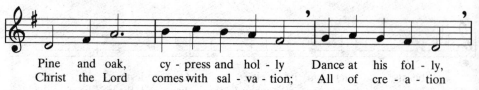

Pine and oak, cy - press and hol - ly Dance at his fol - ly
Christ the Lord comes with sal - va - tion; All of cre - a - tion

1.
sway in his love.
2.
glows with his fire.

Text: Dominic Braud, O.S.B., ©
Music: Dominic Braud, O.S.B.; arr. Robert LeBlanc, b. 1948, ©

89 89 9 10 89
NATURE'S PRAISE

We Gather Together 558

1. We gath - er to - geth - er to sing the Lord's prais - es, To
2. We greet our Lord pres - ent with - in our as - sem - bly; We
3. Since Christ is the vine and his peo - ple the branch - es, In

wor - ship the Fa - ther through Je - sus, his Son. In
hear his good news an - nounced clear - ly to all. Our
him we give praise to the Fa - ther a - bove. He

this cel - e - bra - tion, all sing with ju - bi - la - tion! We
priest is pres - i - ding; in Christ we are a - bid - ing, As
brings ev - 'ry na - tion to learn of his sal - va - tion, That

are his ho - ly peo - ple whose free - dom he won.
we in - voke God's bless - ing and an - swer his call.
all may grow in knowl - edge, in faith, hope, and love.

Text: tr. Omer Westendorf, b. 1916, alt.
Music: Dutch Traditional Melody; arr Edward Kremser, 1838–1914; Instrumental
    Descant: Robert E. Kreutz, b. 1922

Text © 1970, 1973, World Library Publications, Inc.

12 11 12 11
KREMSER

559 All Nations, Clap Your Hands

1. All nations, clap your hands,
2. A - bove our might - y foes
3. With shouts as - cends our King,
4. O sing in joy - ful strains

Let
He
With
And

shouts of tri - umph ring,
gave us pow'r to stand,
tri - umph's stir - ring call;
make his glo - ry known;

For might - y o - ver
And as our her - i -
Praise God, praise God, his
God o - ver all the

all the lands The Lord, Most High is King.
tage he chose The rich and prom - ised land.
prais - es sing, For God is Lord of all.
na - tions reigns, And ho - ly is his throne.

Text: Psalm 47; tr. anon.
Music: Aaron Williams, 1731–1776

66 86
ST. THOMAS (WILLIAMS)

Come, Let Us Join Our Cheerful Songs 560

1. Come, let us join our cheer - ful songs With an - gels round the throne; Ten thou - sand thou - sand are their tongues, But all their joys are one.
2. "Wor - thy the Lamb that died," they cry, "To be ex - alt - ed thus!" "Wor - thy the Lamb," our lips re - ply, "For he was slain for us!"
3. Je - sus is wor - thy to re - ceive Hon - or and pow'r di - vine; And bless - ings, more than we can give, Be, Lord, for - ev - er thine.
4. Let all cre - a - tion join in one To bless the sa - cred name Of him who sits up - on the throne, And to a - dore the Lamb.

Text: Isaac Watts, 1674–1748
Music: Johann Crüger, 1598–1662, alt.

86 86
GRAEFENBERG

561 Come, Let Us Join with One Accord

1. Come, let us join with one ac - cord
2. This is the day that God has blest,
3. Then let us for his com - ing yearn,

In song a - round God's throne: This is the day our
The bright - est of the sev'n, Type of that ev - er -
And for that day pre - pare When our Re - deem - er

ris - ing Lord Did make and call his own.
last - ing rest The saints en - joy in heav'n.
shall re - turn, His glo - ry full to share.

Text: Charles Wesley, Jr., 1757–1834
Music: John B. Dykes, 1823–1876

86 86
BEATITUDO

For the Beauty of the Earth 562

1. For the beau-ty of the earth, For the beau-ty of the skies,
2. For the beau-ty of each hour Of the day and of the night,
3. For the joy of ear and eye, For the heart and mind's de-light,
4. For the joy of hu-man love, Broth-er, sis-ter, par-ent, child,

For the love which from our birth O-ver and a-round us lies,
Hill and vale, and tree and flow'r, Sun and moon and stars of light,
For the mys-tic har-mo-ny Link-ing sense to sound and sight,
Friends on earth and friends a-bove, For all gen-tle thoughts and mild,

REFRAIN

Christ, our God, to thee we raise This our hymn of thank-ful praise.

5. For each perfect gift of thine
   To this world so freely giv'n,
   Graces human and divine,
   Flow'rs of earth and buds of heav'n,
   Refrain

6. For your Church, that evermore
   Lifts its holy hands above,
   Off'ring up on ev'ry shore
   Its pure sacrifice of love,
   Refrain

Higher Key: As With Gladness Men of Old, no. 229
Text: Folliot Sandford Pierpoint, 1835–1917
Music: Conrad Kocher, 1786–1872; arr. William Henry Monk, 1823–1889

77 77 77
DIX

563 From All That Dwell Below the Skies

1. From all that dwell be - low the skies,
2. E - ter - nal are your mer - cies, Lord;
3. Your loft - y themes, all mor - tals, bring;
4. In ev - 'ry land be - gin the song;

Let the Cre - a - tor's praise a - rise;
E - ter - nal truth at - tends your word:
In songs of praise di - vine - ly sing;
To ev - 'ry land the strains be - long;

Let the Re - deem - er's name be sung,
Your praise shall sound from shore to shore,
The great sal - va - tion loud pro - claim,
In cheer - ful sounds all voic - es raise,

Through ev - 'ry land by ev - 'ry tongue.
Till suns shall rise and set no more.
And shout for joy the Sav - ior's name.
And fill the world with loud - est praise.

Lower Key: I Know That My Redeemer Lives!, no. 293

Text: Isaac Watts, 1674–1748, vs. 1 & 2; anon. vv. 3 & 4; para. Psalm 117
Music: John Hatton, c. 1710–1793

88 88
DUKE STREET

God, My King, Your Might Confessing 564

1. God, my King, your might con - fess - ing,
2. All your saints shall praise your glo - ry,
3. Full of kind - ness and com - pas - sion,
4. All your works, O Lord, shall bless you.

Ev - er will I bless your name; Day by day your
On your might and great - ness dwell, Speak of your great
Slow to an - ger, vast in love, God is good to
All the saints shall you a - dore. King su - preme shall

throne ad - dress - ing, Still will I your praise pro - claim.
acts the sto - ry, And your deeds of won - der tell.
all cre - a - tion; All his works his good - ness prove.
they con - fess you, And pro - claim your sov - 'reign pow'r.

Text: Bishop Richard Mant, 1776–1848; para. Psalm 145
Music: Christian Friedrich Witt, 1660–1716; adapt. Henry John Gauntlett, 1805–1876

87 87
STUTTGART

565 I Sing the Almighty Power of God

1. I sing the almighty power of God, That made the mountains rise,
2. I sing the goodness of the Lord, That filled the earth with food;
3. There's not a plant or flower below, But makes thy glories known;

That spread the flowing seas abroad And built the lofty skies.
He formed the creatures with his word, And then pronounced them good.
And clouds arise, and tempests blow, By order from thy throne;

I sing the wisdom that ordained The sun to rule the day;
Lord, how thy wonders are displayed, Where'er I turn my eye,
While all that borrows life from thee Is ever in thy care,

The moon shines full at his command, And all the stars obey.
If I survey the ground I tread, Or gaze upon the sky!
And ev-'ry-where that I could be, Thou, God, art present there.

Alt. Tune: O Little Town of Bethlehem, no. 198

Text: Isaac Watts, 1674–1748, alt.

Music: English Folk Song; harm. Ralph Vaughan Williams, 1872–1958, ©

86 86 86 86
FOREST GREEN

Immortal, Invisible, God Only Wise 566

1. Im - mor - tal, in - vis - i - ble, God on - ly wise, In
2. Un - rest - ing, un - hast - ing, and si - lent as light, Nor
3. To all life thou giv - est, to both great and small; In
4. Great Fa - ther of glo - ry, pure Fa - ther of light, Thine

light in - ac - ces - si - ble hid from our eyes, Most
want - ing, nor wast - ing, thou rul - est in might; Thy
all life thou liv - est, the true life of all; We
an - gels a - dore thee, all veil - ing their sight; Of

bless - ed, most glo - rious, the An - cient of Days, Al -
jus - tice like moun - tains high soar - ing a - bove, Thy
blos - som and flour - ish as leaves on a tree, And
all thy rich grac - es this grace, Lord, im - part: Take the

might - y, vic - to - rious, thy great name we praise.
clouds which are foun - tains of good - ness and love.
with - er and per - ish: but nought chang - eth thee.
veil from our fac - es, the veil from our heart.

Text: Walter Chalmers Smith, 1824–1908
Music: Welsh Melody

11 11 11 11
ST. DENIO

567 Let All Things Now Living

1. Let all things now liv-ing A song of thanks-giv-ing
2. His law he en-forc-es, The stars in their cours-es,

To God our Cre-a-tor tri-um-phant-ly raise;
The sun in its or-bit o-be-dient-ly shine,

Who fash-ioned and made us, Pro-tect-ed and stayed us,
The hills and the moun-tains, The riv-ers and foun-tains,

By guid-ing us on to the end of our days.
The depths of the o-cean pro-claim God di-vine.

God's ban-ners are o'er us, Pure light goes be-fore us,
We, too, should be voic-ing Our love and re-joic-ing

A pil-lar of fire shin-ing forth in the night:
With glad ad-o-ra-tion, a song let us raise:

Till shad-ows have van-ished And dark-ness is ban-ished,
Till all things now liv-ing U-nite in thanks-giv-ing,

As for-ward we trav-el from light in-to light.
To God in the high-est, ho-san-na and praise.

Text: Katherine K. Davis, 1892–1980, ©
Music: Welsh tune; harm. Gerald H. Knight, 1908–1979, ©

12 11 12 11 D
ASH GROVE

Holy God, We Praise Thy Name 568

1. Ho - ly God, we praise thy name. Lord of
2. Hark the loud ce - les - tial hymn; An - gel
3. Lo! the a - pos - to - lic train Join, the

all we bow be - fore thee. All on earth thy
choirs a - bove are rais - ing, Cher - u - bim and
sa - cred name to hal - low; Proph - ets swell the

scep - ter claim. All in heav'n a - bove a -
ser - a - phim, In un - ceas - ing chor - us
loud re - frain, And the white - robed mar - tyrs

dore thee. In - fin - ite thy vast do - main,
prais - ing; Fill the heav'ns with sweet ac - cord:
fol - low; And from morn to set of sun,

Ev - er - last - ing is thy reign.
Ho - ly, ho - ly, ho - ly Lord.
Through the Church the song goes on.

In - fin - ite thy vast do - main,
Fill the heav'ns with sweet ac - cord:
And from morn to set of sun,

Ev - er - last - ing is thy reign.
Ho - ly, ho - ly, ho - ly Lord.
Through the Church the song goes on.

4. Holy Father, Holy Son,   Undivided God we claim thee;
Holy Spirit, Three we name thee;   And adoring bend the knee,
While in essence only One,   While we own the mystery.

Text: Ignaz Franz, 1719–1790, Attr.; tr. Clarence Augustus Walworth, 1820–1900   78 78 77 77
Music: Katholisches Gesangbuch, 1686; alt. Cantate, 1851; arr. Sr. Theophane Hytrek, O.S.F., ©   TE DEUM (GROSSER GOTT)

569 Let Us Praise God Together

1. Let us praise God to-geth-er on our knees.
2. Let us make this a new world with the Lord.
3. Let us all help the poor with the Lord.
4. Let us all work to-geth-er with the Lord.

Let us praise God to-geth-er on our knees.
Let us make this a new world with the Lord.
Let us all help the poor with the Lord.
Let us all work to-geth-er with the Lord.

REFRAIN

When I fall on my knees with my face to the ris-ing sun,

O Lord, have mer-cy on me.

5. Let us all heal the sick with the Lord.
   Let us all heal the sick with the Lord.
   Refrain

Text: Afro-American Spiritual
Music: Afro-American Spiritual, adpt.

10 10 with Refrain
LET US BREAK BREAD

Now Thank We All Our God 570

1. Now thank we all our God, With heart, and hands, and voic - es,
2. O may this boun-teous God Through all our life be near us!
3. All praise and thanks to God The Fa - ther now be giv - en,

Who won-drous things hath done, In whom his world re - joic - es:
With ev - er - joy - ful hearts And bless-ed peace to cheer us:
The Son, and him who reigns With them in high-est heav - en,

Who from our moth - er's arms Has blessed us on our way
And keep us in his grace, And guide us when per - plex'd,
The one e - ter - nal God, Whom heav'n and earth a - dore;

With count-less gifts of love, And still is ours to - day.
And free us from all ills In this world and the next.
For thus it was, is now, And shall be, ev - er - more.

Text: Martin Rinkart, 1586–1649; tr. Catherine Winkworth, 1827–1878, alt.
Music: Johann Crüger, 1598–1662; harm. William Henry Monk, 1823–1889,
after Felix Mendelssohn-Bartholdy, 1809–1847

67 67 66 66
NUN DANKET

571 O Worship the King

1. O wor - ship the King, all glo - rious a - bove,
2. O tell of his might, O sing of his grace,
3. The earth with its store of won - ders un - told,
4. Thy boun - ti - ful care, what tongue can re - cite?

O grate - ful - ly sing his pow'r and his love;
Whose robe is the light, whose can - o - py space;
Al - might - y, thy pow'r hath found - ed of old,
It breathes in the air, it shines in the light;

Our Shield and De - fend - er, the An - cient of Days,
His char - iots of wrath the deep thun - der - clouds form,
Hath root - ed it fast by a change-less de - cree,
Thy mer - cies how ten - der, how firm to the end,

O laud him in splen - dor, and ren - der him praise.
And dark is his path on the wings of the storm.
And round it hath cast, like a man - tle, the sea.
Our Mak - er, De - fend - er, Re - deem - er and Friend.

Text: Robert Grant, 1779–1838
Music: William Croft, 1678–1727, attr.

10 10 11 11
HANOVER

Praise the Lord of Heaven 572

1. Praise the Lord of heav - en; Praise him in the height!
2. Praise the Lord, ye foun - tains Of the depths and seas,
3. Praise him, all ye na - tions, Rul - ers and all kings;

Praise him all ye an - gels; Praise him, stars and light;
Rocks and hills and moun - tains, Ce - dars and all trees;
Praise him, men and maid - ens, All cre - a - ted things;

Praise him, earth and wa - ters, Praise him, all ye skies;
Praise him, clouds and va - pors, Snow and hail and fire,
Glo - ri - ous and might - y Is his name a - lone;

When his word com - mand - ed, All things did a - rise.
Na - ture all ful - fill - ing On - ly his de - sire.
All the earth his foot - stool, Heav - en is his throne.

Text: Thomas B. Browne, 1805–1874, alt.; para. Psalm 148
Music: French Noel, adapt.

65 65 65 65
UNE VAINE CRAINTE

573 Praise the Lord! Ye Heavens, Adore Him

1. Praise the Lord! Ye heav'ns, a - dore him; Praise him, an - gels in the height.
2. Praise the Lord! For he is glo - rious; Nev - er shall his prom - ise fail;
3. Praise the Lord! His might con - fess - ing; Laud him ev - er; bless his name.
4. Wor - ship, hon - or, glo - ry, bless - ing, Lord, we of - fer un - to thee;

Sun and moon, re - joice be - fore him; Praise him, all ye stars of light.
God hath made his saints vic - to - rious; Sin and death shall not pre - vail.
An - gels, saints, his throne ad - dress - ing, Wor - ship him, his pow'r pro - claim.
Young and old, thy praise ex - press - ing, In glad hom - age bend the knee.

Praise the Lord! For he hath spo - ken; Worlds his might - y voice o - beyed;
Praise the God of our sal - va - tion! Hosts on high, his pow'r pro - claim;
Praise the Lord of all cre - a - tion, Praise the glo - rious King of might;
All the saints in heav'n a - dore thee; We would bow be - fore thy throne:

Laws which nev - er shall be bro - ken For their guid - ance he hath made.
Heav'n and earth and all cre - a - tion, Laud and mag - ni - fy his name.
Praise the God of our sal - va - tion; Praise him, praise him in the height.
As thine an - gels serve be - fore thee, So on earth thy will be done.

Alt. tune: Alleluia, Sing to Jesus, no. 504

Text: From the Foundling Hospital Collection, 1796, vv. 1 & 2; Edward Osler, 1798–1863, v. 3; John Dunn, v. 4, ©
Music: Franz Josef Haydn, 1732–1809

87 87 87 87
AUSTRIA

Praise We Our God With Joy 574

1. Praise we our God with joy And gladness never ending;
2. He is our Shepherd true; With watchful care unsleeping,
3. Graces in copious stream From that pure fount are welling,
4. All praise and thanks to God The Father now be given,

Angels and saints with us Their grateful voices blending.
On us, his erring sheep, An eye of pity keeping;
Where, in our heart of hearts, Our God has set his dwelling.
The Son, and Holy Ghost Enthroned in highest heaven;

He is our Shepherd true, With watchful care and love;
So with a mighty arm The bonds of sin he breaks,
His word our lantern is, His peace our comfort still,
The one, eternal God, Whom earth and heav'n adore;

His mercies without end He showers from above.
And to our burdened hearts In words of peace he speaks.
His sweetness all our rest, Our law, our life, his will.
For thus it was, is now, And shall be evermore.

Text: Frederick Oakeley, 1802–1880, and others; tr. Catherine Winkworth, 1827–1878, alt.
Music: Ahasuerus Fritsch, 1629–1701 (Melody); acc. J.S. Bach, 1685–1750

67 67 66 66
DARMSTADT

575 The Olive Tree

1. For I am like a grow-ing ol-ive tree In the
2. For I am like a grow-ing al-mond tree In the
3. For I am like a fig tree bear-ing fruit In the
4. For I am like a grow-ing ap-ple tree In the

house of God my Sav-ior; For I am like a

1. grow-ing ol-ive tree In the house of the Lord for-ev-er.
2. grow-ing al-mond tree In the house of the Lord for-ev-er.
3. fig tree bear-ing fruit In the house of the Lord for-ev-er.
4. grow-ing ap-ple tree In the house of the Lord for-ev-er.

REFRAIN

I will sing your good-ness all the day, Will for-

Text: Psalm 52; adapt. Henry Bryan Hays, O.S.B., b. 1920, ©
Music: Henry Bryan Hays, O.S.B., b. 1920, ©

10 8 10 9 with Refrain
OLIVE TREE

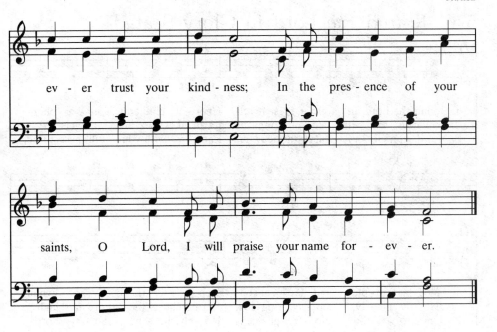

ev - er trust your kind - ness; In the pres - ence of your

saints, O Lord, I will praise your name for - ev - er.

5. For I am like a growing walnut tree
   In the house of God my Savior;
   For I am like a growing walnut tree
   In the house of the Lord forever.
   Refrain

6. For I am like a fragrant cinnamon
   In the house of God my Savior;
   For I am like a fragrant cinnamon
   In the house of the Lord forever.
   Refrain

576 Round the Lord in Glory Seated

1. Round the Lord in glo - ry seat - ed Cher - u - bim and ser - a - phim
2. Heav'n is still with glo - ry ring - ing; Earth takes up the an - gels' cry:
3. "Lord, your glo - ry fills the heav - en, Earth is with your full - ness stored:

Filled his tem - ple and re - peat - ed Each to each the roy - al hymn:
"Ho - ly, ho - ly, ho - ly," sing - ing, "Lord of hosts, the Lord most high."
Un - to you be glo - ry giv - en, Ho - ly, ho - ly, ho - ly Lord."

"Lord, your glo - ry fills the heav - en, Earth is with your full - ness stored:
With his an - gel hosts be - fore him, With his ho - ly Church be - low,
Thus your glo - rious name con - fess - ing, With your an - gel hosts we cry,

Un - to you be glo - ry giv - en, Ho - ly, ho - ly, ho - ly Lord!"
Thus u - nite we to a - dore him, Bid we thus our prais - es flow:
"Ho - ly, ho - ly, ho - ly," bless - ing You, the Lord of hosts Most High.

Text: Richard Mant, 1776–1848
Music: Gerard F. Cobb, 1838–1904

87 87 87 87
MOULTRIE

To God With Gladness Sing 577

1. To God with glad - ness sing, Your Rock and Sav - ior
2. He cra - dles in his hand The heights and depths of
3. Your heav'n - ly Fa - ther praise, Ac - claim his on - ly

bless; With - in his tem - ple bring Your songs of
earth; He made the sea and land, He brought the
Son, Your voice in hom - age raise To him who

thank - ful - ness! O God of might, To
world to birth! O God most high, We
makes all one! O Dove of peace, On

you we sing, En - throned as King On heav - en's height!
are your sheep, On us you keep Your shep - herd's eye!
us de - scend That strife may end And joy in - crease!

Text: James Quinn, S.J., b. 1919; para. Psalm 95, © 1969
Music: John Darwall, 1731–1789 (Melody & Bass); harm. William Henry Monk, 1823–1889

66 66 44 44
DARWALL'S 148TH

578 Ye Watchers and Ye Holy Ones

1. Ye watch-ers and ye ho - ly ones, Bright ser - aphs, cher - u - bim, and thrones, Raise the glad strain, Al - le - lu - ia! Cry out, do - min - ions, prince-doms, pow'rs, Vir -

2. O high - er than the cher - u - bim, More glo - rious than the ser - a - phim, Lead their prais - es, Al - le - lu - ia! Thou bear - er of the e - ter - nal Word, Most

3. Re - spond, ye souls in end - less rest, Ye pa - tri - archs and proph - ets blest, Al - le - lu - ia! Al - le - lu - ia! Ye ho - ly twelve, ye mar - tyrs strong, All

4. O friends, in glad - ness let us sing, Su - per - nal an - thems ech - o - ing, Al - le - lu - ia! Al - le - lu - ia! To God, the Fa - ther, God the Son, And

Text: John Athelstan Riley, 1858–1945, ©
Music: Geistliche Kirchengesange, Cologne, 1623;
*   harm. Ralph Vaughan Williams, 1872–1958, ©*

88 44 88 with Alleluias
LASST UNS ERFREUEN (VIGILES ET SANCTI)

tues, arch - an - gels, an - gels' choirs,
gra - cious, mag - ni - fy the Lord,
saints tri - um - phant, raise the song:
God the Spir - it, Three in One,

REFRAIN

Al - le - lu - ia! Al - le - lu - ia! Al - le -

lu - ia! Al - le - lu - ia! Al - le - lu - ia!

579 We Praise You, God

1. We praise you, God, we name you Lord. E-ternal Fa-ther, earth a-dores, And heav-en's choirs for ev-er praise, Ho-ly, ho-ly, is our God, Most ho-ly is the Lord of all.

2. Your maj-es-ty fills earth and sky. A-pos-tles, proph-ets, mar-tyrs join With all cre-a-tion prais-ing you, North and south and east and west The Church pro-claims her faith in you.

3. Your glo-ry, Fa-ther, has no end, Your true and on-ly Son is love, The Ho-ly Spir-it pleads for us. Christ, you are our glo-rious king, The Fa-ther's own e-ter-nal Son.

4. Be-com-ing man to save us all, You did not scorn a vir-gin's womb, De-stroy-ing death tri-um-phant-ly, Christ, you o-pened heav-en's gates To all be-liev-ers in your word.

Text: Te Deum, tr. Bro. Louis Blenkner, O.S.B., b. 1922, ©
Music: Henry Bryan Hays, O.S.B., b. 1920, ©

888 78
MONTANA

5. You are enthroned at God's right hand,
   And we believe you come to judge,
   You shed your precious blood for us.
   Grant your servants grace and aid;
   Admit us all among your saints.

Songs of Praise the Angels Sang 580

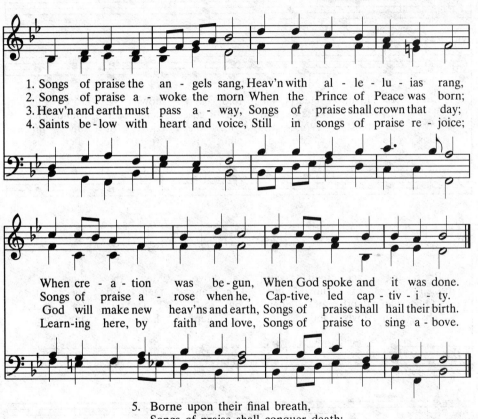

1. Songs of praise the an - gels sang, Heav'n with al - le - lu - ias rang,
2. Songs of praise a - woke the morn When the Prince of Peace was born;
3. Heav'n and earth must pass a - way, Songs of praise shall crown that day;
4. Saints be - low with heart and voice, Still in songs of praise re - joice;

When cre - a - tion was be - gun, When God spoke and it was done.
Songs of praise a - rose when he, Cap-tive, led cap - tiv - i - ty.
God will make new heav'ns and earth, Songs of praise shall hail their birth.
Learn-ing here, by faith and love, Songs of praise to sing a - bove.

5. Borne upon their final breath,
   Songs of praise shall conquer death;
   Then, amidst eternal joy,
   Songs of praise their pow'rs employ.

Text: James Montgomery, 1771–1854, alt.
Music: Anon., 1704; adapt. John Antes, 1740–1811; arr. John B. Wilkes, 1785–1869

77 77
MONKLAND

581 Joyful, Joyful, We Adore Thee

1. Joy - ful, joy - ful, we a - dore thee, God of glo - ry,
2. All thy works with joy sur - round thee, Earth and heav'n re -
3. Thou art giv - ing and for - giv - ing, Ev - er bless - ing,
4. Mor - tals, join the might - y cho - rus Which the morn - ing

Lord of love; Hearts un - fold like flow'rs be - fore thee,
flect thy rays, Stars and an - gels sing a - round thee,
ev - er blest, Well - spring of the joy of liv - ing,
stars be - gan; Love di - vine is reign - ing o'er us,

Prais - ing thee, their sun a - bove. Melt the clouds of
Cen - ter of un - bro - ken praise; Field and for - est,
O - cean - depth of hap - py rest! Thou our Fa - ther,
Hu - man love, God's ho - ly plan. Ev - er sing - ing,

sin and sad - ness; Drive the dark of doubt a - way;
vale and moun - tain, Bloom - ing mead - ow, flash - ing sea,
Christ our broth - er, All who live in love are thine;
march we on - ward, Vic - tor's in the midst of strife;

Text: Henry van Dyke, 1852–1933, alt., ©
Music: Ludwig van Beethoven, 1770–1827; adapt. Edward Hodges, 1796–1867

87 87 87 87
HYMN TO JOY

Text: Courtesy of Charles Scribner's Sons

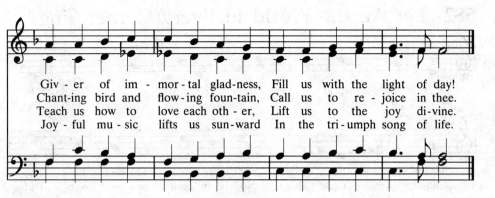

Giv - er of im - mor - tal glad-ness, Fill us with the light of day!
Chant-ing bird and flow - ing foun-tain, Call us to re - joice in thee.
Teach us how to love each oth - er, Lift us to the joy di - vine.
Joy - ful mu - sic lifts us sun-ward In the tri - umph song of life.

582 Let All the World in Every Corner Sing

1. Let all the world in ev-'ry cor-ner sing, My God and King! The
2. Let all the world in ev-'ry cor-ner sing, My God and King! The

heav'ns are not too high, His praise may thi-ther fly; The
Church with psalms must shout, No door can keep them out; But

earth is not too low, His prais-es there may grow. Let all the
a-bove all, the heart Must bear the long-est part. Let all the

world in ev-'ry cor-ner sing, My God and King!
world in ev-'ry cor-ner sing, My God and King!

Text: George Herbert, 1593–1632
Music: Henry Bryan Hays, O.S.B., b. 1920, ©

EZRA CHURCH

583 When in Our Music God Is Glorified

1. When in our mu - sic God is glo - ri - fied,
2. How of - ten, mak - ing mu - sic, we have found
3. So has the Church in lit - ur - gy and song,
4. And did not Je - sus sing a psalm that night

And ad - o - ra - tion leaves no room for pride,
A new di - men - sion in the world of sound,
In faith and love, through cen - tu - ries of wrong,
When ut - most e - vil strove a - gainst the Light?

It is as though the whole cre - a - tion cried
As wor - ship moved us to a more pro - found
Borne wit - ness to the truth in ev - 'ry tongue,
Then let us sing, for whom he won the fight,

Al - le-lu - ia!   Al - le-lu - ia!

5. Let ev'ry instrument be tuned for praise!
Let all rejoice who have a voice to raise!
And may God give us faith to sing always
Alleluia!

Text: Fred Pratt Green, b. 1903
Music: Charles V. Stanford, 1852–1924

10 10 10 with Alleluias
ENGELBERG

Text © Hope Publishing Co.

Truly His 584

1. If you think that the o - cean surf is beau - ti - ful,
2. If you think that a moun-tain range is beau - ti - ful,
3. If you think that a bud - ding rose is beau - ti - ful,
4. If you think that a bird in flight is beau - ti - ful,

And the o - cean surf most cer-tain-ly is,
And a moun - tain range most cer-tain-ly is,
And a bud - ding rose most cer-tain-ly is,
And a bird in flight most cer-tain-ly is,

Then be sure that our God is still more beau-ti-ful, For the whole world is

tru - ly his, For the whole world is tru - ly his!

5. If you think that the falling snow is beautiful,
And the falling snow most certainly is,
Then be sure that our God is still more beautiful,
For the whole world is truly his,
For the whole world is truly his!

6. If you think that your mother's face is beautiful,
And your mother's face most certainly is,
Then be sure that our God is still more beautiful,
For the whole world is truly his,
For the whole world is truly his!

Text: Willard F. Jabusch, b. 1930, ©
Music: Willard F. Jabusch, b. 1930; acc. S. R. Rudcki, b. 1928, ©

585 Send Out Your Spirit, Lord

1. Send out your Spir - it, Lord, this earth re - new - ing!
2. You spread the heav - ens, Lord, like a pa - vil - ion,
3. Here is your sea, O Lord, vast and so might - y,
4. You bring us bread, O Lord, your wine will glad - den;
5. Crea - tures all look to you; fill them with good things,

You're clothed in glo - ry and robed in great light!
Rid - ing the clouds on the wings of the storm.
Where ships are sail - ing and whales glide and play,
You make our fac - es shine bright with your oil.
Lest they should per - ish, re - turn - ing to dust.

How man - y crea - tures you've made in your wis - dom!
Springs bub - ble forth and flow down through the val - leys;
Quick - ly be - com - ing so rest - less and trou - bled
You've made the moon and the sun fit to mea - sure,
When you send forth your own Spir - it re - new - ing,

1.–4.
You give them food when the time is right.
Birds on their banks wel - come each new morn.
If you should take food and breath a - way.
Night - time for rest and the day for toil.

Final Ending
Each heart fills up with fresh joy and trust.

Text: Willard F. Jabusch, b. 1930; para. Psalm 104, ©
Music: Alexis Lvov, 1799–1870; acc. David Kraehenbuehl, b. 1923, ©

11 10 11 9
RUSSIA

586 Sing a New Song

1. Sing a new song to the Lord of the world, Speak of his glo - ry and
2. Sing a new song to the Lord of the world, God is a - lone to be
3. Sing a new song to the Lord of the world, Praise to the name of the
4. Sing a new song to the Lord of the world, O - cean and earth sing his
5. Sing a new song to the Lord of the world, Praise to the name of the

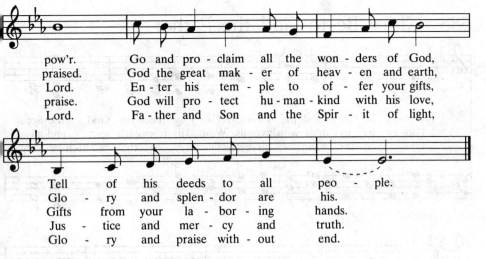

pow'r.	Go and pro - claim	all the	won - ders of God,
praised.	God the great mak - er	of	heav - en and earth,
Lord.	En - ter his tem - ple	to	of - fer your gifts,
praise.	God will pro - tect	hu - man - kind	with his love,
Lord.	Fa - ther and Son	and the	Spir - it of light,

Tell	of	his	deeds	to	all	peo - ple.
Glo -	ry	and	splen - dor	are	his.
Gifts	from	your	la - bor - ing	hands.
Jus -	tice	and	mer - cy	and	truth.
Glo -	ry	and	praise with - out	end.

Text: Psalm 96; tr. Luke Connaughton and Kevin Mayhew, adapt., ©
Music: Jerome Coller, O.S.B., b. 1929, ©

10 7 10 7

Come Before Him Singing 587

1. Come be - fore him singing, thanks and prais - es bring. Shout that
2. Come and bow be - fore him, to him bend your knee. We're his
3. Praise the Lord for - ever in his ho - ly house; Praise him

he's our safety, he's our Rock and King. Depths of
flock and surely he'll our Shep - herd be. Hard - en
for his wonders in his ho - ly house. Let the

earth are his: high - est moun - tains his! He made
not your hearts, like your el - ders' hearts; For - ty
horns re - sound; let the flutes all sound; Drums and

land and sea and all things that live.
years they wan - dered so far a - stray.
crash - ing cym - bals sing praise to God.

Text: Willard F. Jabusch, b. 1930; Psalm 95, para., ©
Music: Robert E. Kreutz, b. 1922

588 Glory Be to God the Father

1. Glo-ry be to God the Fa-ther, Glo-ry be to God the Son,
2. Glo-ry be to him who loves us, Washed us from each spot and stain!
3. Glo-ry to the King of an-gels, Glo-ry to the Church's King,

Glo-ry be to God the Spir-it, Glo-ry to the Three in One!
Glo-ry be to him who bought us, Made us heirs with him to reign!
Glo-ry to the King of na-tions! Heav'n and earth, your prais-es sing;

Glo-ry, hon-or, praise, and bless-ing, While e-ter-nal ag-es run.
Glo-ry, hon-or, praise, and bless-ing, While e-ter-nal ag-es run.
Glo-ry, hon-or, praise, and bless-ing, While e-ter-nal ag-es run.

Text: Horatius Bonar, 1808–1889, alt.
Music: Henry Smart, 1813–1879

87 87 87
REGENT SQUARE

With Joyful Hearts We Enter/Vayamos 589

REFRAIN

With joy-ful hearts we en-ter the ho-ly place of God!
Va-ya-mos ju-bi-lo-sos al al-tar de Dios!

VERSES

1. May your faith-ful-ness and jus - tice Draw us
2. Let us praise our God and Sav - ior Who re-
1. Al sa - gra - do al - tar nos gui - en su Ver-
2. Al Dios san - to ce - le - bre - mos; Que nos

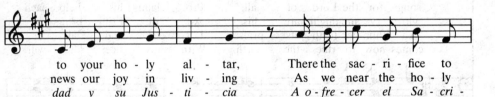

to your ho - ly al - tar, There the sac - ri - fice to
news our joy in liv - ing As we near the ho - ly
dad y su Jus - ti - cia A o - fre - cer el Sa - cri-
lle - na de al - e - gría Y sub - am - os has - ta el

Repeat Refrain

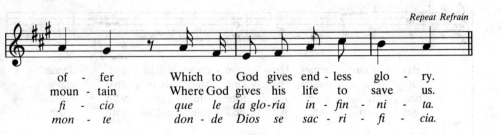

of - fer Which to God gives end - less glo - ry.
moun - tain Where God gives his life to save us.
fi - cio que le da glo-ria in - fin - ni - ta.
mon - te don - de Dios se sac - ri - fi - cia.

3. Let us offer there together
   God's own Son, the saving Victim,
   Who by dying makes us sharers
   In his light and life eternal.
   Refrain

4. Glory be to God the Father,
   Glory be to Christ, our leader;
   And to God the Holy Spirit
   Praise be given without ending.
   Refrain

Text: E.G. Arrondo, C.SS.R., and A. Danoz, C.SS.R; tr. John Patrick Earls, O.S.B., b. 1935, ©
Music: E.G. Arrondo, C.SS.R., and A. Danoz, C.SS.R, ©

88 88 with Refrain
VAYAMOS JUBILOSOS

590 The Song of the Trees

1. O sing to the Lord a song that's new, A song for the Lord of all. Pro - claim his help each day that comes, His won - drous works and deeds.

2. In - deed he is worth - y to be praised; All glo - ry and might are his. An of - f'ring bring in - to his courts, His king - ship there pro - claim.

3. Let heav - en ex - ult and earth be glad, The sea thun - der forth its praise. Let earth and all it bears re - joice Be - fore the Lord who comes.

4. The pres - ence of God is ev - 'ry - where, He comes now to rule the earth. With jus - tice he will gov - ern all, All peo - ple judge with truth.

REFRAIN

Let the trees of the woods all clap their hands, All

Text: Psalm 96; tr. Henry Bryan Hays, O.S.B., b. 1920, ©
Music: Henry Bryan Hays, O.S.B., b. 1920, ©

97 86 with Refrain
SAYLOR'S CREEK

sing and shout for joy At the sight of the Lord, for he

comes, he comes, For he comes to rule the earth.

591 How Great Thou Art

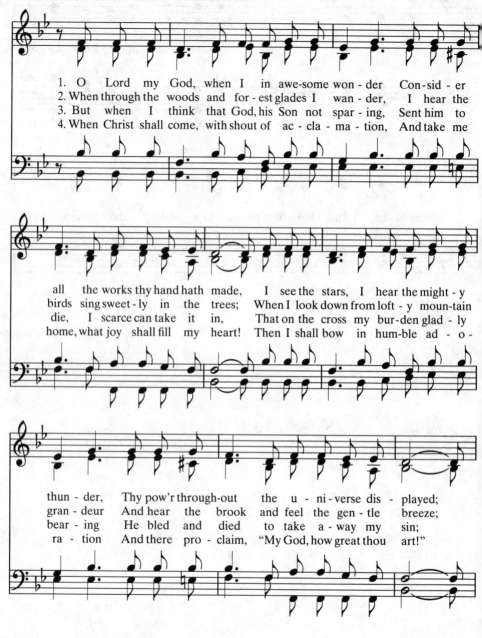

1. O Lord my God, when I in awe-some won-der Con-sid-er
2. When through the woods and for-est glades I wan-der, I hear the
3. But when I think that God, his Son not spar-ing, Sent him to
4. When Christ shall come, with shout of ac-cla-ma-tion, And take me

all the works thy hand hath made, I see the stars, I hear the might-y
birds sing sweet-ly in the trees; When I look down from loft-y moun-tain
die, I scarce can take it in, That on the cross my bur-den glad-ly
home, what joy shall fill my heart! Then I shall bow in hum-ble ad-o-

thun-der, Thy pow'r through-out the u-ni-verse dis-played;
gran-deur And hear the brook and feel the gen-tle breeze;
bear-ing He bled and died to take a-way my sin;
ra-tion And there pro-claim, "My God, how great thou art!"

Text: Stuart K. Hine, b. 1899
Music: Stuart K. Hine, b. 1899; instrumental descant: Sr. Maurita Bernet, O.S.F.

11 10 11 10 with Refrain
O STORE GUD

REFRAIN

Then sings my soul, my Sav - ior God, to thee, How great thou

art! How great thou art! Then sings my soul, my Sav - ior God, to

thee, How great thou art! How great thou art!

592 Praise to the Lord, the Almighty

1. Praise to the Lord, the Al - might - y, the King of cre - a - tion! O my soul, praise him for he is your health and sal - va - tion. All you who hear, Now to his al - tar draw near;

2. Praise to the Lord, let us of - fer our gifts at the al - tar. Let not our sins and trans - gres - sions now cause us to fal - ter. Christ the high priest Bids us all join in his feast,

3. Praise to the Lord, who will pros - per our work and de - fend us; Sure - ly his good - ness and mer - cy here dai - ly at - tend us; Pon - der a - new What the Al - might - y can do,

4. Praise to the Lord! O let all that is in us a - dore him! All that has life and breath, come now in prais - es be - fore him! Let the A - men Sound from his peo - ple a - gain,

Text: Joachim Neander, 1650–1680; tr. Catherine Winkworth, 1827–1878, and others
Music: Erneuerten Gesangbuch, 1665; instrumental descant: Sr. Maurita Bernet, O.S.F., ©

14 14 4 7 8
LOBE DEN HERREN

Join in pro - found a - do - ra - tion.
Vic - tims with him on the al - tar.
Who with his love will be - friend us.
Now as we wor - ship be - fore him.

593 Clap Your Hands

1. Clap your hands, you joy - ful peo - ple, Shout to God with voice of praise.
2. All the princ - es of the peo - ples Now u - nit - ed to God's own,

He is Lord most high a - bove us, Reign - ing un - to length of days.
Come with seed of A - bra - ham and Tri - bute pay the Lord a - lone.

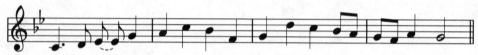

An in - her - i - tance he has giv'n To those who love his won - drous ways.
For ex - alt - ed is our God Up - on his high e - ter - nal throne.

God goes up with shouts of sing - ing, God goes up with trum - pet sound.
Prais - es be to God the Fa - ther, Prais - es be to God the Son,

Sing to him a song of glo - ry; Let praise to his name re - dound.
Prais - es to the Ho - ly Spir - it, Per - sons Three, but na - ture One.

God is king of all the earth; In him a - lone is jus - tice found.
May they ev - er be ex - alt - ed, While un - ceas - ing ag - es run.

Text: Henry Bryan Hays, O.S.B., b.1920; Psalm 47, adapt., ©
Music: Henry Bryan Hays, O.S.B., b. 1920, ©

87 87 78 87 87 78
MARK'S MILL

All Things Bright and Beautiful 594

REFRAIN

All things bright and beau - ti - ful, All crea - tures great and small,

All things wise and won - der - ful: The Lord God made them all.

VERSES

1. Each lit - tle flow'r that o - pens, Each lit - tle bird that sings:
2. The cold wind in the win - ter, The pleas-ant sum-mer sun,
3. The pur - ple head - ed moun - tain, The riv - er run-ning by,
4. He gave us eyes to see them, And lips that we might tell

Repeat Refrain

He made their glow-ing col - ors, He made their ti - ny wings.
The ripe fruits in the gar - den: He made them ev - 'ry one.
The sun - set and the morn - ing That bright-ens up the sky.
How great is God Al-might - y, Who has made all things well.

Text: Cecil Frances Alexander, 1818–1895
Music: William Henry Monk, 1823–1889

76 76 with Refrain
ALL THINGS BRIGHT AND BEAUTIFUL

595 You Are God

1. You are God: we praise you; You are the Lord: we ac - claim you;

2. You are the e - ter - nal Fa - ther: All cre - a - tion wor - ships you.

3. To you all an - gels, all the pow'rs of heav - en,

Cher - u - bim and Ser - a - phim, sing in end - less praise:

4. Ho - ly, ho - ly, ho - ly Lord, God of pow'r and might,

Text: Te Deum, St. Nicetas, ca. 415, attr.; tr. ICET, ©
Music: Slavonic Chant; adapt. and harm. Mason Martens, b. 1933, ©

heav'n and earth are full of your glo - ry.

5. The glo - rious com - pany of a - pos - tles praise you.

The no - ble fel - low - ship of pro - phets praise you.

The white-robed ar - my of mar - tyrs praise you.

6. Through-out the world the ho - ly Church ac - claims you; Fa - ther, of

ma - jes - ty un - bound - ed, your true and on - ly Son, wor - thy

of all wor - ship, and the Ho - ly Spir - it, ad - vo - cate and guide.

7. You, Christ, are the King of glo - ry, the e - ter - nal Son of the Fa - ther.

8. When you be - came man to set us free you did not shun the Vir - gin's womb.

You o - ver - came the sting of death and o - pened the king - dom of heav - en

596 On This Day, the First of Days

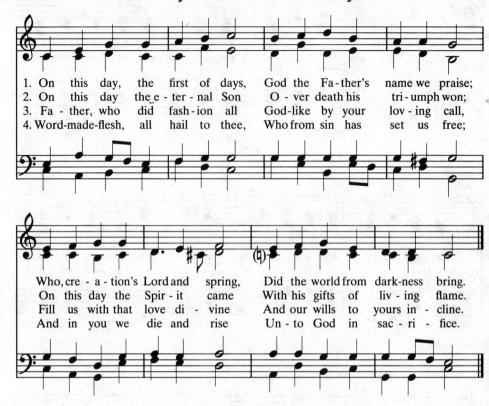

1. On this day, the first of days, God the Fa-ther's name we praise;
2. On this day the e-ter-nal Son O-ver death his tri-umph won;
3. Fa-ther, who did fash-ion all God-like by your lov-ing call,
4. Word-made-flesh, all hail to thee, Who from sin has set us free;

Who, cre-a-tion's Lord and spring, Did the world from dark-ness bring.
On this day the Spir-it came With his gifts of liv-ing flame.
Fill us with that love di-vine And our wills to yours in-cline.
And in you we die and rise Un-to God in sac-ri-fice.

5. Holy Spirit, you impart
Gifts of love to ev'ry heart;
Give us light and grace, we pray;
Fill our hearts this holy day.

6. God, the blessed Three-in-One,
May your holy will be done;
In your word our souls are blest,
As with you this day we rest.

Text: Carcassonne Breviary, 1745; tr. Henry W. Baker, 1821–1877, alt.
Music: J. A. Freylinghausen, 1670–1739; adapt. and harm. William Henry
Havergal, 1793–1870, and William Henry Monk, 1823–1889

77 77
LUBECK

For Your Gracious Blessing 597

For your gra - cious bless - ing We give thanks, O Lord.

For your lov - ing kind - ness We give thanks, O Lord.

Text: Unknown

Dona Nobis Pacem 598

1. Do - na no - bis pa - cem, pa - cem.

2. Do - na no - bis pa - cem.

3. Do - na no - bis pa - cem.

Do - na no - bis pa - cem.

Do - na no - bis pa - cem.

Do - na no - bis pa - cem.

Text: Anonymous
Music: Traditional Round

599 O God of Love, O King of Peace

1. O God of love, O King of peace, Make
2. Whom shall we trust but you, O Lord? Where
3. Where saints and an-gels dwell a-bove, All

wars through-out the world to cease; Our vio-lent ways help
rest but on your faith-ful word? None ev-er called on
hearts are joined in ho-ly love; O bind us in that

us con-tain; Give peace, O God, give peace a-gain!
you in vain; Give peace, O God, give peace a-gain!
heav'n-ly chain; Give peace, O God, give peace a-gain!

* May be sung as a two– or four–voice canon.
Text: Henry W. Baker, 1821–1877
Music: Thomas Tallis, c. 1505–1585

88 88
TALLIS' CANON

Before Thy Throne, O God, We Kneel 600

1. Be - fore thy throne, O God, we kneel: Give us a con-science quick to feel, A read - y mind to un - der - stand The mean - ing of thy chas-t'ning hand; What - e'er the pain and shame may be; Bring us, O Fa - ther, near - er thee.

2. Search out our hearts and make us true; Help us to give to all their due. From love of plea-sure, lust of gold, From sins which make the heart grow cold, Wean us and train us with thy rod; Teach us to know our faults, O God.

3. For sins of heed-less word and deed, For pride am - bi - tious to suc - ceed, From craft - y trade and sub - tle snare To catch the sim - ple un - a - ware, For lives be - reft of pur - pose high, For - give, for - give, O Lord, we cry.

4. Let the fierce fires which burn and try, Our in - most spir - its pu - ri - fy: Con - sume the ill; purge out the shame; O God, be with us in the flame; A new - born peo-ple may we rise, More pure, more true, more no - bly wise.

Alt. Tune: Faith of Our Fathers, no. 634
Text: William Boyd Carpenter, 1841–1918, alt.
Music: La Scala Santa, 1681; harm. A. Gregory Murray, b. 1905, ©

88 88 88
COLERAINE (LA SCALA SANTA)

601 Eternal Father, Strong to Save

1. E - ter - nal Fa - ther, strong to save, Whose arm has bound the
2. O Christ, the Lord of hill and plain O'er which our traf - fic
3. O Spir - it, whom the Fa - ther sent To spread a - broad the
4. O Trin - i - ty of love and pow'r, Our loved ones shield in

rest - less wave, Who bid the might - y o - cean deep Its
runs a - main By moun - tain pass or val - ley low; Wher -
fir - ma - ment; O wind of heav - en, by your might Save
dan - ger's hour; From rock and tem - pest, fire and foe, Pro -

own ap - point - ed lim - its keep: To you we pray most
ev - er, Lord, your peo - ple go, Pro - tect them by your
all who dare the ea - gle's flight, And keep them by your
tect them ev - 'ry - where they go; Thus ev - er - more with

ear - nest - ly For those in per - il on the sea.
guard - ing hand From ev - 'ry per - il on the land.
watch - ful care From ev - 'ry per - il in the air.
thanks shall we Give praise from air and land and sea.

Text: William Whiting, 1825–1878, alt. vs. 1 & 4; Robert Nelson Spencer, 1877–1961, vs. 2 & 3
Music: John Bacchus Dykes, 1823–1876

88 88 88
MELITA

Alternative Text

Hymn for the Seriously Ill   602

1. O God, who gave us life and breath,
   Come help our brother (sister) now near death.
   Your healing hand can conquer hell;
   Lord, raise him (her) up and make him (her) well.
   We pray with Christ your only Son:
   Your kingdom come, your will be done!

2. Lord, while he (she) struggles be his (her) guide
   And stand steadfast right by his (her) side.
   As once you helped King David fight,
   Now stay with him (her) all through the night.
   And when the war at last is won,
   Your kingdom come, your will be done!

3. There was a time when he (she) was here,
   Both day by day and year by year.
   We come together as before;
   Lord, let him (her) pray with us once more!
   That in the Church we may be one,
   Your kingdom come, your will be done!

4. If now the end is drawing near,
   Then keep him (her) strong and free of fear,
   And help him (her) win the crown of gold
   You promised you would not withhold.
   And when the final race is run,
   Your kingdom come, your will be done!

Text: Michael Gilligan
Text © ACP

88 88 88
MELITA

SOCIAL CONCERN

603 Go Forth for God;
Go to the World in Peace

1. Go forth for God; go to the world in peace;
2. Go forth for God; go to the world in love;
3. Go forth for God; go to the world in strength;
4. Go forth for God; go to the world in joy;

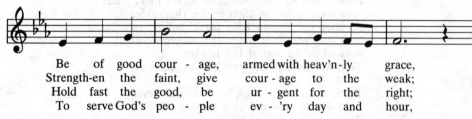

Be of good cour - age, armed with heav'n-ly grace,
Strength-en the faint, give cour - age to the weak;
Hold fast the good, be ur - gent for the right;
To serve God's peo - ple ev - 'ry day and hour,

In God's good Spir - it dai - ly to in -
Help the af - flict - ed; rich - ly from a -
Ren - der to no one e - vil; Christ at
And serv - ing Christ, our ev - 'ry gift em -

crease, Till in his king-dom we be - hold his face.
bove His love sup - plies the grace and pow'r we seek.
length Shall o - ver - come all dark - ness with his light.
ploy, Re - joic-ing in the Ho - ly Spir - it's pow'r.

Text: John Raphael Peacey, 1896–1971, and English Praise, 1975, alt., ©
Music: Erik Routley, 1917–1982

10 10 10 10
LITTON

Music © 1984, Hope Publishing Co.

God, Who Stretched the Spangled Heavens   604

1. God, who stretched the span - gled heav - ens In - fi - nite in
2. We have ven - tured worlds un - dreamed of Since the child-hood
3. As each far ho - ri - zon beck - ons, May it chal-lenge

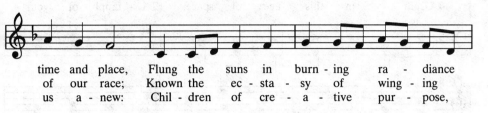

time and place, Flung the suns in burn - ing ra - diance
of our race; Known the ec - sta - sy of wing - ing
us a - new: Chil - dren of cre - a - tive pur - pose,

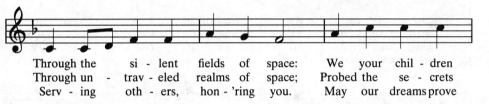

Through the si - lent fields of space: We your chil - dren
Through un - trav - eled realms of space; Probed the se - crets
Serv - ing oth - ers, hon - 'ring you. May our dreams prove

in your like - ness, Share in - ven - tive pow'rs with you;
of the at - om, Yield - ing un - i - mag - ined pow'r,
rich with prom - ise; Each en - deav - or well be - gun;

Great Cre - a - tor, still cre - at - ing, Show us what we yet may do.
Fac - ing us with life's de - struc-tion Or our most tri - um-phant hour.
Great Cre - a - tor, give us guid - ance Till our goals and yours are one.

Text: Catherine Cameron, b. 1927
Music: William Moore, 1835; harm. Charles Anders, b. 1929, ©

Text © 1967, Hope Publishing Co.

87 87 87 87
HOLY MANNA

605 God's Blessing Sends Us Forth

1. God's bless - ing sends us forth, Strength-ened for our
2. God's news in spo - ken word Joy - ful - ly our
3. We by one liv - ing bread As one bod - y
4. Grant in this age of space Tri - umph of your

task on earth, Re - freshed in soul, and re -
hearts have heard; O may the seed of God's
have been fed, So we are one as we
truth and grace; Lord, you a - lone are un -

newed in mind. May God with
love now grow. May we in
share this food; How gra - cious
chang - ing truth. Pre - serve and

us re - main, Through us his Spir - it reign That
fruit - ful deeds Glad - ly serve oth - ers' needs That
to be - hold All mem - bers of one fold Who
ev - er guide As your fair spot - less bride, Your

Text: Omer Westendorf, b. 1916
Music: Schlesische Volkslieder, 1842; acc. Guido de Sutter, b. 1931

Irregular
CRUSADER'S HYMN

Text and music accompaniment © 1964, World Library Publications, Inc.

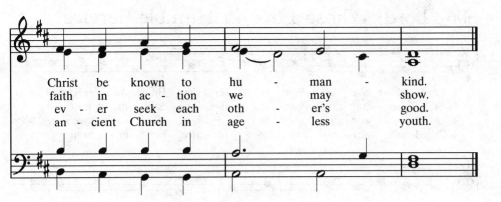

Christ   be   known   to   hu - man - kind.
faith   in   ac - tion   we   may   show.
ev - er   seek   each   oth - er's   good.
an - cient   Church   in   age - less   youth.

606 Lord, Whose Love in Humble Service

1. Lord, whose love in hum-ble ser-vice Bore the weight of
2. Still your chil-dren wan-der home-less; Still the hun-gry
3. As we wor-ship, grant us vi-sion, Till your love's re-
4. Called from wor-ship in-to ser-vice, Forth in your great

hu-man need, Who did on the cross, for-
cry for bread; Still the cap-tives long for
veal-ing light, In its height and depth and
name we go, To the child, the youth, the

sak-en, Show us mer-cy's per-fect deed;
free-dom; Still in grief we mourn our dead.
great-ness Dawns up-on our hu-man sight:
a-ged, Love in liv-ing deeds to show;

We, your ser-vants, bring the wor-ship Not of
As, O Lord, your deep com-pas-sion Healed the
Mak-ing known the needs and bur-dens Your com-
Hope and health, good-will and com-fort, Coun-sel,

voice a-lone, but heart: Con-se-crat-ing
sick and freed the soul, Use the love your
pas-sion bids us bear, Stir-ring us to
aid, and peace we give, That your chil-dren,

to your pur-pose Ev-'ry gift which you im-part.
Spir-it kin-dles Still to save and make us whole.
faith-ful ser-vice. Your a-bun-dant life to share.
Lord, in free-dom, May your mer-cy know and live.

Text: Albert F. Bayly, 1901–1984, alt. ©
Music: Traditional Dutch Melody; harm. Charles Winfred Douglas, 1867–1944, ©

87 87 87 87
IN BABILONE

Peace I Leave with You 607

REFRAIN

Peace I leave with you, my friends, peace the world can-not give. Peace I leave with you, my friends, so that your joy be ev - er full.

VERSES

1. The Fa - ther's love I came to give,
2. Take his gift and be at peace;
3. By this love which you should have
4. Take my words of life to heart,
5. All I have I give to you;
6. I came so that you may have life,
7. If you love me keep my word,

To Refrain

to be the hope for all who live.
the Spir - it of our love I bring.
all will know you are my friends.
and you will live with hope and joy.
I share with you the Fa - ther's love.
and have it to the full.
and our home we'll make with you.

Final Ending

full. Peace I leave with you, my friends, so that your joy be ev - er full.

Text: Gregory Norbet, O.S.B., b. 1940, ©
Music: Gregory Norbet, O.S.B., b. 1940; acc. Sr. Mary David Callahan, O.S.B., b. 1923, ©

608 Prayer of St. Francis

1. Make me a chan-nel of your peace. Where there is ha-tred,
2. Make me a chan-nel of your peace. Where there's de-spair in

let me bring your love. Where there is in-ju-ry, your par-don, Lord. And
life, let me bring hope. Where there is dark-ness on-ly light, And

1.
where there's doubt, true faith in you.
2.
where there's sad-ness ev-er joy. O

VERSE 3

Mas-ter, grant that I may nev-er seek So much to be con-

soled as to con-sole. To be un-der-stood as to un-der-

stand. To be loved, as to love with all my soul.

VERSE 4

Make me a chan-nel of your peace. It is in par-don-

ing that we are par-doned. In giv-ing of our-selves that we re-

ceive, And in dy-ing that we're born to e-ter-nal life.

Text: Sebastian Temple, b. 1928, ©
Music: Sebastian Temple, b. 1928; arr. Gerard Farrell, O.S.B., b. 1919, ©

Whatsoever You Do 609

REFRAIN

What-so - ev - er you do to the least of my

peo - ple, that you do un - to me. *Fine*

VERSES

1. When I was hun - gry, you gave me to eat;
2. When I was home - less, you o - pened your door;
3. When I was wea - ry, you helped me find rest;
4. When I was lit - tle, you taught me to read;

When I was thirst - y, you gave me to drink.
When I was na - ked, you gave me your coat.
When I was anx - ious, you calmed all my fears.
When I was lone - ly, you gave me your love.

D. S.

Now en - ter in - to the home of my Fa - ther.

5. When in a prison, you came to my cell;
   When on a sickbed, you cared for my needs.

6. In a strange country, you made me at home;
   Seeking employment, you found me a job.

7. Hurt in a battle, you bound up my wounds;
   Searching for kindness, you held out your hand.

8. When I was Black or Latino or White,
   Mocked and insulted, you carried my cross.

9. When I was aged, you bothered to smile;
   When I was restless, you listened and cared.

10. You saw me covered with spittle and blood;
    You knew my features, though grimy with sweat.

11. When I was laughed at, you stood by my side;
    When I was happy, you shared in my joy.

Text: Willard F. Jabusch, b. 1930, ©
Music: Willard F. Jabusch, b. 1930, ©

610 Great God, Our Source

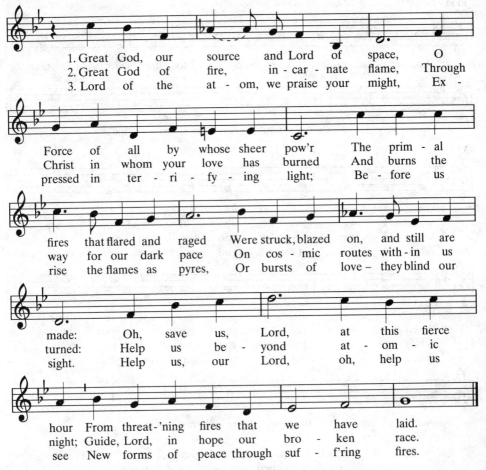

1. Great God, our source and Lord of space, O Force of all by whose sheer pow'r The prim - al fires that flared and raged Were struck, blazed on, and still are made: Oh, save us, Lord, at this fierce hour From threat-'ning fires that we have laid.

2. Great God of fire, in - car - nate flame, Through Christ in whom your love has burned And burns the way for our dark pace On cos - mic routes with - in us turned: Help us be - yond at - om - ic night; Guide, Lord, in hope our bro - ken race.

3. Lord of the at - om, we praise your might, Ex - pressed in ter - ri - fy - ing light; Be - fore us rise the flames as pyres, Or bursts of love – they blind our sight. Help us, our Lord, oh, help us see New forms of peace through suf - f'ring fires.

Text: George Utech, b. 1931, ©
Music: Richard Hillert, b. 1923, ©

88 88 88
SOURCE

611 O Jesus Christ, May Grateful Hymns Be Rising

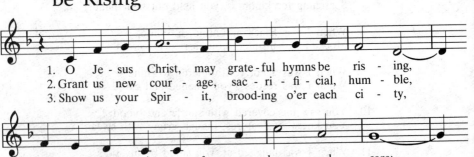

1. O Je - sus Christ, may grate - ful hymns be ris - ing, In ev - 'ry ci - ty for your love and care;

2. Grant us new cour - age, sac - ri - fi - cial, hum - ble, Strong in your strength to ven - ture and to dare;

3. Show us your Spir - it, brood-ing o'er each ci - ty, As you once wept a - bove Je - ru - sa - lem,

In - spire our wor - ship, grant the glad sur - pris - ing
To lift the fall - en, guide the feet that stum - ble,
Seek - ing to gath - er all in love and pi - ty,

That your blest Spir - it rous - es ev - 'ry - where.
Seek out the lone - ly and God's mer - cy share.
And heal - ing those who touch your gar - ment's hem.

Text: Bradford Gray Webster, b. 1898, alt., ©
Music: David Evans, 1874–1948, ©

11 10 11 10
CHARTERHOUSE

Lord of All Nations, Grant Me Grace 612

1. Lord of all na - tions, grant me grace To love all
2. Break down the wall that would di - vide Your chil - dren,
3. For - give me, Lord, where I have erred By love - less
4. Give me your cour - age, Lord, to speak When - ev - er

peo - ple, ev - 'ry race: To see each mor - tal as I
Lord, on ev - 'ry side. My neigh-bor's good let me pur -
act and thought-less word. Make me to see the wrong I
strong op - press the weak. Should I my - self as vic - tim

ought, My kin - dred, whom your love has bought.
sue, Let Chris - tian love bind warm and true.
do Will cru - ci - fy my Lord a - new.
live, Re - mem - b'ring you, may I for - give.

5. With your own love may I be filled
And by your Holy Spirit willed,
That all whose lives are touched by mine,
May know your healing touch divine.

Text: Philippians 2:1–18; Olive W. Spannaus, b. 1916, alt., ©
Music: Samotulsky Kancional, Slovak, 1561; harm. Richard Hillert, b. 1923, ©

88 88
BEATUS VIR

613 The Church of Christ in Every Age

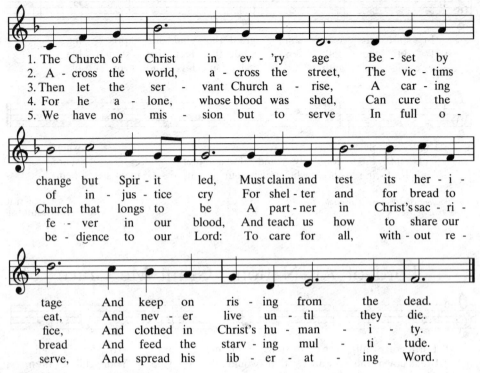

1. The Church of Christ in ev - 'ry age Be - set by
2. A - cross the world, a - cross the street, The vic - tims
3. Then let the ser - vant Church a - rise, A car - ing
4. For he a - lone, whose blood was shed, Can cure the
5. We have no mis - sion but to serve In full o -

change but Spir - it led, Must claim and test its her - i -
of in - jus - tice cry For shel - ter and for bread to
Church that longs to be A part - ner in Christ's sac - ri -
fe - ver in our blood, And teach us how to share our
be - dience to our Lord: To care for all, with - out re -

tage And keep on ris - ing from the dead.
eat, And nev - er live un - til they die.
fice, And clothed in Christ's hu - man - i - ty.
bread And feed the starv - ing mul - ti - tude.
serve, And spread his lib - er - at - ing Word.

Text: Fred Pratt Green, b. 1903
Music: Vernon Griffiths, 1894–1985, ©

88 88
DUNEDIN

Text © 1971, Hope Publishing Co.

614 We've Come to Hear

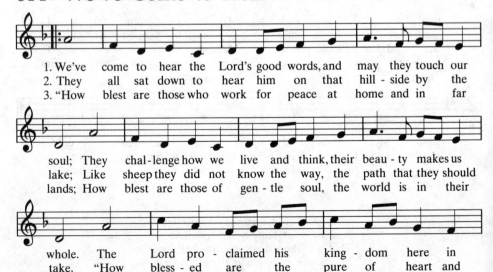

1. We've come to hear the Lord's good words, and may they touch our
2. They all sat down to hear him on that hill - side by the
3. "How blest are those who work for peace at home and in far

soul; They chal - lenge how we live and think, their beau - ty makes us
lake; Like sheep they did not know the way, the path that they should
lands; How blest are those of gen - tle soul, the world is in their

whole. The Lord pro - claimed his king - dom here in
take. "How bless - ed are the pure of heart and
hands; And blest are those who mer - cy show for

words both clear and strong. No place with - in that
bless - ed are the poor; And all who thirst for
they shall mer - cy find; And those who suf - fer

king - dom now for self - ish - ness and wrong!
jus - tice find their hap - pi - ness is sure!
for the right will see the Lord is kind!"

Text: Willard F. Jabusch, b. 1930, ©
Music: Willard F. Jabusch, b. 1930, ©

86 86 86 86

With Jesus for Hero 615

1. With Je - sus for he - ro, for teach - er and friend,
2. His king - dom is com - ing, God's will shall be done,
3. God's name shall be hal - lowed, his love un - der - stood,
4. To God be the glo - ry, to Christ be the praise,

The world to the pur - pose of God shall as - cend:
And kind - ness and jus - tice and peace shall be won;
The Fa - ther pro - tect - ing the wise and the good:
To God be our ser - vice, in Christ be our ways:

We strug - gle and quar - rel, but he brings re - lease,
Then learn we that gos - pel of love to o - bey,
All peo - ple shall see him in truth as he is,
O Spir - it e - ter - nal, in you be our rest,

And shows us the way to his wis - dom and peace.
Till sick - ness and want and dis - putes pass a - way.
The heart of the world shall for - ev - er be his.
Be - yond us, with - in us, our goal and our guest!

Text: Percy Dearmer, 1867–1936, ©
Music: Gaelic tune; harm. Richard Proulx, b. 1937, ©

11 11 11 11
SIOBAN NI LAOGHAIRE

616 The Voice of God Speaks But of Peace

1. The voice of God speaks but of peace;
2. Mer - cy and faith - ful - ness have met,
3. The Lord shall bless our dai - ly work;

Peace for all his friends. For those who
Jus - tice and peace em - braced. God's love smiles
Earth shall yield its fruit. Jus - tice shall

turn to him their heart, His help is al - ways near.
up from earth be - low, His jus - tice down from heav'n.
march be - fore the Lord, And peace be - hind his steps.

REFRAIN

Re - store a - gain our life, O Lord, May we re - joice in

Text: Psalm 85; adapt. Henry Bryan Hays, O.S.B., b. 1920, ©
Music: Henry Bryan Hays, O.S.B., b. 1920, ©

85 85 with Refrain
SHALOM

you! Your mer - cy let us see,

O Lord, Give us your sav - ing help.

617 Lord Christ, When First You Came to Earth

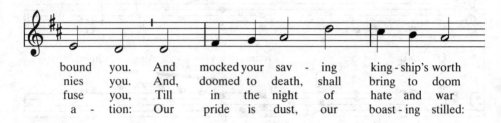

1. Lord Christ, when first you came to earth, Up - on a cross they
2. O awe - some Love, which finds no room In life where sin de -
3. New ad - vent of the love of Christ, Will we a - gain re -
4. O wound - ed hands of Je - sus, build In us your new cre -

bound you. And mocked your sav - ing king - ship's worth
nies you. And, doomed to death, shall bring to doom
fuse you, Till in the night of hate and war
a - tion: Our pride is dust, our boast - ing stilled:

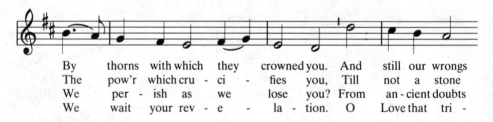

By thorns with which they crowned you. And still our wrongs
The pow'r which cru - ci - fies you, Till not a stone
We per - ish as we lose you? From an - cient doubts
We wait your rev - e - la - tion. O Love that tri -

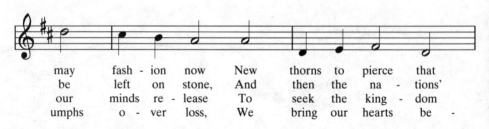

may fash - ion now New thorns to pierce that
be left on stone, And then the na - tions'
our minds re - lease To seek the king - dom
umphs o - ver loss, We bring our hearts be -

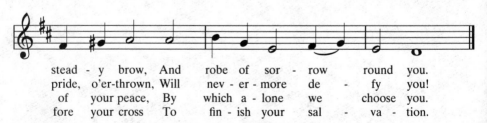

stead - y brow, And robe of sor - row round you.
pride, o'er-thrown, Will nev - er - more de - fy you!
of your peace, By which a - lone we choose you.
fore your cross To fin - ish your sal - va - tion.

Text: Walter Russell Bowie, 1882–1969, alt., ©
Music: Une Pastourelle gentille, 1529, adapt.; harm. Ralph Vaughan Williams, 1872–1958, ©

87 87 887
MIT FREUDEN ZART

When Israel Was in Egypt's Land 618

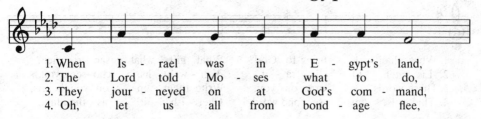

1. When Is - rael was in E - gypt's land,
2. The Lord told Mo - ses what to do,
3. They jour - neyed on at God's com - mand,
4. Oh, let us all from bond - age flee,

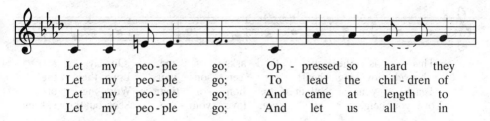

Let my peo - ple go; Op - pressed so hard they
Let my peo - ple go; To lead the chil - dren of
Let my peo - ple go; And came at length to
Let my peo - ple go; And let us all in

could not stand, Let my peo - ple go.
Is - rael through, Let my peo - ple go.
Ca - naan's land, Let my peo - ple go.
Christ be free, Let my peo - ple go.

REFRAIN

Go down, Mo - ses, way down in E - gypt's land;

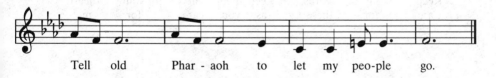

Tell old Phar - aoh to let my peo-ple go.

Text: Afro-American Spiritual
Music: Afro-American Spiritual; harm. from English Praise, 1975, ©

85 85 with Refrain
GO DOWN MOSES

619 What Shall I Bring

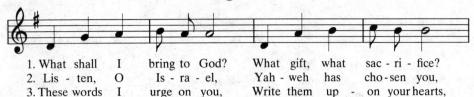

1. What shall I bring to God? What gift, what sac-ri-fice?
2. Lis-ten, O Is-ra-el, Yah-weh has cho-sen you,
3. These words I urge on you, Write them up - on your hearts,
4. This is my sec-ond word, Cher-ish it as the first:

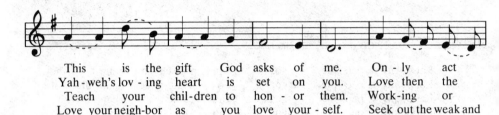

This is the gift God asks of me. On-ly act
Yah-weh's lov-ing heart is set on you. Love then the
Teach your chil-dren to hon-or them. Work-ing or
Love your neigh-bor as you love your-self. Seek out the weak and

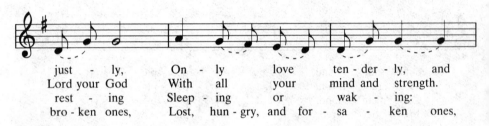

just - ly, On - ly love ten-der-ly, and
Lord your God With all your mind and strength.
rest - ing Sleep-ing or wak - ing:
bro-ken ones, Lost, hun-gry, and for-sa-ken ones,

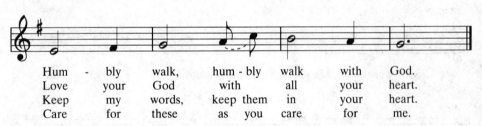

Hum - bly walk, hum-bly walk with God.
Love your God with all your heart.
Keep my words, keep them in your heart.
Care for these as you care for me.

Text: Sr. Kieran Sawyer, S.S.N.D., ©
Music: Czech hymn: harm. Sr. Anita Smisek, O.P. and Joel Blahnik, ©

Irregular
ANDĚLSKYCHLEBE

O Holy City, Seen of John   620

1. O ho-ly cit-y, seen of John, Where Christ, the Lamb, does reign, With-in those four-square walls shall come No night, nor need, nor pain, And where the tears are wiped from eyes That shall not weep a-gain.

2. O shame to us who rest con-tent While lust and greed for gain In street and shop and ten-e-ment Wring gold from hu-man pain, And bit-ter lips in blind de-spair Cry, "Christ has died in vain."

3. Give us, O God, the strength to build The cit-y that has stood Too long a dream, whose laws are love, Whose ways, the com-mon good, And where the shin-ing sun be-comes God's grace for hu-man good.

4. Al-read-y in the mind of God That cit-y ris-es fair: Lo, how its splen-dor chal-leng-es The souls that great-ly dare: Yea, bids us seize the whole of life And build its glo-ry there.

Text: W. Russell Bowie, 1882–1969, alt.
Music: Elkanah Kelsay Dare, 1782–1826; acc. C. Winfred Douglas, 1867–1944, ©

86 86 86
MORNING SONG (CONSOLATION)

621 Our Father, by Whose Name

1. Our Fa - ther, by whose name All par - ent - hood is
2. O Christ, your - self a child With - in an earth - ly
3. O Ho - ly Spir - it, bind Our hearts in u - ni -

known, In love di - vine you claim Each fam - 'ly as your
home, With heart still un - de - filed To full a - dult-hood
ty And teach us how to find The love from self set

own. Bless moth-ers, fa - thers, guard - ing well, With con-stant
come; Our chil-dren bless in ev - 'ry place That they may
free, In all our hearts such love in - crease That ev - 'ry

love as sen - ti - nel, The homes in which your peo - ple dwell.
all be - hold your face And know-ing you may grow in grace.
home, by this re-lease, May be the dwell-ing - place of peace.

Text: F. Bland Tucker, 1895–1984, ©
Music: John Edwards, 1806–1885, ©

66 66 888
RHOSYMEDRE

When Christ Was Lifted From the Earth 622

1. When Christ was lift - ed from the earth, His arms stretched out a - bove Through ev - 'ry birth, To draw an an - swering love.
2. Still east and west his love ex - tends And al - ways, near or far, He calls and claims us as his friends And loves us as we are.
3. Where gen - er - a - tion, class, or race Di - vide us to our shame, He sees not la - bels but a face, A per - son, and a name.
4. Thus free - ly loved, though ful - ly known, May I in Christ be free To wel - come and ac - cept his own As Christ ac - cept - ed me.

Text: Brian A. Wren, b. 1936
Music: Gordon Slater, 1896–1979, ©

Text © 1980, Hope Publishing Company

86 86
ST. BOTOLPH

This Day at Thy Creating Word 623

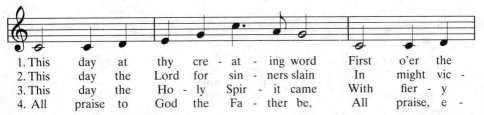

1. This	day	at	thy	cre - at - ing word	First	o'er	the
2. This	day	the	Lord	for	sin - ners slain	In	might	vic -
3. This	day	the	Ho - ly	Spir - it came	With	fier -	y
4. All	praise	to	God	the	Fa - ther be,	All	praise,	e -

earth	the	light	was poured;	O	Lord, this	day	up - on	us	shine And
to - rious rose	a - gain;	O	Je - sus,	may	we	lift - ed	be From
tongues of	clo - ven flame;	O	Spir - it,	fill	our hearts this day With
ter - nal	Son,	to	thee,	Whom, with the	Spir - it,	we	a - dore For

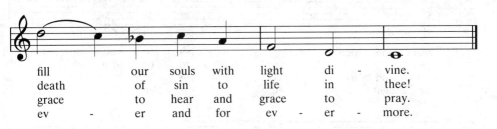

fill	our	souls	with	light	di	-	vine.
death	of	sin	to	life	in		thee!
grace	to	hear	and	grace	to		pray.
ev	-	er	and	for	ev	- er -	more.

Alt. Tunes: On Jordan's Bank, no. 182, This is My Will, no. 480
Text: William Walsham How, 1823–1897, alt.
Music: Henry G. Ley, 1887–1962, ©

88 88
RUSHFORD

624 Gather Us In

1. Here in this place, new light is stream-ing,
2. We are the young our lives are a mys-t'ry,
3. Here we will take the wine and the wa-ter,
4. Not in the dark of build-ings con-fin-ing,

now is the dark-ness van-ished a-way, See, in this space, our
we are the old who yearn for your face, We have been sung through-
here we will take the bread of new birth, Here you shall call your
not in some heav-en, light years a-way, but here in this place, the

fears and our dream-ings, brought here to you in the
out all of his-t'ry, called to be light to the
sons and your daugh-ters, call us a-new to be
new light is shin-ing, now is the king-dom,

light of this day.
whole hu-man race.
salt for the earth.
now is the day.

Ga-ther us in, the lost and for-sa-ken,
Ga-ther us in, the rich and the haugh-ty,
Give us to drink the wine of com-pas-sion,
Ga-ther us in and hold us for-ev-er,

Ga-ther us in, the blind and the lame; Call to us now, and
Ga-ther us in, the proud and the strong; Give us a heart so
Give us to eat the bread that is you; Nour-ish us well, and
Ga-ther us in and make us your own; Ga-ther us in, all

Text: Marty Haugen, b. 1952, ©
Music: Marty Haugen, b. 1952, ©

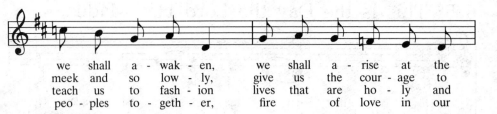

we	shall	a -	wak - en,	we	shall	a -	rise	at	the
meek	and	so	low - ly,	give	us	the	cour - age	to
teach	us	to	fash - ion	lives	that	are	ho - ly	and
peo -	ples	to -	geth - er,	fire	of	love	in	our

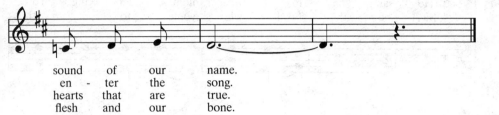

sound	of	our	name.
en -	ter	the	song.
hearts	that	are	true.
flesh	and	our	bone.

625 This Is the Day the Lord Has Made

1. This is the day the Lord has made; He
2. To - day he rose and left the tomb, And
3. Ho - san - na to th'a - noint - ed King, To
4. Blest be the Lord who comes to all With

calls the hours his own; Let heav'n re - joice, let
con - quered death and sin. Let all the saints with
Da - vid's ho - ly Son, Make haste to help us,
mes - sag - es of grace; Who comes, in God his

earth be glad, And praise sur - round his throne.
joy pro - claim The vic - t'ry he did win.
Lord, and send Sal - va - tion from your throne.
Fa - ther's name, To save our sin - ful race.

5. "Hosanna" in the highest strains
   The Church on earth shall raise;
   The highest heav'ns in which he reigns
   Shall give him nobler praise.

6. O give all praise this holy day
   To God, the Three in One,
   To Father, Son, and Spirit blest,
   Who reign while ages run.

Text: Isaac Watts, 1674–1748
Music: A Collection of Hymns and Sacred Poems, Dublin, 1749

86 86
IRISH

Come, You Thankful People, Come 626

1. Come, you thank-ful peo - ple, come, Raise the song of har - vest home:
2. All the world is God's own field, Fruit un - to his praise to yield;
3. For the Lord our God shall come, And shall take his har - vest home;
4. E - ven so, Lord, quick - ly come To your fi - nal har - vest home;

All is safe - ly gath - ered in, Ere the win - ter storms be - gin;
Wheat and tares to - geth - er sown, Un - to joy or sor - row grown:
From his field shall in that day All of - fens - es purge a - way;
Gath - er all your peo - ple in, Free from sor - row, free from sin;

God, our Mak - er, does pro - vide For our wants to be sup - plied;
First the blade, and then the ear, Then the full corn shall ap - pear:
Give his an - gels charge at last In the fire the tares to cast,
There, for ev - er pu - ri - fied, In your pres-ence to a - bide:

Come to God's own tem - ple, come, Raise the song of har-vest home.
Grant, O har - vest Lord, that we Whole-some grain and pure may be.
But the fruit - ful ears to store In his gar - ner ev - er - more.
Come, with all your an - gels, come, Raise the glo-rious har-vest home.

Text: Henry Alford, 1810–1871
Music: George Elvey, 1816–1893, ©

77 77 77 77
ST. GEORGE'S WINDSOR

627 Thanksgiving Carol

1. Fields of corn, give up your ears, Now your ears are heav - y,
2. Vines, send in your bunch of grapes, Now the bunch is clus - tered,
3. Gar - den, give your gay - est flow'rs, Hedge, your wild - est bring in,

Wheat and oats and bar - ley - spears, All your har - vest - le - vy.
Be your gold and pur - ple shapes Round the al - tar mus - tered.
Turn the church - es in - to bow'rs Lit - tle birds shall sing in.

Where your sheaves of plen - ty lean, we once more the
Where the hang - ing bunch - es shine we once more shall
Where the chil - dren sing their glee we once more the

grain shall glean Of the ev - er - liv - ing,
taste the wine Of the ev - er - liv - ing,
flow'r shall see Of the ev - er - liv - ing,

Text: Der Tag, der ist so freudenreich, tr. Eleanor Farjeon, 1881–1965, ©
Music: German carol 15th c.; harm. Geoffrey Shaw, ©

God the Lord will bless the field, Bring-ing in its
God the Lord will bless the root, Bring-ing in its
God the Lord will bless the throng, Lift-ing up its

au - tumn yield glad - ly to thanks - giv - ing.
au - tumn fruit glad - ly to thanks - giv - ing.
au - tumn song glad - ly to thanks - giv - ing.

628 We Plow the Fields and Scatter

1. We plow the fields and scat - ter The good seed on the land, But it is fed and wa - tered By God's al - might - y hand; He sends the snow in win - ter, The
2. He on - ly is the Mak - er Of all things near and far; He paints the way - side flow - er, He lights the eve - ning star. The winds and waves o - bey him, By
3. We thank you, then, dear Fa - ther, For all things bright and good: The seed - time and the har - vest, Our life, our health, our food. And all that we can of - fer Your

Text: Matthias Claudius, 1740–1815; tr. Jane Montgomery Campbell, 1817–1878
Music: Johann Abraham Peter Schulz, 1747–1800, attr.

76 76 76 76
WIR PFLUGEN

warmth to swell the grain, The breez - es and the
him the birds are fed: Much more to us his
bound - less love im - parts, The gifts to you most

sun - shine, And soft re - fresh - ing rain:
chil - dren, He gives our dai - ly bread:
pleas - ing Are hum - ble, thank - ful hearts:

REFRAIN

All good gifts a - round us Are sent from heav'n a - bove, So

thank the Lord, O thank the Lord For all his love.

629 God, Whose Farm Is All Creation

1. God, whose farm is all cre - a - tion,
Take the grat - i - tude we give;
Take the fin - est of our har - vest,
Crops we grow that all may live.

2. Take our plow - ing, seed - ing, reap - ing,
Hopes and fears of sun and rain,
All our think - ing, plan - ning, wait - ing,
Rip - ened in this fruit and grain.

3. All our la - bor, all our watch - ing,
All our cal - en - dar of care,
In these crops of your cre - a - tion,
Take, O God: they are our prayer.

Text: John Arlott, b. 1914, ©
Music: English Traditional Melody; harm. Ralph Vaughan Williams, 1872–1958, ©

87 87
SHIPSTON

Sing to the Lord of Harvest 630

1. Sing to the Lord of har - vest, Sing songs of love and praise;
2. God makes the clouds drop fat - ness, The des-erts bloom and spring,
3. Bring to this sa - cred al - tar The gifts his good-ness gave,

With joy - ful hearts and voic - es Your al - le - lu - ias raise.
The hills leap up in glad - ness, The val - leys laugh and sing.
The gold - en sheaves of har - vest, The souls Christ died to save.

By him the roll - ing sea - sons In fruit - ful or - der move;
God fills them with his full - ness, All things with large in - crease;
Your hearts lay down be - fore him When at his feet you fall,

Sing to the Lord of har - vest A joy - ous song of love.
He crowns the year with good - ness, With plen - ty and with peace.
And with your lives a - dore him Who gave his life for all.

Text: John S.B. Monsell, 1811–1875, alt., ©
Music: Johann Steurlein, 1546–1613, ©

76 76 76 76
WIE LIEBLICH IST DER MAIEN

631 Almighty God, Your Word Is Cast

1. Al - might - y God, your word is cast Like
2. Let not our self - ish - ness and hate This
3. Let not the world's de - ceit - ful cares The
4. And when the pre - cious seed is sown Your

seed in - to the ground, Now let the dew of
ho - ly seed re - move, But give it root in
ris - ing plant de - stroy, But let it yield a
quick - 'ning grace be - stow, That all whose souls the

heav'n de - scend And right - eous fruits a - bound.
ev - 'ry heart To bring forth fruits of love.
hun - dred - fold The fruits of peace and joy.
truth re - ceive Its sav - ing pow'r may know.

Text: John Cawood, 1775–1852
Music: Scottish Psalter, 1615; acc. Thomas Ravenscroft, c. 1590–1633

86 86
DUNDEE (FRENCH)

Almighty God, Your Word Is Cast 632

1. Al - might - y God, your word is cast Like
2. Let not our self - ish - ness and hate This
3. Let not the world's de - ceit - ful cares The
4. And when the pre - cious seed is sown Your

seed in - to the ground, Now let the dew of
ho - ly seed re - move, But give it root in
ris - ing plant de - stroy, But let it yield a
quick-'ning grace be - stow, That all whose souls the

heav'n de - scend And right - eous fruits a - bound.
ev - 'ry heart To bring forth fruits of love.
hun - dred - fold The fruits of peace and joy.
truth re - ceive Its sav - ing pow'r may know.

Text: John Cawood, 1775–1852
Music: Jane Manton Marshall, b. 1924, ©

86 86
WALDEN

633 Battle Hymn of the Republic

1. Mine eyes have seen the glo - ry of the
2. I have seen him in the watch - fires of a
3. He has sound - ed forth the trum - pet that shall
4. In the beau - ty of the lil - ies Christ was

com - ing of the Lord; He is tram - pling out the
hun - dred cir - cling camps; They have build - ed him an
nev - er call re - treat; He is sift - ing out all
born a - cross the sea, With a glo - ry in his

vin - tage where the grapes of wrath are stored; He has
al - tar in the eve - ning dews and damps; I can
hu - man hearts be - fore his judg - ment seat; O be
bos - om that trans - fig - ures you and me; As he

loosed the fate - ful light - ning of his ter - ri - ble swift
read the right - eous sen - tence by the dim and flar - ing
swift, my soul, to an - swer him; be ju - bi - lant, my
died to make us ho - ly, let us die that all be

Text: Julia Ward Howe, 1819–1910
Music: John William Steffe, ca. 1911, attr.

15 15 15 6 with Refrain
BATTLE HYMN OF THE REPUBLIC

sword; His truth is march - ing on.
lamps; His day is march - ing on.
feet! Our God is march - ing on.
free! While God is march - ing on.

REFRAIN

Glo - ry! Glo - ry! Hal - le - lu - jah! Glo - ry!

Glo - ry! Hal - le - lu - jah! Glo - ry! Glo - ry! Hal - le -

lu - jah! His truth is march - ing on.

634 Faith of Our Fathers

1. Faith of our fa - thers! liv - ing still
2. Our fa - thers, chained in pris - ons dark,
3. Faith of our fa - thers! Mar - y's prayers
4. Faith of our fa - thers! we will love

In spite of dun - geon, fire, and sword;
Were still in heart and con - science free:
Shall win our coun - try un - to thee;
Both friend and foe in all our strife,

Oh, how our hearts beat high with joy
And blest would be their chil - dren's fate,
And through the truth that comes from God
And preach thee, too, as love knows how,

When - e'er we hear that glo - rious word:
If we, like them, should die for thee!
Our peo - ple shall be tru - ly free:
By kind - ly deeds and vir - tuous life:

Alt. Tune: Before Thy Throne, O God, We Kneel, no. 600
Text: Frederick Wm. Faber, C.O., 1814–1868, alt.
Music: Henry Frederick Hemy, 1818–1888; adapt. and arr., James George Walton
1821–1905

88 88 88
ST. CATHERINE (TYNEMOUTH)

REFRAIN

Faith of our fa - thers, ho - ly faith!

We will be true to thee till death.

635 Go Make of All Disciples

Text: Leon M. Adkins, b. 1896, alt., ©
Music: Gesangbuch de Herzogl, Wirtemberg, 1784

Text: Copyright ©, 1955, 1964, Abingdon Press. From THE BOOK OF HYMNS

76 76 76 76
ELLACOMBE

dai - ly   liv - ing   Re - veal   you   ev - 'ry - where.
soul and   bod - y   By   wa - ter   and the   Word.
in our   wit - ness   The   Mas - ter   Teach-er's   art.
earth your   pow - er   Shall   bring God's   king - dom   here.

636 God of Mercy, God of Grace

1. God of mer - cy, God of grace, Show the bright - ness of thy face. Shine up - on us, Sav - ior, shine, Fill thy Church with light di - vine, And thy sav - ing health ex - tend Un - to earth's re - mot - est end.

2. Let the peo - ple praise thee, Lord; Be by all that live a - dored. Let the na - tions shout and sing: Glo - ry to their Sav - ior King! At thy feet their tri - bute pay And thy ho - ly will o - bey.

3. Let the peo - ple praise thee, Lord; Earth shall then her fruits af - ford. God to us a bless - ing give, We to God de - vot - ed live; All be - low, and all a - bove, One in joy and light and love.

Text: H.F. Lyte, 1793–1847; Psalm 67; para., alt.
Music: Johann Gottlob Werner, 1777–1822

77 77 77
RATISBON

God of Mercy, God of Grace 637

1. God of mer - cy, God of grace, Show the bright - ness of thy
2. Let the peo - ple praise thee, Lord; Be by all that live a -
3. Let the peo - ple praise thee, Lord; Earth shall then her fruits af -

face. Shine up - on us, Sav - ior, shine, Fill thy
dored. Let the na - tions shout and sing: Glo - ry
ford. God to us a bless - ing give, We to

Church with light di - vine, And thy sav - ing health ex -
to their Sav - ior King! At thy feet their tri - bute
God de - vot - ed live; All be - low, and all a -

tend Un - to earth's re - mot - est end.
pay And thy ho - ly will o - bey.
bove, One in joy and light and love.

Text: Psalm 67; para. H.F. Lyte, 1793–1847, alt.
Music: David Evans, 1874–1948, ©

77 77 77
LUCERNA LAUDONIAE

638 Lord of Light

1. Lord of light, your name out-shin-ing All the stars and suns of space, Use our tal-ents in your king-dom As the ser-vants of your
2. By the toil of faith-ful work-ers In some far out-ly-ing field, By the cour-age where the ra-diance Of the cross is still re-
3. Grant that knowl-edge, still in-creas-ing, At your feet may low-ly kneel; With your grace our tri-umphs hal-low, With your char-i-ty our
4. By the prayers of faith-ful watch-ers, Nev-er si-lent day or night; By the cross of Je-sus, bring-ing Peace to all and heal-ing

Alt. Tune: Alleluia, Sing to Jesus, no. 504

Text: Howell E. Lewis, 1860–1953, alt., ©
Music: Cyril V. Taylor, b. 1907

87 87 87 87
ABBOT'S LEIGH

Music © Hope Publishing Co.

grace; Use us to ful - fill your pur - pose
vealed, By the vic - to - ries of meek - ness,
zeal; Lift the na - tions from the shad - ows
light; By the love that pass - es knowl-edge,

In the gift of Christ your Son:
Through re - proach and suf - f'ring won:
To the glad - ness of the sun:
Mak - ing all your chil - dren one:

REFRAIN

Fa - ther, as in high - est heav - en,

So on earth your will be done.

639 Lord, You Give the Great Commission

1. Lord, you give the great com - mis - sion:
2. Lord, you call us to your ser - vice:
3. Lord, you make the com - mon ho - ly:
4. Lord, you show us love's true meas - ure:

"Heal the sick and preach the word."
"In my name bap - tize and teach."
"This my bod - y, this my blood."
"Fa - ther, what they do, for - give."

Lest the Church ne - glect its mis - sion,
That the world may trust your pro - mise,
Let us all, for earth's true glo - ry,
Yet we hoard as pri - vate treas - ure

And the Gos - pel go un - heard,
Life a - bun - dant meant for each,
Dai - ly lift life heav - en - ward,
All that you so free - ly give.

Alt. Tune: Alleluia, Sing to Jesus, no. 504

Text: Jeffrey Rowthorn, b. 1934, ©
Music: Cyril V. Taylor, b. 1907

87 87 87 87
ABBOTT'S LEIGH

Help us wit - ness to your pur-pose With re -
Give us all new fer - vor, draw us Clos - er
Ask - ing that the world a - round us Share your
May your care and mer - cy lead us To a

newed in - teg - ri - ty;
in com - mun - i - ty;
chil - dren's lib - er - ty; With the Spir - it's
just so - ci - e - ty;

gifts em - pow'r us For the work of min - is - try.

5. Lord, you bless with words assuring:
   "I am with you to the end."
   Faith and hope and love restoring,
   May we serve as you intend,
   And, amid the cares that claim us,
   Hold in mind eternity;
   With the Spirit's gifts empow'r us
   For the work of ministry.

640 O Spirit of the Living God

1. O Spir-it of the liv-ing God, In all the
2. Give tongues of fire and hearts of love To preach the
3. Be dark-ness, at your com-ing, light; Con-fu-sion,
4. O Spir-it of the Lord, pre-pare A sin-ful

full-ness of your grace, Wher-ev-er hu-man
re-con-cil-ing word; Give pow'r and unc-tion
or-der in your path; Souls with-out strength in-
world its God to meet; And breathe a-broad like

feet have trod, des-cend on our re-bel-lious race.
from a-bove, Wher-e'er this bless-ed sound is heard.
spire with might; Let mer-cy tri-umph o-ver wrath.
morn-ing air, Till hearts of stone be-gin to beat.

5. Proclaim the Gospel far and wide;
   The triumphs of the cross record;
   The name of Christ be glorified;
   Let ev'ry people call him Lord!

Alt. Tune: This Is My Will, no. 480
Text: James Montgomery, 1771–1854, alt.
Music: Percy Carter Buck, 1871–1947, ©

88 88
GONFALON ROYAL

Forth in the Peace of Christ 641

1. Forth in the peace of Christ we go; Christ to the world with joy we bring; Christ in our minds, Christ on our lips, Christ in our hearts, the world's true King.

2. Priests of the world, Christ sends us forth The world of time to con - se - crate, This world of sin by grace to heal, Christ's world in Christ to re - cre - ate.

3. Christ's are our lips, his word we speak; Proph - ets are we whose deeds pro - claim Christ's truth in love that we may be Christ in the world to spread Christ's name.

4. We are the Church; Christ bids us show That in his Church all na - tions find Their hearth and home where Christ re - stores True peace, true love, to hu - man - kind.

Text: James Quinn, S.J., b. 1919, © 1969
Music: Welsh Caniadan y Cyssegr, 1893

88 88
LLEDROD

642 God Is Working His Purpose Out

1. God is work-ing his pur-pose out As
2. From ut-most east to ut-most west, Wher-
3. March we forth in the strength of God, With the
4. All we can do is worth-less toil Un-

year suc-ceeds to year: God is work-ing his
ev-er foot has trod, By the mouth of man-y
ban-ner of Christ un-furled, That the light of the glo-rious
less God bless-es the deed; Vain-ly we hope for the

pur-pose out, And the time is draw-ing near;
mes-sen-gers Goes forth the voice of God;
gos-pel of truth May shine through-out the world:
har-vest-tide Till God gives life to the seed; Yet

Near-er and near-er draws the time, The time that shall sure-ly
Give ear to me, you con-ti-nents, You isles, give ear to
Fight we the fight with sor-row and sin To set their cap-tives
near-er and near-er draws the time, The time that shall sure-ly

be, When the earth shall be filled with the glo-ry of God As the
me, That the earth may be filled with the glo-ry of God As the
free, That the earth may be filled with the glo-ry of God As the
be, When the earth shall be filled with the glo-ry of God As the

1.–3.
wa-ters cov-er the sea.
wa-ters cov-er the sea.
wa-ters cov-er the sea.

4.
wa-ters cov-er the sea.

Text: Arthur C. Ainger, 1841–1919, alt.
Music: Martin Shaw, 1875–1958, ©

Irregular
PURPOSE

We Are the Light of the World 643

1. Bless - ed are they who are poor in spir - it,
2. Bless - ed are they who are meek and hum - ble,
3. Bless - ed are they who will mourn in sor - row,
4. Bless those who hun - ger and thirst for jus - tice,

Theirs is the king - dom of God. Bless us, O
They will in - her - it the earth. Bless us, O
They will be com - fort - ed. Bless us, O
They will be sat - is - fied. Bless us, O

Lord, make us poor in spir - it; Bless us, O Lord, our God.
Lord, make us meek and hum-ble; Bless us, O Lord, our God.
Lord, when we share their sor - row; Bless us, O Lord, our God.
Lord, hear our cry for mer - cy; Bless us, O Lord, our God.

REFRAIN

We are the light of the world; May our light shine be - fore all,

That they may see the good that we do, And give glo - ry to God.

5. Blessed are they who show others
   mercy,
   They will know mercy, too.
   Bless us, O Lord, hear our cry
   for mercy;
   Bless us, O Lord, our God.
   Refrain

6. Blessed are hearts that are clean
   and holy,
   They will behold the Lord,
   Bless us, O Lord, make us pure
   and holy;
   Bless us, O Lord, our God.
   Refrain

7. Blessed are they who bring peace
   among us,
   They are the children of God.
   Bless us, O Lord, may your
   peace be with us;
   Bless us, O Lord, our God.
   Refrain

8. Bless those who suffer from
   persecution,
   Theirs is the kingdom of God.
   Bless us, O Lord, when they
   persecute us;
   Bless us, O Lord, our God.
   Refrain

Text: Jean Anthony Greif, 1898–1981, ©
Music: Jean Anthony Greif, 1898–1981, ©

644 Amid the World's Bleak Wilderness

1. A - mid the world's bleak wil - der-ness A
2. His love se - lect - ed this ter - rain; His
3. We are his branch - es, cho - sen, dear, And
4. From him we draw the juice of life, For

vine - yard grows with prom - ise green,
vine with love he plant - ed here
though we feel the dress - er's knife,
him sup - ply his win - er - y

The plant - ing of the Lord him - self.
To bear the choic - est fruit for him.
We are the ob - jects of his care.
With fruit from which true joys de - rive.

VERSE 5

Vine, keep what I was meant to be: Your

branch, with your rich life in me.

Text: Jaroslav J. Vajda, b. 1919, ©
Music: Richard W. Hillert, b. 1923, ©

888
GRANTON

645 If Anyone Would Follow

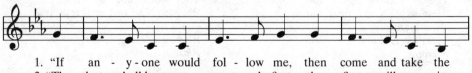

1. "If an - y - one would fol - low me, then come and take the
2. "The last shall be ac - count - ed first, the first will come in
3. How strange, yet good, sound Je - sus' words, what wis - dom they con -

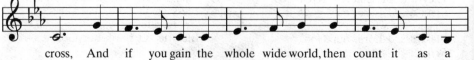

cross, And if you gain the whole wide world, then count it as a
last; The poor will eat at heav - en's feast, the rich will have to
tain; They touch our souls all parched and bleak like sum - mer's heal - ing

loss." His words are hard, a - gainst the grain and yet they still com -
fast." Who give their lives for Je - sus' sake will live to share his
rain. No eas - y grace he of - fers us to lull a laz - y

pel To fol - low Christ, to seek his way, and ev - 'ry-thing to sell.
joy, But what the world con - sid - ers great is like an in-fant's toy.
mind; His words of chal-lenge, words of hope, are of a bet-ter kind.

Text: Willard F. Jabusch, b. 1930, ©
Music: American Melody; acc. S.R. Rudeki, b. 1928, ©   **86 86 86 86**

God Is My Strong Salvation 646

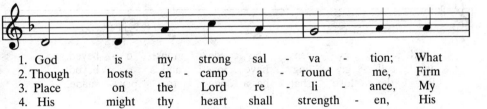

1. God   is   my   strong   sal - va - tion;   What
2. Though   hosts   en - camp   a - round   me,   Firm
3. Place   on   the   Lord   re - li - ance,   My
4. His   might thy   heart   shall   strength - en,   His

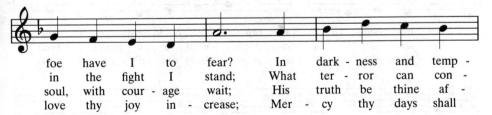

foe   have   I   to   fear?   In   dark - ness   and   temp -
in   the   fight   I   stand;   What   ter - ror   can   con -
soul, with cour - age   wait;   His   truth   be   thine   af -
love   thy   joy   in - crease;   Mer - cy   thy   days   shall

ta - tion My light, my help is near.
found me, With God at my right hand?
fi - ance, When faint and des - o - late.
length - en; The Lord will give thee peace.

Text: James Montgomery, 1771–1854; Psalm 27, para.
Music: Henry Bryan Hays, O.S.B., b. 1920, ©   **76 76**
                                                                    DINWIDDIE

647 When Jesus Came Preaching The Kingdom of God

1. When Je - sus came preach - ing the King-dom of God
2. Since Je - sus came preach - ing the King-dom of God,
3. Still Je - sus comes preach - ing the King-dom of God

With the love that has pow'r to per - suade,
What a change in our lives he has made!
In a world that is sick and a - fraid:

The sick were made whole, both in bod - y and soul,
How man - y have shared in the joy of their Lord.
His gos - pel has spread like the leav - en in bread

And ev - en the de - mons o - beyed.
In self - giv - ing have loved and o - beyed!
By the love that has a pow'r to per - suade.

But he need - ed a few he could trust to be true,
But let none of us doubt what re - li - gion's a - bout,
So let none of us swerve from our mis - sion to serve.

To share in his work from the start:
Or by what it is shamed and be - trayed:
That has made us his Church from the start,

When Je - sus came preach-ing the King - dom of God.
Do just - ly, love mer - cy, walk hum - bly with God.
May Je - sus, the light of the world, send us out

God's gift to the hum-ble of heart.
Is the rule of life Je-sus o-beyed.
In the strength of the hum-ble of heart.

Text: Fred Pratt Green, b. 1903
Music: Richard Hillert, b. 1923, ©

Text © 1974, Hope Publishing Co.

118 118 118 118
KINGDOM OF GOD

We're Called to Be Disciples 648

1. We're called to be dis - ci - ples of Je - sus Christ, our King;
2. He came to bring his free - dom to all who sit in chains;
3. He gave to us a gos - pel, a won-drous thing to speak,

We have a no - ble rea - son to cel - e - brate and sing.
He brings the sick and wound - ed an oint-ment for their pains;
Re - fresh-ment for the wear - y and cour - age for the weak;

We're called to spread his king - dom, that is our no - ble
His words can mean sal - va - tion, the words that we re -
The sad will have true glad - ness, the cap - tive a re -

call, our call, To tell an anx-ious peo - ple that Je - sus died for all!
peat, re-peat, And give us hope for mer - cy be-fore the judg-ment seat,
lease, re-lease, To walk a-gain in free-dom and fol-low ways of peace.

To tell an anx-ious peo - ple that Je - sus died for all!
And give us hope for mer - cy be - fore the judg-ment seat.
To walk a - gain in free - dom and fol - low ways of peace.

Text: Willard F. Jabusch, b. 1930, ©
Music: German Melody; acc. S.R. Rudcki, b. 1928, ©

76 76 76 76

649 Lord, When You Came /
Pescador de Hombres

VERSES

1. Lord, when you came to the sea - shore You weren't
2. Lord, you knew what my boat car - ried: Nei - ther
1. *Tú has ve - ni - do a la o - ri - lla, no has bus -*
2. *Tú sa - bes bien lo que ten - go, en mi*

seek - ing the wise or the wealth-y, But on - ly ask - ing
mon - ey nor weap-ons for fight - ing, But nets for fish - ing,
ca - do ni a sa - bios, ni a ri - cos, tan só - lo quie - res
bar - ca no hay o - ro ni es - pa - das, tan só - lo re - des

REFRAIN

that I might fol - low. O Lord, in my eyes you were
my dai - ly la - bor.
que yo te si - ga. Se - ñor, me has mi - ra - do a los
y mi tra - ba - jo.

gaz - ing, Kind - ly smil - ing, my name you were say - ing;
o - jos, son - ri - en - do has di - cho mi nom - bre,

All I treas - ured, I have left on the sand there;
en la a - re - na he de - ja - do mi bar - ca,

D.S.

Close to you, I will find oth - er seas.
jun - to a tí bus - ca - re o - tro - mar.

Text: Cesareo Gabarain (Spanish Text), Willard F. Jabusch, b. 1930 (English), ©
Music: Cesareo Gabarain, arr. Robert E. Kreutz, b. 1922

Spanish Text and Music © 1979, Ediciones Paulinas, Spain; Keyboard & Flute Arrangement © 1983, Oregon Catholic Press

3. Lord, have you need of my labor,
   Hands for service, a heart made
      for loving,
   My arms for lifting the poor and broken?
   Refrain

3. *Tú necesitas mis manos,*
   mi cansancio que a otros descanse,
   amor que quiera seguir amando.
   Refrain

4. Lord, send me where you
      would have me,
   To a village, or heart of the city;
   I will remember that you are with me.
   Refrain

4. *Tú pescador de otros, mares,*
   ansia eterna, almas que esperan.
   Amigo bueno, que a-sí me llamas.
   Refrain

In Christ There Is No East or West 650

1. In Christ there is no east or west, In him no south or north, But one great fel-low-ship of love, Through-out the whole wide earth.
2. Join hands, dis-ci-ples of the faith, What-e'er your race may be! Who serves my Fa-ther as his child Is sure-ly kin to me.
3. In Christ now meet both east and west, In him meet south and north, All Christ-ly souls are one in him, Through-out the whole wide earth.

Text: John Oxenham, 1852–1941, alt., ©
Music: Afro-American Spiritual; adapt. and arr. Harry T. Burleigh, 1866–1949, ©

86 86
MCKEE

651 Take Up Your Cross

1. Take up your cross, the Sav - ior said, If you would
2. Take up your cross, let not its weight Fill your weak
3. Take up your cross, heed not the shame, And let your
4. Take up your cross, then, in his strength, And calm - ly

my dis - ci - ple be; Take up your cross with will - ing
spir - it with a - larm; His strength shall bear your spir - it
fool - ish heart be still; The Lord for you ac - cept - ed
ev - 'ry dan - ger brave: It guides you to a bet - ter

heart, And hum - bly fol - low af - ter me.
up, And brace your heart, and nerve your arm.
death Up - on a cross, on Cal - v'ry's hill.
home And leads to vic - t'ry o'er the grave.

5. Take up your cross, and follow Christ,
   Nor think till death to lay it down;
   For only those who bear the cross
   May hope to wear the glorious crown.

Alt. Tune: O Christ Our True and Only Light, no. 456

Text: Charles William Everest, 1814–1877
Music: Felix Mendelssohn-Bartholdy, 1809–1847, attr.

88 88
BRESLAU

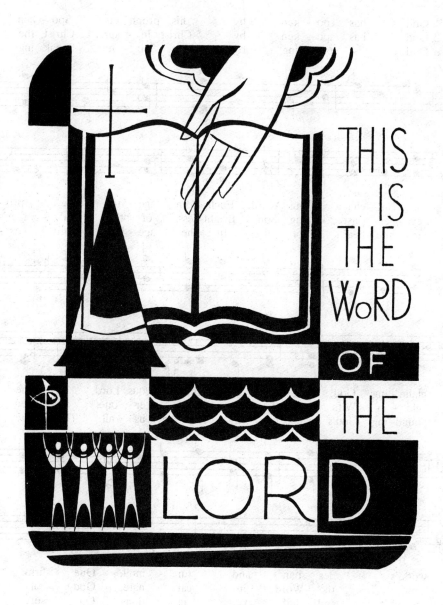

THIS
IS
THE
WORD
OF
THE
LORD

652 God Has Spoken by His Prophets

1. God has spo - ken by his proph - ets, Spo - ken
his un - chang - ing Word; Each from age to age pro -
claim - ing God, the one, the right - eous Lord. In the
world's de - pair and tur - moil, One firm

2. God has spo - ken by Christ Je - sus, Christ, the
ev - er - last - ing Son, Bright-ness of the Fa - ther's
glo - ry, With the Fa - ther ev - er one; Spo - ken
by the Word in - car - nate, God of

3. God is speak - ing by his Spir - it, Speak - ing
to the hearts of all, In the age - less Word ex -
pound - ing God's own mes - sage for us all. Through the
rise and fall of na - tions One sure

Text: George W. Briggs, 1875–1959, alt., ©
Music: Charles H. H. Parry, 1848–1918, ©

87 87 87 87
RUSTINGTON

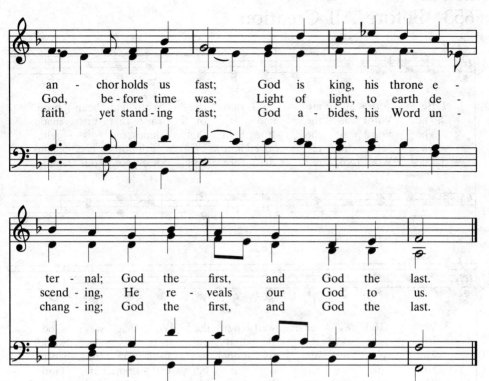

an - chor holds us fast; God is king, his throne e -
God, be - fore time was; Light of light, to earth de -
faith yet stand - ing fast; God a - bides, his Word un -

ter - nal; God the first, and God the last.
scend - ing, He re - veals our God to us.
chang - ing; God the first, and God the last.

653 Before All Creation

1. Be - fore all cre - a - tion the Word had been born,
2. The Word was the mak - er of all that was made;
3. The Word was the true light that shines on us all.
4. To all who re - ceived him by faith in his name
5. The Word took our na - ture and dwelt in our midst,

With God ev - er dwell - ing, the Word that was God.
In him was the life that en - light - ens the world.
The world knew him not, though he dwelt in the world;
His gift was the pow'r to be chil - dren of God,
The pre - sence of God in his tem - ple of flesh.

Be - fore the be - gin - ning, when time was not yet,
The light shines in dark - ness, and dark - ness is gone.
The world of his mak - ing its Mak - er dis - owned;
Of blood not be - got - ten, nor will of the flesh,
We saw him in glo - ry as God's on - ly Son,

Text: James D. Quinn, S.J., b. 1919, © 1969, 1988
Music: Irish Traditional Melody; arr. Robert S. Ross

11 11 11 11
COLUMCILLE (2)

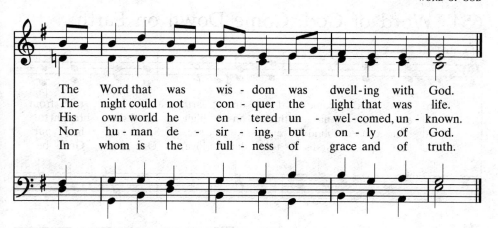

The Word that was wis - dom was dwell - ing with God.
The night could not con - quer the light that was life.
His own world he en - tered un - wel - comed, un - known.
Nor hu - man de - sir - ing, but on - ly of God.
In whom is the full - ness of grace and of truth.

654 Word of God, Come Down on Earth

1. Word of God, come down on earth, Liv-ing rain from
2. Word e-ter-nal, throned on high, Word that brought to
3. Word that caused blind eyes to see, Speak and heal our
4. Word that speaks God's ten-der love, One with God be-

heav'n de-scend-ing; Touch our hearts and bring to birth
life cre-a-tion, Word that came from heav'n to die,
mor-tal blind-ness; Deaf we are: our heal-er be;
yond all tell-ing, Word that sends us from a-bove,

Faith and hope and love un-end-ing. Word al-might-y,
Cru-ci-fied for our sal-va-tion, Sav-ing Word, the
Loose our tongues to tell your kind-ness. Be our Word in
God the Spir-it, with us dwell-ing, Word of truth, to

we re-vere you; Word made flesh, we long to hear you.
world re-stor-ing, Speak to us, your love out-pour-ing.
pit-y spo-ken, Heal the world, by our sin bro-ken.
all truth lead us, Word of life, with one Bread feed us.

Text: James Quinn, S.J., b. 1919, © 1969
Music: Johann R. Ahle, 1625–1673; arr. George H. Palmer, 1846–1926

78 78 88
LIEBSTER JESU

Alternative Text

Blessed Jesus, At Thy Word 655

1. Blessed Jesus, at thy word
   We are gathered all to hear thee;
   Let our hearts and souls be stirred
   Now to seek and love and fear thee;
   By thy teachings pure and holy,
   Drawn from earth to love thee solely.

2. All our knowledge, sense, and sight
   Lie in deepest darkness shrouded,
   Till thy Spirit breaks our night
   With the beams of truth unclouded;
   Thou alone to God canst win us;
   Thou must work all good within us.

3. Gracious Lord, thyself impart!
   Light of Light, from God proceeding,
   Open thou our ears and heart,
   Help us by thy Spirit's pleading.
   Hear the cry thy Church upraises;
   Hear, and bless our prayers and praises.

Text: Benjamin Schmolck, 1672–1737; tr. Catherine Winkworth, 1827–1878, alt.

78 78 88
LIEBSTER JESU

Song of Good News 656

1. O - pen your ears, O Chris - tian peo - ple;
2. They who have ears to hear his mes - sage;
3. Is - ra - el comes to greet the Sav - ior;

O - pen your ears and hear good news! O - pen your hearts, O
They who have ears, then let them hear! They who would learn the
Ju - dah is glad to see his day! From East and West the

roy - al priest - hood; God has come to you.
way of wis - dom, Let them hear God's word.
peo - ple trav - el; He will show the way.

REFRAIN

God has spo-ken to his peo-ple, Hal - le - lu - jah! And his words are

Repeat Refrain | Last Time

words of wis - dom, Hal - le - lu - jah, jah.

Text: Willard F. Jabusch, b. 1930, ©
Music: Jewish Folk Tune; acc. Willard F. Jabusch, b. 1930, ©

98 95 with Refrain
YSRAEL V'ORAITA

657 O Word of God Incarnate

1. O Word of God in-car-nate, O Wis-dom from on high,
2. The Church from you, dear Mas-ter, Re-ceived the word di-vine;
3. O make your Church, dear Sav-ior, A lamp of bur-nished gold,

O Truth un-changed, un-chang-ing, O Light of our dark sky:
And still that light is lift-ed O'er all the earth to shine.
To bear be-fore the na-tions Your true light, as of old;

We praise you for the ra-diance That from the scrip-ture's page,
It is the chart and com-pass That all life's voy-age through,
O teach your wan-d'ring pil-grims By this their path to trace,

A lan-tern to our foot-steps, Shines on from age to age.
'Mid mists and rocks and quick-sands Still guides, O Christ, to you.
Till, clouds and dark-ness end-ed, They see you face to face.

Text: William W. How, 1823–1897, alt.
Music: Neu-vermehrtes Gesangbuch, Meiningen, 1693; adapt. and arr. Felix Mendelssohn–Bartholdy, 1809–1847

76 76 76 76
MUNICH

America 658

1. My country, 'tis of thee, Sweet land of liberty, Of thee I sing; Land where my fathers died, Land of the pilgrims' pride, From ev'ry mountain-side Let freedom ring.

2. My native country, thee, Land of the noble free, Thy name I love; I love thy rocks and rills, Thy woods and templed hills; My heart with rapture thrills Like that above.

3. Let music swell the breeze, And ring from all the trees Sweet freedom's song: Let mortal tongues awake; Let all that breathe partake; Let rocks their silence break, The sound prolong.

4. Our fathers' God, to thee, Author of liberty, To thee we sing: Long may our land be bright With freedom's holy light; Protect us by thy might, Great God, our King.

Text: Samuel Francis Smith, 1808–1895
Music: Anonymous

664 6664
AMERICA

659 America the Beautiful

1. O beau - ti - ful for spa - cious skies, For am - ber waves of grain, For pur - ple moun-tain maj - es - ties A - bove the fruit - ed plain! A - mer - i - ca! A - mer - i - ca! God shed his grace on thee, And crown thy

2. O beau - ti - ful for pil - grim feet, Whose stern, im - pas-sioned stress A thor - ough-fare for free - dom beat A - cross the wil - der - ness! A - mer - i - ca! A - mer - i - ca! God mend thine ev - 'ry flaw, Con - firm thy

3. O beau - ti - ful for he - roes proved In lib - er - at - ing strife, Who more than self their coun - try loved, And mer - cy more than life! A - mer - i - ca! A - mer - i - ca! May God thy gold re - fine, Till all suc-

4. O beau - ti - ful for pa - triot dream That sees be - yond the years Thine al - a - bas - ter cit - ies gleam, Un - dimmed by hu - man tears! A - mer - i - ca! A - mer - i - ca! God shed his grace on thee, And crown thy

Text: Katherine Lee Bates, 1859–1929
Music: Samuel Augustus Ward, 1848–1903

86 86 86 86
MATERNA

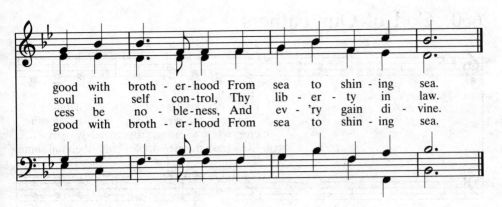

good with broth - er - hood From sea to shin - ing sea.
soul in self - con - trol, Thy lib - er - ty in law.
cess be no - ble - ness, And ev - 'ry gain di - vine.
good with broth - er - hood From sea to shin - ing sea.

660 God of Our Fathers

1. God of our fa - thers, whose al - might-y hand Leads forth in beau - ty all the star-ry band Of shin - ing worlds in splen-dor through the skies, Our grate - ful songs be - fore thy throne a - rise.

2. Thy love di - vine hath led us in the past, In this free land by thee our lot is cast; Be thou our rul - er, guard-ian, guide, and stay, Thy word our law, thy paths our cho - sen way.

3. From war's a - larms, from dead - ly pes - ti - lence, Be thy strong arm our ev - er sure de - fense; Thy true re - li - gion in our hearts in - crease, Thy boun - teous good - ness nour - ish us in peace.

4. Re - fresh thy peo - ple on their toil-some way, Lead us from night to nev - er-end-ing day; Fill all our lives with love and grace di - vine, And glo - ry, laud, and praise be ev - er thine.

Text: Daniel Crane Roberts, 1841–1907
Music: George William Warren, 1828–1902

10 10 10 10
NATIONAL HYMN

O Lord of Nations 661

1. O Lord of na-tions look to us Your peo-ple of this land, Where
2. O sov-'reign Lord, we look to you With heart-felt thanks and praise. We
3. May ev-er these U-nit-ed States Ac-claim the Lord a-bove. May

boun-teous bless-ings ev-er flow From your al-might-y hand. Let
beg that jus-tice, sown in peace, Bring har-vest in our days. Your
na-tional bound-aries nev-er set The lim-its to our love. One

us as stew-ards tend this realm, And guard each hu-man right, That
right arm be our strength and pow'r, Your truth our guid-ance be, Where
fam-'ly of A-mer-i-cans, On soil where pa-triots trod, Let

this our ho-ly her-i-tage Be pleas-ing in your sight.
just and e-qual laws pre-vail A-mong a peo-ple free.
us with all the na-tions be One fam-'ly un-der God.

Text: Omer Westendorf, b. 1916, ©
Music: Robert E. Kreutz, b. 1922, ©

86 86 86 86

662 The Star-Spangled Banner

1. O say can you see by the dawn's ear - ly
2. On the shore, dim - ly seen thro' the mists of the
3. O thus be it ev - er, when free - men shall

light, What so proud - ly we hailed at the twi - light's last
deep, Where the foe's haugh - ty host in dread si - lence re -
stand Be - tween their loved homes and the war's des - o -

gleam-ing, Whose broad stripes and bright stars, through the per - il - ous
pos - es, What is that which the breeze, o'er the tow - er - ing
la - tion! Blest with vic - t'ry and peace, may the heav'n-res - cued

fight, O'er the ram - parts we watched, were so gal - lant - ly
steep, As it fit - ful - ly blows half con - ceals half dis -
land Praise the Pow'r that hath made and pre - served us a

Text: Francis Scott Key, 1779–1843
Music: Anon.; acc. John Stafford Smith, 1750–1836, attr.

Irregular
NATIONAL ANTHEM

663 Asperges me

(Outside the Easter Season)

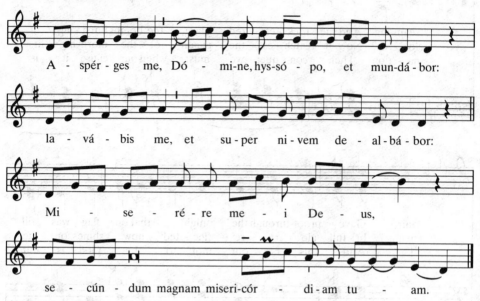

A - spér - ges me, Dó - mi-ne, hys-só - po, et mun-dá - bor:

la - vá - bis me, et su - per ni - vem de - al - bá - bor:

Mi - se - ré - re me - i De - us,

se - cún - dum magnam miseri-cór - di - am tu - am.

Text: Graduale Romanum, 1979
Music: Plainchant, Mode VII; acc. Rev. Bartholomew Sayles, O.S.B., b. 1918; and Sr. Cecile Gertken, O.S.B., b. 1902, ©

664 Vidi Aquam

(From Easter Sunday until Pentecost inclusive)

Vi - di a - quam e - gre - di - én - tem de tem - plo,

a lá - te - re dex - tro, al - le - lú - ia: et om - nes

ad quos per - vé - nit a - qua i - sta sal - vi fac - ti

sunt, et di - cent, al - le - lú - ia, al - le - lú - ia.

Text: Liber Cantualis, 1983
Music: Plainchant, Mode VIII; acc. Rev. Bartholomew Sayles, O.S.B., b. 1918; and Sr. Cecile Gertken, O.S.B., b. 1902, ©

Jubilate Deo 665

Kyrie

Ký-ri - e e - lé - i - son. Ký-ri - e e - lé - i - son.

Chri - ste e - lé - i - son. Chri - ste e - lé - i - son.

Ký-ri - e e - lé - i - son. Ký-ri - e e - lé - i - son.

Text: Gradual Romanum, 1979
Music: Plainchant; acc. Rev. Bartholomew Sayles, O.S.B., b. 1918, and Sr. Cecile Gertken, b. 1902, ©

Sanctus

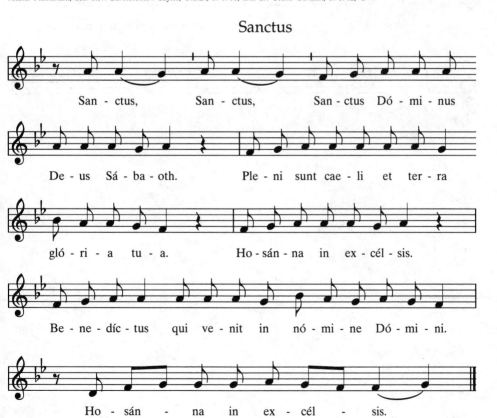

San - ctus, San - ctus, San - ctus Dó - mi - nus

De - us Sá - ba - oth. Ple - ni sunt cae - li et ter - ra

gló - ri - a tu - a. Ho - sán - na in ex - cél - sis.

Be - ne - díc - tus qui ve - nit in nó - mi - ne Dó - mi - ni.

Ho - sán - na in ex - cél - sis.

Text: Gradual Romanum, 1979
Music: Plainchant, Mass XVIII; acc. Rev. Bartholomew Sayles, O.S.B., b. 1918 and Sr. Cecile Gertken, O.S.B., 1902, ©

Agnus Dei

A - gnus De - i, qui tol - lis pec - cá - ta mun - di:

mis - se - ré - re no - bis. A - gnus De - i,

qui tol - lis pec - cá - ta mun - di: mis - se - ré - re no - bis.

A - gnus De - i, qui tol - lis pec - cá - ta mun - di:

do - na no - bis pa - cem.

Text: *Gradual Romanum, 1979*
Music: *Plainchant, Mass XVIII; acc. Rev. Bartholomew Sayles, O.S.B., b. 1918 and Sr. Cecile Gertken, O.S.B., b. 1902,* ©

Mass VIII 666

Kyrie

Ký-ri - e * e - lé - i - son.

Ký-ri - e e - lé - i - son.

Chri-ste e - lé - i - son.

Chri-ste e - lé - i - son.

Ký-ri - e e - lé - i - son.

Ký - ri - e *

** e - lé - i - son.

Text: Kyriale, Mass VIII
Music: Plainchant, Mode V; acc. Rev. Bartholomew Sayles, O.S.B., b. 1918, and Sr. Cecile Gertken, O.S.B., b. 1902, ©

Gloria

Gló-ri - a in ex-cél-sis De - o. Et in ter-ra pax ho-mí - ni-bus

bo - nae vo-lun-tá - tis. Lau-dá — mus te.

Be-ne-dí-ci-mus te. A-do-rá — mus te.

Glo-ri-fi-cá-mus te. Grá-ti-as á-gi-mus ti - bi

prop-ter ma-gnam gló-ri-am tu - am. Dó-mi-ne De-us, Rex cae-lé - stis,

De-us Pa-ter om-ní - po-tens. Dó-mi-ne Fi-li u-ni-

gé-ni-te Je - su Chri-ste. Dó-mi-ne De-us, A-gnus De - i,

Fí-li-us Pa - tris. Qui tol-lis pec-cá-ta mun - di,

mi-se-ré — re no - bis. Qui tol-lis pec-cá-ta mun-di,

Text: Kyriale, Mass VIII
Music: Plainchant, Mode V; acc. Rev. Bartholomew Sayles, O.S.B., b. 1918, and Sr. Cecile Gertken, O.S.B., b. 1902, ©

sú-sci-pe de-pre-ca-ti-ó-nem no - stram. Qui se-des ad déx-te-ram Pa-tris,

mi - se - ré - re no - bis. Quó-ni - am tu so - lus san - ctus.

Tu so - lus Dó - mi - nus. Tu so-lus al - tís - si - mus,

Je - su Chri - ste. Cum San - cto Spí - ri - tu,

in gló-ri - a De - i Pa - tris. A - men.

Gospel Acclamation

Laus ti - bi, Chri - ste, Rex ae - tér-nae gló - ri - ae.

Credo III

Cre - do in u - num De - um, Pa - trem om - ni - po - tén - tem,

fa - ctó - rem cae - li et ter - rae, vi - si - bí - li - um óm - ni - um,

et in - vi - si - bí - li - um. Et in u - num Dó - mi - num

Je - sum Chri - stum, Fí - li - um De - i u - ni - gé - ni - tum.

Et ex Pa - tre na - tum an - te óm - ni - a saé - cu - la.

De - um de De - o, lu - men de lú - mi - ne, De - um ve - rum de De - o ve - ro.

Gé - ni - tum, non fa - ctum, con - sub - stan - ti - á - lem Pa - tri,

per quem óm - ni - a fa - cta sunt. Qui pro - pter nos hó - mi - nes,

et pro - pter no - stram sa - lú - tem de - scén - dit de cae - lis.

Text: Kyriale, Credo III
Music: Plainchant, Mode V; acc. Rev. Bartholomew Sayles, O.S.B., b. 1918, and Sr. Cecile Gertken, O.S.B., b. 1902, ©

Et in-car-ná-tus est de Spí-ri-tu Sán-cto ex Ma-rí-a Vír-gi-ne:

Et ho-mo fa-ctus est. Cru-ci-fí-xus é-ti-am pro no-bis

sub Pón-ti-o Pi-lá-to pas-sus, et se-púl-tus est.

Et re-sur-ré-xit tér-ti-a di-e, se-cún-dum Scrip-tú-ras.

Et a-scén-dit in cae-lum: se-det ad déx-te-ram Pa-tris.

Et í-te-rum ven-tú-rus est cum gló-ri-a,

ju-di-cá-re vi-vos et mór-tu-os, cu-jus re-gni non e-rit fi-nis.

Et in Spí-ri-tum San-ctum Dó-mi-num, et vi-vi-fi-cán-tem:

qui ex Pa-tre Fi-li-ó-que pro-cé-dit. Qui cum Pa-tre et Fí-li-o

si-mul a-do-rá-tur, et con glo-ri - fi - cá-tur: qui lo-cú-tus est per pro-phé-tas.

Et u-nam, san-ctam, ca-thó-li-cam et a - po-stó - li-cam Ec-clé - si - am.

Con-fí - te - or u-num bap - tí-sma in re-mis-si - ó-nem pec-ca - tó - rum.

Et ex - spé - cto re - sur - rec - ti - ó - nem mor - tu - ó - rum.

Et vi - tam ven-tú - ri saé - cu - li. A -

- men.

Sanctus

San - ctus, San - ctus, San - ctus

Dó - mi - nus De - us Sá - ba - oth

Ple-ni sunt cae - li et ter - ra gló-ri - a tu - a.

Text: Kyriale, Mass VIII
Music: Plainchant, Mode VI, acc. Rev. Bartholomew Sayles, O.S.B., b. 1918, and Sr. Cecile Gertken, O.S.B., b. 1902, ©

Ho - sán - na in ex - cél - sis.

Be-ne - dí - ctus qui ve - nit in nó-mi-ne Dó - mi-ni.

Ho-sán - na in ex - cél - sis.

Memorial Acclamation

My - sté - ri - um fí - de - i Mor-tem tu - am an-nun - ti - á - mus,

Dó - mi - ne, et tu - am re - sur - rec - ti - ó -

nem con - fi - té - mur, do - nec vé - ni - as.

Great Amen

A - men, A - men, A - men.

Agnus Dei

A - gnus De - i *qui tol - lis pec-cá - ta mun - di:

mi - se - ré - re no - bis. A - gnus De - i qui tol - lis

pec-cá - ta mun - di: mi - se - ré - re no - bis.

A - gnus De - i, qui tol - lis pec-cá - ta

mun - di: do - na no - bis pa - cem.

Text: Kyriale, Mass VIII
Music: Plainchant, Mode VI; acc. Rev. Bartholomew Sayles, O.S.B., b. 1918, and Sr. Cecile Gertken, O.S.B., b. 1902

Copyrights

INDEX OF SCRIPTURAL REFERENCES RELATED TO HYMNS

8	487	6:41-51	380
8:1	647	6:41-59	504
8:22-25	452, 601	6:49-58	396
9:1-6	540, 641	6:51	390, 510
9:18-24	651	6:62	296, 351, 378, 390
9:28-36	253, 518	6:68-69	405
10:27	387	7:37-39	351
10:38-42	241, 647	8	588
11:1	244	8:12	424, 453
11:2	552	8:31-36	634
11:4	608	9:1-41	357, 447
13:13	241	9:4	467
13:29	650	10:1-30	241, 372, 396, 389, 458, 460
14:25-33	651	11:1-45	358
15:1-3	401	12:12-16	177, 256, 257
15:3-7	660	12:20-33	291, 445
15:11-13	401	12:46	424
18:9-14	624	14	413
19:37-38	256, 257	14:1-3	287
19:41	467	14:1-12	293
21:28	430	14:6	520, 532
22:12	393	14:15-21	498
22:39-46	264	14:16	520, 532
22:61	241	14:18	504
23	261	14:24-26	297, 298, 299, 300, 302, 304,
23:33, 44, 50-53	262		352, 353, 501
23:39-43	369, 370	14:27	607
24	276	15	612
24:1-2	262	15:1-8	214
24:1-8	596	15:12-17	473, 480
24:1-12	290, 623	16:13	307
24:28-35	390	17	366
24:34	286, 289	17:20-26	366
24:29	241	18:16-17, 25-27	336
24:30-35	388	19	259, 530
24:46-48	635	19:2	263
24:46-53	295	19:2-5	261
24:50-51	287	19:2-5, 17-31	260
24:50-53	504	19:16-37	264
24:51-53	454	19:25	235, 236, 316, 323, 324
		19:34	262, 351, 380, 381, 545
		19:33-34	503
		19:34-35	526
JOHN		20	284, 290
		20:1	623
1:1	538	20:1-18	271, 276, 278, 285, 286, 288
1:1-5	225	20:11-18	286, 289
1:1-5, 9-14	653	20:17	296
1:1-18	212, 220, 222, 225, 654	20:19-31	282, 290, 464
1:9	220, 225, 436, 453	20:22-23	294
1:15-18	182	20:24-29	336, 363, 369, 370
1:19-23	171	21:1-19	448
1:29-36	231, 545	21:15-17	336
2:1-11	231, 545	21:18-19	345
2:1-12	405		
2:13-25	485		
3	488	**ACTS**	
3:1-8	283		
3:4-8	347	1:8	297, 298, 299, 304, 501, 502
3:5	222	1:9	504
3:14-21	258	1:9-11	295
3:16	485, 530	2	347, 623
4:5-42	453	2:1-3	354, 502
4:10	378	2:1-4	596
4:12-16	387	2:1-11	297, 304
4:13-14	356	2:36	516
4:14	453	3:14-15	258
6	367, 374, 510	4:11-12	489
6:25-59	545	4:12	538
6:25-69	375	7:54-60	336
6:32-59	275	8:14-17	641
6:32, 54-56, 68-69	376, 378	9:1-19	336
6:35, 51	376, 377		

4:3-7	634	4:12, 16	386, 387
4:7-8	336	5:6-8	351

HEBREWS

1:3	515
1:1-12	225
2:9-10	516
2:14-18	253
2:17–10:25	362, 378, 504
4:16	378, 397, 509
9:11-14	378, 504
9:23-26	545
9 & 10	541
10:1-22	378, 397, 545
11	636
11:32-40	636
12:1	336
12:1-3	568, 595, 651
12:28	373
13:5	452
13:6	458
13:8	293

JAMES

1:10-17	566
1:17	562, 563, 565, 628, 659
2:1	650
3:1–5:6	600
5:13-16	406, 408, 449

1 PETER

1:3	410
1:18-19	489
2:4-6	485, 487, 488
2:21-14	276

2 PETER

1:4	452
1:19	424
12:4-5	386, 387
13:11-12	186

1 JOHN

2:27	298, 299, 304, 354
3:18	634
4:7-17	454
4:9-10	530
4:10-16	386, 387

REVELATION

1:4-7	377
1:6	641
1:8	220, 378
1:12-18	533
1:18	276, 287, 515, 520
2:10	336
2:28	424
3:4-5	411, 412
3:7	179
3:21	509, 545
4	306, 568
4:5	306, 568, 595
4:6	504
4:6-11	576, 568
4:8-11	306, 307, 377, 454
4:10	454
4:11	374, 507
5	265
5:6-14	265, 504, 530, 545, 560
5:9	268, 504, 525, 546
5:11-14	521. 560
5:12	335
5:12-13	519
5:13	566, 567
6:9-11	521, 568
7:2-4, 9-14	336
7:9-12	519, 563
7:9-17	578
7:12	554
7:12-17	335
7:13-17	346
11:15-18	525
14:1-5	530
14:13	336, 411, 412
14:17-20	633
15:4	306
17:14	516
19:1-9	530
19:6-9	186, 268
19:11-16	307, 377
19:12	525
19:16	516
21:1-4	469, 620
21:2-27	411, 412, 485
21:2-22:5	469, 620
21:9-22:5	469, 620
21:19-27	186
22:1	351
22:5	487
22:16	214, 424, 552
22:17	283, 453
22:20	430

INDEX OF TEXT SOURCES

INDEX OF COMPOSERS AND ARRANGERS

INDEX OF TUNE SOURCES

LONG METRE WITH ALLELUIA

LM with Alleluia
88 88 with Alleluia
Erschienen ist der herrlich Tag 335

LONG METRE WITH REFRAIN

LM with Refrain
88 88 with Refrain
Englert 355,356
Sweet Sacrament 544
Vayamos Jubilosos 589
Veni, veni, Emmanuel 179

LONG METRE DOUBLED

LMD 88 88 D
Deirdre (St. Patrick's Breastplate) 305
Magnificat 433

44 6 D with Refrain

Coventry Carol 209

46 46 46 44

Dufner 471

55 54 D

Bunessan 425, 426

65 65 with Refrain

Adorote 369
Bgdzic Pozdnowiona 391
Lourdes (Massabielle) 316

65 65 D

King's Weston 538
Une Vaine Crainte 572

664 6664

America 658
Italian Hymn 307, 308

666 666

Laudes Domini 488

66 66 88

Darwall's 148th 515, 577
Love unknown 258

66 66 888

Rhosymedre 621

667 667

Nunc Dimittis 436

66 77 78 55

In dulci jubilo 190

66 86 66

Coela 554

66 11 D

Down Ampney 498

67 67 66 66

Darmstadt 486, 574
Nun Danket 570

75 75 slightly Irregular

Assumpta Est 322

75 75 with Refrain

King of Glory 541

76 76

De Eersten Zijn De Laatsten 345
Dinwiddie 646
Non Dignus (Claribel) 376

76 76 and Repeat

Cherry Tree Carol 172

76 76 with Refrain

All things Bright and Beautiful 594
Fulda Melody 257, 382
Go Tell It On the Mountain 217
Gott Vater, Sei Gepriesen 309
Valet Will Ich Dir Geben 256

76 76 D

Aurelia 397, 405, 488, 489
Ave Virgo Viriginum 320
Ellacombe 175, 278, 635
Gaudeamus Pariter 279
Munich 657
Neshanic 401
Passion Chorale 259, 383
Wie Lieblich ist det Maien 630

76 76 D with Refrain

Wir Pflügen 628

76 76 676

Es ist ein Ros 191

76 76 77 with Refrain

Messiah 255

87 87

Charlestown 467
Credo 505
Drakes Boughton 392
Merton 176
St. Columba (Erin) 246, 460
Shipston 629
Stuttgart 230, 404, 564

87 87 with Refrain

Greensleeves 215
Ich Glaub an Gott 546

87 87 D

Abbot's Leigh 638, 639
Alle Tage Sing und Sage 313
Au Sang Qu'un Dieu 449
Austria 573
Domhnach Trionoide 481
Geneva 466
Holy Anthem 280
Holy Manna 604
Hyfrydol 454, 504
Hymn to Joy 581
In Babilone 606
Moultrie 576
Nettleton 446
Pleading Savior 323
Rustington 652
Sabine Crossroads 459

87 87 D with Refrain

Ecclesia 490

87 87 444 77

Bryn Calfaria 545

87 87 66 66 7

Ein Feste Burg 487

87 87 77

Coblenz 398
Irby 212
Unser Herrschen 285, 496
Zeuch mich, zeuch mich 346

87 87 87 74

Christ Lag in Todesbande 275

87 87 78 D

Mark's Mill 593

87 87 87

Komm, O Komm du Geist des Lebens 353
Laude Anima 513
Pange Lingua Gloriosi 361
Picardy 377

Regent Square 206
Richard's Shop 249
St. Thomas 379
St. Thomas (Webbe) 364
Sun Journey 251
Westminister Abbey 485

87 87 87 with Refrain

Corde Natus 220
Den des Vaters Sinn geboren 321

87 87 887

Mit Freuden Zart 617

87 87 88 77

Jesu, Joy 410

87 98 87

Besancon Carol 183

88 with Alleluias and Refrain

Puer Natus in Bethlehem 203, 204

88 with Refrain

Alleluia No. 1 292

88 446 with Refrain

Kings of Orient 232

88 44 88 with Alleluias

Lasst uns erfreuen 272, 578

88 44 88 with Refrian

Lasst uns erfreuen 555

88 86

Inniskeen 196

886 D

Song 18 507

887

Burrill 236
Stabat Mater 235

888

Granton 644

888 with Alleluias

Beverly 540
Gelobt sei Gott 271
O Filii et Filiae 290
Victory 276

88 78

Montana 579

88 888

Holy Spirit 299

88 88 88

Coleraine (La Scala Santa) 600
Melita 601, 602
Newmark, alt. 492
St. Catherine (Tynemouth) 634
Source 610
Stella 315
Surrey 354

88 88 88 with Refrain

Beverly Shores 396

89 89 9 10 89

Nature's Praise 557

97 96 with Refrain

Saylor's Creek 590

98 95 with Refrain

Ysrael V'oraita 656

98 98

Eucharistic Hymn 556
O Waly, Waly 393

98 98 D

Rendez a Dieu 374, 375

98 98 6

Maryhaven 202, 493

99 99

Neri 281

10 4 10 4 10 10

Alberta 455

10 7 10 7

Sicilian Mariner's 318

10 8 10 9 with Refrain

Olive Tree 575

10 9 8 10

Ag an Bposadh 417

10 9 10 9

New River 350

10 10

Caena Domini 378

10 10 with Refrain

Crucifer 542
Let us Break Bread 569

10 10 9 10

Slane 531

10 10 10 with Alleluia

Engelberg 283, 583

10 10 10 with Alleluias

O'Leary 547
Sine Nomine 336

10 10 10 10

Anima Christi 385
Consolamini 171
Eventide 431
Litton 603
National Hymn 660
Renewing Death 445
Song 22 523

10 10 10 10 10

Old 124th 551

10 10 10 10 10 10

Unde et Memores 366

10 10 11 11

Hanover 571
Laudate Dominun 519, 550
Paderborn (Maria Zu Leiben) 317, 341

10 11 11 12

Slane 524

11 8 11 8 D

Kingdom of God 647

11 10 10 11

Noel Nounelet 291

11 10 11 9

Russia 585

METRICAL PSALMS AND HYMNS BASED ON PSALMS

SERVICE MUSIC

ORDER OF MASSES

CANTICLES

SEQUENCES

LATIN TEXTS

LITURGICAL INDEX

HOLY ORDERS

MARRIAGE

PASTORAL CARE OF THE SICK AND DYING

PENANCE/RECONCILIATION

RELIGIOUS PROFESSION

BLESSINGS

TOPICAL INDEX

ANGELS

521 ALL HAIL THE POWER OF JESUS'
NAME
206 ANGELS FROM THE REALMS OF
GLORY
219 ANGELS WE HAVE HEARD ON HIGH
560 COME, LET US JOIN OUR CHEERFUL
SONGS
337 HAIL REDEEMER, KING MOST
BLEST!
222 HARK! THE HERALD ANGELS SING
568 HOLY GOD, WE PRAISE THY NAME
306 HOLY, HOLY, HOLY, LORD GOD
ALMIGHTY
195 IT CAME UPON THE MIDNIGHT
CLEAR
549 O GOD, YOU ARE THE FATHER
382 O JESUS, WE ADORE THEE
573 PRAISE THE LORD! YE HEAVENS,
ADORE HIM
574 PRAISE WE OUR GOD WITH JOY
576 ROUND THE LORD IN GLORY
SEATED
580 SONGS OF PRAISE THE ANGELS
SANG
517 THE LORD IS KING! LIFT UP YOUR
VOICE
519 YE SERVANTS OF GOD, YOUR
MASTER PROCLAIM
578 YE WATCHERS AND YE HOLY ONES

CHRISTIAN LIFE

359 A GRACIOUS GUIDE THE LORD
431 ABIDE WITH ME!
467 ALL WHO LOVE AND SERVE YOUR
CITY
447 AMAZING GRACE
443 AS A CHALICE CAST OF GOLD
444 AS THOSE WHO SERVE
445 BEFORE THE FRUIT IS RIPENED BY
THE SUN
234 BELOVED SON AND DAUGHTER
DEAR
450 BLEST ARE THE PURE IN HEART
497 BREATHE ON ME, BREATH OF GOD
462 BRING JUDGMENT, LORD, UPON
THE EARTH
540 CHRIST IS THE KING! O FRIENDS
REJOICE
448 CHRISTIAN, DO YOU HEAR THE
LORD?
446 COME, THOU FOUNT OF EVERY
BLESSING
466 FATHER, LORD OF ALL CREATION
483 FATHER OF HEAVEN, WHOSE LOVE
PROFOUND
641 FORTH IN THE PEACE OF CHRIST
WE GO
635 GO MAKE OF ALL DISCIPLES
449 GOD OF MERCY AND COMPASSION
465 GRANT TO US, O LORD, A HEART
RENEWED
476 HAPPY ARE THEY
482 HOSEA
452 HOW FIRM A FOUNDATION
451 HOW LOVELY IS YOUR DWELLING
PLACE

453 I HEARD THE VOICE OF JESUS SA'
468 I LOVE YOU, O MY LORD, MOST
HIGH
477 IN MY NAME
469 JERUSALEM, MY HAPPY HOME
493 JESUS RENEWS THE PARISH
455 LEAD KINDLY LIGHT
484 LIVING STONES
638 LORD OF LIGHT
639 LORD, YOU GIVE THE GREAT
COMMISSION
454 LOVE DIVINE, ALL LOVES
EXCELLING
470 MY GOD, ACCEPT MY HEART
458 MY SHEPHERD WILL SUPPLY MY
NEED
456 O CHRIST, OUR TRUE AND ONLY
LIGHT
478 O FOR A CLOSER WALK WITH GO
400 O GOD OF GREAT COMPASSION
457 O GOD, OUR HELP IN AGES PAST
549 O GOD, YOU ARE THE FATHER
474 O LORD, OUR FATHERS OFT HAVE
TOLD
621 OUR FATHER, BY WHOSE NAME
475 REDEMPTION FROM CAPTIVITY
471 STAND FIRM IN FAITH
651 TAKE UP YOUR CROSS
613 THE CHURCH OF CHRIST IN EVER
AGE
460 THE KING OF LOVE MY SHEPHERD
479 THE LORD'S MY SHEPHERD
575 THE OLIVE TREE
461 THE THIRSTY DEER WILL YEARN
AND DREAM
472 THERE IS A BALM IN GILEAD
473 THIS IS MY COMMANDMENT
480 THIS IS MY WILL
481 THOSE WHO LOVE AND THOSE WI
LABOR
463 TO YOU, O LORD, I LIFT MY SOUL
395 WE LONG FOR YOU, O LORD
464 WE WALK BY FAITH
614 WE HAVE COME TO HEAR
619 WHAT SHALL I BRING
583 WHEN IN OUR MUSIC GOD IS
GLORIFIED
520 YOU ARE THE WAY

CHRISTIAN UNITY

359 A GRACIOUS GUIDE THE LORD
366 AT THAT FIRST EUCHARIST
485 CHRIST IS MADE THE SURE
FOUNDATION
540 CHRIST IS THE KING, O FRIENDS
REJOICE
487 CHRIST'S CHURCH SHALL GLORY I
HIS POWER
634 FAITH OF OUR FATHERS
466 FATHER, LORD OF ALL CREATION
374 FATHER, WE THANK THEE WHO
HAST PLANTED
563 FROM ALL THAT DWELL BELOW
THE SKIES
624 GATHER US IN
396 GIFT BREAD
389 GIFT OF FINEST WHEAT
605 GOD'S BLESSINGS SENDS US FORTH

HURCH

COMFORT AND CONSOLATION

COMMITMENT

COURAGE AND STRENGTH

CREATION

HOPE AND TRUST

HUMILITY

JESUS CHRIST

JOY AND GLADNESS

PRESENCE OF GOD

PROVIDENCE OF GOD

WORD OF GOD

YOUTH HYMNS

INDEX OF FIRST LINES AND COMMON TITLES

First Lines and Common Titles